DO FEDERAL SOCIAL PROGRAMS WORK?

DO FEDERAL SOCIAL PROGRAMS WORK?

David B. Muhlhausen

 PRAEGER

AN IMPRINT OF ABC-CLIO, LLC
Santa Barbara, California • Denver, Colorado • Oxford, England

Library of Congress Cataloging-in-Publication Data

Muhlhausen, David B.
  Do federal social programs work? / David B. Muhlhausen.
    pages cm
  Includes bibliographical references and index.
  ISBN 978-1-4408-2803-4 (hbk. : alk. paper) — ISBN 978-1-4408-2804-1 (ebk.)
  1. Public welfare—United States. 2. United States—Social policy.
  I. Title.
HV95.M845   2013
361.60973—dc23   2012051078

ISBN: 978-1-4408-2803-4
EISBN: 978-1-4408-2804-1

17 16 15 14   2 3 4 5

This book is also available on the World Wide Web as an eBook.
Visit www.abc-clio.com for details.

Praeger
An Imprint of ABC-CLIO, LLC

ABC-CLIO, LLC
130 Cremona Drive, P.O. Box 1911
Santa Barbara, California 93116-1911

This book is printed on acid-free paper ∞

Manufactured in the United States of America

First, to my parents, Marvin and Barbara Muhlhausen, for the love, patience, guidance, and support they have provided to me. There is no effective substitute for caring and supportive parents. Second, to social engineers of all stripes. This book would not be necessary without their indelible belief that government can make people better. I can only hope that this book will encourage some humility among them.

Contents

Acknowledgments

Do Federal Social Programs Work? owes its existence to my work at the Heritage Foundation trying to inform policymakers, media, and the public about the need to determine the effectiveness of federal social programs. While the underlying idea for this book had been percolating in my head for a few years, the genesis of the decision to write it came from discussions among my Heritage Foundation colleagues and a supporter of Heritage. I owe them a debt of gratitude for getting me focused on writing the book.

Over the years, I have been the beneficiary of a talented boss, Bill Beach, the former Director of the Heritage Foundation Center for Data Analysis. Bill and a colleague, David Azerrad, reviewed parts of the manuscript. Special thanks go to John Fleming for creating the charts and graphs used in Chapters 2 and 3. I owe a debt of gratitude to Praeger editor Beth Ptalis, who shepherded me through the publishing process, and the editors who cleaned up my sometimes garbled words and clarified the message I sought to convey.

While given tremendous advice on the contents of this book, the views expressed in this book are entirely my own and may not reflect the opinion of the Heritage Foundation and those who reviewed sections of it or discussed the need for me to write the book in the first place. Despite all the assistance given to me, any mistakes in the text are entirely my own.

Chapter 1

Introduction

This book asks a simple question: Do federal social programs work? While the question may be straightforward, getting to an answer is complicated. To answer in the affirmative, federal social programs must ameliorate the social problems they target. In other words, social programs are intended to enhance the welfare of recipients. In essence, social programs seek to improve human behavior in ways that will make people better off. For example, the social programs of the Great Society sought to eradicate the fundamental causes of poverty by providing opportunity for the poor to join other Americans in prosperity.[1]

As we will see, the provision of funding for social programs is often confused with effectiveness. The intentions of program supporters do not automatically translate into the desired results. Although this fact is seldom discussed openly, much less analyzed, by program supporters, the goal of the book is for supporters of federal social programs to seriously reassess their faith in the ability of the federal government to solve social problems.

With unrestrained spending and surging public debt threatening our nation's stability, determining whether the hundreds of billions of dollars spent each year on federal social programs are worth the cost is now more important than ever. Federal social programs are included in what are considered as discretionary and "other mandatory" domestic programs. This classification includes numerous education, welfare, housing, and employment programs.

While the major contributors to the nation's debt crisis are health and income support entitlement programs, such as Medicare and Social Security, Congress must still take tough action on discretionary and other mandatory programs to reduce spending and reach a balanced budget. Most of the nation's poverty programs are classified as other mandatory to distinguish them from Social Security and Medicare. Americans fearful or skeptical of plans to reduce spending on federal social programs need to be convinced that fear tactics offered by those against budget cuts are unwarranted.

What Is a Social Program?

What is a social program? The term "social program," as used in this book, refers to social programs funded by the federal government that attempt to improve human behavior by increasing skills or awareness chiefly through noncompensatory services. In essence, these programs engage in social engineering to enhance the well-being of citizens. Social programs are intended to fix social problems that individuals are assumed to be unable to solve themselves. These programs are expected to break the link between a lack of resources, whether physical, mental, or financial, with negative outcomes. Some social programs are intended to fix the perceived defects of capitalism. For example, the federal government funds many social programs that are intended to assist low-income individuals escape poverty.

Consider Head Start—a classic example of a social program. Created as part of the War on Poverty in 1965, Head Start is a preschool community-based program funded by the federal government. By providing education, nutrition, and health services, Head Start is intended to provide a boost to disadvantaged children before they enter elementary school. Its goal is to help disadvantaged children catch up to children living in more fortunate circumstances.

Social programs, as the term is used in this book, do not include economic incentive policies that compensate participants with wages and salaries. For example, taxation policies like the Earned Income Tax Credit, child tax credit, and the mortgage interest deduction are not included as social programs for the purposes of this book. Tax credits and deductions are compensatory policies that provide incentive for the adoption of certain behaviors. However, in a later chapter, we will explore social programs that offer small stipends or cash incentives in addition to other services.

Further, the term social program does not include entitlement programs, such as Social Security, Unemployment Insurance, and veteran's benefits. For each of these entitlement programs, the receipt of benefits is based on employment history or participation in the U.S. Armed Services. A retired individual receiving Social Security benefits has at least 40 quarters of employment history prior to the receipt of benefits. A veteran receiving healthcare benefits has earned this benefit based on his military service.

While there are certainly questions over the cost and effectiveness of these entitlement programs, they are not the focus of this book.

An individual receiving the services or benefits of a social program has not earned entry into the program like a retiree has done with Social Security or a veteran with healthcare benefits. Participation in social programs is not based on service or employment, but on the individual being in some form of an undesirable condition. Undesirable conditions can include poor academic achievement, poverty, or lack of employable skills.

Further, social programs do not include regulations. Government-established rules of conduct from such regulatory agencies as the Occupational Safety and Health Administration and the Environmental Protection Agency do not count. Regulatory agencies concerning themselves with consumer safety issues and financial transactions do not count either.

Solving Social Problems

Social problems can be mind-bogglingly complicated to solve. This book is about the federal government's efforts at solving social problems. For example, can the federal government alleviate poverty by raising the incomes of welfare participants through employment and training services? The heart and soul of the book is an *objective* analysis of whether federal social programs have achieved their goals. Underpinning the entire book are the following questions: Have federal programs lived up to their promises? Readers should ask themselves whether they, as taxpayers, can live without these programs?

The answers to these questions are particularly relevant to our nation's current political debate over the federal government's debt. Many of the budget plans in Congress reduce the rate of increase in spending on federal social programs. Very few plans actually propose real spending reductions. Opponents of these plans assert that any real reduction or slowing in the growth of spending on social programs will have disastrous effects on society. Using evidence from scientifically rigorous evaluations of national programs, this book tests the credibility of this assertion.

In general, Americans badly want to believe that our elected national leaders can solve social problems. This belief did not start with the ascension of Barack Obama to the presidency of the United States. Since the Progressive Era, New Deal, and Great Society, when faced with a social problem, many Americans have instinctively looked to the federal government for a solution. President Lyndon B. Johnson promised to eradicate poverty with the Great Society. President George W. Bush advocated a massive increase in the federal government's role in education so that no child would be left behind. Is lack of success in these endeavors the result of electing the wrong leaders? Or, is it because we have an inflated sense of what the federal government can achieve?

The theme of this book will not be that all federal programs are ineffective. NASA's Apollo program was wonderfully successful. Sending Americans safely to and from the moon was a singular achievement. While the U.S. Armed Forces have had great difficulty in nation-building in Iraq and Afghanistan, there is little uncertainty related to the lethality of U.S. troops. However, when rigorously evaluated, federal social programs intended to change human behavior have not had similar success. Furthermore, fears of harmful effects resulting from substantially reduced funding for federal social programs are not justified.

The arguments for reducing social program spending will be supported by an objective review of the evaluation literature. Social programs should be carefully evaluated to determine whether they do, in fact, work. Impact evaluations attempt to isolate the direct effects of social programs apart from other factors that affect the outcome of interest. If the program does not achieve the intended results, then the program has failed. For example, a job-training program intended to improve the employment prospects of individuals living in an urban neighborhood might well appear to be very successful, until one becomes aware that an upturn in the local economy is really responsible for employment gains. To reliably sort out the job-training program's effects or any other social program's effects from confounding factors is a difficult task.

The results of objective scientific evaluations that rely on randomized assignment are used to underpin this book's arguments. Determining whether federal social programs work or do not work is based on credible and rigorous evidence. Experimental evaluations are the "gold standard" of evaluation designs because the use of random assignment helps to ensure that the control group is equivalent to the intervention group in composition, predispositions, and experiences.[2] Relying on this experimental method limits the book's content to federal social programs that have undergone rigorous scientific evaluations.

Specifically, this book relies on multisite experimental evaluations. Because these evaluations assess the effectiveness of federal social programs in multiple locations, the results tell us about the performance of national programs. While individual programs operating in single locations may undergo experimental evaluations, these small-scale, single-site evaluations do not inform policymakers of the general effectiveness of national programs. Small-scale evaluations assess the impact on only a small fraction of people served by federal social programs. The success of a single program that serves a particular jurisdiction or population does not necessarily mean that the same program will achieve similar success in other jurisdictions or among different populations. Thus, small-scale evaluations are poor substitutes for large-scale evaluations. In addition, a multisite experimental evaluation that examines the performance of a particular program in numerous and diverse settings can potentially produce results that are more persuasive to policymakers than results from a single locality. Social programs are the major focus of this book because these programs are the most likely to undergo such evaluations.

A major advantage of using rigorous multisite scientific evidence is that the conclusions about the federal government's ability to solve social problems are objective and nonpartisan. Those on the Left and on the Right, and in the Democrat and Republican Parties, all have favored social programs over the years. Some may mistakenly assume that Democrats support increased spending on federal social programs, while Republicans do not. While social program spending experienced its slowest growth during Ronald Reagan's presidency, as we will see in Chapter 2, substantial increases in spending on social programs occurred during the administrations of Richard Nixon, George H. W. Bush, and George W. Bush. In addition, the experimental evaluations covered in later chapters include assessments of federal social engineering programs favored by liberals and many conservatives, primarily social conservatives. This approach of relying on rigorous scientific evaluations should have great appeal to audiences that genuinely care about whether federal social programs are effective.

The American public should have nothing to fear from the elimination of ineffective programs. In February 2012, Rasmussen Reports asked a nationally representative sample of likely U.S. voters the following questions: "As the nation searches for solutions to the federal budget crisis, should thoughtful spending cuts be considered in every program of the federal government?" Sixty-four percent of respondents agreed with the need for spending cuts, while 22 percent disagreed, and 12 percent were unsure.[3] A follow-up poll by Rasmussen Reports after the November 2012 presidential election found that 65 percent of likely voters approved of the need for spending cuts, while 20 percent disagreed and 15 percent undecided.[4] Americans appear to be ready for spending cuts.

However, opponents of reduced spending often engage in scaremongering. Coming out against reduced Head Start spending, President Obama in July 2011 referred to spending on the program as "investments," suggesting that Head Start benefits children participating in the program.[5] Obama's implication is clear: Increased spending produces beneficial outcomes, decreased spending produces negative outcomes.

Others have made similar statements. In April 2011, Senate majority leader Harry Reid claimed that an effort in the House of Representative to reduce the growth in spending "kicks hundreds of thousands of boys and girls out of Head Start . . ."[6] Senator Bernard Sanders called proposed cuts to Head Start "devastating."[7] Representative Xavier Becerra concluded that reduced funding would mean that children "would lose the opportunity to get better educated on their route to becoming America's future leaders . . ."[8] Are these dire observations likely to occur?

In April 2012, President Obama called the budget plan passed by the Republican-controlled U.S. House of Representations a "Trojan Horse" and "thinly veiled social Darwinism."[9] The president further criticized the budget plan as making "draconian cuts" to federal spending programs.[10] In particular, the president said, "If this budget becomes law and the cuts were applied evenly, starting in 2014, over 200,000 children would lose their chance to get an early education in the Head Start program."[11] On the 2012 campaign trail, Obama repeatedly made this claim. The clear implication is that over 200,000 children will somehow be harmed by not attending Head Start. This would be true only if Head Start is an effective program that actually benefits the children it serves.

Senator Tom Harkin, chair of the Senate Committee on Health, Education, Labor, and Pensions, in July 2012 asserted that proposed cuts to domestic programs will "have destructive impacts on the whole array of programs that undergird the middle class in this country—everything from education to job training, medical research, child care, food safety, national parks, border security and safe air travel. These essential government services and programs directly touch every family in America, and they will be subject to deep, arbitrary cuts under sequestration."[12]

This book, however, shows that rigorous scientific evidence demonstrates that children participating in Head Start perform no better in academic achievement than similar children excluded from participating in Head Start. Simply put, Head Start is a failed social program. I do not offer this assessment flippantly. Perhaps one of the most rigorous scientific evaluations ever conducted on a federal social program found that Head Start fails by a large margin to achieve its goals. Thus, reducing funding or even eliminating the ineffective Head Start program will not harm children. This book makes similar arguments for other social programs.

As later chapters demonstrate, the federal government has great difficulty in operating national social programs based on "proven" small-scale social programs. In a 2011 issue of *Time*, journalist Joel Klein acknowledges the ignored reality that national-scale programs based on effective pilot programs frequently do not yield the same successful results.[13] His case in point is Head Start—a "Great Society" preschool program intended to provide a boost to disadvantaged children before they enter elementary school. Head Start was based on a few pilot programs, such as the Perry Preschool program, that were believed to be effective. Advocates asserted that a national preschool program for disadvantaged children would yield the same positive results. However, a scientifically rigorous evaluation of multiple Head Start sites throughout the nation clearly found that the program is ineffective. The program has little to no positive effects for children granted access to it.

Klein asks, "Why do so many succeed as pilots and fail when taken to scale?"[14] The answer to his question is twofold. First, national programs often do a poor job of replicating the crucial factors found in the pilot programs that are necessary for producing the same successful results, such as hiring highly skilled staff. Second, the social conditions contributing to the success of a particular pilot program are often not present in other settings. A very poignant example of why caution should be exercised when generalizing findings based on a single pilot program is the case of police departments performing mandatory arrests in domestic violence incidents.

Despite the scare tactics used by social engineering advocates, some policy experts reluctantly admit that federal social programs have rarely been demonstrated to work. According to Isabel V. Sawhill, a senior fellow at the Brookings Institution, and Jon Baron, president of the Coalition for Evidence-Based Policy:

> Since 1990, there have been 10 instances in which an entire federal social program has been evaluated using the scientific "gold standard" method of randomly assigning individuals to a program or control group. Nine of these evaluations found weak or no positive effects, for programs such as the $1.5 billion Job Corps program (job training for disadvantaged youth); the $300 million Upward Bound program (academic preparation for at-risk high school students); the $1.2 billion 21st Century Community Learning

Centers (after-school programs for disadvantaged youth); and, most recently, the $7 billion Head Start preschool program. Only one program— Early Head Start (a sister program to Head Start, for younger children)— was found to produce meaningful, though modest, positive effects.[15]

However, as is detailed in Chapter 4, Early Head Start is not as effective as Sawhill and Baron believe. In addition, while often ignored, evaluations of federal social programs often indicate that these programs produce harmful outcomes.

Chapter Outline

The book is organized around federal social programs intended to benefit (1) children and families and (2) workers. Chapter 2 addresses our nation's budget crisis. At the end of fiscal year (FY) 2012 on September 30, 2012, the Office of Management and Budget estimated that the federal government's gross debt will reach 104.8 percent of gross domestic product (GDP), or $16.4 trillion.[16] In November 2012, the Congressional Budget Office confirmed that the nation's debt stood at $16.3 trillion.[17] This amount—over $16 trillion—is a staggering sum. How did we accumulate this massive debt? Basically, the ends of government as originally set forth in the Declaration of Independence have evolved over time. Starting with the Progressive Era, running through the New Deal, and ending with the Great Society, the original constitutionalism of the American Founding was rewritten with the call for a much more activist federal government. The chapter demonstrates that the growth of social program spending has far exceeded our nation's population and GDP growth. The chapter reveals how the ever-expanding budgets of federal social programs have contributed to our nation's budget crisis. The chapter concludes by making the case that the best way to get the economy moving again and reduce the federal debt is to cut spending.

The first topic of Chapter 3 is the importance of holding government programs accountable. For too many federal programs, we do not even know if they are effective because systematic evaluations are absent. Billions of dollars are spent each year on federal programs for which we do not even know if they achieve their stated mission. If Americans are serious about trying to deal with the budget crisis, then tax dollars must be spent as efficiently as possible. Finding out what works and does not work through rigorous scientific evaluation of federal social programs is a necessary step to regaining control over unnecessary spending.

The second topic of Chapter 3 is the problem of selection. Before we can judge a government program to be effective, we first must understand the importance of selection. It can be astoundingly difficult to distinguish between what is working and what is not, and nowhere is this predicament truer than when government tries to change human behavior. For example, individuals seeking entry into federal job-training programs may be more motivated than individuals not seeking to acquire new skills. Such motivational factors and other similar factors are often invisible to those assessing effectiveness. Failure to account for these crucial factors can produce a spurious association between job-training and employment outcomes. Thus, the chapter will introduce the reader to scientific methods for assessing the effectiveness of federal government programs.

Chapter 4 examines the effectiveness of federal social programs intended to benefit children and families, while Chapter 5 examines employment programs intended to benefit workers. Each of these chapters answers the following questions:

- Have federal social programs lived up to their promises?
- How have these programs benefited children and families or workers?

When policymakers begin to discuss cutting a federal program's budget, advocates of the program often assert that any amount of spending cuts will harm the intended beneficiaries. This argument automatically assumes that the programs in question are beneficial to society, without any objective analysis of whether these programs actually work. Any consideration of the unintended negative consequences of these programs is often overlooked. Clearly, there is little merit in claims that eliminating programs that are ineffective to begin with will produce harmful effects, as suggested by program advocates. For instance, eliminating an educational program that failed to affect academic achievement would not hurt the academic achievement of students. Because these programs do not work in the first place, Chapters 4 and 5 counterclaims that cutting social programs will lead to harmful consequences.

The concluding chapter (Chapter 6) presents the way forward for America. Based on the previous two chapters, the last chapter concludes that there are an ample number of programs that can be eliminated or have their budgets significantly reduced. Supporters of federal social engineering, whether liberal or conservative, Democrat or Republican, have an inflated sense of what federal social programs can achieve that is not backed up by multisite experimental evaluations. In addition, Chapter 6 calls for a new effort to hold federal programs accountable by ensuring that programs are evaluated for their effectiveness. Demonstrating results should be tied to funding decisions.

Chapter 2

Budget Crisis

On December 31, 2011, the gross debt racked up by the federal government reached $15.2 trillion—the legal limit as authorized by Congress.[1] In response, on January 12, 2012, President Barack Obama formally notified Congress of his intent to raise the nation's debt ceiling by $1.2 trillion—from $15.2 to $16.4 trillion.[2]

The Congressional Budget Office (CBO) reported throughout 2012 that the federal deficit for fiscal year (FY) 2012 will be nearly $1.1 trillion.[3] "Measured as a share of gross domestic product (GDP)," the CBO reports, "that shortfall will be 7.0 percent, which is nearly two percentage points below the deficit recorded last year but still higher than any deficit between 1947 and 2008."[4] GDP is the total market value of all officially recognized goods and services produced within a country in a given year. FY 2012 is the fourth year in a row that the federal government has posted a deficit exceeding $1 trillion.[5] In 2009, the CBO warned that these "Large budget deficits would reduce national savings, leading to more borrowing from abroad and less domestic investment, which in turn would depress economic growth in the United States. Over time, the accumulation of debt would seriously harm the economy."[6]

At the end of calendar year 2011, the Office of Management and Budget (OMB) estimated that at the end of FY 2012 on September 30, 2012, the federal government's gross debt will reach 104.8 percent of GDP, or $16.4 trillion.[7] In November 2012, the CBO reported that the nation's gross debt stood at $16.3 trillion.[8] This amount is a staggering sum that is difficult for Americans to comprehend. If we did, we would be truly frightened at the prospect of paying it off. How did we accumulate this massive debt?

To arrive at an answer, we first need to understand how the scope, power, and responsibilities of the federal government greatly expanded overtime. Starting with the Progressive Era, running through the New Deal, and ending with the Great Society, the original understanding of the role of government in protecting our freedoms established during the American

Founding was redefined with the call for a much more activist federal government.[9] Each of these political waves sought to transform the United States into something very different than the Founding Fathers envisioned.[10] President Obama's 2012 reelection campaign Internet tool, "The Life of Julia," is a modern illustration of how much the role of the federal government has grown.[11] The fictional "Julia" represents a woman who benefits from federal government programs advocated by President Obama over the course of her entire life. Through successive government interventions, Julia's life is effectively made better. For example, Julia at age three is enrolled in Head Start to help her get ready for school. Later, Julia's son benefits from attending schools with good teachers due federal education programs. At each successive stage of her life, Julia's life is improved due to various interventions by the federal government. The apparent counterfactual condition is that Julia's life would have been vastly diminished without benefiting from federal government interventions throughout her life. There was a time when such federal government interventions in the lives of Americans would have been unimaginable.

The American Founding

The purpose of this book is not to present in full the political theory underpinning the American Founding.[12] However, to properly understand the overall growth in federal spending and, in particular, spending on social programs, the new conception of freedom, established during the Progressive Era, that substantially expanded the purpose of the federal government needs to be discussed. The progressives replaced the Founders' notion of formal freedom with a new positive, or "effective," freedom that required government to assist individuals in achieving their full potential as human beings.

This change drastically expanded the power and scope of the federal government. To accomplish the task of understanding the impact of the progressive definition of freedom—and to better understand how the role and power of the federal government was transformed—the principals of the American Founding need to be briefly presented.

In 1776, the Declaration of Independence not only declared that the American colonies were free and independent states, but also established the ends of government. The most famous line of the Declaration reads: "We hold these truths to be self-evident, that all men are created equal, that they are endowed by their Creator with certain unalienable rights, which among these are Life, Liberty and the pursuit of Happiness." The purpose of government is to establish the conditions that allow individuals to freely exercise these formal rights, or freedoms. The Founders used different language to describe the origin of rights. For example, some Founding documents credit the origin of rights as coming from a deity or God, as in the Declaration of Independence's use of "Creator," while other documents credit rights as a birthright when individuals enter society or resulting from nature. Based on nature, the Massachusetts Constitution of 1780 asserted that rights are "natural, essential, and unalienable."[13] Taking the birthright approach, the 1776 Virginia Declaration of Rights declared "That all men are by nature equally free and independent, and have certain inherent rights, of which, when they enter into a state of society . . ."[14] The unifying theme among these origins is that rights are not derived from government.

Four important factors regarding natural rights need to be made clear. First, natural rights exist before the creation of government and thus cannot be created or altered by government. "The rights of nature, as the Founders saw it," according to Thomas G. West, a professor of politics at Hillsdale College, "are based on what man is and has by nature—his life, his liberty, and his ability to acquire property and pursue happiness."[15] In practice, this conception of rights means that an individual is free to follow his or her pursuits with the expectation that others leave him or her alone. Successfully obtaining the object of an individual's pursuits is not guaranteed and does not assert a rightful claim that others must ensure that the individual is successful. The protection of our freedoms by government does not mean that the government must ensure that our freedoms are successfully exercised.

Second, rights are considered to be equally held by all individuals. This notion of equality meant that individuals are politically equal, not equal in all aspects, such as intelligence, thrift, and skill.[16] Third, drawing from the principle of equality means that there are no natural rulers among human beings:

> Since all men are created equal, all men are also by nature free or, put differently, have the natural right to rule themselves. More precisely, every ordinary adult human being has a natural right to do anything that does not violate the laws of nature, meaning chiefly, but not exclusively, the like right of another to rule himself.[17]

Fourth, rights are considered to be universal. According to Bradley C. S. Watson, a professor of political science at Saint Vincent College, these unalienable rights, as understood by the Founders, "were held not to be culturally determined or time-bound or subject to infinite incremental growth."[18] In other words, as culture changes and technology advances, natural rights remain fixed in meaning. For example, the right of free speech retains its same essential meaning, even though the free speech of today as expressed through current technology was unknown and unforeseen by the Founders.

The power of the federal government in general, and the power of Congress in particular, is limited to activities that allow individuals to enjoy their formal freedoms, or natural rights.[19] The implication is that legislative power is primarily negative, meaning that laws are needed to protect the natural rights of individuals from encroachment by others.[20] The Founders' understanding of natural rights, combined with the U.S. Constitution that placed formal limits on the scope and power of the federal government, meant that the federal government had virtually no role in operating the types of federal social programs administered today. While the Founders were concerned with protecting freedom by limiting the power of the federal government, the states retained broad police powers. Based on the Founders' conception, once government secures our natural rights, the responsibility for obtaining our hopes, desires, and economic security, while not guaranteed, is up to us. As we shall see, the notion of natural rights was successfully challenged.

The Transformation of America: The Progressive Era, New Deal, and Great Society

During the late nineteenth century, the political theory of the Founding began to fade for many Americans.[21] The transition was accomplished through a dismissal of the principles of the American Founding and a new understanding of freedom. Instead of government based on natural rights as expressed in the Declaration of Independence, the progressive doctrine based on historicism—the assertion that "values" evolve over time—began to dominate.[22]

The political science of the Founders focused on the protection of formal freedoms as the central goal of government by arranging limits and checks on government power.[23] The progressives rejected limits and checks on government in favor of action.

Frank Johnson Goodnow, the first president of the American Political Science Association, asserted that the old conception of rights based on individuals worked in the past when progress was viewed in terms of individuals. As society advanced, however, the individual-based conception of rights became a "menace" to the increasing need for more social organization through government action.[24] In 1916, Goodnow concluded that "We no longer believe as we once believed that a good social organization can be secured merely through stressing our rights. The emphasis is being laid more and more on social duties."[25]

Before Woodrow Wilson became president, he had a long and influential academic career as a political scientist. Based on historicism, Wilson concluded that the natural rights expressed in the Declaration of Independence were not universal. According to Wilson's view of the Declaration of Independence,

> It expressly leaves to each generation of men the determination of what they will do with their lives, what they will prefer as the form and object of their liberty, in what they will seek their happiness. . . . In brief, political liberty is the right of those who are governed to adjust the government to their own needs and interests.[26]

In essence, principals of the Founding, according to Wilson, were out of date. Wilson was not the only progressive to think that the principals of the Founding were outdated.

According to leading progressive John Dewey, American individualism was on the wane.[27] The Founders' conception of natural rights, according to Dewey, was "located in the clouds" and the "falsity" of natural rights "may easily be demonstrated both philosophically and historically."[28] Further, "Natural rights and natural liberties exist only in the kingdom of mythological social zoology."[29]

In 1903, Charles E. Merriam, an influential political scientist at the University of Chicago, asserted: "In the new view, the state . . . is not limited to the negative function of preventing certain kinds of action, but may positively advance the general welfare by means and measures expressly directed to that end."[30] While progressives, such as Merriam, dismissed the principles of the Founding as outdated, they did credit the Founders for bringing forth political changes that were correct for their time. As Merriam wrote:

> The Revolutionary doctrines of an original state of nature, natural rights, the social contract, the idea that the function of government is limited to the

protection of person and property,—none of these finds wide acceptance among leaders in the development of political science. The great service rendered by these documents, under other and earlier conditions, is fully recognized, and the presence of a certain element of truth in them is freely admitted, but they are no longer generally received as the best explanation for political phenomena.[31]

Seconding Merriam, Dewey and his coauthor, James H. Tufts, affirmed that formal freedom is "absolutely indispensable."[32] With the principles of the American Founding considered outdated, the progressives then set themselves toward redefining the traditional understanding of freedom.

The progressives' conception of freedom rejected the notion that it is something individuals naturally possess; instead, it is something the state must help individuals achieve.[33] Securing formal freedoms is not enough to allow individuals to be truly free. Individuals must be given the capacity and resources to achieve effective freedom.[34] Instead of protecting our formal freedoms as understood by the Founders, Wilson asserted that government must be more active. According to the future president, "the individual must be assured the best means, the best and fullest opportunities, for complete self-development."[35]

According to Dewey and Tufts, formal freedom, while indispensible, is not enough:

> The freedom of an agent who is merely released from direct external obstructions is formal and empty. If he is without resources of personal skill, without control of the tools of achievement, he must inevitably lend himself to carrying the directions and ideas of others.[36]

Therefore, they proposed effective freedom.[37] Relating to the individual, effective freedom creates "a moral demand that the practical limitations which hem him in should be removed; that practical conditions should be afforded which will enable him effectively to take advantage of the opportunities formally open."[38]

To be effectively free, individuals must also acquire the necessary resources needed to benefit from formal freedom. Individuals cannot be truly free when only their natural rights are secured. What good is your right to life when you live in poverty and despair? Through increased social organization, the state must provide the conditions necessary for individuals to possess effective freedom.[39] Thus,

Organized social planning, put into effect for the creation of an order in which industry and finance are socially directed on behalf of institutions that provide the material basis for the cultural liberation and growth of individualism is now the sole method of social action by which liberalism can realize its professed alms.[40]

Foreshadowing the Great Society, Dewey's progressivism envisioned a society in which individuals could achieve their full potential as human beings only through government assistance.

After replacing the Founders' notion of formal freedom with a new positive (effective) freedom, the progressive doctrine stressed the need for increased social organization—meaning expansive new legislative powers in general, and the power to create new government programs focused on solving social problems in particular.

As the story is traditionally told, the advent of the Industrial Revolution brought about new problems that made the political theory of the Founding outdated. Instead of freedom as defined by the Founders, with its formal protections against being injured by others, the progressive conception of effective freedom held that rendering such protections was meaningless if individuals did not have the means to achieve their fulfillment. Effective freedom means that government programs must be provided to those thought to not have enough talents, wealth, housing, education, health, and so forth.[41] No longer fixed in human nature and universal, rights are derived from the current state of society.[42]

How did the Industrial Revolution bring about the need for a new conception of the proper role of government? Spanning from the 1820s to the 1920s, the nation's cities underwent rapid growth in industry and manufacturing. In turn, this industrialization made cities centers of economic power and attracted immigrants searching for a better life. As employment shifted from farming to factory work, new social problems arose. For example, debilitating injuries resulting from factory work lead to workers being unable to provide for their families. These new problems gave rise to the belief that government must be more active. People could not be left alone to solve problems that only collective efforts could adequately address.

Despite the prevailing view that people were left on their own to solve their problems, there is a rich history of Americans providing voluntary mutual aid before and during the Progressive Era. Assistance was often provided by private charity, mutual aid societies, and state and local governments.[43] Before the advent of the national welfare state, millions of

Americans received mutual aid from fraternal societies.[44] These fraternal societies were characterized by "an autonomous system of lodges, a democratic form of internal government, a ritual, and the provision of mutual aid for members and their families."[45]

For example, a considerable share of the Masonic mutual aid involved employment-seeking assistance, short-term housing, and character references.[46] Other organizations, like the Ancient Order of United Workmen, offered life insurance to members.[47] While the exact numbers are unknown, University of Alabama professor of history David T. Beito estimates that fraternal life insurance societies in 1910 had at least 13 million members.[48]

Local governments provided assistance as well. Several states offered mother's pension programs that provided financial assistance to widows with children.[49] From 1921 to 1931, the number of families receiving these pensions rose from 45,825 to 93,620.[50]

However, the rise of the welfare state assumed much of the social responsibility that was once the province of voluntary associations.[51] The year after the Social Security Act of 1935 saw the beginning of benefit retrenchment by fraternal societies and their eventual decline.[52] The decline in mutual aid societies and the growth of federal domestic programs are direct results of the Progressive Era. The Progressive Party platforms of 1912 and 1924 called for an expanded role of government in the regulation of economic activity.[53]

While the policy successes of the Progressive Era mainly focused on the creation of regulations intended to protect workers from unsafe and unfair working conditions and regulate business activity, the passage of the Sixteenth Amendment to the U.S. Constitution in 1913 allowed for an infusion of cash into the federal treasury. The federal income tax and later U.S. Supreme Court decisions—for example, *United States v. Butler* in 1936—granted the federal government an unlimited spending power that allowed the creation of new domestic programs that were unheard of before. The policy changes during the Progressive Era, and more importantly, the new definition of freedom, laid the groundwork for creating and funding the New Deal and Great Society.

The stock market crash in 1929 was the start of the Great Depression. While the stock market nearly returned to its full precrash value within several months, reactions by President Herbert Hoover, Congress, and the Federal Reserve to fix the problem contributed to the banking collapse and the deepening of the Depression.[54] For example, the Smoot-Hawley

Tariff Act of 1930 established the highest tariffs in the nation's history, which harmed the economy.[55] In addition, Hoover—with the approval of Congress—tried to spend his way out of the Depression on public works projects.[56]

According to Census Bureau data, the civilian labor force unemployment rate increased over five times, from 3.2 percent in 1929 to 16.3 percent in 1931.[57] The unemployment rate peaked in 1933 at 25.2 percent and remained in the double digits until 1941.[58] Over the years, economists have developed an alternative series of unemployment numbers based on the Census Bureau data that include unemployed individuals participating in New Deal relief programs, such as the Civilian Conservation Corps, and prisoners.[59] According to economist Stanley Lebergott,

> These [Census Bureau] estimates for the years prior to 1940 are intended to measure the number of persons who are totally unemployed, having no work at all. For the 1930's this concept, however, does not include one large group of persons who had both work and income from work—those on emergency work. In the United States we are concerned with measuring lack of regular work and do not minimize the total by excluding persons with made work or emergency jobs. This contrasts sharply, for example, with the German practice during the 1930's when persons in labor force camps were classed as employed, and Soviet practice which includes employment in labor camps, if it includes it at all, as employment.[60]

Using the alternative measure, the civilian labor force unemployment rate increased by almost five times, from 3.2 percent in 1929 to 15.9 percent in 1931.[61] The unemployment rate peaked in 1933 at 24.9 percent and remained in the double digits until 1940.[62] Regardless of which series of unemployment numbers are used, the unemployment rate remained high for several years. The economic crisis provided ample opportunity to increase the role of the federal government in the everyday lives of Americans.

The policy changes brought about by the New Deal were grounded in a conception of freedom that is different from the Founders'. While campaigning for the presidency in 1932, Franklin D. Roosevelt asserted that "Every man has a right to life; and this means that he has also a right to make a comfortable living."[63] Instead of requiring Americans to not harm each other, we are, according to Roosevelt, obligated to ensure that we have a comfortable living.

During Roosevelt's 1944 State of the Union address to Congress, he called for a new Bill of Rights.[64] The political rights established under the original Bill of Rights, such as the rights of free speech, free press, and trial by jury, had, he said, "proved inadequate to assure us equality in the pursuit of happiness" as the nation's industrial economy expanded.[65] Because "true individual freedom cannot exist without economic security and independence," Roosevelt's proposed second Bill of Rights guaranteed Americans material comfort and a pass on the hardships of life. These proposed rights included rights to useful and remunerative jobs; adequate food, clothing, and recreation; decent homes; medical care; and good education.[66] In essence, individuals cannot be truly free unless they are given the necessary resources (provided by others) to effectively exercise their freedom. While his Second Bill of Rights was not added to the Constitution, Roosevelt redefined freedom in terms of economic security.

The welfare state, created during the New Deal, was an attempt to compensate for capitalism's perceived defects. The New Deal was based on "the assumption that the nation's greatest problems were rooted in the structure of modern industrial capitalism and that it was the mission of government to deal somehow with the flaws in that structure."[67] The welfare state compensates the losers of capitalism by distributing income and resources to the poor from capitalism's winners, the rich. "The intention is to secure more for those who have too little," according to William Voegeli of Claremont McKenna College, "as the sensibilities of the welfare state's architects and advocates define as a minimum level of decency."[68]

While much of the New Deal was devoted to the regulation of business and economic development, such as the Tennessee Valley Authority, the New Deal also created new relief and jobs programs. Prior to 1935, the federal government had no role in cash assistance for poor children and families. The 1935 Social Security Act not only created Social Security, but also established Aid to Dependent Children (ADC), an income maintenance program for widowed, deserted, and other unmarried women with children. ADC allowed its beneficiaries to stay at home and care for their children instead of working. ADC was subsequently changed to Aid to Families with Dependent Children (AFDC) in 1950.

Other programs provided government-paid jobs to the unemployed. The Civilian Conservation Corps (CCC), just one of several programs created in 1933, employed young men "to stop soil erosion, plant trees, fight forest fires, create parks, build or repair roads and bridges, and do other work in rural and suburban areas."[69] The Public Works Administration (PWA) focused on the provision of jobs through the creation of large-scale construction projects like dams and tunnels.[70] However, the PWA failed to have enough impact on unemployment, so the Civilian Works

Administration (CWA) was created as a replacement to employ more unskilled labor in such activities as road construction.[71] The CWA had a short life and was superseded by the Works Progress Administration (WPA) in 1934. In addition to the construction of public facilities, the WPA "staffed clinics, supervised playgrounds, preserved historic records and buildings, revised traditional crafts, excavated archeological sites, painted pictures, produced plays and concerts, and recycled clothing and toys."[72] These programs focused on providing work opportunities to the unemployed and were not engaged in social engineering by changing human behavior.

Under the New Deal, the Social Security Act of 1935 created four entitlement programs: (1) the Social Security income program for the elderly, (2) the means-tested Social Security Disability Insurance (SSDI) program for unemployable people with disabilities, (3) unemployment insurance, and (4) the previously mentioned ADC.

While Social Security, SSDI, and ADC were permanent programs, most of the New Deal programs intended to provide temporary relief.[73] For example, President Franklin D. Roosevelt originally rejected the notion that work relief programs should be long-term public employment programs.[74] However, the advent of the 1960s brought about a change in policy thinking. Unlike the New Dealers, the advocates of the Great Society did not seek to provide relief and social insurance programs, but to socially engineer a better society.[75]

The 1960s were a tumultuous decade that saw major cultural, political, and policy changes. Early in this decade, the federal government established job-training programs for people who were unemployed and economically disadvantaged. These programs provided a combination of remedial education, vocational training, on-the-job training, subsidized work experience, basic life-skills training, and job search assistance. Programs funded under the Manpower Development and Training Act (MDTA) of 1962 were originally intended to retrain workers dislocated by technological advances, but MDTA was later converted into a job-training program for people who were economically disadvantaged.[76]

In May 1964, President Lyndon B. Johnson gave his call for a "Great Society" at a University of Michigan commencement ceremony. The primary principles of the Great Society were "amelioration and opportunity."[77] Johnson believed that federal social programs had the ability to ameliorate hardships facing many Americans and, simultaneously, provide opportunities for Americans to improve their own lives.[78] The Great

Society through its " 'War on Poverty' would rehabilitate families and rebuild communities in the process of providing education, training, and jobs."[79] While the New Deal was intended to relieve the effects of poverty and provide economic security, the Great Society sought to eradicate the fundamental causes of poverty by providing opportunity for the poor to join other Americans in prosperity and ultimately make redistribution unnecessary.[80] People cannot be effectively free when they are in poverty. For example, the New Deal did little related to education policy, which was a major component of the Great Society.[81] The Great Society was recognition that the New Deal had not solved the problem of poverty.[82]

Johnson challenged Americans "to enrich and elevate our national life, and to advance the quality of our American civilization."[83] He envisioned the Great Society as

> a place where every child can find knowledge to enrich his mind and to enlarge his talents. It is a place where leisure is a welcome chance to build and reflect, not a feared cause of boredom and restlessness. It is a place where the city of man serves not only the needs of the body and the demands of commerce but the desire for beauty and the hunger for community.[84]

While Roosevelt defined freedom in terms of material security, Johnson expressed freedom in terms of reaching the highest ideals. Despite the difference in ends, Johnson was not breaking away from the progressives. He was attempting to fully realize their goal of bringing forth effective freedom. To accomplish the Great Society's task, Johnson pledged to "assemble the best thought and the broadest knowledge from all over the world" to create federal social programs to solve all social ills.[85]

A month later, Johnson proclaimed, "We stand at the edge of the greatest era in the life of any nation. For the first time in world history we have the abundance and the ability to free every man from hopeless want, and to free every person to find fulfillment in the works of his mind or the labor of his hands."[86] Instead of setting the minimum conditions to protect life and liberty and allow for the pursuit of happiness, the Great Society promised freedom from material hardship and the realization of individual fulfillment for Americans.

Legislatively, a tidal wave of new laws was passed that greatly expanded the power of the federal government. The Eighty-Eighth Congress (January 3, 1963 to January 3, 1965) passed the Economic Opportunity Act of 1964 that created the Office of Economic Opportunity (OEO). The OEO operated

Volunteers in Service to America (VISTA), Job Corps, Community Action Program, Upward Bound, and Head Start.

The Eighty-Ninth Congress (January 3, 1965 to January 3, 1967) passed 181 major pieces of legislation asked for by Johnson.[87] These laws addressed civil rights, education, health, poverty, housing, and transportation issues facing the nation. For example, in 1965, a banner year for social policy legislation, Congress passed:

- The Elementary and Secondary Education Act
- The Social Security Act
- The Voting Rights Act
- The Housing and Urban Development Act
- The Public Works and Economic Development Act
- The Higher Education Act
- The Vocational Rehabilitation Act

Johnson believed that the problem of poverty resided in individuals who lacked the necessary skills to obtain good-paying jobs.[88] To solve this problem, the federal government needed to create job-training and education programs to help the poor become effectively free. The Elementary and Secondary Education Act of 1965 was intended to promote greater economic and social opportunity.[89]

Underpinning the Great Society was the belief by social scientists that they were equally capable of analyzing problems and developing national policies to eliminate poverty.[90] As a whole, the diverse set of Great Society programs "reflected the judgment that public measures could alter both the performance of the economy and the characteristics of the poor and thereby improve their economic status. Nearly every hypothesis regarding why the poor performed weakly in the labor market was reflected in some program."[91]

From the Progressive Era, through the New Deal, to the Great Society, the role of the federal government was greatly expanded. The purpose of government in protecting freedom as conceived by the Founders gradually gave way to a greatly expanding notion of freedom. Instead of securing our natural rights based on the principals of the Founding, the current mission of the federal government revolves around the Great Society's objective of providing effective freedom that alleviates material hardship and promotes the realization of individual fulfillment for Americans. Simply put, the mission of the federal government was to make us better.

The federal social programs created over the decades have received support from Democrats and Republicans in Congress and presidents of both political parties. Further, the support for an activist role of the federal government crosses ideological lines. Liberals of today support the very activist agenda of the federal government trying to make people better, as do many conservatives, especially social conservatives. For example, presidential appointees in the Department of Health and Human Services during the George W. Bush administration sought to inject marriage promotion projects into various social programs, including Head Start.[92]

While merits of the expansion of the federal government due to the Progressive Era, New Deal, and Great Society deserve careful consideration, a detailed discussion of this topic is beyond the scope of this book. While some agree with the progressives' dismissal of the principles of the American Founding and their new understanding of freedom, others disagree. One area where there should be total agreement is that the transformation did occur.

Spend, Spend, and Spend Some More

The enormous growth of the role of the federal government in the ordinary lives of Americans has been accompanied by excessive growth in spending. A characteristic of this growth in spending is the persistent imbalance between revenues and spending. The public's increased demand for services provided by the federal government and their reluctance to accept higher levels of taxation, combined with the inability of Congress to make hard choices, has led to the persistent revenue-spending imbalance.

The OMB's historical tables that supplement each year's budget proposal by the president of the United States include detailed information on budget surpluses, deficits, and total debt.[93] The OMB's annual surplus and deficit data as reported in dollars dates back to 1901, but 1930 will be used as the starting year for our purposes because the OMB provides these surpluses and deficits as a percentage of GDP starting in 1930. While the federal government has consistently run deficits since the 1930s, as detailed in Chart 2.1, the size of the deficits steadily increased in the 1970s. The data presented in Chart 2.1 are in 2010 dollars to account for inflation. During the 1980s, the deficits rapidly increased. The trend reversed from 1998 to 2001 with the surpluses, meaning that the federal government's revenues exceeded its spending. There has been much debate over what caused the reversal, with many crediting a booming economy

Chart 2.1: Budget Surplus or Deficit, 1930–2011

IN BILLIONS OF 2010 DOLLARS

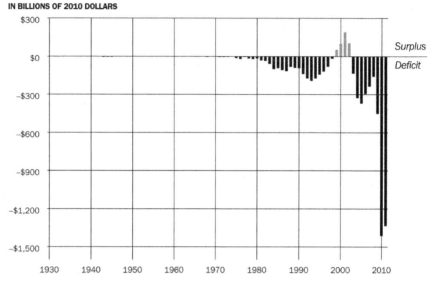

Source: Office of Management and Budget, *Historical Tables, Budget of the United States, Fiscal Year 2013* (Washington DC: U.S. Government Printing Office, 2011), Table 1.1.

that increased revenues along with budgetary compromises between President William J. Clinton and the Republican-controlled Congress. However, these surpluses were short lived.

In 2002, the federal government's surpluses disappeared. The nation's economy, already in an economic recession from March 2001 to November 2001, was hard hit by the September 11, 2001, terrorist attacks. While the economy slowed, federal spending steadily increased. Deficits sharply climbed from 2002 to 2004 and then began to decline from 2005 to 2007.

The events of 2008—the bursting of the housing market bubble and the global financial crisis—led to a drastic decline in economic activity that has not been seen since the Great Depression. The economic crisis that led to a drastic reduction in revenues was also accompanied by an unprecedented increase in domestic spending. Passed by Congress and signed into law by President Barack Obama, the American Recovery and Reinvestment Act of 2009 was an economic stimulus package estimated to cost $787 billion. Revised estimates by the CBO put the cost of the stimulus package at $814 billion.[94] For the first time in the nation's history, deficits reached into trillions of dollars.

Chart 2.2: Budget Surplus or Deficit as Percentage of GDP, 1930–2011

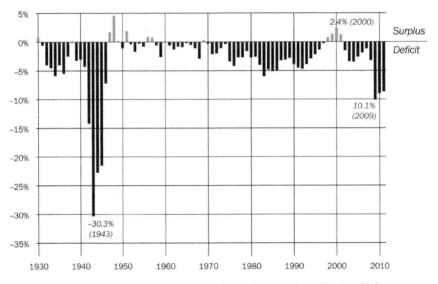

Source: Office of Management and Budget, *Historical Tables, Budget of the United States, Fiscal Year 2013* (Washington DC: U.S. Government Printing Office, 2011), Table 1.2.

Another way of presenting surpluses and deficits is to express the figures as a percentage of GDP. Chart 2.2 presents deficits and surpluses as the percentage of GDP from 1930 to 2011. Over this 82-year period, the federal government reported deficits in 69 (84.1%) of these years.

From the Great Depression during the 1930s through the close of World War II, the federal government ran staggering deficits, especially during the war. During World War II, the deficit as a percentage of GDP reached a high of 30.3 percent in 1943—a share that has yet to be replicated.[95] Five years later, the federal government in 1948 ran the highest surplus as of yet at 4.6 percent.[96] From the 1950s to the early 1970s, deficits fluctuated and were occasionally interrupted with short-lived surpluses.

Between 1974 and 1981, the federal government consistently ran deficits that ranged from 1.6 to 4.2 percent of GDP.[97] Then from 1982 to 1997, the federal government persistently ran deficits that ranged from 3 to 5 percent until the deficits began to diminish in 1996 and 1997.[98]

In 1998, for the first time in 29 years, the federal government ran a surplus. The surplus was 0.8 percent of GDP.[99] For four years, surpluses were

Chart 2.3: Escalating Gross Federal Debt, 1940–2011

From 1940 to 2011, gross federal debt rose 1,713 percent.

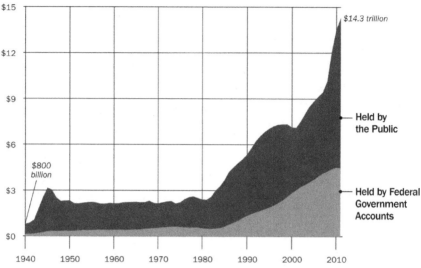

IN TRILLIONS OF 2010 DOLLARS

Source: Office of Management and Budget, *Historical Tables, Budget of the United States, Fiscal Year 2013* (Washington DC: U.S. Government Printing Office, 2011), Table 7.1.

reported, with the peak being 2.4 percent in 2000.[100] As previously mentioned, the deficits returned in 2002 and exploded in size in 2009. As a percentage of GDP, the deficits under the Barack Obama administration have been the highest since World War II. In 2009, the deficit reached 10.1 percent of GDP.[101] Since then, the deficit declined from 9.0 percent in 2010 to 8.7 percent in 2011.[102]

The cumulative effect of these persistent deficits is the national gross debt reached $16.3 trillion in November 2012.[103] From 1940 to 2011, as presented in Chart 2.3, the national gross debt increased from $0.8 trillion in constant 2010 dollars to $14.3 trillion—a 1,713 percent increase. Expressing the figures in constant 2010 dollars allows for the removal of the distorting effects of inflation. The first thing to notice about Chart 2.3 is that gross debt is comprised of debt held by the public and debt held by federal government accounts. The debt held by the public consists of the total amount borrowed to cover the federal government's accumulated deficits. The debt held by federal government accounts consists of money the federal government has loaned itself from trust funds, like Social Security, to fund current operations. For example, instead of reserving Social Security revenue surpluses to be paid to future retirees, the federal government automatically spends these surpluses on current government programs and promises to pay back the borrowed funds in the future.

During World War II, the gross debt increased to $3.2 trillion in 1945 and then dropped to $2.5 trillion in 1947. From then until 1983, the gross debt remained steady in the low to mid $2 trillion range. In 1983, the gross debt reached $3.0 trillion and steadily climbed thereafter. By 1989, the gross debt had reached $5.0 trillion. Jumping another $2.3 trillion, the gross debt reached $7.3 trillion in 1999. A decade later and showing no signs of slowing in growth, the gross debt was $12.1 trillion. Two years and $2.3 trillion later, the gross debt reached $14.3 trillion in 2011.

Over this 72-year period—from 1940 to 2011—the annual rate of growth in gross debt was 4.1 percent, while the annual growth rate of GDP was 3.5 percent. For much of this time span, however, the growth in the federal government's gross debt was flat. If we start with 1981 as the beginning point, when the gross debt started to increase, then the annual rate of growth is 6.2 percent. From 1981 to 2011, the annual growth rate of GDP was 2.8 percent. During this time period, the debt was growing at more than twice the rate of GDP.

From 1940 to 2011, as presented in Chart 2.4, the debt held by the public increased from $0.67 trillion in constant 2010 dollars to $9.82 trillion—a 1,466 percent increase. During World War II, the debt held by the public increased to $3.85 trillion in 1945 and then dropped to $1.77 trillion in 1952. From then until 1977, the public debt fluctuated between $1.59 trillion and $1.83 trillion. In 1977, the public debt reached $1.98 trillion and steadily climbed thereafter. By 1989, the public debt reached $2.85 trillion. Jumping another $0.9 trillion, the public debt reached $4.75 trillion in 1999. A decade later and showing no signs of slowing in growth, the public debt was $7.67 trillion in 2009. Two years and $2.15 trillion later, the public debt reached $9.82 trillion in 2011.

Over this 72-year period—from 1940 to 2011—the annual rate of growth in the public debt was 3.9 percent, while the annual growth rate of GDP was 3.5 percent. At this rate, the public debt doubles every 20 years. For much of this time span, however, the growth in the federal government's gross debt was flat. If we start with 1981, then the annual rate of growth is 5.65 percent. From 1981 to 2011, the annual growth rate of GDP was 2.8 percent. At this rate, the public debt doubles every 14 years. During this

Chart 2.4: Escalating Gross Federal Debt Held by the Public, 1940–2011

From 1940 to 2011, federal debt held by the public rose 1,466 percent.

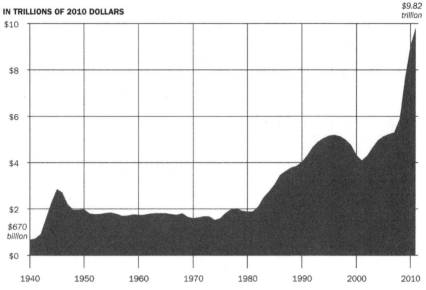

Source: Office of Management and Budget, *Historical Tables, Budget of the United States, Fiscal Year 2013* (Washington DC: U.S. Government Printing Office, 2011), Table 7.1.

time period, the public debt was growing at more than twice the rate of GDP.

How does the federal government's gross debt compare to the size of the national economy? Chart 2.5 presents the gross debt as a percentage of GDP from 1940 to 2011. The gross debt increased from 52 percent of GDP in 1940 to 99 percent of GDP in 2011. While the gross debt as a percentage of GDP almost doubled between 1940 and 2011, this comparison does not adequately tell the story of federal spending over this 72-year period.

During World War II, America fought to save the United Kingdom and the entire continent of Europe from German totalitarianism and to rescue the Pacific region from Japanese imperialism. As a result of the war effort, the gross debt skyrocketed from 52 percent of GDP in 1940 to 122 percent of GDP in 1946. Gross debt as a share of GDP steadily fell from the late 1940s to a low of 33 percent from 1979 to 1981. During the 1980s, the gross debt rapidly increased, reaching 53 percent in 1989. From 1994 to

Chart 2.5: Gross Debt as Percentage of GDP, 1940–2011

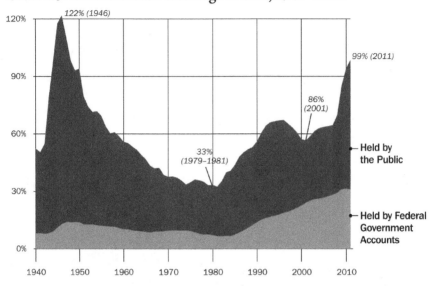

Source: Office of Management and Budget, *Historical Tables, Budget of the United States, Fiscal Year 2013* (Washington DC: U.S. Government Printing Office, 2011), Tables 7.1 and 10.1.

1997, the gross debt peaked at 67 percent and then declined to 56 percent in 2001. From 2002 to 2007, the gross debt incrementally grew to 65 percent. In 2008, the gross debt jumped 5 percent to 70 percent. By 2011, the gross debt dramatically increased by 29 percent to 99 percent.

Chart 2.6 presents the debt held by the public as a percentage of GDP from 1940 to 2011. The public debt increased from 44.2 percent of GDP in 1940 to 67.7 percent of GDP in 2011. While the public debt as a percentage of GDP increased an additional 22.5 percent between 1940 and 2011, this comparison does not adequately tell the story of federal spending over this 72-year period.

As with gross debt, the trend in public debt was greatly affected by World War II. As a result of the war effort, the public debt skyrocketed from 44.2 percent of GDP in 1940 to 108.7 percent of GDP in 1946. Public debt as a share of GDP steadily fell from the late 1940s to a low of 23.9 percent in 1974. During the 1980s, the public debt rapidly increased, reaching 40.6 percent in 1989. The public debt reached 49.2 in 1993 percent and then declined to 32.5 percent in 2001. From 2002 to 2007, the public debt slowly grew to 36.3 percent. In 2009, the public debt jumped an additional 17.8 percent

Chart 2.6: Debt Held by the Public as Percentage of GDP, 1940–2011

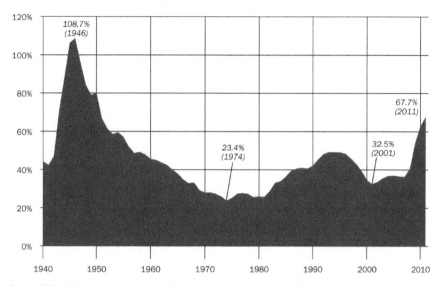

Source: Office of Management and Budget, *Historical Tables, Budget of the United States, Fiscal Year 2013* (Washington DC: U.S. Government Printing Office, 2011), Tables 7.1 and 10.1.

to 54.1 percent. By 2011, the debt dramatically increased by another 13.6 percent to 67.7 percent. In June 2012, the CBO projected that the public debt will reach 70 percent of GDP by the end of calendar year 2012.[104] If Congress keeps its current tax and spending policies in place, the CBO estimates that public debt will reach 90 percent of GDP by 2022.[105]

Defining and Measuring Spending on Federal Social Programs

How does spending on federal social programs fit into the picture of fiscal irresponsibility that has been presented so far? Chart 2.7 breaks down total federal spending for FY 2011 by mandatory, discretionary, and interest categories. Mandatory spending composed of entitlement programs accounted for 59 percent of all federal spending. Within the mandatory spending category, 20.1 percent was allocated for Social Security, 14.6 percent for Medicare, 7.2 percent for Medicaid, and 17.1 percent for other mandatory spending programs.

Discretionary spending accounted for 35 percent of federal spending in FY 2011 with defense comprising 18.3 percent and non-defense spending

Chart 2.7: Federal Spending, Fiscal Year 2011

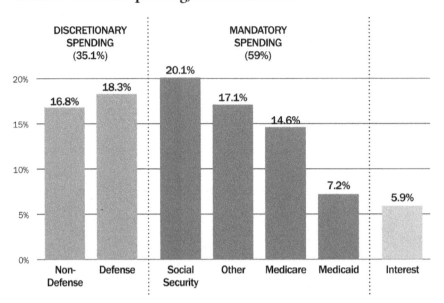

Source: Congressional Budget Office, *The Budget and Economic Outlook: Fiscal Years 2012 to 2022*, (Washington DC: U.S. Government Printing Office) January 2012, Table 3.1, p. 49.

consisting of 16.8 percent. Interest payments accounted for 5.9 percent of total spending.

Each February, the OMB releases the president's proposed budgets for the federal government. Within the proposals are numerous policy suggestions laying out each aspect of the president's agenda for the nation. Of particular interest to us are the OMB's historical tables that include a breakdown of federal spending by broad classifications, called superfunctions, and the narrower classifications, called functions and subfunctions.

Obtaining exact data on how much the federal government spends on social programs is difficult. William Voegeli used the superfunction Human Resources as a proxy for the amount of money spent on the welfare state.[106] To measure the growth of federal social programs, we will have to dive deeper into the OMB data by using the function and subfunction classifications. The OMB started classifying spending by subfunction categories in 1962, so this will be our starting year.

The Education, Training, Employment, and Social Services function and the Housing Assistance, Food and Nutrition Assistance, Other Income

Chart 2.8: Spending on Federal Social Programs, 1962–2011

From 1962 to 2011, social program spending increased by 1,789 percent.

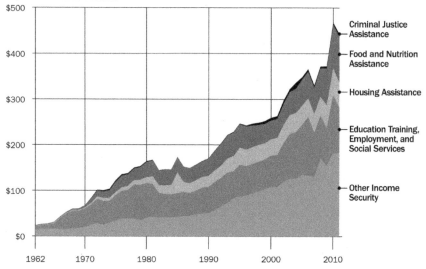

IN BILLIONS OF 2010 DOLLARS

Criminal Justice Assistance

Food and Nutrition Assistance

Housing Assistance

Education Training, Employment, and Social Services

Other Income Security

Source: Office of Management and Budget, *Historical Tables, Budget of the United States, Fiscal Year 2013* (Washington DC: U.S. Government Printing Office, 2011), Tables 3.2 and 10.1.

Security, and Criminal Justice Assistance subfunctions are used to estimate the amount of taxpayer dollars spent on federal social programs.[107] Within these categories are a range of social programs intended to change human behavior for the better. While this measure is imperfect, it is a practical estimate of social program spending. A sampling of social programs funded under these categories include Temporary Assistance for Needy Families (TANF), job-training and education programs, and juvenile delinquency prevention programs. The figures presented include only federal outlays and ignore the amount spent by state and local governments.

Chart 2.8 illustrates spending on federal social programs in 2010 dollars over 50 years, from 1962 to 2011. In 1962, total spending on federal social programs was $23.4 billion. In 2011, federal social program spending had increased to $442.8 billion—a 1,789 percent increase compared to spending in 1962. The growth in spending over this 50-year period represents an annual growth rate of 6.2 percent. An annual growth rate of 6.2 percent means that spending on social programs will double in size every 17 years.

Most of the growth in social programs is from the Other Income Security subfunction, which includes TANF, the successor of AFDC. From 1962 to 2001, social program spending increased at a steady rate, with a dip in spending from 1982 to 1990 that was interrupted by a spike in spending in 1985. Spending on social programs experienced the largest decrease in 1982, with a 13.8 percent reduction compared to spending in 1981. After 2001, the rate of spending growth increased. From 2001 to 2002, spending increased by 12.8 percent—from $263.4 billion to $297.2 billion. From 2003 to 2006, spending continued to increase, albeit with smaller percentage increases. Then, spending experienced a 9.7 percent decrease from 2006 to 2007. However, spending resumed its climb by jumping by 12.6 percent from 2007 to 2008. Spending virtually flatlined in 2009 before experiencing the largest percentage increase (25.8%) in 2010 since the 38.2 percent increase in 1966. In 2011, spending declined from $468.2 billion in 2010 to $442.8 billion—a decrease of 5.4 percent.

As Chart 2.8 demonstrates, spending on federal social programs has steadily increased, despite adjusting for inflation. However, Chart 2.8 does not account for population growth. Some may argue that the large increase in social program spending reflects population growth more than the ever-expanding budgets of social programs. Thus, the annual 6.2 percent growth rate really reflects population growth.

A growing population means more spending on social programs. To account for population growth, Chart 2.9 presents the spending on a 2010 dollar per capita basis. In 1962, social program spending was $125.67 per capita. In 2011, the figure increased to $1,421.02 per capita—a 1,031 percent increase. In 1962, the total population of the United States was 186,537,737 people.[108] The total population of the nation grew to 311,591,917 people in 2011—an annual growth rate of 1.1 percent.[109] An annual growth rate of 1.1 percent means that the total population will double in size every 91 years. In contrast, the annual growth rate of 5.1 percent in social program spending per capita means spending in this category doubles every 19 years.

Others will posit that the growth in social program spending reflects the growing economy of the nation. They will say that spending has not really grown that much. It is just keeping pace with economic growth. Chart 2.10 puts this hypothesis to rest. From 1962 to 2011, spending on social programs as a percentage of the nation's GDP increased from 0.1 percent to 3.1 percent. The growth in spending over this 50-year period represents an annual rate of 7.3 percent per year for social programs, while the annual growth rate of the economy as measured in GDP was 3.1 percent. An annual growth rate of

Chart 2.9: Per-Capita Spending on Federal Social Programs, 1962–2011

From 1962 to 2011, per-capita spending on social programs increased by 1,031 percent.

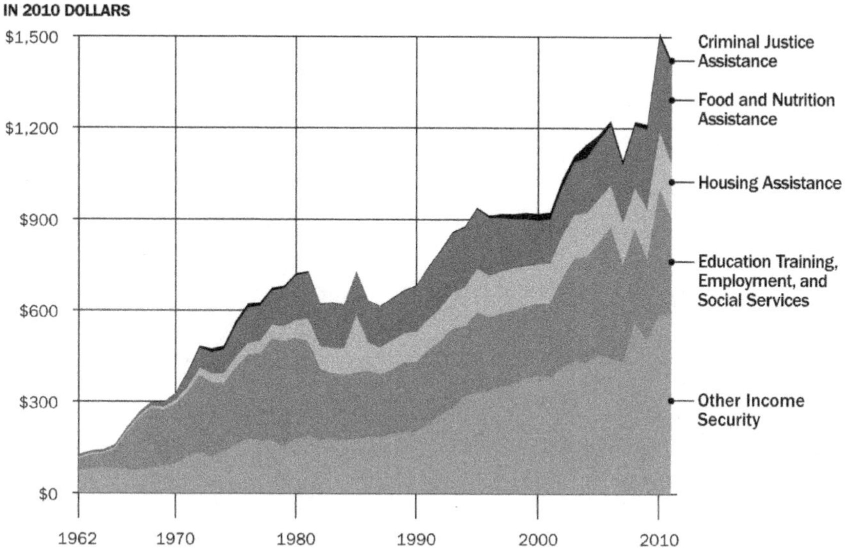

IN 2010 DOLLARS

Sources: Office of Management and Budget, *Historical Tables, Budget of the United States, Fiscal Year 2013* (Washington DC: U.S. Government Printing Office, 2011), Tables 3.2 and 10.1; U.S. Census Bureau, Population Estimates Program, Population Division, "Historical National Population Estimates."

7.3 percent means that spending on social programs will double in size every 15 years. At a 3.1 percent growth rate, the nation's economy will take just under 33 years to double in size.

How has the change in spending on federal social programs varied by presidential administration? Federal social programs have generally experienced generous spending increases no matter whether the president was a Democrat or Republican. Table 2.1 presents the total percentage increase and annual growth rate by each presidential term from John F. Kennedy to Barack Obama.

The 2010 dollar figures presented in the table are for each president's term in office. The total increase in real, per capita social program spending represents the percentage change in spending during the president's term or terms in office. The annual per capita growth rates are the average spending increase per year during a president's term or terms in office.

Since OMB began cataloging spending by subfunction only in 1962, Table 2.1 uses 1962, instead of 1961, as the base year for the combined first

Chart 2.10: Spending on Federal Social Programs as Percentage of GDP, 1962–2011

From 1962 to 2011, social program spending as a percentage of GDP grew 7.3 percent annually. During that same period, the economy grew by only 3.1 percent per year.

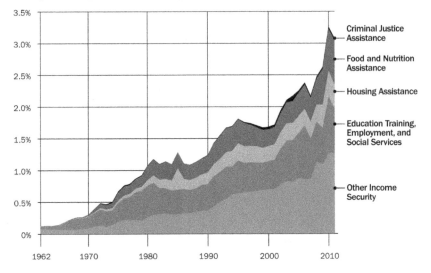

Source: Office of Management and Budget, *Historical Tables, Budget of the United States, Fiscal Year 2013* (Washington DC: U.S. Government Printing Office, 2011), Tables 3.2 and 10.1.

term of John F. Kennedy and Lyndon B. Johnson. Using 1962 as the base year likely understates the growth in social program spending. Unsurprisingly, the presidential term that experienced the largest total percentage change in per capita social program spending of 87.3 percent is Lyndon B. Johnson's second term (his first term elected as president). During Johnson's second term, the annual growth rate was 17.0 percent. Overall, the Kennedy/ Johnson administrations experienced the largest increase of spending— 136.0 percent—with an annual growth rate of 13.1 percent.

Coming in second are the administrations of Richard Nixon and Gerald Ford. During Nixon's first term, spending increased by 59.9 percent, with an annual growth rate of 12.5 percent. Over the course of the Nixon and Ford administrations, spending increased by 111.1 percent, with an annual growth rate of 9.8 percent.

The most frugal president is Ronald Reagan. During his first term in office, the trend in social program spending was flat, with 0.0 percent change in total spending and annual growth rates. During his second term, total spending declined by 8.4 percent, with an annual decrease of 2.2 percent. Overall

TABLE 2.1.   Growth Rates of Real, Per Capita Social Program Outlays by Presidential Term and Presidency

Presidency	First and Final Years	Number of Years	Total Increase in Real, Per Capita Social Program Outlays	Annual Growth Rate of Real, Per Capita Social Program Outlays
Kennedy/Johnson	1962–1965*	3	26.0%	8.0%
Johnson	1965–1969	4	87.3%	17.0%
Kennedy/Johnson	**1961–1969**	**8**	**136.0%**	**13.1%**
Nixon I	1969–1973	4	59.9%	12.5%
Nixon II/Ford	1973–1977	4	32.0%	7.2%
Nixon/Ford	**1969–1977**	**8**	**111.1%**	**9.8%**
Carter	**1977–1981**	**4**	**16.3%**	**3.8%**
Reagan I	1981–1985	4	0.0%	0.0%
Reagan II	1985–1989	4	−8.4%	−2.2%
Reagan	**1981–1989**	**8**	**−8.4%**	**−1.1%**
George H.W. Bush	1989–1993	4	28.8%	6.5%
Clinton I	1993–1997	4	7.0%	1.7%
Clinton II	1997–2001	4	0.5%	0.1%
Clinton	**1993–2001**	**8**	**7.6%**	**0.9%**
George W. Bush I	2001–2005	4	27.4%	6.3%
George W. Bush II	2005–2009	4	2.9%	0.7%
George W. Bush	**2001–2009**	**8**	**31.2%**	**3.5%**
Obama	2009–2011	2	17.2%	8.3%

*The first year that OMB catalogued spending by subfunctions was for FY 1962, so the base year for the Kennedy administration (1961) is excluded.

Source: Office of Management and Budget. *Historical Tables, Budget of the United States, Fiscal Year 2013.* Washington, DC: U.S. Government Printing Office, 2011, Tables 3.2 and 10.1; U.S. Census Bureau, Population Estimates Program, Population Division, "Historical National Population Estimates." http://www.census.gov/population/estimates/nation/popclockest.txt (accessed December 12, 2012).

during both of Reagan's terms, spending declined by 8.4 percent, with an annual decrease of 1.1 percent.

The second most frugal president is William Clinton. During Clinton's first term, spending increased by 7.0 percent, with an annual growth rate of 1.7 percent. The trend reversed during his second term, with a spending increase of 0.5 percent and annual growth rate of 0.1 percent. Over the course of both of his terms, spending increased by 7.6 percent, with an annual growth rate of 0.9 percent. While Clinton deserves credit for being the most frugal Democratic president during this time span, the contribution of a Republican-controlled Congress toward slowing spending increases should not be ignored.

While Barack Obama successfully ratcheted up spending during his first year in office with the annual appropriations process and the American Recovery and Reinvestment Act, how he will compare to previous presidents remains to be seen. During his first two years in office, spending increased by 17.2 percent, with an annual increase of 8.3 percent. These calculations compare his 2009 base year of $1,212.09 spending per capita to $1,421.02 per capita in 2011, so the comparison can be a little misleading. During 2010, spending was $1,513.57 per capita on social programs. The 2010 elections that resulted in a Republican-controlled House of Representatives appear to have slowed the growth in social program spending.

Another observation for Table 2.1 is that spending on social programs appears to be the greatest after a president is first elected. For example, after Johnson was first elected president, spending increased by 87 percent. During Nixon's first term, spending increased by 59.9 percent. During the first terms of George H. W. Bush and George W. Bush, spending increased by 28.8 percent and 27.4 percent, respectively.

How the Federal Government's Debt Harms Us All

America's debt is out of control, and Congress and recent presidents have done little to decrease spending and reduce the debt. Our current fiscal path will debilitate our economy, substantially weaken our prosperity, and lead to massive tax burdens to be faced by future generations.

Carmen M. Reinhart of the Peterson Institute for International Economics and Kenneth S. Rogoff of Harvard University created a unique data set of financial crises covering eight centuries. Reinhart and Rogoff conclude that a unifying problem among the financial crises they analyzed is government debt.[110] They coined the "this-time is different syndrome," that is, the "belief that financial crises are things that happen to other people in other countries at other times; crises do not happen to us, here and now. We are doing things better, we are smarter, we have learned from past mistakes."[111] This syndrome is often displayed despite indicators of a forthcoming financial crisis being apparent to all. Our federal government has accumulated a debt of staggering proportions. CBO estimates strongly suggest that the federal government's spending pattern is unsustainable.

The United States has four basic options to prevent out-of-control debt from devastating our economy. The first is to raise taxes. The second is to cut spending. The third is to print more money to pay down the debt, while increasing inflation. The last is to default. While the "correct" option is often based on one's ideology, there is a body of empirical research that indicates that our best option is to cut spending.

Harvard University professor of economics Alberto Alesina and his coauthors analyzed the effect of large government fiscal adjustments—substantial spending cuts or tax increases—on economic growth and government deficits and debt from 1970 to 2007 in 21 countries with membership in the Organization for Economic Co-operation and Development (OECD).[112] OECD is an international economic association of economically advanced democracies that promotes economic progress and world trade. Alesina and his coauthors' research attempts to determine whether tax cuts or spending increases have more expansionary effects on the economy. Their second question is whether spending reductions or tax increases are more likely to reduce deficits and debt. They found that fiscal stimuli based on tax cuts were more likely to be associated with increased economic growth than were spending increases. Further, fiscal adjustments based on spending reductions accompanied by no tax increases were much more effective than tax increases at reducing deficits and debt, and avoiding economic downturns. As an added bonus, they found that spending cuts intended to reduce deficits were associated with economic expansions rather than recessions. Commenting on the current fiscal crisis that the United States is facing, Alesina and Ardagna conclude that their analysis "suggests that unless primary [government] spending is cut, it is difficult to achieve fiscal stability because spending may rise faster than tax revenue."[113]

In another study, Alesina and his coauthors analyzed the effect of large government fiscal adjustments—substantial spending cuts or tax increases—on profits and business investments in 18 OECD countries from 1960 to 1996.[114] Alesina and his colleagues found that increases in government spending are associated with reduced private sector profits. In particular, a 1 percent increase in the ratio of government spending to GDP results in an immediate decrease of private sector investment of 0.15 percent and has a cumulative negative impact of 0.74 percent after five years.[115] The impact is even stronger when the increase in spending is limited to government wages. A 1 percent increase in the ratio of government wage spending to GDP results in an immediate decrease of private sector investment of 0.48 percent and has a cumulative negative impact of 2.56 percent after five years.[116]

In addition, Alesina and his colleagues found that tax increases reduce private sector profits and investments, with taxes on labor having the largest negative effect. However, the negative effect of increased taxation is less than the effect of increased government spending.

Most important for the topic of this book is that Alesina and his colleagues found that "fiscal stabilizations that have led to an increase in economic growth consist mainly of spending cuts, particularly in government wages and transfers, while those associated with an economic downturn are characterized by tax increases."[117] Cutting government spending is considered "expansionary" because of the increase in economic growth that results, while tax increases are considered "contractionary" because they led to economic downturns.[118]

Harvard University professor of economics Silvia Ardagna found that increased spending on government employees and transfer payments has a contractionary effect on the economy that is similar to raising taxes.[119] His research also indicates that cutting spending increases the welfare of households and is more effective at reducing government deficits and debt than increases in tax rates.

Bertrand Gruss of the International Monetary Fund and Jose L. Tores of the University of Málaga in Spain have concluded that if the United States fails to address its fiscal imbalances for a prolonged period, the nation will experience a significant crowding-out of private investment and an acute drag on economic growth.[120] The continuation of current spending policies over the next two decades, as opposed to stabilizing federal debt at pre-2008 levels, will result in a permanent loss of around 17 percent in the nation's economic output.[121] Further, "The associated drop in per-capita consumption, combined with the worsening of wealth concentration that the model suggests, would cause a large average welfare loss in the long-run, equivalent to about 7 percent of lifetime consumption."[122]

This body of literature suggests a clear path for America: cutting spending, while apparently politically painful for members of Congress, will boost the economy and reduce debt. A good place to start is with the elimination of funding for ineffective social programs.

Chapter 3

Assessing Effectiveness: The Problem of Selection

Holding Social Programs Accountable

Given the fiscal crises the federal government is facing, holding federal social programs accountable for their performance is necessary to regain control over excessive spending. Why should Congress routinely spend taxpayer dollars on failed social programs that we know do not work?

Operating with increasingly scarce resources, federal policymakers need to start denying funds to ineffective programs, even if calls for funding these programs *seem* morally compelling. Calling for more spending on social programs may seem morally compelling, but is it moral to continue spending taxpayer dollars on programs that do not produce their intended results?

Social programs should be carefully evaluated to determine whether they do, in fact, work. But how do we know when these programs work? To reliably sort out the effect of a social program from confounding factors is a difficult task.

Some will argue that we need to attack fraud and abuse in federal social programs. While this approach is noble, it still fails to address the problem of spending taxpayer dollars on ineffective programs. While preventing fraud and abuse in social programs will produce some cost savings, such actions will not reform a program that has been found highly ineffective. Besides, eliminating fraud and abuse will never bring the federal government's overspending under control.

Science versus Anecdotal Observations

Many people believe that social programs are effective based on their personal opinions and observations. There are numerous methods of making sense of the world around us. We frequently make personal observations of events around us to bring order to our lives. We often assign cause-and-effect relationships to events we personally experience. For instance, learning that touching a hot stove will burn you is an easy cause-and-effect association that does not need to be tested more than once. We can easily correlate the act of touching the stove with the pain felt. Firsthand experience is often instrumental to developing knowledge. We make personal observations every day that guide us in our activities. We often seek the advice of others based on their personal experiences.

However, the usefulness of personal observations or experiences can be undermined when we are assessing complex social interactions that can have multiple causes. This problem is particularly acute when assessing the effectiveness of social programs where multiple factors can cause the outcomes of interest.

Congress frequently seeks policy advice through hearings. At congressional hearings, congressional committees seek the testimony of experts. On many occasions, these committees are collecting advice on the merits of social programs. As is often the case at these hearings, the invited panelists offer their opinions of the pros and cons of the social program of interest. A frequent type of panelist is an administrator of a social program that is financially dependent on continued federal funding.

In 2010, I had the honor of being asked to testify on a piece of legislation reauthorizing the Second Chance Act of 2007 before the U.S. House of Representative Committee on the Judiciary, Subcommittee on Crime, Terrorism, and Homeland Security.[1] The Second Chance Act provides federal funds for the operation of prisoner reentry programs. Prisoner reentry programs help former prisoners transition back into society after their release from prison. On the panel were administrators of prisoner reentry programs from the Richmond, Virginia, Second Chance Re-Entry Program and the Illinois Department of Corrections. Both administrators provided anecdotal examples and observations based on their personal experience that their programs are effective and worthy of federal funding. The chairman of the Committee on the Judiciary, John Conyers, sitting in on the subcommittee hearing, asked me, "I am wondering, as you have heard the other four panelists with you that have all talked about the benefits and the positive influence of this prisoner reentry concept, were you impressed with any of the benefits that they talked about that resulted from the programs?"[2] I replied,

> [T]he ultimate judge of whether or not programs work is a rigorous scientific study . . . while we may have anecdotal examples of where programs can be a

success, often those anecdotal stories are biased or sometimes mistaken, or sometimes they are [from] people seeking additional funding, and so they are not going to say, "You know what? My program really stinks." They are not going to say that.[3]

My point was that no one who comes before Congress with hat in hand seeking federal funding is going to admit that they do not know if their program works or that their program is ineffective. A key problem with anecdotal observations is the absence of a counterfactual condition—the ability to know what would have happened in the absence of the social program. The congressmen were holding a hearing to justify reauthorization of the Second Chance Act. However, they had no solid evidence that federal funding of prisoner reentry programs was effective. With the federal government spending hundreds of billions of dollars per year on social programs, we should expect Congress to not rely on personal opinions that are too often self-serving.

Federal social programs should be carefully evaluated to determine whether they do, in fact, work. The best way to gain this knowledge is to conduct large-scale, multisite experimental evaluations that attempt to isolate the direct effects of social programs apart from other factors that affect the outcomes of interest.

Evidence-Based Policy

The social sciences can make important contributions to policymaking. Perhaps the greatest contribution is the evidenced-based policy movement that seeks to inform and influence policymakers through scientifically rigorous evaluations of the effectiveness of government programs.[4] The evidence-based policy movement, in other words, seeks to inform policymakers about what works and what does not work. According to Ron Haskins of the Brookings Institution, "Evidence-based policy is especially important today because the nation's major social intervention programs in preschool, the public schools, delinquency, employment and training, and many other areas usually do not have significant impacts on the social problems they were designed to address."[5]

The notion that public policy should be informed by social science has gained widespread acceptance. The evaluation of federal social programs, using scientific techniques, offers policymakers and the public ample opportunities to learn about the effectiveness of social programs. Despite the availability of evaluation methods, the effectiveness of federal social programs is unknown in far too many cases. Many programs operate for decades without ever undergoing thorough scientific evaluations. For example, a 1997 report commissioned by the U.S. Department of Justice (DOJ) and authored by criminologists at the University of Maryland looked at 500 evaluations of crime-prevention programs.[6] While the study did not evaluate specific programs, it reviewed scientific studies of programs and judged them on their scientific merit. The report noted that many of the DOJ's crime-prevention programs either were evaluated as ineffective or escaped scrutiny altogether. It added, "By scientific standards, there are very few 'programs of proven effectiveness.'"[7] A 2002 update to the University of Maryland report similarly found that few criminal justice programs could be considered effective at reducing crime.[8] Yet, the DOJ continues to spend billions of dollars on criminal justice programs that are unknown to be effective.

With the enormous federal debt increasingly shaping policy debates in Washington, DC, Congress should subject all federal social programs to rigorous evaluations to determine what works and what does not work. Scientifically rigorous impact evaluations are necessary to determine whether these programs actually produce their intended effects. Thus, the implementation of rigorous impact evaluation offers policymakers excellent opportunities to exercise oversight of government programs. Policymakers are shirking their responsibilities to taxpayers if they continue to fund social programs that are unknown to work or that do not work at all. Obviously, there is little merit in continuing programs that fail to ameliorate their targeted social problems.

However, there is disagreement over what can be counted as evidence.[9] For example, should high-quality quasi-experiments be given the same level of scientific credibility as experimental evaluations? Despite such disagreements, this chapter argues that experimental evaluations are the most credible and accurate method by which to assess effectiveness.

What Are Evaluations?

According to Carol H. Weiss, a professor of education at Harvard University, "Evaluation is the systematic assessment of the operation and/or the outcomes of a program or policy, compared to a set of explicit or implicit standards, as a means of contributing to the improvement of the program or policy."[10] This definition is too broad for our purposes because it includes several types of evaluations.

Our focus is on impact evaluations, which are also commonly called impact assessments or outcome evaluations. Impact evaluations use social science research methods to *systematically examine* through *counterfactual conditions* the *effectiveness* of programs or policies intended to *ameliorate social conditions*. To *systematically examine* means using research procedures conducted formally and with rigor according to accepted social science research cannons. *A counterfactual condition* "is a comparison of what did appear after implementing the program with what would have appeared had the program not been implemented."[11] Unfortunately, many evaluation methods have great difficulty in establishing a credible counterfactual condition. *Effectiveness* refers to answering whether the program produced outcomes that achieved the program's goals. The change produced by the social program should not have occurred without the intervention. *Ameliorate social conditions* refers to the degree to which the social program lessoned or improved upon the social problems it targeted. Basically, did the program provide some social benefit?

Any impact evaluation of a social program should judge "the quality of a program's performance as it relates to some aspect of its effectiveness in producing social benefits."[12] Does the program achieve its goals and objectives? Does the intervention have beneficial or detrimental effects on participants? Are some participants affected more or less by the intervention than others? Is the problem that the intervention is intended to address made better?

Impact evaluations often assess impacts by comparing treatment or intervention groups to control or comparison groups. In experimental impact evaluations, the treatment or intervention is randomly assigned to one group, while the other group does not receive the treatment or intervention. The group randomly receiving the services is called the intervention or treatment group, while the group not receiving the services is the control group. The findings for the control group serve as the counterfactual condition.

Broadly speaking, there are two types of evaluation designs: experimental and quasi-experimental.[13] Experimental evaluations, often called randomized field or control trials, randomly assign individuals to the intervention and control groups. Random assignment means that each subject has the same probability of being assigned to the intervention or control group.

Impact evaluations that assign subjects to the intervention and comparison groups through some other method than random assignment are quasi-experimental. The group that serves as the counterfactual condition in quasi-experimental impact evaluations is called a comparison group, instead of control group in the case of experimental impact evaluations. As will be demonstrated later in this chapter, the absence of random assignment can lead to serious limitations on demonstrating effectiveness.

The other types of evaluations are needs assessments, program theory assessments, process evaluations, and efficiency assessments. Needs assessments answer questions about the social conditions that a program is intended to ameliorate and need for the program.[14] What are the nature, extent, and distribution of the social problem? Does the social problem rise to a level that needs a formal intervention? What are the needs of the population needing assistance? For example, a needs assessment that examines the prevalence of homelessness in a city should be conducted before a homeless assistance program is created. What are the characteristics of the homeless population? How many of these individuals suffer from mental illness and drug and alcohol dependency? Needs assessments help policymakers better understand the problem of interest and also provide useful information that can be used in designing the program.

Program theory assessments answer questions about the program's conceptualization and design.[15] These assessments describe program theory and frequently use logic models. For example, Head Start operates on a program theory that the provision of education, nutrition, and health services to preschool children from low-income families will help them catch up to the academic achievement levels of children from higher-income families. Head Start operates under the theory that the services it provides will translate into beneficial outcomes for the children later in life.

Process evaluations answer questions about program implementation, operation, and service delivery.[16] Through program monitoring, these evaluations assess the activities and operations of the program. Essentially, they provide feedback on current operations. Is the program serving its targeted population? What amount of services is provided to participants? Are participants completing or graduating from the program? For example, a process evaluation of Head Start may determine how many children are served and how much each child receives in educational, nutrition, and health services. Process evaluations are very common and can often add insight to why an impact evaluation found a particular program to be effective or ineffective.

The last type of evaluation is efficiency assessments, which attempt to answer questions about cost-benefit or cost-effectiveness ratios.[17] Are program resources being used efficiently? Is the cost of the program reasonable in relation to the benefits produced? Would alternative programs generate similar benefits at less cost? Efficiency assessments take into account costs and effectiveness. The evaluations can be cost-effectiveness or cost-benefit studies. Efficiency assessments are often combined with impact evaluations.

Demonstrating Causality

While we can never actually prove causality with 100 percent certainty, we can, through rigorous scientific methods, rule out alternative explanations or hypotheses. If X is thought to cause Y, then what we are saying is that a change in X is probabilistically followed by a change in Y. Causal hypotheses are probabilistic, rather than deterministic, because there are numerous causes and degrees of effects.[18]

Despite the scientific difficulty, "Causality is central to the scientific endeavor."[19] For most causal relationships, there is an asymmetry, with one variable having an effect on the other, but not the other way around.[20] Symbolically, a relationship between two variables, X and Y, can be drawn with an arrow between the two variables to signify a causal association. The variable that the arrow points toward is the dependent variable. Thus, X → Y, indicates an explanatory variable X having a causal influence on dependent variable Y.

If we believe that a particular variable is causally related to another, how do we determine whether there is a causal relationship? A relationship between two variables must comply with three criteria to be regarded as a causal one.[21] The three criteria are:

- An association between the variables
- An appropriate time order
- The elimination of alternative explanations or hypotheses[22]

If one or more of these criteria fails to be satisfied, then we cannot assert that a causal relationship exists. If all three are met, then the scientific evidence supports our belief that a causal relationship exists.

Association between the Variables

If X is thought to cause Y (X → Y), then what we are saying is that a change in X is probabilistically followed by a change in Y. For our purposes, participation in a social program is expected be associated with a beneficial outcome. When the social program intervention occurs, we tend to see certain outcomes. For example, a statistical test finds that participation in an early childhood education program, X, is associated with an increase in academic achievement, Y.

Statistical testing relies on determining statistical significance. A "statistically significant" finding indicates that the effect of a particular intervention is statistically distinguishable from no effect. For example, if an analysis finds that an early childhood education program has a statistically significant effect on a particular outcome, then social scientists can conclude with a high degree of confidence that the result was caused by the program, not by chance.

A "statistically insignificant" finding indicates that the effect of a particular intervention is, for statistical purposes, no different from zero. For example, if an early childhood education program is found to have a statistically insignificant effect on a particular outcome, the probability that the effect was caused by chance is too great for social scientists to conclude with confidence that the program produced the effect. In other words, access to the early childhood education program had no statistically measurable effect on the particular outcome. Another way of phrasing statistical insignificance is to state that the effect of the program is indistinguishable from zero.

The common standard among social scientists for declaring a finding statistically significant is the five percent significance level ($p \le 0.05$). This means that there is at least a 95 percent statistical probability that the program caused the effect and at most a five percent probability that the program had no measurable effect. Most social scientists use this rigorous standard of statistical significance because they want a high degree of confidence in their findings. Policymakers who make decisions based on social science research should also want a high degree of confidence. The one percent significance level ($p \le 0.01$) is an even more rigorous standard, meaning that there is only a one percent probability that results were the product of chance.

Sometimes, social scientists will use the less rigorous standard of 10 percent ($p \le 0.10$). Under this looser standard, social scientists are willing to risk a 10 percent chance of mistakenly concluding that the program had an effect, when it really had no effect at all. The 10 percent significance standard can be justified when social scientists are analyzing small samples, such as 100 cases. Studies using small sample sizes are less likely than studies using much larger sample sizes to be sensitive enough to find statistically significant findings at the five percent significance level.[23] Thus, social scientists sometimes use the less rigorous 10 percent significance level for small sample sizes.

In contrast, the larger the sample size used in a study, the more sensitive the study will be in finding statistically significant effects. For this reason, most social scientists use the five percent confidence level when working with large sample sizes.

In some cases, authors of large-scale evaluations of social programs report statistically significant impacts based on the 10 percent significance level ($p \leq 0.10$). However, this level of statistical significance is hard to justify with large samples of individuals participating in the evaluations. Thus, the findings presented in Chapters 4 and 5 that include confidence levels of 10 percent are considered as only suggestive and marginally statistically significant. When considering the results presented in these chapters, more weight should be given to results that are statistically significant at least at the five percent confidence level.

An Appropriate Time Order

Cause must precede effect. The change in X must come before the change in Y. In other words, the intervention of the social program, X, must occur before the observed outcome, Y. For example, a change in academic achievement, Y, must come after participation in Head Start, X.

The Elimination of Alternative Explanations or Hypotheses

Plausible rival explanations must be ruled out to fulfill this criterion. This criterion is the most difficult to satisfy. It is a common mistake to assume that if the association and time order criteria are met, then a causal association had been established. For example, one can observe an unemployed person entering a job-training program with the hope of boosting her skills to make herself more employable. After receiving training, she quickly finds a new job. The two variables, job training and employment, have the appropriate time order with the cause preceding the effect. The person found a job, so to the casual observer, there appears to be an association. For many, this is enough evidence to make the causal observation that the job-training program is effective.

To the scientific observer, however, there may be many alternative explanations that are more or at least as likely to explain the outcome. While the job trainee was receiving training, the local economy may have rebounded, with employers needing more workers. Instead of receiving training, the person could have sat on her couch all day watching television and still have been hired for the job. Another plausible explanation is that the person is more motivated to find employment than others. This is demonstrated by her seeking training to improve her job skills. Another just as motivated unemployed person who did not receive any training may have found a similar job. Each of these alternative explanations is plausible. Thus, based solely on the association and time order criteria, the casual observer does not have a strong case that the job-training program was effective.

To summarize, to support the hypothesis that the social program causes the outcome, we must show that participation in the social program and the outcome of interest are statistically dependent. Then, we must be certain that the outcome was observed after participation in the social program. Last and most difficult, alternative explanations must be ruled out as the cause for participation in the social program to be considered the cause of the outcome.

Threats to Internal and External Validity

The ability to make causal observations comes down to handling threats to internal and external validity. Validity refers to the truth or falsity of statements about cause and effect. Internal validity is the "basic minimum without which any experiment is uninterpretable."[24] Did in fact the social program being evaluated make a difference in this specific instance? To establish internal validity, some kind of control condition is required in order to determine what would have happened to the people in the intervention group had they not received the intervention. Any threat to internal validity is a hazard to the ability of the evaluation to make causal inferences.

External validity deals with questions of generalizability. To what populations, settings, and times can the effect of a social program be generalized? For example, can the results of an evaluation of a delinquency prevention program in Baltimore, Maryland, be generalized to a similar program operating in Little Rock, Arkansas? Threats to external validity cast doubts on the extent to which the results of the social program as conducted would be duplicated with the same program at a different time, or place, or with different participants. Evaluators of social programs should strive to select evaluation designs that are strong in both external and internal validity.

Experimental evaluations are, by far, the best design for dealing with threats to internal validity. What about external validity? Experimental evaluations that are large scale—meaning large sample sizes—and are conducted in multiple sites have the most validity for making generalizations.

Threats to Internal Validity

Internal validity is concerned with making causal inferences.[25] Did, in fact, social program X cause outcome Y? There are several factors that threaten internal validity. A threat to internal validity is an objection that an evaluation design allows the causal link between the intervention and outcome to remain uncertain. The design is weak in some way. The design does not allow the person assessing effectiveness to have confidence in the results. If uncontrolled, these factors confound real effects. The most common threats to internal validity are listed and defined in Table 3.1.

The internal validity threat of *history* occurs when events taking place concurrently with the intervention could cause the observed effect.[26] Some change in the experimental condition other than the intervention by the social program has an effect on the outcome. For example, an evaluation of a job-training program that compared the employment status and earnings of program participants without a control group may conclude that the program was effective. After participating in the training, individuals found jobs and experienced increased earnings. However, the absence of a control group means that history is a serious threat to the internal validity

TABLE 3.1.   Threats to Internal Validity

1. *History*: Events taking place concurrently with the intervention could cause the observed effect.
2. *Maturation*: Natural changes in participants that occur over time could be confused with an observed outcome.
3. *Testing*: Taking a test can affect scores on subsequent exposures to that test, an occurrence that can be confused with an intervention effect.
4. *Instrumentation*: The nature of an outcome measure or the observers administering the measure may change over time that could be confused with an outcome.
5. *Statistical regression*: When participants are selected for their extreme scores, they will often have less extreme scores on other variables, an occurrence that can be confused with an observed outcome.
6. *Selection bias*: Systematic differences in the characteristics of intervention and control/comparison group participants that could also cause the observed outcome.
7. *Attrition or experimental mortality*: Differential loss of intervention and control/comparison participants due to the intervention or to the measurement process can produce artifactual or spurious effects.

Sources: William R. Shadish, Thomas D. Cook, and Donald T. Campbell, *Experimental and Quasi-Experimental Designs for Generalized Causal Inference* (Boston: Houghton Mifflin Company, 2002), Table 2.4, 54; Donald Campbell and Julian C. Stanley, *Experimental and Quasi-Experimental Designs for Research* (Boston: Houghton Mifflin Company, 1963), 5–6.

of the evaluation. Other factors, such as a newly thriving economy, could be responsible for the positive effects. If a control group was used, then the control group members may have had similar successful outcomes compared to the intervention group. In such cases, one would not be able to conclude that the job-training program was effective.

Maturation occurs when natural changes in participants that occur over time could be confused with an observed outcome.[27] This threat can include "growing older, growing hungrier, growing more tired, and the like."[28] Maturation covers all biological and psychological processes that systematically and independently vary with the passage of time. For example, the cognitive abilities of children naturally evolve with age. Maturation means that the observed gains found in education research can be strongly influenced by the natural biological and psychological developmental process of children. Evaluations of education programs without control groups cannot isolate the effect of maturation on the measured outcomes.

The internal validity threat of *testing* occurs when the initial act of taking a test or some other type of examination affects subsequent exposures to the test or examination.[29] "Practice, familiarity, or other forms of reactivity" that influence observed outcomes could be mistaken for program effects.[30] For example, testing can occur in evaluations of education programs when the outcome measure is based on tests administered at the beginning (pretest) and end (posttest) of the school year. In this example, the effect of initially taking a pretest influences the results of the posttest. After the pretest, students may adapt and learn how to perform better on the year-end test. Testing prevents us from determining whether the students became better test takers by themselves or the education program actually helped them to improve their academic skills.

Instrumentation occurs when "changes in calibration of a measuring instrument or changes in the observers or scores used may produce changes in the obtained measurements."[31] For example, "human observers may become more experienced between pretest and posttest and so report more accurate scores at later points in time."[32]

Statistical regression occurs when participants have been selected on the basis of their extreme scores.[33] This type of selection process can cause "regression to the mean," which refers to the fact that those with extreme scores on any measure at one point in time will very likely have less extreme scores on later tests. Individuals scoring toward extremes are likely to drift naturally toward less extreme scores over time. For example, when selection into a social program is based on low scores, individuals may perform better on a retest of the original assessment and other similar, but different measures.

Selection bias is, perhaps, the most problematic threat to internal validity for evaluations of social programs. When systematic differences in the characteristics of intervention and comparison participants are present, the observed outcomes may be the result of selection bias and not the effect of the social program.[34] This threat is common in quasi-experimental designs when the estimate of the counterfactual derives from a comparison group. Pre-existing differences can become confounded with the effects of the intervention.

Consider judging the effectiveness of drug courts. Drug courts have become a popular alternative for addressing nonviolent drug offenders. Typically, drug courts process offenders through either diversion or post-adjudication programs that allow participants to escape harsher penalties in exchange for voluntarily participating in drug treatment. Individuals volunteering to enter into a drug court program may be more motivated than individuals not seeking the benefits of a drug treatment program. Such motivational factors and other similar factors are often invisible to those assessing effectiveness. Failure to account for these crucial factors can produce a spurious association between drug court participation and recidivism and substance abuse outcomes.

Another common case of selection bias in the evaluation of drug courts is the too frequent comparison of drug court graduates to nongraduates.[35] The intervention group is comprised of those participants who successfully completed the drug court, while the comparison group consists of drug court participants who were kicked out of the program or dropped out. The "much-heralded findings" based on this faulty methodology "show that the successes succeed and the failures fail."[36] This type of comparison is incapable of providing a scientifically valid assessment of the effectiveness of drug courts.

A similar example is a quasi-experimental evaluation of the InnerChange Freedom Initiative (IFI), a faith-based prison rehabilitation program operated by Prison Fellowship in a Texas prison.[37] While the author of evaluation, Byron R. Johnson, a professor of social sciences at Baylor University, concluded that while "participation in the IFI program is not related to recidivism reduction," program graduates "are significantly less likely to be either arrested or incarcerated during the two-year period following release from prison[, which] represents initial evidence that program completion of this faith-based initiative is associated with lower rates of recidivism."[38] However, the counterfactual condition in this case is IFI individuals who failed to complete the program. The successful graduates may have been just as likely to not recidivate without participating in the faith-based program. Obviously, this evaluation tells us nothing more than successes succeed and failures fail. The individuals completing the program may have been more motivated to rehabilitate themselves, so the lack of an adequate counterfactual condition renders the results meaningless for determining if faith-based prison programs are effective at reducing recidivism.

Attrition or mortality is the differential loss of participants from the control or comparison group.[39] Participants from the intervention group and the control or comparison groups sometimes fail to complete participation in the evaluation. Accordingly, "If different kinds of people remain to be measured in one condition versus another, then such differences could produce posttest outcome differences even in the absence of treatment."[40] Evaluations, even random experiments, that exclude dropouts from outcome assessments may inadvertently engage in "creaming of the crop," in which those least likely to succeed drop out, leaving behind an intervention group composed of individuals most likely to succeed. This type of attrition breaks equivalence between the intervention and control groups, thus biasing the impact estimates.

Differential attrition can be a problem, for example, in an evaluation of a drug treatment program where less motivated members of the intervention group drop out of treatment. Thus, the intervention group becomes disproportionately composed of individuals with greater motivations to beat their addiction compared to the composition of the comparison group.

Threats to External Validity

External validity is concerned with questions of generalizability. To what populations, settings, and times can the particular effect of a social program be generalized? Threats to external validity casts doubts on the extent to which the results of a social program as conducted would be duplicated with the same program at a different time, or place, or with different participants.[41] In regards to social programs, there are four patterns of generalization. The *narrow-to-broad* generalization occurs when someone infers a causal relationship from the particular persons, setting, treatments, and outcomes of the original social program to a larger population.[42] This generalization can occur, for example, when a particular social program operating in Baltimore, Maryland, is assumed to have the same effect if implemented as a nation-wide program. Just because the social program worked in Baltimore does not mean that it will work everywhere. Some social programs will work under at least some conditions and not under others. Another example is the assumption that all types of drug treatment programs are effective based on the results of a particular drug treatment program.

The reverse of the narrow-to-broad generalization is the *broad-to-narrow* generalization.[43] This potential error can occur, for example, when the results of a prison rehabilitation program for the general prison population that includes individuals convicted of all offenses are inferred to have the same successful results if the same program was applied exclusively to prisons convicted of violent crimes.

The *at-a-similar-level* generalization occurs when a social program that is found to be effective in a particular jurisdiction is assumed to be effective in similar jurisdictions. This error can occur when a preschool education program in Boston, Massachusetts, is assumed to have the same results in the similarly sized city of Memphis, Tennessee. Another example can occur when the results of a particular statewide social program are assumed to remain the same when implemented in a different state.

Last, *to-a-similar-or-different-kind* generalization occurs when the results of a social program targeting particular types of individuals is assumed to work for (1) similarly situated individuals in a different setting or time or (2) completely different individuals.[44] For example, a job-training program for unemployed males in Lubbock, Texas, should not be automatically assumed to be just as effective if implemented as a national program for all unemployed males. This generalization error is similar to the narrow-to-broad generalization. An example of a to-a-different-kind generalization is the assumption that a program found to be effective at preventing the delinquency of juveniles from upper-class families will have the same effect as a program serving juveniles from families living in poverty. A similar example is the assumption that marriage counseling programs judged to be effective for keeping the marriages of middle- to upper-class couples intact will be successful at encouraging lower-class unmarried couples with children to marry.

Internal and external validity are particularly important issues when assessing the effectiveness of social programs.

The Advantages of Experimental Evaluations

The impact of social programs cannot be estimated with 100 percent certainty. All such impact evaluations face formidable control problems that make valid estimates difficult. As a general rule, the more rigorous the research methodology is, the more reliable the evaluation's findings are.

Determining the impact of social programs requires comparing the conditions of those who received assistance with the conditions of an equivalent group that did not experience the intervention. However, evaluations differ by the quality of methodology used to separate the net impact of programs from other factors that may explain differences in outcomes between comparison and intervention groups.

Experimental evaluations are the "gold standard" of evaluation designs. Randomized experiments attempt to demonstrate causality by (1) holding all possible causes of the outcome constant, (2) deliberately altering only the possible cause of interest, and (3) observing whether the outcome differs between the intervention and control groups. In reality, we can never be 100 percent sure that all the potential causes (confounding factors) were held constant.

When conducting an impact evaluation of a social program, identifying and controlling for all the possible factors that influence the outcomes of interest is impossible. We simply do not have enough knowledge to accomplish this task. Even if we had the capability to identify all possible causal factors, collecting complete and reliable data on all these factors would likely still be beyond our abilities. For example, it is impossible to isolate a person participating in a social program from his family in order to "remove" the influences of family. This is where the benefits of random assignment become clear.

Because we do not know enough about all possible causal factors to identify and hold them constant, randomly assigning test subjects to intervention and control groups allows us to have a high degree of confidence that these unidentified factors will not confound our estimate of the intervention's impact.

Random assignment helps to ensure that the control group is equivalent to the intervention group in composition, predispositions, and experiences.[45] First, randomization means that the intervention and control groups will have an identical composition. The groups are comprised of the same types of individuals in terms of their program-related and outcome-related characteristics. Second, the intervention and control groups will have identical predispositions. Members of both groups "are equally disposed toward the program and equally likely, without intervention, to attain any given outcome status."[46] Third, the intervention and control groups will have identical experiences with regards to time-related processes, such as maturation, and history.

Because the intervention and control groups differ from one another by chance only, factors outside of the intervention that are related to the outcomes are assumed to be equally present in each group. Subjects whose characteristics may make them more responsive to treatment are just as likely to be in either the intervention or control groups. The intervention and control groups should have the same portion of subjects favorably predisposed to benefit from the intervention. Thus, outcome differences should be attributable to the intervention. In sum, randomization eliminates any systematic association between intervention status and the observed and unobserved participant characteristics, thus largely eliminating the selection bias that potentially contaminates other evaluation designs.[47]

According to Jim Manzi, a senior fellow at the Manhattan Institute,

The purposes of randomization, therefore, are (1) to help prevent experimenter bias from assigning systematically different patients to the test versus control groups, consciously or unconsciously, and (2) more subtly, yet more profoundly, to hold approximately equal those potential sources of bias between the test and control groups of which we are ignorant. It is a method designed to create controlled experiments in the presence of rampant, material hidden conditionals.[48]

Demonstrating impact can be measured as simply as I – C, where I is the outcome for the intervention group and C is the outcome for the control or comparison group. Consider the hypothetical example of an experimental evaluation of a correctional rehabilitation program, where the intervention group (I) has a recidivism rate of 48 percent and the control group has a recidivism rate of 60 percent.

$$I - C = 48 \text{ percent} - 60 \text{ percent} = -12 \text{ percent}$$

What does a difference of 12 percent mean about the effectiveness of the rehabilitation program? When this difference is based on random assignment, then answering the question is made vastly easier than if the result was based on a quasi-experimental evaluation.

We need to return to our criteria for establishing causality. The first criterion—an association between the variables—is satisfied if we performed a statistical test that indicated whether the effect of 12 percent is statistically distinguishable from no effect. If the statistical test indicates a statistically significant effect on recidivism, then we can conclude with a high degree of confidence that the result was caused by the program, not by chance.

The second criterion—an appropriate time order—is fulfilled because the rehabilitation program (the cause) preceded the reduction in recidivism (the effect.). The last criterion—the elimination of alternative explanations—is largely satisfied due to the nature of random assignment. Weaker evaluation designs are often plagued by unobserved differences between the intervention and control groups, which make drawing reliable casual conclusions impossible.

Randomized evaluations ensure that preprogram differences between the intervention and control groups do not confound or obscure the true impact of the programs being evaluated. Random assignment allows the evaluator to test for differences between the experimental and control groups that are due to the intervention and not to preintervention discrepancies between the groups. Because they draw members of the interaction and comparison groups from the same pool of eligible participants, these experimental evaluations are superior to other evaluations that use weaker designs.

In addition, the experimental design's methodology is easier to describe to policymakers and layperson than other evaluation methods that use sophisticated statistical modeling techniques,[49] which often have significant weaknesses in determining program impact. Further, the results of a quasi-experimental evaluation using sophisticated statistical modeling techniques can "become entangled in a protracted and often inconclusive scientific debate about whether the findings of a particular study are statistically valid."[50] Alternatively, the results of experimental evaluations are more straightforward and can be easily grasped: "Compared to the control group, the intervention group that participated in the program experienced a 10% increase in the outcome measure."[51]

In quasi-experimental designs, failure to remove the influence of differences that affect program outcomes leaves open the possibility that the underlying differences between the groups, not the program, caused the net impact. While quasi-experimental designs often use sophisticated techniques, experimental evaluations are still considered better at producing reliable estimates of program effects. Evidence in criminal justice policy indicates that quasi-experimental evaluations tend to find results contrary to the findings of experimental evaluations.[52]

After conducting a meta-analysis of 308 criminal justice program evaluations, Professor David Weisburd of George Mason University and his colleagues found that weaker evaluation designs are more likely to find favorable intervention effects and less likely to find harmful intervention effects.[53] They caution that quasi-experimental designs, no matter how well designed, may be incapable of controlling for the unobserved factors that make individuals more likely to respond favorably to the intervention.

Given that experimental evaluations produce the most reliable results, Congress should promote the use of experimental evaluations to assess the effectiveness of federal programs. Congress has a responsibility to ensure that experimental evaluations are used to assess the impact of federal social programs. Quasi-experimental designs, no matter how well designed, may be incapable of controlling for nonprogram factors that influence how participants respond to the intervention.

Given the importance of criminal justice policy, Weisburd argues that researchers have a moral imperative to conduct randomized experiments[54] because of their "obligation to provide valid answers to questions about the effectiveness of treatments, practices, and programs."[55] This moral imperative also applies to Congress, which spends hundreds of billions of dollars on social programs every year. Yet Congress has seldom supported the experimental evaluation of federally funded grant programs.

Addressing Threats to Internal Validity

The remaining task regarding the merits of random assignment is to demonstrate that this method is the most capable of handling threats to internal validity. Experimental evaluations do so by distributing internal validity threats randomly of intervention conditions.[56] Intervention group members will have the same average characteristics as control group members. Random assignment, however, does not prevent alternative factors from influencing outcomes. Random assignment simply ensures that these factors or events are no more likely to happen to intervention group members than to control group members. The only systematic difference between the groups will be the intervention. For example, consider an experimental evaluation of a social program intended to help disadvantaged high school students attend college. Family breakup, such as divorce, may have a casual impact on whether students attend college. Random assignment ensures that family breakup is no more likely to happen to intervention group members than to control group members. Quasi-experimental designs cannot make such guarantees.

Selection bias is the only internal validity threat that random assignment prevents from occurring.[57] Selection bias implies that a systematically biased method was used for selecting units into groups. Chance can have no systematic bias.

Random assignment ensures that confounding variables are unlikely to be correlated with intervention conditions.[58] The random chance of being selected is unrelated to the pre-existing conditions of the pool of individuals being allocated to the intervention or control groups. Consider a coin toss as the process for allocating individuals to the groups. The results of the coin toss are unrelated to the individuals' race, ethnicity, age, income, or anything else.

Therefore, we can expect that the preintervention correlation between intervention assignment and potential confounding factors should not be significantly different from zero.[59] For statistical purposes, this zero correlation is extremely helpful.

Consider a linear regression model of a job-training evaluation:

$$Y_i = \alpha + \beta_X X_i + \beta_T T_i + \epsilon_i$$

where Y is the income of an individual after random assignment, α is the constant or intercept, β_X is the regression coefficient for observed characteristics, X is a set of observed factors, β_T is the regression coefficient that measures the impact of program participation, T is a dummy variable coded as 0 when the individual is in the control group and 1 when the individual is in the intervention group, ϵ is an error term reflecting the unobserved factors that also affect Y, and the subscript i ranges from the first individual to the last individual in the study. If β_T is significantly different than zero, then job training had a significant effect on income. That is, if β_T is positive and statistically significant, then participation in the job-training program was associated with increased income. The opposite would be indicated if β_T was negative and statistically significant. If β_T is statistically indistinguishable from zero, then job training had no impact on income.

However, for this model to provide us with valid impact estimates, T must not be correlated with ϵ. The statistical procedure used in the linear regression model chooses values of β_T, so the correlations between the ϵ and the T are zero. The statistical model makes this zero correlation assumption whether or not the correlation really was zero in the study.

Random assignment guarantees that the correlation between ϵ and the T in the study will be zero. However, in quasi-experimental evaluations, many confounding factors are likely to be correlated with assignment to the intervention. The statistical procedure still chooses the same value for β, even though the error term will be correlated with β. This yields an incorrect estimate of the treatment effect, meaning the value of β_T will an incorrect or biased measure of the effect of job training.

However, estimating this equation when assignment to the job-training program is not based on random assignment poses a serious threat to yielding unbiased impact estimates. When members of the intervention group are purposely selected by job-training administrators or they enter into the job-training program through self-selection, selection bias is going to be a problem. When selection is based on unobserved factors, ϵ will contain factors that are also correlated with T. The evaluator cannot measure and account for the influence of these unobserved factors. Thus, T and ϵ are correlated, leading to biased estimates of program effect.

Consider an example of a quasi-experimental evaluation of a smoking cessation program. If the intervention group is solely comprised of smokers seeking assistance in quitting their habit and the comparison group consists of smokers unwilling to seek help in quitting their habit, T and ϵ are very likely to be correlated. Why? The selection effect—the higher motivation to quit—is unlikely to be observed and accurately measured by the evaluator. Controlling for the race, age, and education levels of participants is easier. Controlling for motivation of the individual participants is vastly more difficult. The unobserved selection process will be captured by ϵ, making it correlated with program participation, T. The effect of selection bias in this case means that the quasi-experimental evaluation will almost certainly overstate the effectiveness of the smoking cessation program.

While random assignment does not prevent the other threats to internal validity, it distributes them equally among the intervention and control groups. In an experimental evaluation, the effect of *history*—outside events occurring after the evaluation began—will have an equal influence on members of the intervention and control groups. Consider an example of an experimental evaluation of a home mortgage education program that attempts to educate future homebuyers on how to apply for mortgages from banks. After random assignment occurs, an event of history such as mortgage lenders tightening or loosening lending standards will influence the outcome of interest—successfully obtaining a mortgage. However, the effect of this event of history will be equally distributed among the intervention and control groups.

The same equal distribution will occur with maturation. For example, consider a child malnutrition program designed to help children living in poverty gain weight as they naturally grow. Through natural biological processes, children will gain weight, thus affecting the outcome of interest.

Random assignment ensures that the effect of maturation is distributed equally among the intervention and control group members.

The internal validity threat of testing can still affect experimental evaluations that compare pretest results to posttest results. Thus, experimental evaluations that use only posttests are effective at reducing this threat.

Random assignment does not eliminate the threat of instrumentation. Statistical regression is not a problem because random assignment assigns individuals to the intervention and control groups by pure chance and not on the basis of extreme scores.

The differential loss of participants in the intervention and control groups—attrition—can still be a problem after random assignment. If more members of either the intervention or control group drop out of the study, the final results could be biased. The threat of attrition can be particularly acute when it is associated with being assigned to the intervention group. Differential attrition can be a problem, for example, in an evaluation of a weight loss program based on physical exercise. If members of the intervention group drop out because they find the rigor of the exercise program too strenuous, the intervention group may become disproportionately composed of individuals with higher motivation to lose weight compared to the composition of the control group. In this case, the evaluation will likely overstate the effectiveness of the weight loss program.

In short, random assignment facilitates our ability to make causal inferences about social programs by equating intervention and control groups before and after the intervention begins, making alternative explanations implausible and creating error terms that are uncorrelated with the intervention variable.

Limitations of Random Assignment

So far, this chapter has focused on the strengths and benefits of impact evaluations using random assignment. There are, however, some limitations with random assignment. Some people will assert that ethical considerations will arise when eligible individuals are deliberately refused participation in a federal social program so that they can serve as members of the control group. Random assignment, according to the detractors, unfairly confers a perceived benefit to some individuals while denying it to others. The reasons why this position does not have merit are twofold.

First, as previously mentioned in this chapter, experimental evaluations are the best method for accurately assessing the effectiveness of social programs. If we do not possess reliable knowledge about the effectiveness of the social program in question, then we cannot know if limiting participation for evaluation purposes actually raises ethical concerns. Barring control group members from participating in a social program that has little to no effect does not leave these individuals worse off. An example of where there should definitely be no ethical concerns about limiting participation is when demand of participation outstrips the supply of open slots. When demand for a social program is greater than the number of slots available for participation, there should be no objections to random assignment. A simple lottery could be used to assign eligible participants to the intervention and control groups. An example of a federal social program where demand outstrips supply is the Pell grant program. For the 2010–2011 school year, there were 18.6 million valid applicants, and during fiscal year 2011, there were 8.6 million grant recipients.[60] Demand clearly outstrips supply. Despite being an ideal candidate for a large-scale multisite experimental evaluation, the effectiveness of Pell grants has not been assessed.

Second, as previously mentioned, Congress has the moral imperative to assess whether the hundreds of billions of dollars it spends on social programs every year are being spent wisely. In fiscal year 2011, Congress allocated over $41 billion for Pell grants, a program that lacks rigorous scientific evidence of effectiveness.[61] Others will say that large-scale multisite experimental evaluations are too expensive. Given the hundreds of billions of dollars spent on federal social programs each year, setting aside 5 to 10 percent of this tidy sum to fund large-scale multisite experimental evaluations would be a wise investment.

What about High-Quality Quasi-Experimental Evaluations?

Some will argue that high-quality quasi-experimental designs, such as regression discontinuity designs and propensity score matching, are suitable alternatives to experimental evaluations.

Regression Discontinuity Designs

In experimental evaluations, the selection procedure is random assignment. In quasi-experimental evaluations, as previously discussed, selection is a nonrandom process. This problem renders most quasi-experimental evaluations susceptible to selection bias. Instead of trying to figure out what variables are related to selection, in regression-discontinuity designs, the evaluator has the selection variable. Many consider regression-discontinuity designs to be the second best evaluation design, behind experimental evaluations, because they are believed to yield the least biased impact estimates of quasi-experimental designs.[62]

Regression-discontinuity designs work by applying a case-by-case allocation rule for parsing subjects into the intervention and comparison groups according to their "scores" on the selection variable. For this method, the selection procedure is some quantitative assignment variable, A, such that one group is made of subjects with scores below some cut point on A and the other group comprises those subjects whose scores on A are above that cut point. The selection variable is formally called the quantitative assessment variable (QAV). It is also called the cutting-point or cut-off variable because it applies a cutting point to some continuum of need, merit, or other selection variable. Using values along the continuum of the selection variable, subjects with scores over a certain point—cutting point—are assigned into one group, and those with scores under the cutting point are assigned to the other group.

The advantage of the regression-discontinuity design is that the selection procedure is explicitly known. Each participant is selected based on his or her score—a measured variable. Thus, the design allows for the statistical control of selection bias. Regression-discontinuity designs are considered to approximate randomized experiments with regards to yielding unbiased estimates.[63] Selection procedures in impact evaluations are good to the extent that they tend to leave the treatment variable T unrelated to the outcome variable Y, except for the effects of the program.

As indicated by its name, regression analysis is essential to this design. The regression-discontinuity design operates as follows. First, assignment of subjects to the intervention (T) is based on their scores on the quantitative assignment variable (A). Those above the cut point go into one group. Those below the cut point go into the other group. The quantitative assignment variable (A) may be related to Y.

This can make T related to Y, even without T having a "true" causal impact on Y. This happens because T is merely a division of the subjects into high and low groupings on A.[64] However, this relationship can be controlled in the regression analysis.

An intervention effect is present when there is a difference between the two regression lines in height, slope, or both.

Displayed in Chart 3.1 is an example of a regression-discontinuity design indicating a positive impact on the outcome variable. The individuals with a

Chart 3.1: Regression-Discontinuity Design: Change in Intercept

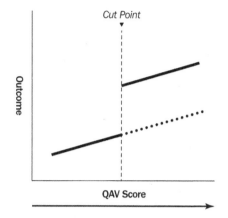

QAV score below the cut-off point are placed in the comparison group, while the individuals scoring at or above the cut-off point on the QAV score are placed in the intervention group. After the cut point, the regression line makes an abrupt and positive change in height. The shift in height indicates that the subjects participating in the intervention experienced an increase in the outcome measure. The estimated Y counterfactual condition for all treatment subjects is provided by the simple extension of the outcome line for participants (the dashed line). Since the lines are assumed to be straight and have the same slope, the distance between the dashed line (the estimated counterfactual condition) and the actual treatment outcome is the same along the lines.

In Chart 3.2, the intervention has no impact because the two regression lines have the same intercept and slope. The absence of an abrupt shift or change in the slope after the cuff-off point means that, compared to the comparison group, being placed in the intervention group had no effect on the outcome variable of interest.

Chart 3.3 is an example of an abrupt shift after the cuff-off point and a change in slope. In this example, program participation appears not only to have an abrupt impact, but the impact has a positive interaction, with the QAV score represented by the positive change in slope. For the intervention group, the impact of program participation on the outcome variable increases as the QAV score increase.

Chart 3.2: Regression-Discontinuity Design: No Impact

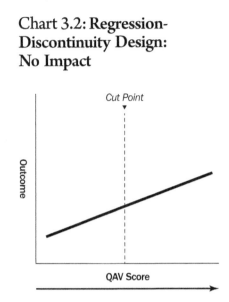

The example presented in Chart 3.4 is similar to Chart 3.3, but there is no abrupt shift in height after the cut-off point. However, there is a change in slope, suggesting, for the intervention group, the impact of

Chart 3.3: Regression-Discontinuity Design: Change in Intercept and Slope

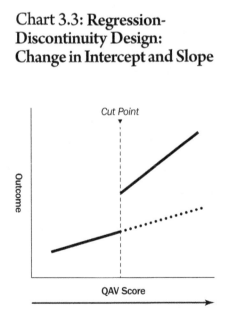

Chart 3.4: Regression-Discontinuity Design: Change in Slope

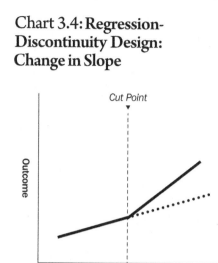

the program on the outcome variable increases as the QAV score increases.

For a more detailed example, consider a hypothetical social program intended to boost the academic achievement of economically disadvantaged children attending elementary school. The educational program provides intervention T with the expectation that academic achievement, Y, will increase. However, all economically disadvantaged children cannot be in the program because of limited resources. Thus, the program administrators decide that the intervention will be given to the neediest students. Selection into the program is determined by a poverty index, called A. The poverty index is based on family income and living conditions. The lower the index score, the greater level of poverty. The cuff-off point for A is 70. Children scoring below 70 get are assigned to the intervention group, while those scoring 70 or above are assigned to the comparison group.

The following equation represents the regression-discontinuity model:

$$Y_i = \alpha_0 + \beta_A A_i + \beta_T T_i + \beta_{TA} T_i A_i + \beta_x X_i + \epsilon_i$$

where Y is the outcome for academic achievement of an elementary student after selection into the intervention or comparison group; α is the constant or intercept; β_A is the regression coefficient for the effect of the A, the poverty score; β_T is the regression coefficient that measures the impact of program participation; T is a dummy variable coded as 0 when the individual is in the comparison group (A ≥ 70) and 1 when the individual is in the intervention group (A < 70); β_{TA} is regression coefficient for the change in slope caused by the interaction between T and A; β_X is the regression coefficient for observed characteristics; X is a set of observed factors; ϵ is an error term reflecting the unobserved factors that also affect Y; and the subscript i ranges from the first individual to the last individual in the study.

β_T and β_{TA} are the combined effect of the intervention. If β_T is significantly different than zero, then the education program had a significant effect on academic achievement. That is, if β_T is positive and statistically significant, then participation in the program is associated with increased academic achievement as illustrated in Chart 3.5. The opposite would be indicated if β_T was negative and statistically significant. If β_T is statistically indistinguishable from zero, then the education program had no impact on academic achievement.

In addition to the change in height as illustrated in Chart 3.5, participation in the program has a positive interaction with the poverty index, represented by the positive change in slope. For the intervention group, the impact of program participation on the outcome variable increases as the QAV score increases. Notice that the slope for those in the intervention group has a greater angle than the slope for those in the comparison group.

Chart 3.5: Hypothetical Elementary Education Program of Children in Poverty

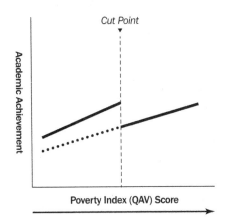

The goal of any comparison group design is to provide an estimate of the counterfactual condition that avoids selection bias. The regression-discontinuity design accomplishes this goal by a combination of two factors. First, through rigid assignment procedures, the selection of subjects into the intervention group must occur with no exceptions.[65] In the preceding example, a student with a score of 70 or 71 must be excluded from the intervention group. The cut-off point needs to be followed for all subjects in the evaluation. If the cut-off point is fuzzy, then the design will not work

Second, the regression model must be properly specified.[66] If poverty index A is associated with academic achievement (Y), and if the intervention group was selected based only on A, then a regression analysis with variable A included as an explanatory variable will put the evaluator in a good position to estimate intervention effects.[67]

The only large-scale multisite regression-discontinuity evaluation that appears to have been conducted of a federal social program is the Reading First Impact Study.[68] The No Child Left Behind Act of 2001 (NCLB), a singular legislative achievement of President George W. Bush, created the Reading First Program. The lofty goal of the social program was to ensure that all children can read at or above grade level by the end of the third grade. The assumed innovation of the Reading First Program was that it was based on instructional practices that have been found to be effective based on scientific research.

The Reading First Impact Study employed a regression-discontinuity design based on the systematic processes some school districts used to allocate Reading First funding after their states had received it.[69] Eligible schools were ranked based on a QAV, such as an indicator of previous student performance or poverty.[70] A cut-point based on the rank order was used to create intervention and comparison groups. The evaluation was based on 248 schools from 13 states—125 of these schools were assigned to the intervention group—from 17 school districts and one statewide program.[71] While the Reading First Program appears to have increased the total time teachers spent on reading instruction practices promoted by the program, the program failed to have a statistically significant impact on reading comprehension test scores in the first, second, and third grades.[72]

While regression-discontinuity designs are considered second only to designs using random assignment, this method has limited applications because of the need for the QAV. Few social programs strictly follow a QAV score for the allocation of program services. In addition to limited applications, regression-discontinuity designs have two noteworthy weaknesses.

First, compared to randomized experiments, regression-discontinuity designs require more assumptions on the proper way to specify the regression model.[73] Second, randomized experiments are more powerful in their ability to detect impacts than regression-discontinuity designs.[74] Regression-discontinuity designs require 2.7 times more study participants to have the same statistical power in detecting statistically significant outcomes compared to experimental designs.[75]

Given that there appears to be only one large-scale multisite regression-discontinuity evaluation of a federal social program, Reading First, and that this book is focused exclusively on the most scientifically rigorous evaluation design, experimental evaluations, the results of the Reading First evaluation, while confirming the argument of this book, will be excluded from Chapter 4, which covers federal social programs targeting children and families.

Propensity Score Matching

During the 1970s, the National Supported Work (NSW) Demonstration evaluated, through random assignment, voluntary training and assisted work programs targeting long-term participants in Aid to Families with Dependent Children (AFDC) at 12 sites across the nation. In 1986, Robert J. LaLonde compared the experimental evaluation's results to quasi-experimental methods.[76] Specifically, LaLonde used data on the NSW intervention group and constructed comparison groups using data from the Panel Study of Income Dynamics (PSID) and Current Population Survey (CPS) to serve as the counterfactual conditions, instead of the data from the NSW demonstration control group. The comparison groups were carefully constructed from the PSID and CPS to be as similar in earnings histories as possible to the NSW intervention group. According to LaLonde, the results of quasi-experiment "often differ significantly from experimental results."[77] Further, "this evidence suggests that policymakers should be aware that the available nonexperimental evaluations of employment and training programs may contain large and unknown biases resulting from specification errors."[78]

The sophistication of quasi-experimental methods has substantially grown since LaLonde's 1986 study. Using propensity score matching, Rejeev H. Dehejia and Sadek Wahba produced results that were close to the results of the NSW Demonstration.[79] Propensity score matching carefully matches intervention groups to nonexperimental comparison groups on their likelihood of participating in an intervention based on preintervention characteristics. The matching process yields a single propensity score for each member of the intervention and comparison groups. In theory, this propensity score summarizes the preintervention characteristics and, thus, can be used to control for the preintervention differences between the experimental intervention group and the nonexperimental comparison group. Their comparison groups were derived from the PSID and CPS. According to Dehejia and Wahba, their method obtained "estimates of the treatment impact that are much closer to the experimental treatment effect than LaLonde's nonexperimental estimates."[80]

However, Jeffrey A. Smith and Petra E. Todd found that that the propensity score matching by Dehejia and Wahba worked well only for a precise subsample of the NSW Demonstration data.[81] For example, Dehejia and Wahba's propensity score modeling excluded almost 40 percent of LaLonde's observations due to the inclusion of an additional variable in their propensity score model.[82] Despite excluding such a large portion of the data, Dehejia and Wahba's estimates were close to the original NSW Demonstration results.

However, Larry L. Orr and his coauthors conclude that these propensity score matching studies "are less encouraging than they might originally seem."[83] A 2005 study by Jeffrey A. Smith and Petra E. Todd found that the results from Dehejia and Wahba's study were extremely sensitive to sample selection and the specification of matching variables used to create the propensity scores.[84] While Dehejia and Wahba were able to produce similar results using a particular subsample, Smith and Todd were unable to produce similar results when they applied the same modeling methods to other reasonable subsamples.[85] Smith and Todd conclude that their "findings make it clear that propensity score matching does not represent a 'magic bullet' that solves the selection problem in every context."[86] Based on the analysis by Smith and Todd, Larry L. Orr and his coauthors concluded that while "it was possible to find a nonexperimental approach that yielded estimates similar to the (known) experimental results, equally plausible approaches—in fact, only slight variations in the nonexperimental methods—yielded results different (sometimes very much so) from the experimental results."[87]

Daniel Friedlander and Philip K. Robins attempted to replicate the results of welfare-to-work experimental evaluations done in the 1980s.[88] While they found that the results using in-state comparison groups produced some improvement compared to the results using out-of-state comparison groups, both techniques were problematic because they yielded inaccuracies.[89] Using propensity score methods, another analysis by Wang-Sheng Lee attempted to replicate the experimental evaluation of an

Indiana welfare-to-work program.[90] Even when the comparison group had similar labor market characteristics, the quasi-experimental methods yielded biased impact estimates that were quite large.

In the education policy field, propensity score matching has not been successful at replicating the results of experimental evaluations. Roberto Agodini and Mark Dynarski attempted to use propensity score matching to replicate the results of an experimental evaluation of middle and high school dropout prevention programs.[91] They found "no consistent evidence that propensity-score methods replicate experimental impacts of the dropout prevention programs ... In fact, we find that evaluating these programs using propensity-score methods might have led to misleading inferences about the effectiveness of the programs."[92] Another propensity score matching study by Elizabeth Ty Wilde and Robinson Hollister attempted to replicate the experimental evaluation results of the Tennessee's Student Teacher Achievement Ratio Project (Project STAR)—a class size reduction program.[93] Based on their rigorous assessment, "propensity score estimators do not perform very well when judged by standards of how close they are to the 'true' impacts estimated from experimental estimators based on a random assignment design."[94] Further, "We hope that this study raises a flag of caution for decision-makers: Do not rush to adopt a propensity score matching estimator thinking it will be an adequate substitute for one derived from a true experimental design."[95]

Steven Glazerman and his coauthors reviewed 12 studies of nonexperimental statistical techniques, including propensity score matching, used to replicate the results of experimental evaluations of job-training and welfare-to-work programs.[96] While they found that some of the statistical techniques reduced the bias of quasi-experimental methods to some degree, none of the individual techniques reliably replicated the experimental results.[97]

According to Howard L. Bloom and his coauthors, the basic problem is that

[A]ll propensity-score balancing or matching methods have the limitation that they can balance only measured characteristics. If all relevant characteristics are measured and included in the estimated propensity score, then balancing the program and comparison groups with respect to this score eliminates selection bias. But if some important characteristics are not measured—perhaps because they cannot be—selection bias might remain. Thus, the quality of program impact estimates obtained from propensity-score balancing methods depends on how well the comparison group matches the program group before matching and on the nature and quality of the data available to measure (and thus further balance) sample members' characteristics. As for any impact estimation procedure, the result is only as good as the research design that produced it.[98]

Propensity score matching in the subject area of voter mobilization has similarly failed to accurately replicate the results of an experimental evaluation.[99]

All of the propensity score matching comparisons studies have attempted to replicate the results of previously conducted experimental evaluations. As far as I am aware, no one has first conducted a propensity score evaluation of a social program and then confirmed the quasi-experimental results by performing an experimental evaluation. All of the propensity score comparison studies reviewed in this chapter carefully attempted to replicate experimental results with known benchmarks in mind. These studies are an academic exercise in replicating true experimental results with quasi-experimental techniques. No one has done the opposite by demonstrating *ex ante* that propensity score matching results can be replicated using experimental methods. Without the true experimental results as the target, evaluators using propensity score matching have no guide in doing their statistical analysis. As succinctly put by Phoebe H. Cottingham, and Douglas J. Besharov, "The propensity score approach has to rely on modeling using observable baseline data, so one cannot know for sure whether the unobservables are introducing substantial bias into the findings."[100]

In sum, propensity score matching is not a valid substitute for experimental evaluations. Propensity score matching's main failing is that the method is unable to remove the effects of selection bias caused by unobserved variables. No matter the level of statistical sophistication, the method cannot account for unobserved factors like the ability of random assignment. This conclusion is important because, as will be discussed in Chapter 5, the U.S. Department of Labor failed to conduct an experimental evaluation of the Workforce Investment Act job-training program as mandated by Congress. Instead, they commissioned a propensity score quasi-experimental evaluation that that concluded the program was effective.[101]

Can Effective Programs Be Replicated?

Policymakers and advocates often assume that a social program that is effective in one setting will automatically produce the same results in other settings. Policymakers should not make this assumption.

Many advocates of social programs have adopted the language of the "evidence-based" policy movement. Under the evidence-based policy movement, programs found to be effective using rigorous scientific methods are deemed "effective" or "evidence-based" and held up as "model" programs.

However, many of the programs labeled as "evidence-based"—often by program advocates—have been evaluated in only a single setting, so the results cannot necessarily be generalized to other settings. In addition, these evidence-based programs have often been implemented by highly trained professionals operating under ideal conditions. These programs are carefully monitored to ensure that the participants receive the intended level of treatment. In the real world, program conditions are often much less than optimal.

The success of replicating evidence-based programs often depends on implementation fidelity—the degree to which programs follow the theory underpinning the program and how correctly the program components are put into practice. Incorrect implementation often accounts for the failures of previously successful or model programs when implemented in other jurisdictions.

Reconnecting Youth

A good example of a "successful" program that has not been found to be effective when replicated in the real world is Reconnecting Youth, a school-based substance abuse program. Reconnecting Youth was designated as a "model program" by the Substance Abuse and Mental Health Services Agency (SAMSHA)[102] and as a "research-based" program by the National Institute on Drug Abuse.[103] These classifications are important because schools receiving Safe and Drug-Free Schools and Communities grants under the No Child Left Behind Act of 2001 must select only drug prevention programs that have been previously designated as effective.[104]

Denise Hallfors, a senior research scientist at the Pacific Institute for Research and Evaluation, and her colleagues evaluated the effectiveness of Reconnecting Youth in real-world conditions.[105] In a random experiment, 1,370 high-risk youths in nine high schools in two large urban school districts were assigned to intervention and control groups. Overall, Reconnecting Youth had no effect on academic performance, truancy, or substance abuse. However, Reconnecting Youth participants showed statistically significant decreases in conventional peer bonding and prosocial weekend activities (e.g., doing homework, club or church activities, and family activities), and a statistically significant increase in high-risk peer bonding.[106]

Hallfors and her colleagues concluded that "Reconnecting Youth failed to meet the requirement to do more good than harm."[107] Further, programs found to be effective in a single location "do not provide adequate evidence for widespread dissemination or designation as 'model' programs."[108]

MST

Multisystemic therapy (MST) is another program model that has been labeled effective. It has shown promise in reducing the delinquency of youth who display serious antisocial behavior. As a highly intensive and tailored counseling program aimed at individuals, not groups, MST recognizes that antisocial behavior is influenced by three areas where youth interact: family, school, and peer associations.[109] Highly trained MST counselors work with parents, usually in the home, to improve discipline, enhance family relationships, increase youth interactions with prosocial peers, and improve school performance.[110]

Several randomized experiments by its developers have linked MST to reductions in offending by participants.[111] However, there is some debate about whether MST is truly effective and can be replicated successfully across the nation.

Professor Julia H. Littell of Bryn Mawr College and her colleagues have pointed out that some of MST's experimental evaluations have suffered from attrition in which subjects in the evaluation dropped out of treatment and were not included in the final analysis.[112] Evaluations, even random experiments, that exclude dropouts from outcome assessments may inadvertently engage in creaming of the crop, in which those least likely to succeed drop out, leaving behind an intervention group composed of individuals most likely to succeed. This type of attrition breaks equivalence between the intervention and control groups, thus biasing the impact estimates.

Further, the successful MST effects have yet to be replicated in other settings. An experimental evaluation of MST in Ontario, Canada, included intervention dropouts in its final outcome measures to avoid the problem of attrition. This evaluation, unbiased by attrition, found that MST failed to reduce delinquency.[113] In Norway, MST was found to be effective based on intermediate measures, but delinquency was not measured.[114]

After conducting a meta-analysis of MST, Littell and her colleagues concluded that "it is not clear whether MST has clinically significant advantages over other services."[115] While the debate over MST's effectiveness is not yet settled, evaluations suggest that MST has had little success when replicated in other settings.

These examples illustrate why programs should be evaluated in multiple settings before being labeled evidence-based. Generalizing from a single evaluation conducted in one setting is, at best, premature.

An alternative to replication, especially in the case of federal social programs, is to evaluate the effectiveness of social programs based on multiple sites. Federal social programs operate under various conditions that single-site evaluations cannot address; thus, evaluations of these programs should be done in ways that will tell Congress and taxpayers how these programs operate nationally.

Standards for Assessing the Effectiveness of Federal Social Programs

Congress can take several steps to ensure that federal social programs are properly assessed using experimental evaluations. These experimental evaluations should be large in scale and based on multiple sites to avoid problems of external validity. Given the multitude of confounding factors that may influence the performance of social programs, the larger the size of the evaluation, the more likely the social program will be assessed under all the conditions that it operates under.

When Congress creates social programs, especially state and local grant programs, the funded activities are implemented in multiple cities or towns. Federal social programs are intended to be spread out across the nation. For this reason, Congress should require national, multisite experimental evaluations of these programs.

While individual social programs funded by the federal government may undergo experimental evaluations, these small-scale, single-site evaluations do not inform policymakers of the general effectiveness of national social programs. Small-scale evaluations assess only the impact on a small fraction of people served by federal social programs. The success of a single program that serves a particular jurisdiction or population does not necessarily mean that the same program will achieve similar success in other jurisdictions or among different populations. Simply, small-scale evaluations are poor substitutes for large-scale evaluations. Thus, federal social programs should be evaluated in multiple sites so that social programs can be tested in the various conditions they operate under and the numerous types of populations they serve.

Consider the following analogy: If Congress wanted to know the characteristics of the population served by Head Start, conducting a survey of a single Head Start program operating in Houston, Texas, would not tell us much about the national population served by Head Start. To find out the characteristics of the population served by Head Start, a national representative sample of Head Start programs would need to be used. The same reasoning holds for evaluating effectiveness. If we want to find out the effectiveness of Head Start as a national program, then we cannot rely on examining the effects of a single Head Start center. The obvious scientific approach would be to undertake a multisite evaluation of Head Start that reflects the various conditions that the program operates under nationally.

In addition, a multisite experimental evaluation that examines the performance of a particular program in numerous and diverse settings can potentially produce results that are more persuasive to policymakers than results from a single locality.[116]

The case of police departments performing mandatory arrests in domestic violence incidents is a poignant example of why caution should be exercised when generalizing findings from a single evaluation. During the 1980s, criminologists Lawrence W. Sherman and Richard A. Berk analyzed the impact of mandatory arrests for domestic violence incidents on future domestic violence incidents in Minneapolis, Minnesota.[117] Compared to less severe police responses, the Minneapolis experiment found that mandatory arrests lead to significantly lower rates of domestic violence. Sherman and Berk urged caution, but police departments across the nation adopted the mandatory arrest policy based on the results of one evaluation conducted in one city.

However, what worked in Minneapolis did not always work in other locations. Experiments conducted by Sherman and others in Omaha, Nebraska; Milwaukee, Wisconsin; Charlotte, North Carolina; Colorado Springs, Colorado; and Dade County, Florida, found mixed results.[118] Experiments in Omaha, Milwaukee, and Charlotte found that mandatory arrests lead to long-term *increases* in domestic violence. Apparently, knowing that they would automatically be arrested prompted repeat offenders to become more abusive. It seems that the following sick logic occurred: If I'm going to automatically spend the night in jail, I might as well beat my wife extra good. In a subsequent analysis of the disparate findings, Sherman postulated that arrested individuals who lacked a stake in conformity within their communities were significantly more likely to engage in domestic violence after arrest, while married and employed arrested individuals were significantly less likely to commit further domestic violence infractions.[119]

Contradictory results from evaluations of similar social programs implemented in different settings are a product not only of implementation fidelity, but also of the enormous complexity of the social context in which these programs are implemented. Jim Manzi, a senior fellow at the Manhattan Institute, uses the conflicting results of experimental evaluations to explain the influence of "causal density" on the social sciences.[120] "Casual density," a term coined by Manzi, is "the number and complexity of potential causes of the outcomes of interest."[121] Manzi postulates that as causal density rises, social scientists will find greater difficulty in identifying all of the factors that cause the outcome of interest.

The confounding influence of causal density likely contributed to contradictory effects of mandatory arrest policies by location. To address casual density, experimental impact evaluations of federal social programs should be conducted using multiple sites. In fact, the total sum of the multiple sites should be a nationally representative of the populations served by the social program being evaluated.

Large-Scale Multisite Experimental Evaluation of Federal Social Programs

Despite the trillions of dollars that Congress has spent on federal social programs, only a few programs have undergone large-scale experimental impact evaluations. I have made the best effort to include all the relevant evaluations of federal social programs that have been published since 1990. Evaluations of the following social programs are reviewed in Chapters 4 and 5:

- Early Head Start
- Enhanced Early Head Start with Employment Services
- Head Start
- Even Start Family Literacy Program
- 21st Century Community Learning Centers
- Abstinence Education
- Upward Bound
- Food Stamp (renamed SNAP) Employment and Training Program

- Welfare-to-Work
- Employment Retention and Advancement (ERA) Project
- Building Strong Families
- Supporting Healthy Marriage
- Moving to Opportunity
- Section 8 Housing Vouchers
- Job Training Partnership Act (JTPA) programs
- Unemployment Insurance (UI) Self-Employment Demonstrations
- Project GATE (Growing America Through Entrepreneurship)
- Job Corps
- JOBSTART
- Center for Employment Training (CET) Replication
- Quantum Opportunity Program Demonstration

Chapter 4

Children and Families

This chapter covers federal social programs that are intended to benefit a wide range of clients—from infants and toddlers all the way to adult household heads. In between, these social programs serve prekindergarten children, elementary and middle school students, high school students, and families. A whole host of social problems are targeted for amelioration, including low academic skills, poverty, sex outside of marriage, out-of-wedlock births, unemployability and low wages, bad parenting, and romantic relationship problems in and outside of marriage. Before the progressive transformation of America, these social problems were rightly considered personal problems. In 2005, for example, the Government Accountability Office (GAO) identified 69 federal programs that provide support for prekindergarten and childcare. According to a conservative estimate, the federal government spent more than $25 billion on these programs in FY 2009.[1] There appears to be almost no personal or social problem that the supporters of social engineering are not willing to tackle.

Early Head Start

Commenting on the lack of demonstrated effectiveness of federal social programs over the last 20 years in 2010, Isabel V. Sawhill of the Brookings Institution and Jon Baron of the Coalition for Evidence-Based Policy wrote, "Only one program—Early Head Start (a sister program to Head Start, for younger children)—was found to produce meaningful, though modest, positive effects."[2] While the short-term results of the evaluation were publicly available at the time Sawhill and Baron made this statement that Early Head Start produced beneficial impacts, a subsequent long-term follow-up study, released in 2012, found that the short-term beneficial impacts quickly faded way (not an uncommon finding for social programs).

Early Head Start, created during the 1990s, is a federally funded community-based program that serves low-income families with pregnant women, infants, and toddlers up to age 3. It is called a two-generation program because the program provides services to children and their parents. Through three different service models—home-based, center-based, and mixed approaches—Early Head Start's child development services include home visitations, childcare, case management, parenting education, healthcare and referrals, and family support.[3] Through these types of interventions, Early Head Start is expected "to improve the cognitive, social, and emotional development of infants and toddlers in low income families."[4]

Home-based programs provide child development services predominately through home visits, while center-based programs provide these services primarily through childcare in Early Head Start centers. The mixed approach provides home-based services to some families, center-based services to some families, and a mix of home- and center-based services to other families.

Short-Term Impacts of Early Head Start

The Administration on Children, Youth and Families within the Department of Health and Human Services selected 17 Early Head Start sites for a large-scale, multisite experimental evaluation.[5] The initial impact findings released in a report titled *Making a Difference in the Lives of Infants and Toddlers and Their Families: The Impacts of Early Head Start* strongly suggested that Early Head Start was an effective program. Between 1996 and 1998, 3,001 families were randomly assigned to intervention and control groups.[6] Control group families were barred from receiving Early Head Start services until their applicant child reached the age of 3, when the child would be no longer eligible for services.[7] Nevertheless, control group families were allowed to seek early childhood services provided by other programs. The 17 sites were selected based on the belief that they were generally representative of the programs funded during 1995 and 1996. However, "Because the 17 research programs were not randomly selected, the impact results cannot be formally generalized to all Early Head Start programs funded during 1995 and 1996."[8] Despite this word of caution, authors of the evaluation assert that because the features of the 17 programs are similar to all Early Head Start programs, "our findings about effective program practices and their impacts on children and families are likely to pertain to Early Head Start programs more broadly."[9]

The outcome variables of the Early Head Start evaluation focused on three categories: service use, child development and parenting, and family development.[10] Intervention group families, on average, participated in the program for 21 months, with almost half of the families participating for at least two years.[11] The evaluation also recorded the race and ethnicity of the primary caregivers of the children participating in the 17 Early Head Start sites. Blacks comprised 34 percent of primary caregivers, while Hispanics and whites made up 24 percent and 37 percent, respectively, of primary caregivers.[12] The remaining five percent were primary caregivers that fell into the "other" category.[13] These figures can be considered as a close approximation of the race and ethnicity of the families receiving Early Head Start services.

Impact on Service Outcomes.   The service outcome measures are intermediate outcome measures. While intermediate measures, such as being provided program services, are important, these outcomes are not the ultimate goal of Early Head Start. If Early Head Start participant children do not improve upon childhood developmental measures, for example, then the intermediate outcomes are irrelevant to judging whether the program is effective.

While control group families could seek similar early childhood services, intervention group families received more child development and case management services.[14] For example, 92.9 percent of the intervention group and 57.8 percent of the control group received at least the minimal cores services—a statistically significant difference of 35.1 percent at the one percent confidence level.[15] Core services focus on health and social, cognitive, and language development. In addition, 87.2 percent of participating families received at least one home visit, compared to 33.7 percent of control group families—a statistically significant difference of 53.5 percent at the one percent confidence level.[16]

Twenty-six months after random assignment, 86.1 percent of program group families received some form of childcare, while 80.2 percent of control group families received some form of childcare—a statistically significant difference of 5.9 percent at the one percent confidence level.[17] The average total number of hours of any kind of childcare received was 1,544 hours for the intervention group and 1,224 hours for the control group.[18] This difference of 320 hours is statistically significant at the one percent confidence level.

Overall, parents in the intervention group were more likely to receive parental education services than control group parents. For example,

94.0 percent of intervention group parents and 64.4 percent of control group parents received some form of parenting education 28-months after random assignment.[19] The difference of 29.6 percent is statistically significant at the one percent confidence level.

Similarly, intervention group families were more likely to receive case management services. For instance, 87.0 percent of intervention group families experienced at least one case management meeting, compared to 55.3 percent for control group families—a statistically significant difference of 31.7 percent at the one percent confidence level.[20]

In this chapter and the next, tables are used to summarize the findings of the evaluations reviewed. Many of the evaluations assessed program impacts on numerous outcomes. In several cases, there are far too many findings to be summarized in a concise manner. However, the most important findings are summarized in the tables. In the tables, the statistical significance and effects (beneficial or harmful) of the social programs are marked the following classifications:

- 0   Finding was not statistically significant
- Pos   Positive or beneficial impact
- Neg   Negative or harmful impact
- *   Marginally statistically significant at the 10 percent confidence level ($p \leq 0.10$)
- **   Statistically significant at the five percent confidence level ($p \leq 0.05$)
- ***   Statistically significant at the one percent confidence level ($p \leq 0.01$)
- n/a   No measure was assessed or reported
- †   No statistical significance test was performed

For example, an indicator of 0 means that the program failed to have a statistically measurable impact on a particular outcome measure. However, a Pos** indicator means that the program had a statistically significant impact at the five percent confidence level, which is considered to be a beneficial result, while a Neg*** indicates a harmful finding at the one percent confidence level.

Impact on Child Development.   Table 4.1 summarizes the selected findings for the impact of Early Head Start by age 3. Compared to control group children, intervention group children scored higher on a number of cognitive and receptive language development measures.[21] The standard scores for the Bayley Mental Development Index (MDI)—a measure of

TABLE 4.1. Selected Findings for the Early Head Start Evaluation, Outcomes at Age 3

Outcomes at Age 3	Overall	Black	Hispanic	White
Child Cognitive and Language Development				
Bayley Mental Development Index (MDI) standard score	Pos**	0	0	0
Percentage with Bayley MDI below 85	Pos*	0	0	0
Peabody Picture Vocabulary Test (PPVT-III) standard score	Pos*	Pos**	0	0
Percentage with PPVT-III below 85	Pos**	0	0	0
Test de Vocabulario Imagenes Peabody (TVIP) standard score	0	n/a	n/a	n/a
Percentage with TVIP below 100	0	n/a	n/a	n/a
Child Social-Emotional Development				
Engagement of parent during parent-child semistructured play	Pos***	Pos***	0	0
Sustained attention to objects during parent-child semistructured play	Pos***	Pos***	0	0
Engagement of parent during parent-child puzzle challenge task	0	Pos***	0	0
Persistence during parent-child puzzle challenge task	0	Pos**	0	0
Bayley Behavior Rating Scale (BRS): Emotional regulation	0	0	0	0
Bayley BRS: Orientation/Engagement	0	0	Pos**	0
Negatively toward parent during parent-child semistructured play	Pos**	Pos***	0	0
Frustration with parent-child puzzle challenge task	0	0	0	0
Child behavior checklist: aggressive behavior	Pos**	Pos**	0	0
Impact on Parenting				
Emotionally Supportive Parenting				
Home Observation for Measurement of the Environment: Warmth	Pos*	Pos**	0	0
Supportiveness during parent-child semistructured play	Pos***	Pos***	0	0
Supportive presence during parent-child puzzle challenge task	0	Pos**	0	0
Home Environment and Parent Stimulation of Language and Learning				
Home Observation for Measurement of the Environment: Total score	Pos**	Pos***	0	0

TABLE 4.1. (Continued)

Outcomes at Age 3	Overall	Black	Hispanic	White
Percentage of parents who set a regular bedtime for child	0	Pos**	0	0
Percentage of parents and children who have regular bedtime routines	0	0	0	0
Support of language and learning	Pos**	Pos**	0	0
Parent-child play	Pos*	0	0	0
Quality of assistance during parent-child puzzle challenge task	Pos*	Pos**	Pos*	0
Percentage of parents who read to child every day	Pos**	0	Pos**	0
Percentage of parents who regularly read to child at bedtime	0	Pos*	0	0
Internal physical environment	0	0	0	0
Negative Aspects of Parenting Behavior				
Detachment during parent-child semistructured play	Pos*	0	0	0
Intrusiveness during parent-child semistructured play	0	Pos*	0	0
Detachment during parent-child puzzle challenge task	0	0	0	0
Intrusiveness during parent-child puzzle challenge task	0	Pos*	0	0
Negative regard during parent-child semistructured play	0	0	0	0
Home Observation for Measurement of the Environment: Harshness	0	0	0	0
Percentage of parents who spanked the child during the previous week	Pos***	0	0	0
Parenting Knowledge: Safety and Discipline Strategies				
Percentage of parents who always use car seat for child	0	0	0	0
Percentage of parents who suggested responses to the hypothetical situation with child:				
Prevent or distract	0	n/a	n/a	n/a
Remove child or object	0	n/a	n/a	n/a
Talk and explain	0	n/a	n/a	n/a
Time out	0	n/a	n/a	n/a
Threaten or command	Pos**	n/a	n/a	n/a
Shout	0	n/a	n/a	n/a

(continued)

TABLE 4.1. (Continued)

Outcomes at Age 3	Overall	Black	Hispanic	White
Physical punishment	Pos**	n/a	n/a	n/a
Percentage of parents suggesting only mild responses to the hypothetical situations	Pos*	0	0	0
Index of severity of discipline strategies suggested	Pos**	Pos**	0	0
Parent Health, Mental Health, and Family Functioning				
Parent's health status	0	0	0	0
Parenting Stress Index (PSI): Parental distress	0	Pos*	0	0
PSI: Parent-child dysfunctional interaction	0	Pos*	0	Neg**
CES-Depression Scale (CES-D; short form)	0	0	0	0
CES-D: Severe depressive symptoms	0	0	0	0
Family Environment Scale—Family Conflict (Average score)	0	0	0	0
Parental Self-Sufficiency Activities during First 26 Months				
Percentage of parents ever employed or in an education or job-training program	Pos**	Pos***	0	0
Average hours per week employed at all jobs and in any education or training	Pos*	Pos*	Pos**	0
Percentage of parents ever employed	Pos*	Pos***	0	0
Average hours per week employed at all jobs	0	0	0	0
Percentage of parents who ever participated in an education or training program	Pos***	0	Pos**	Pos**
Average hours per week in an education program	Pos***	Pos**	Pos***	0
Parental Attainment of Educational Degrees and Credentials during First 26 Months				
Highest grade completed	0	n/a	n/a	n/a
GED certificate	0	0	0	0
High school diploma	0	0	0	0
Vocational, business, or secretarial diploma	0	n/a	n/a	n/a
Associate's degree	0	n/a	n/a	n/a
Bachelor's degree	0	n/a	n/a	n/a

TABLE 4.1.   (Continued)

Outcomes at Age 3	Overall	Black	Hispanic	White
Parental Welfare Participation during First 26 Months				
Percentage of parents who received any welfare benefits	0	0	Neg*	0
Total welfare benefits received	0	Pos**	0	0
Percentage of parents who received AFDC or TANF benefits	0	0	Neg***	0
Total AFDC or TANF benefits received	0	Pos**	0	0
Ever received food stamp benefits	n/a	0	Neg*	0
Average total food stamp benefits received	0	0	0	0

Key: 0   Finding was not statistically significant
　　Pos Positive or beneficial impact
　　Neg Negative or harmful impact
　　*   Statistically significant at the 10 percent confidence level ($p \leq 0.10$)
　　**   Statistically significant at the 5 percent confidence level ($p \leq 0.05$)
　　*** Statistically significant at the 1 percent confidence level ($p \leq 0.01$)
　　n/a No measure was assessed or reported
　　†   No statistically significance test was performed
Source: John M. Love, Ellen Eliason Kisker, Christine M. Ross, Peter Z. Schochet, Jeanne Brooks-Gun, Diane Paulsell, Kimberly Boller, Jill Constantine, Cheri Vogel, Allison Sidle Fulingi, and Christi Brady-Smith, *Making a Difference in the Lives of Infants and Toddlers and Their Families: The Impacts of Early Head Start, Volume 1: Final Technical Report* (Princeton, NJ: Mathematica Policy Research, June 2002), Table V.1, 201; Table V.2, 203; Table V.3, 207; Table V.4, 211; Table V.5, 215; Table V.6, 219; Table V.7, 221; Table V.8, 227; Table V.9, 229; Table V.10, 232; Table V.11, 235; Table VII.11, 381–385; Table VII.12, 386–388.

cognitive, language, and personal-social development—for the intervention group children averaged 91.4, while the average score for the control group children was 89.9—a statistically significant difference of 1.6 at the five percent confidence level. In addition to the Bayley MDI average scores, the evaluators assessed the percentage of children scoring below a Bayley MDI score of 85, which "measures the proportion with delayed performance, or scores one standard deviation or more below the mean for their age in the nationally representative, standardization sample."[22] Of those children scoring below 85 on the Bayley MDI, 27.3 percent and 32.0 percent were intervention group and control group children, respectively—a marginally statistically significant difference of 4.7 percent at the less rigorous 10 percent confidence level.

For receptive language development, intervention group children had an average Peabody Picture Vocabulary Test (PPVT-III) standard score of 83.3, compared to the average score of 81.1 for the control group children—a statistically significant difference of 2.1 at the five percent confidence level.[23]

The PPVT-III assesses the listening comprehension of spoken words in standard English for children.[24] In addition to the PPVT-III average scores, the evaluators assessed the percentage of children scoring below a PPVT-III score of 85, which also "measures the proportion with scores one standard deviation or more below the mean for their age in the nationally representative, standardization sample."[25] Of intervention group children, 51.1 percent scored below a PPVT-III score of 85, compared to 57.1 percent of the control group children—a statistically significant difference of 6.0 percent at the five percent confidence level. While this is a positive result, it is worth noting that the majority of intervention group children still scored below a PPVT-III score of 85.

The last language development measure, Test de Vocabulario en Imagenes Peabody (TVIP), assessed the listening comprehension of spoken words in Spanish for Spanish-speaking and English-Spanish bilingual children.[26] For Spanish-speaking children, the intervention and control group children had average TVIP scores of 97.2 percent and 94.9 percent, respectively.[27] This difference of 2.3 percent was statistically indistinguishable from zero, meaning that the program had no effect on the outcome. For those scoring below the mean score of 100 for their age based on a nationally representative sample, 36.2 percent of intervention group children fell into this category, compared to 41.2 percent for control group children—a difference of five percent that is statistically indistinguishable from zero.

Impact on Child Social-Emotional Development.   Compared to control group children, intervention group children scored higher on only two out of six positive measures of child social-emotional development.[28] The average scores for a seven-point scale measuring child behavior during parent-child semistructured play was assessed, with the intervention group children averaging 4.8, while the control group children averaged 4.6—a statistically significant difference of 0.2 at the one percent confidence level. Another seven-point scale for assessing the sustained attention to objects during parent-child semistructured play had intervention and control group children averaging 5.0 percent and 4.8 percent, respectively. The difference of 0.2 is statistically significant at the one percent confidence level. Early Head Start failed to have statistically measurable impacts on the remaining four positive measures of child social-emotional development.

Compared to control group children, intervention group children scored lower on two-thirds of negative measures of child social-emotional development.[29] Intervention group children were less likely to be observed engaging in negativity toward parent during parent-child semistructured play. In addition, the intervention group children were less likely to be observed displaying aggressive behavior. Both of these positive effects were statistically significant at the five percent confidence level. However, participation in Early Head Start did not affect the display of frustration during parent-child puzzle challenges.

Impact on Parenting.   Overall, participation in Early Head Start was associated with improved emotionally supportive parenting.[30] During home visitations, the evaluators assessed the "warmth" of the responsive and supportive behavior of parents. Based on a zero to three scale, intervention group parents averaged a score of 2.6, compared to the average score of 2.5 for the control group parents. The difference of 0.1 is statistically significant at the less rigorous 10 percent confidence level. The result for the supportiveness of the parent during parent-child semistructured play was more impressive. Based on a seven-point scale, intervention and control group parents averaged 4.0 and 3.9 on the scale, respectively—a statistically significant difference of 0.1 at the one percent confidence level. Despite these positive findings, Early Head Start had no effect on the supportiveness of the parent during parent-child puzzle challenge tasks.

The evaluation also assessed the overall home environment and parent stimulation of language and learning based on nine outcome measures. Of the nine measures, five measures yielded statistically significant results.[31] However, only three of these measures were at least statistically significant at the five percent confidence level. Home Observation for Measurement of the Environment (HOME) assesses the quality of stimulation and support provided to children in their home environments.[32] This measure has a maximum score of 37. The higher the score, the better the home environment. The average total scores for this measure for the intervention and control groups were 27.6 and 27.0, respectively.[33] The difference of 0.5 was statistically significant at the five percent confidence level.[34] For measures focusing on structuring the child's day, Early Head Start failed to affect the percentage of parents who set a regular bedtime for their children and the percentage of parents who have regular bedtime routines with their children.

The results for parent-child activities and learning support were more impressive. At the five percent confidence level, participation in Early Head Start had positive impacts on support in the home for language and learning, and for the percentage of parents who read to their child every day.[35] At the less rigorous 10 percent confidence level, the intervention group performed better on measures of parent-child play and the quality of assistance during parent-child puzzle challenge tasks. Early Head Start failed to affect the percentage of parents who regularly read to their child at bedtime and the internal physical environment measure that assessed the cleanliness, organization, and warmth of the home environment.

As for negative aspects of parenting behavior, Early Head Start was largely ineffective. On the four measures of parental insensitivity, Early Head Start had only one statistically significant finding.[36] At the less rigorous 10 percent level of confidence, parents in the intervention group were less likely to display detachment during parent-child semistructured play. For measures assessing parental displays of hostility and punishment, Early Head Start failed to have an impact on two out of three of the outcomes.[37] Involvement in the program did not affect displays of negative regard during parent-child semistructured play and harshness or punitive behavior by the parents. Despite these findings, the intervention group parents were less likely to spank their children—46.7 percent of intervention group parents spanked their children, while 53.8 percent of control group parents did the same. The difference of 7.1 percent in favor of Early Head Start was statistically significant at the one percent confidence level.

The Early Head Start evaluation also assessed the safety and disciplinary strategies used by parents. For the 10 outcome measures, the program had statistically significant impacts on four measures.[38] For the intervention and control group parents, 69.8 percent and 70.8 percent, respectively, reported always using car seats for their children. This difference of 0.9 in favor of the control group was statistically indistinguishable from zero.

Hypothetically, the parents were provided with four potential conflict situations with the child and asked how they would respond: (1) the child persists in playing with breakable things, (2) the child declines to eat, (3) the child pitches a temper tantrum in a public place, and (4) the child strikes the parent in anger.[39] On all four of the positive parental responses (prevent or distract, remove child or object, talk and explain, and offer a time out), Early Head Start had no statistically measurable impact. On the three negative parental responses (threaten or command, shout, and physical punishment), the program had positive impacts. Parents in the intervention group were a little less likely to offer threatening or commanding and physical punishment responses, compared to the control group parents. These differences were statistically significant at the five percent confidence level. Overall, 44.7 percent of parents in the intervention group and 40.5 percent of parents in the control group offered only mild responses to the hypothetical situations. The difference of 4.2 percent was statistically significant at the less rigorous 10 percent confidence level. The last safety and disciplinary outcome measure was the index of severity of discipline strategies (a score ranked one through five) suggested as answers to the hypothetical situations. The lower the index score, the lower the severity of the parental response. Parents in the intervention group had an average index score of 3.4, while the control group parents averaged 3.5—a statistically significant difference of 0.2 in favor of the intervention at the five percent confidence level.[40]

Early Head Start failed to have any statistically measurable impact on the physical and mental health of parents and family functioning. On 10 measures that assessed parental distress, dysfunctional parent-child interactions, and family conflict, not a single measure indicated Early Head Start had beneficial or harmful impacts.[41]

The results for Early Head Start fared better for the measures of parental self-sufficiency 26-months after random assignment.[42] For the percentage of parents ever being employed or participating in an education or job-training program, 93.9 percent of the intervention group parents reported in the affirmative, while 90.5 percent of the control group parents reported in the affirmative. The difference of 3.4 percent in favor of the intervention group was statistically significant at the five percent confidence level. For the average hours per week employed at all jobs and in any education or training programs, the intervention and control group parents reported averaging 22.3 hours and 20.9 hours, respectively. This difference of 1.5 hours is statistically significant at the less rigorous 10 percent confidence level. The percentage of parents reporting ever being employed was 86.6 percent for intervention group parents and 83.4 percent for control group parents—a statistically significant difference of 3.4 percent at the less rigorous 10 percent confidence level. On average, intervention and control group parents spent 17.1 hours per week employed in any job; thus, Early Head Start had no impact on average hours worked. However, parents in the intervention group were more likely to seek education and training than control group parents. Of intervention group parents, 60 percent were involved in education or training programs, while the figure for control group parents was 51.4 percent—a statistically significant difference of 8.6 percent at the one percent confidence level. Parents in the intervention group averaged 4.6 hours per week participating in education programs, compared to 3.4 hours per week for the control group parents—a statistically significant difference of 1.2 hours at the one percent confidence level.

Despite the positive gains in seeking education or training, Early Head Start had no effect on six measures of parental attainment of educational degrees and credentials, including obtaining General Educational Development (GED) certificates, high school diplomas, and college degrees.[43]

In addition, Early Head Start had no statistically measurable impact on five measures of welfare participation.[44] For example, 68.1 percent of intervention group parents and 66.5 percent of control group parents reported receiving any welfare benefits over the course of 26 months after random assignment. The difference of 1.6 percent was statistically insignificant.

Impacts by Race and Ethnicity.   As can be clearly seen in Table 4.1, almost all of the positive findings for all Early Head Start participants are being driven by the positive findings for blacks.[45] With only a few exceptions, there are few statistically significant impacts for whites and Hispanics, while the findings for blacks closely mirror the overall findings. When there are statistically significant impacts by race and ethnicity, the results generally demonstrate Early Head Start having beneficial impacts. There are, however, a few harmful impacts by race and ethnicity that are worth mentioning. For whites, parents in the intervention group displayed higher dysfunctional parent-child interactions than their counterparts in the control group.[46] The harmful impact was statistically significant at the five percent confidence level. Further, participation in Early Head Start appears to have increased welfare dependency for Hispanics. While 35.5 percent of Hispanics in the intervention group reported ever receiving AFDC or TANF benefits, only 23.3 percent of Hispanics in the control group reported ever receiving AFDC or TANF benefits.[47] The difference of 12.3 percent was statistically significant at the one percent confidence level. At the less rigorous 10 percent confidence level, Hispanics in the intervention group were more likely to have ever received welfare benefits, in general, and food stamps, specifically.

While Early Head Start produced several short-term beneficial impacts, these impacts appear to be driven by race. Sawhill and Baron were correct that some meaningful results were produced; however, these results were almost exclusively benefiting blacks, not whites and Hispanics. Blacks comprised 34 percent of primary caregivers, while Hispanics and whites made up 24 percent and 37 percent, respectively, of primary caregivers.[48] Thus, Early Head Start appears to benefit only a minority of its clientele.

Long-Term Impacts of Early Head Start

In 2012, the follow-up study was titled *Early Head Start Children in Grade 5: Long-Term Follow-Up of the Early Head Start Research Evaluation Project Study Sample: Final Report*.[49] Recall the title of the initial Early Head Start evaluation. There is a good reason for the bland technical title of the follow-up evaluation, which is ambiguous about the effectiveness of Early Head Start. While the previous evaluation assessed the program's short-term impacts at age 3 for the children in the intervention and control groups, the follow-up study assessed impact at fifth grade. For the follow-up study, data from 1,632 sample members were collected.[50]

Overall Long-Term Impacts.   Table 4.2 summarizes the overall findings as well as the findings by race and ethnicity. The overall initial effects of Early Head Start at age 3 have clearly faded by the fifth grade. For the 11 child-social-emotional outcomes, only 1 outcome was marginally statistically significant.[51] For the social-emotional success index, the intervention group children had an average score of 47.2, while the control group children averaged 42.1—a statistically significant difference at the less rigorous 10 percent confidence level. The social-emotional success index assesses "the absence of risk on five social-emotional outcomes: externalizing

TABLE 4.2.   Selected Findings of Early Head Start Evaluation at Grade 5

Child and Family Outcomes at Grade 5	Overall	Black	Hispanic	White
Child Social-Emotional Outcomes				
Child Behavior Checklist CBCL internalizing behavior	0	0	0	0
CBCL externalizing behavior	0	Pos**	0	Pos*
CBCL attention problems	0	Pos**	0	0
Self-reported delinquent behavior	0	0	0	0
Early Childhood Longitudinal Survey-Kindergarten Cohort Self Description Questionnaire (ECLS-K-SDQ) anger/distractibility	0	0	0	0
ECLS-K-SDQ sad/lonely/anxious	0	0	0	0
ECLS-K-SDQ peer relations	0	0	0	0
Self-reporting bullying by peers	0	Pos*	0	0
Attention Deficit Disorder/Attention	0	0	0	0

(continued)

TABLE 4.2. (Continued)

Child and Family Outcomes at Grade 5	Overall	Black	Hispanic	White
Deficit Hyperactivity Disorder (ADD/ ADHD) since first grade (parent report)				
Social-emotional risk index	0	0	0	0
Social-emotional success index	Pos*	0	0	0
Child Negative Social-Emotional Outcomes				
CBCL aggressive behavior	0	Pos**	0	0
CBCL rule-breaking behavior	0	Pos**	0	Pos*
CBCL social problems	0	Pos**	0	0
CBCL anxious/depressed	Pos*	Pos**	0	Pos*
CBCL withdrawn/depressed	0	0	0	0
CBCL somatic complaints	0	0	0	0
CBCL thought problems	0	Pos*	0	0
Child Academic Outcomes				
English receptive vocabulary-Peabody Picture Vocabulary Test-Third Edition (PPPVT-III)	0	0	0	0
PPVT-III standard score below 85	0	0	0	0
Matrix reasoning-Wechsler Intelligence Scale for Children (WISC)	0	0	0	Pos*
Early Childhood Longitudinal Survey-Kindergarten (ECLS-K) reading	0	0	0	0
ECLS-K mathematics	0	0	0	0
Retention (parent report)	0	0	0	0
Chronic absenteeism (parent report)	0	0	0	0
Child has Individualized Education Plan (IEP)-parent report	0	0	0	0
Academic success index	0	0	Neg*	0
Ability success index	0	0	0	0
Child Outcomes: Multidomain Indices				
Cumulative Risk	0	0	0	0
Categorical risk (low, medium, high)	0	0	0	0
Cumulative success	0	0	0	0
Parenting and the Home Environment				
Parent supervision	0	0	0	0
Severity of discipline strategies	0	0	0	0
Family involvement in school	0	Pos***	0	0
Children's books (26 or more)	0	0	0	0
Help with homework	0	0	0	0
HOME total score-sum of the above five measures	0	0	0	0
Total support for education	0	0	0	0
Support for education, internal to the home	0	Pos*	0	0

TABLE 4.2.   (Continued)

Child and Family Outcomes at Grade 5	Overall	Black	Hispanic	White
Support for education, external to the home	0	0	0	0
Family Well-Being and Mental Health				
Center for Epidemiologic Studies Depressive (CES-D) symptoms	0	Pos*	0	0
Parent substance use	0	0	0	0
Parent alcohol use	0	Pos***	0	0
Parenting Stress Index (PSI)-parenting distress	0	0	0	Pos*
Number of moves	0	Pos*	0	0
Homelessness	0	0	0	0
Family Environment Scale (FES)-family conflict	0	0	0	Pos*
PSI Parent-child dysfunctional interaction	0	0	0	0
Child-reported relationship with mother	0	0	0	0
Child-reported relationship with father	0	0	0	0
Child exposure to domestic violence	0	0	0	0
Parent Self-Sufficiency				
Household annual income	0	0	0	0
Income-to-needs ration	0	0	0	0
Mother's highest educational level	0	0	Pos*	0
Mother's employment status	0	0	0	0
Current welfare participation	0	0	0	Pos*

Key: 0   Finding was not statistically significant

Pos   Positive or beneficial impactNeg Negative or harmful impact

*   Statistically significant at the 10 percent confidence level ($p \le 0.10$)

**   Statistically significant at the 5 percent confidence level ($p \le 0.05$)

***   Statistically significant at the 1 percent confidence level ($p \le 0.01$)

n/a   n/a No measure was assessed or reported

†   No statistically significance test was performed

Source: Cheri A. Vogel, Yange Xue, Emily M. Moiduddin, Barbara Lepidus Carlson, and Ellen Eliason Kisker, *Early Head Start Children in Grade 5: Long-Term Follow-Up of the Early Head Start Research Evaluation Project Study Sample: Final Report,* OPRE Report # 2011-8 (Washington, DC: Office of Planning, Research, and Evaluation, Administration for Children and Families, U.S. Department of Health and Human Services, December 2010), Table III.2, 24–25; Table III.3, 26; Table III.6, 31–33; Table III.7, 34.

behavior, internalizing behavior, attention problems, peer bullying, and delinquent behaviors."[52] The higher the index score, the better.

Of the 7 child negative social-emotional outcomes, Early Head Start failed to affect 6 outcomes.[53] On measures of aggressive behavior, rule-breaking behavior, social problems, withdrawal or depression, somatic complaints, and thought problems, the program had no statistically measurable effects on the child by the fifth grade. Early Head Start appears to have had a marginally statistically significant impact on reducing anxious or depressed behavior. The difference between the intervention and control groups was statistically significant at the 10 percent confidence level.

By the fifth grade, Early Head Start failed to have statistically measurable effects on the 10 measures of child academic outcomes.[54] For example, the program appears to be ineffective at affecting reading, vocabulary, and math skills.

For the 3 multidomain indices of child outcomes—measures of cumulative risk factors (e.g., bullying by peers, self-reported delinquency, chronic illness) and success factors (e.g., academic success, peer success)—Early Head Start failed to affect all measures.[55] The same pattern held for measures of parenting and the home environment. On all 9 measures, the program failed to have impacts that were statistically different from zero.[56] Thus, the program was unsuccessful at improving such factors as parenting supervision, disciplinary strategies, family involvement in school, and parental help with homework.

On the 11 measures of family well-being and mental health outcomes, Early Head Start failed to affect all the measures.[57] For instance, the program had no effect on parent illegal substance use, parent alcohol use, family conflict, child-reported relationships with mother and father, and child expose to domestic violence. For the five measures of parent self-sufficiency, the same pattern held.[58] For example, the program failed to affect annual household income, the mother's education level and employment status, and current welfare participation.

In sum, Early Head Start marginally affected only two of the 56 outcome measures. The program failed to affect the remaining 54 outcome measures. Clearly, the overall benefits of Early Head Start for the entire program sample faded away.

Impacts by Race and Ethnicity.   While Early Head Start has little to no effect by the fifth grade for the entire sample, blacks appear to benefit substantially more from the program than whites and Hispanics. As seen in Table 4.2, blacks responded favorably to the program in 13 of the 56 measures. Out of the 11 child social-emotional outcomes, intervention group blacks had two statistically significant positive impacts on externalizing behavior and attention problems, and one marginally statistically significant impact on self-reported bullying by peers, compared to similar members of the control group.[59] For the remaining eight measures, Early Head Start had no effect for blacks.

The effectiveness of Early Head Start for blacks on measures of child negative social-emotional outcomes is the most impressive of all. The program had statistically significant impacts on reducing negative behaviors for four measures and a marginally statistically significant effect on one measure.[60] However, these impressive results did not continue with child academic outcomes. On all 10 academic success measures, Early Head Start had no statistically measurable effect for black children.[61]

For the three multidomain indices of child outcomes, Early Head Start failed to affect all measures for blacks.[62] The same pattern almost held for measures of parenting and the home environment. On seven of the nine measures, the program failed to have impacts there were statistically different from zero (no effect) for blacks.[63] For instance, the program appears to have no effect on parent supervision, parental discipline strategies, and helping with homework. The program did have, however, a positive statistically significant effect on family involvement in school and a marginally statistically significant beneficial effect in internal support for education within the home.

The same pattern held for measures of family well-being and mental health outcomes. For blacks, Early Head Start failed to affect eight out of 11 outcome measures, such as parental substance use, parent distress, homelessness, family conflict, child-reported relationships with mother and father, and child exposure to domestic violence. The program appears to have had a statistically significant beneficial impact on parent alcohol use and marginally statistically significant positive impacts on parental depressive symptoms and number of household moves.

With only a few exceptions, Early Head Start had no statistically measurable effect on the outcomes for whites and Hispanics. For 54 of the 56 outcomes, Early Head Start appears to be ineffective for Hispanics.[64] While only marginally statistically significant at the 10 percent confidence level, the program may be associated with a decrease in academic success for Hispanic children.[65] The program also had a marginally statistically significant effect on slightly raising the education level of Hispanic mothers. Of the 56 outcome measures for whites, Early Head Start failed to affect 49 outcomes.[66] For the remaining seven outcomes, the program had marginally statistically significant beneficial impacts at the 10 percent confidence level.

Thinking about probability, the 10 percent confidence level means that in 100 statistical tests, we can reasonably expect to have 10 statistically significant findings by pure chance alone and not the result of the program being tested. We need to keep this fact in mind when assessing Early Head Start's effectiveness. Thus, we can reasonably expect to find almost six (5.6) of the 56 outcomes measure to be statistically significant at the 10 percent confidence level for each of the white, black, and Hispanics groups. For whites, there were seven outcomes statistically significant at the 10 percent confidence level. We can reasonably conclude that nearly all of these findings are the result of chance and not caused by the program.

For blacks, while the results may appear to be relatively impressive, we need to keep in mind that eight of the beneficial outcomes are statistically significant at the five percent confidence level. Under probability theory, we can expect by pure chance alone about six (5.6) of the outcome measures will be statistically significant at the five percent confidence level. Thus, the majority of these statistically significant impacts for blacks may not be caused by Early Head Start at all.

Enhanced Early Head Start with Employment Services

Enhanced Early Head Start with Employment Services (hereinafter referred to as Enhanced Early Head Start) is a demonstration program that involves regular Early Head Start services with the addition of employment and training services. It is "a proactive program focusing on parental employment and the economic self-sufficiency needs of families."[67] Enhanced Early Head Start employs on-site self-sufficiency specialists that work with regular staff and participating families. The services include "formalized employment and self-sufficiency services" and "community partnerships with local employment-focused and educational agencies."[68]

As with regular Early Head Start, Enhanced Early Head Start targets low-income families with infants, toddlers, and pregnant woman. An experimental evaluation of the program based on two sites in Kansas and Missouri was performed. The Kansas and Missouri sites "were selected based on their histories of delivering high-quality EHS [Early Head Start] services."[69]

To be eligible for participation in the evaluation, families had to (1) have a family income at or below the federal poverty limit, (2) have a child under three years old or be expecting a child, and (3) live in the program's service area.[70] From August 2004 to December 2006, 610 families were randomly assigned, in equal numbers, to intervention and control groups.[71] Two evaluation reports were published on the program. The first evaluation is based on an 18-month follow-up survey, while the second is based on a 42-month follow-up survey.[72] At the time of the 42-month follow-up survey, infants and toddlers in the evaluation were between three and five years old, and between five and seven years old, respectively.[73]

Table 4.3 summarizes selected findings for both reports. Overall, the authors of the 18-month follow-up study concluded that "The results of the evaluation indicate that Enhanced EHS had few overall effects on parental employment, family functioning, and child well-being."[74] The authors

TABLE 4.3.   Selected Findings of Early Head Start Enhanced Services for the Hard-to-Employ

	18-Month Follow-Up	42-Month Follow-Up
Mothers' Quarterly Employment and Earnings		
Quarterly employment (percent)		
Quarter 1 (quarter of random assignment)	0	n/a
Quarter 2	0	n/a
Quarter 3	0	n/a
Quarter 4	0	n/a
Quarter 5	0	n/a
Quarter 6	0	n/a
Annual employment (percent)		
Year 1	n/a	0
Year 2	n/a	0
Year 3	n/a	0
Ever employed, Quarters 1–6	0	n/a
Ever employed (percent), Quarters 2–15	n/a	0
Number of quarters employed, Quarters 2–15	n/a	0
Employed for 8 consecutive quarters (percent)	n/a	0
Quarterly Earnings		
Quarter 1 (quarter of random assignment)	0	n/a
Quarter 2	0	n/a
Quarter 3	0	n/a
Quarter 4	0	n/a
Quarter 5	0	n/a
Quarter 6	0	n/a
Total earnings, Quarters 1–6	0	n/a
Annual earnings ($)		
Year 1	n/a	0
Year 2	n/a	0
Year 3	n/a	0
Total earnings, Quarters (2–15)	n/a	0
Characteristics of Current Job		
Mothers' employment		
Ever worked for pay since random assignment (percent)	0	0

(continued)

TABLE 4.3. (Continued)

	18-Month Follow-Up	42-Month Follow-Up
Working for pay at time of survey (percent)	0	0
Longest job spell since random assignment (months)	0	Neg**
Fathers'/partners'/spouses' employment (percent)		
Ever worked since random assignment	0	0
Working for pay at time of survey	0	0
Characteristics of mothers' jobs		
Hours worked per week	0	0
Not working (percent)	0	0
Working part-time (percent)	0	0
Working full-time	0	0
Earnings per week ($)	0	0
Hourly wage ($)	0	0
Receiving any benefits (percent)	0	0
Receiving sick days with full pay (percent)	0	0
Receiving paid vacation (percent)	0	0
Receiving or offered health care coverage (percent)	0	0
Household Income		
Income source (percent)		
Earnings	0	0
Child support	0	0
Public assistance	0	0
Cash assistance	0	0
Food stamps	0	0
Supplemental Security Income (SSI) or disability income	0	0
Total material income in prior month ($)	0	0
Total household income in prior month ($)	0	0
Percentage of household income from mother	0	0
Does not know household income (percent)	0	0
Poverty status		
Below federal poverty level (percent)	0	0
Parenting Practices and Parental Psychological Well-Being		
Parenting involvement and engagement (percent)		
Frequency of parenting warmth: At least once a day	0	0
Frequency of social play and cognitive stimulation: At least once a day	0	0
Parental disciplinary strategies (percent)		
Suggested using only mild disciplinary strategies in hypothetical situations	0	0
Percentage of parents who spanked their child in past week	0	0

TABLE 4.3. (Continued)

	18-Month Follow-Up	42-Month Follow-Up
Parental psychological well-being		
Parenting stress and aggravation	0	n/a
Parental psychological distress	0	Neg*
Child Outcomes		
Child social and emotional outcomes		
Self-regulation		
Behavioral regulation	Pos**	n/a
Delay of gratification/impulse control	0	n/a
Walk a line: Slowed down	n/a	0
Executive functioning/impulse control (percent)		
Pencil tapping: Passed	n/a	0
Card sorting: Passed	n/a	0
Parent-reported behavioral, social, and emotional adjustment		
Social and emotional problems	0	0
Social and emotional competencies	0	0
Attention and impulsivity problems	n/a	0
Child language and cognitive outcomes		
Verbal comprehension	0	n/a
Early reading skills	0	0
Early math skills	0	0
Child health outcomes		
General health status: Excellent (percent)	0	n/a
Interviewers assessment of child's task orientation	n/a	0

Key: 0 Finding was not statistically significant
    Pos Positive or beneficial impact
    Neg Negative or harmful impact
    * Statistically significant at the 10 percent confidence level ($p \leq 0.10$)
    ** Statistically significant at the 5 percent confidence level ($p \leq 0.05$)
    *** Statistically significant at the 1 percent confidence level ($p \leq 0.01$)
    n/a No measure was assessed or reported
    † No statistically significance test was performed

Source: JoAnn Hsueh, Erin Jacobs, and Mary Farrell, *A Two Generational Child-Focused Program Enhanced with Employment Services: Eighteen-Month Impacts from the Kansas and Missouri Sites of the Enhanced Services for the Hard-to-Employ Demonstration and Evaluation Project*, MDRC, March 2011, Table 5.1, p. 79; Table 5.2, pp. 81-82; Table 5.3, p. 84; Table 6.1, p. 98; and Table 6.3, p. 107 and JoAnn Hsueh and Mary E. Farrell, *Enhanced Early Head Start with Employment Services: 42-Month Impacts from the Kansas and Missouri Sites of the Enhanced Services for the Hard-t0-Employ Demonstration and Evaluation Project*, OPRE Report # 2012-05 (Washington, DC: Office of Planning, Research, and Evaluation, Administration for Children and Families, U.S. Department of Health and Human Services, February 2012), Table 3.1, 34; Table 3.2, 36–37; Table 4.1, 55; Table 4.3, 61.

of the 42-month follow up concluded that Enhanced Early Head Start "did not have significant impacts on parental employment and economic outcomes, parenting, or child outcomes among the full research sample."[75]

Impact on Employment and Earnings

For the 18-month follow-up report, mothers in the intervention and control groups were assessed on their quarterly employment rates and earnings. Participation in Enhanced Early Head Start failed to affect the employment rate of mothers.[76] In each of the quarters, intervention group mothers were no more or less likely to report being employed, compared to control group mothers. For example, the employment rate of intervention group mothers in quarter six was 64.0 percent, while the employment rate for control group mothers was 69.3 percent—a difference of 5.3 percent that was statistically insignificant.

Similarly, the employment findings for the 42-month follow-up survey were entirely consistent with the 18-month follow-up findings. Participation in Enhanced Early Head Start was unsuccessful at increasing the employment rates of mothers three years after random assignment.[77] For example, mothers in the intervention group had an employment rate of 79.0 percent in the second year, while the employment rate of control group mothers was 80.2 percent—a statistically insignificant difference of 1.2 percent. From quarters two through 15, intervention group mothers averaged 8.8 quarters of employment, while the control group mothers averaged 8.7 quarters. The difference was statistically indistinguishable from zero. The majority of both groups of mothers failed to work for eight consecutive quarters over the entire study period. For the 42-month follow-up, 91.8 percent of intervention group mothers reported being ever employed, while the figure for the control group mothers was 89.1 percent—a statistically insignificant difference.

The same pattern held for quarterly earnings. Over six quarters, Enhanced Early Head Start had no effect on earrings for participating mothers during the 18-month follow-up period.[78] For example, the total incomes over six quarters for the intervention and control group mothers were $12,024 and $11,705, respectively The difference of $319 was statistically indistinguishable from zero. For each of the three years after random assignment, the 42-month follow-up study found that the incomes for the intervention and control group mothers did not statistically differ.[79] Total earnings over the three-year period for intervention and control group mothers were $32,537 and $30,096, respectively. The difference of $2,442 was statistically insignificant, suggesting that the program had no impact on the incomes of mothers.

For both follow-up surveys, Enhanced Early Head Start was unsuccessful at affecting total household income and the poverty status of participants.[80] Specifically, the program had no effect on total maternal income and total household income in the prior month. For the first follow-up survey, the percentage of household income earned by mothers in the intervention group was 58.4 percent, while the figure for the control group was 56.6 percent. The difference of 1.8 percent was statistically indistinguishable from zero. By the time of the second follow-up survey, the percentage of household income earned by mothers in the intervention and control groups were 57.0 percent and 60.0 percent, respectively. Again, the difference was statistically insignificant. Despite receiving employment and training services, solid majorities of the intervention group households reported receiving public assistance (e.g., cash assistance, food stamps, and Supplemental Security Income or disability income) for both surveys. For example, at the time of the second survey, 65.2 percent of intervention group households reported receiving public assistance, while the rate for the control group households was 61.1 percent. The difference of 4.1 percent was statistically insignificant. The program also failed to affect the percentage of households with incomes below the federal poverty level. For the first survey, 50.2 percent and 50.9 percent of the intervention and control group households had incomes below the federal poverty threshold, respectively—the difference of 0.7 was statistically insignificant. Interestingly, the poverty rates decreased for the intervention and control groups by the second follow-up survey. Of the intervention group households, 31.1 percent were under the federal poverty level, compared to 31.2 percent of the control group households. The minute difference is statistically indistinguishable from zero.

Characteristics of Current Job

At the time of the 18-month survey, 63.4 percent and 64.4 percent of intervention and control mothers, respectively, reported currently working for pay—a difference of one percent that was statistically insignificant.[81] At the time of the 42-month survey, 58.0 percent and 62.0 percent of intervention and control mothers, respectively, reported currently working for pay—a difference of four percent that was statistically insignificant.[82]

While mothers of both groups had similar longest job spells at the time of the 18-month follow-up survey, mothers in the control group had longer job spells at the time of the 42-month follow-up survey. The mothers in the intervention group had job spells that were, on average, 2.5 months less than the job spells of control group mothers—a statistically significant difference at the five percent confidence level.[83]

For both follow-up surveys, participation in Enhanced Early Head Start had no effect on hours worked per week, working full-time or part-time, earnings per week, hourly wages, and the receipt of job benefits.[84] Participation in the program had no effect on the employment status of fathers for both follow-up periods.

Impacts on Parenting Practices and Parental Psychological Well-Being

Overall, participation in Enhanced Early Head Start failed to influence the outcomes for parenting practices and parental psychological well-being, at least at the five percent confidence level.[85] In both surveys, participation in the program had no effect on parenting factors such as daily displays of parenting warmth, daily displays of social play and cognitive stimulation, and the percentage of parents who spanked their child in the past week. While the program had no effect on parental psychological distress during the first follow-up, parents in the intervention group had marginally higher levels of psychological distress at the time of the second follow-up. Intervention group parents had higher levels of depression and anxiety during the prior month compared to their counterparts. This finding is statistically significant at the less rigorous 10 percent confidence level.

Impacts on Child Outcomes

Of the eight child outcomes that were assessed during the 18-month follow-up survey, only one measure yielded statistically significant results.[86] Children in the intervention group scored higher on their ability for self-regulation of their behavior compared to their counterparts in the control group. This finding is statistically significant at the five percent confidence level. Otherwise, Enhanced Early Head Start was unsuccessful at affecting impulse control, social and emotional problems, verbal comprehension, reading skills, and math skills. By the 42-month follow-up, the program had no statistically measurable effects on the 10 child outcomes that were assessed.[87]

Head Start

Head Start and other early childhood education programs are thought to be effective based largely on two outdated small-scale experiments, the

Carolina Abecedarian Project and the Perry Preschool Project.[88] Created as part of the War on Poverty in 1965, Head Start is a preschool community-based program funded by the federal government. By providing education, nutrition, and health services, Head Start is intended to provide a boost to disadvantaged children before they enter elementary school. Its goal is to help disadvantaged children catch up to children living in more fortunate circumstances. From fiscal year (FY) 1965 to FY 2009, Congress spent $167.5 billion in 2009 dollars on Head Start.[89] From FY 2000 to FY 2009, the average annual appropriation for Head Start was $7.6 billion.

Background on the Head Start Impact Study

Despite Head Start's long life, the program had never undergone a thorough, scientifically rigorous evaluation of its effectiveness until Congress mandated an evaluation in 1998. The Head Start Impact Study began in 2002, and the short-term and long-term results released in 2005 and 2010, respectively, are disappointing. Overall, the evaluation found that the program largely failed to improve the cognitive, social-emotional, health, and parenting outcomes of children who participated compared to the outcomes of similar children who did not participate. According to the report, "the benefits of access to Head Start at age four are largely absent by 1st grade for the program population as a whole."[90]

In 1998, Congress mandated that the Department of Health and Human Services conduct a multisite experimental impact evaluation of Head Start based on a nationally representative sample of the children the program serves. Begun in 2002, the Head Start Impact Study is "based on a nationally representative sample of both Head Start programs and newly entering three- and four-year-old children. That is, children applying for entry into Head Start in fall 2002, from a nationally representative random sample of programs, were selected at random. This makes results generalizable to the entire Head Start program, not just the selected study sample."[91] Approximately, 5,000 children who applied to participate in Head Start were randomly assigned to intervention and control groups.[92] The intervention group participated in Head Start services, while the control group was excluded from Head Start participation. The parents of control group children were free to enroll their children in other early education programs.

The evaluation included two separate samples of children applying for participation in Head Start: a cohort of three-year-olds and a cohort of four-year-olds. The three-year-old cohort was used to study the effects of participating in Head Start for four years, while the four-year-old cohort was used to assess the impact of one year of participation in the program.[93] The greater "dose" of participating in Head Start for an additional year is expected to yield more beneficial impacts for the three-year-old cohort, compared to the impacts for the four-year-old-cohort.

In the 2005 Head Start Impact Study, the results are based on one year of Head Start participation.[94] A follow-up evaluation, the 2010 Head Start Impact Study, assessed the effectiveness of Head Start when children were in kindergarten and the first grade.[95]

While the 2005 Head Start Impact Study found that the program affected a sizable minority of outcome measures, the 2010 Head Start Impact Study found that Head Start largely failed to improve the cognitive, social-emotional, health, and parenting outcomes compared to the outcomes of similar children. The authors disappointingly concluded:

> In sum, this report finds that providing access to Head Start has benefits for both three-year-olds and four-year-olds in the cognitive, health, and parenting domains, and for three-year-olds in the social-emotional domain. However, the benefits of access to Head Start at age four are largely absent by 1st grade for the program population as a whole.[96]

While the results of the 2010 study have been known to officials within the Department of Health and Human Services since the end of the Bush administration, with the passage of the American Recovery and Reinvestment Act of 2009, Congress provided $1 billion in additional funding to the original $7.5 billion in FY 2009 funding for Head Start.[97]

First-Year Findings

The findings for the 2005 Head Start Impact Study are presented by cognitive, social-emotional, health, and parenting outcomes for each cohort. The first-year selected findings are summarized in Table 4.4. To give the reader an overall impression of the effectiveness of Head Start without needlessly going into detail by breaking down the results for each cohort by subgroups (e.g., race, English speaking ability), the discuss will focus on the overall effects for each cohort.

Impacts on Cognitive Development.   For cognitive development of the three-year-old and four-year-old cohorts, the 2005 study assessed 11 first-year outcomes. For the three-year-old cohort, access to Head Start

TABLE 4.4. Findings of Head Start Impact Study, First Year Impacts

	All Language Backgrounds	
Cognitive Outcomes	3-Year-Old Cohort Outcomes	4-Year-Old Cohort Outcomes
Pre-Reading Skills		
Woodcock-Johnson–Letter-Word Identification	Pos***	Pos*
Letter naming task	Pos**	Pos**
Pre-Writing Skills		
Woodcock-Johnson–Spelling	0	Pos*
McCarthy Drawing	Pos*	0
Vocabulary Knowledge		
Peabody Picture Vocabulary Test, 3rd Edition	Pos*	0
Color Naming/Identification	0	0
Oral Comprehension and Phonological Awareness		
Woodcock-Johnson–Oral Comprehension	0	0
CTOPPP Elision (English)	0	0
Early Math Skills		
Woodcock-Johnson–Applied Problems	0	0
Counting Bears	0	0
Parental Perception of Child's Literacy		
Parent Educational Literacy Activities Scale (PELS)	Pos***	Pos***
Social-Emotional Outcomes		
Social Skills and Approaches to Learning		
Social skills scale	0	0
Social competencies	0	0
Problem Behavior		
Total problem Behavior scale	Pos*	0
Aggressive behavior scale	0	0
Hyperactive behavior scale	Pos**	0
Withdrawn behavior scale	0	0
Health Outcomes		
Child has health insurance	0	0
Child health status is excellent or very good	0	0
Child needs ongoing care	0	0
Child had care for injury last month	0	0
Child had dental care	Pos***	Pos**
Parenting Outcomes		
Educational Activities		
Number of times child is read to on average	Pos*	Pos*
Family cultural enrichment scale	Pos**	0

(continued)

TABLE 4.4.   (Continued)

Cognitive Outcomes	All Language Backgrounds	
	3-Year-Old Cohort Outcomes	4-Year-Old Cohort Outcomes
Disciplinary Practices		
Used time out in last week	0	Pos*
Number of times used time out in last week	0	0
Spanked child in last week	Pos*	0
Number of times spanked child in last week	Pos*	0
Safety Practices		
Parental safety practices scale	0	0
Removing harmful objects subscale	0	0
Restricting child movement Subscale	0	0
Safety devices subscale	0	0

Key: 0 Finding was not statistically significant
     Pos Positive or beneficial impact
     Neg Negative or harmful impact
     *   Statistically significant at the 10 percent confidence level ($p \leq 0.10$)
     **   Statistically significant at the 5 percent confidence level ($p \leq 0.05$)
     *** Statistically significant at the 1 percent confidence level ($p \leq 0.01$)
     n/a No measure was assessed or reported
     †   No statistically significance test was performed
Sources: U.S. Department of Health and Human Services, Administration for Children and Families, *Head Start Impact Study: First Year Findings* (Washington, DC, May 2005), Exhibit 5.1-A, 5-14; Exhibit 5.2-A, 5-17; Exhibit 6.1-A, 6-6; Exhibit 6.2-A, 6-9; Exhibit 7.1, 7-6; Exhibit 7.2, 7-7; Exhibit 8.1, 8-9; and Exhibit 8.2, 8-10.

failed to result in at least marginally statistically significant effects on six of the 11 measures of cognitive ability.[98] For the four-year-old cohort, access to the program failed to yield at least marginally statistically significant results on seven of the 11 outcome measures.

Despite failing to affect a majority of cognitive outcomes, access to Head Start appears to improve pre-reading skills for both cohorts. At the one percent and five percent levels of confidence, access to Head Start for the three-year-old cohort improved general pre-reading skills (Woodcock-Johnson: Letter-Word Identification) and letter naming tasks, respectively. On average, the three-year-old intervention group could name 1.3 more letters of the alphabet than control group children.[99] For the Woodcock-Johnson: Letter-Word Identification test, the four-year-old intervention group, on average, had higher scores than their counterparts in the control group. The difference was marginally statistically significant at the less rigorous

10 percent confidence level. At the five percent level of significance, the four-year-old intervention group scored higher on letter naming tasks than the control group. On average, the four-year-old intervention group could name 2.3 more letters of the alphabet than their counterparts.[100]

As for prewriting skills, the effect of Head Start was less consistent. Based on the Woodcock-Johnson: Spelling assessment, which "measures perceptual-motor skills involved in tracing or copying letter shapes and then measures children's ability to draw letters on request, without being shown the shape of the letter in question," access to Head Start failed to improve prewriting skills for the three-year-old cohort.[101] However, the program appears to have had a marginally positive impact at the 10 percent level of confidence on prewriting skills of the three-year-old cohort based on the McCarthy Drawing test, which "measures perceptual-motor skills involved in seeing and copying basic geometric shapes."[102] Alternatively, four-year-old children with access to Head Start scored higher on the Woodcock-Johnson: Spelling assessment, compared to their counterparts. However, this finding is marginally statistically significant at the 10 percent confidence level. For the McCarthy Drawing test, access to the program failed to affect the prewriting skills of the four-year-old cohort.

The same inconsistency continued for the vocabulary knowledge outcome measures.[103] The Peabody Picture Vocabulary Test (3rd edition) "measures children's receptive vocabulary by asking them to select one of four pictures that best represents each of a series of words spoken by the examiner," while the Color Naming test "measures children's ability to name the colors of drawings of bears in 10 different colors."[104] The scores of three-year-old children who had access to Head Start on the Peabody Picture Vocabulary Test were higher than the scores of their counterparts. The difference was statistically significant at the less rigorous 10 percent level of confidence. Despite this marginally positive finding, access to the programs failed to improve vocabulary knowledge of three-year-olds based on the Color Naming test. For the four-year-old cohort, access to the program yielded statistically insignificant results for both vocabulary knowledge measures.

On two measures of oral comprehension and phonological awareness, access to Head Start for the three- and four-year-old cohorts was unsuccessful.[105] The differences between the intervention and control group scores in both cohorts on the Woodcock-Johnson: Oral Comprehension test and the Elision task from the Comprehensive test of Print and Phonological Processing—Preschool edition (CTOPPP) yielded statistically indistinguishable results. The Woodcock-Johnson: Oral Comprehension test measures "the ability of children to understand and make inferences from spoken phrases and sentences," while the CTOPPP test measures "a child's understanding that spoken sentences are made of component words, compound words are made up of simpler words, and that even simple words are made up of component syllables and sounds."[106]

Access to Head Start for the three-year-old and four-year-old cohorts was unsuccessful at improving the early math skills of children on the Woodcock-Johnson: Applied Programs and Counting Bears tests.[107] The Woodcock-Johnson: Applied Problems test assesses "children's proficiency at solving simple word problems that involve counting, simple arithmetic, and basic measurement."[108] The Drawing Bears test evaluates "how well children had done at one-to-one counting of a set of drawings of 10 bears."[109]

Last, access to Head Start appears to have increased the perception by parents that the literacy of their children is improving.[110] On average, the scores on the Parent Educational Literacy Activities Scale for parents of three- and four-year-old children in the intervention group were higher than the scores for parents of children in the control group. The differences in parental perception for both cohorts were highly statistically significant at the one percent confidence level.

Impacts on Social-Emotional Development.   For social-emotional development, the 2005 study assessed six parent-reported outcomes for both cohorts. For the three-year-old cohort, access to Head Start failed to produce at least marginally statistically measurable effects on four of the six outcomes.[111] Access to Head Start failed to affect all six of the outcome measures for the four-year-old cohort.[112]

For the three-year-old cohort, the program failed to improve parental assessments of social skills and approaches to learning, while having a mixed impact on aggressive behavior. Head Start failed to affect parental assessments of aggressive and withdrawal behaviors. However, the differences of parental perceptions of total problem behavior were lower for the intervention group, compared to the control group. This difference is marginally statistically significant at the 10 percent confidence level. The results for hyperactive behavior can be held with higher confidence. At the five percent confidence level, parents of the intervention group children perceived their children to be less hyperactive than did parents of the control group children.

Impacts on Child Health Outcomes.   For parent-reported child health, the 2005 study assessed five outcomes for each cohort. For both cohorts, access to Head Start failed to affect four of the five health outcome measures.[113] Access to Head Start had no statistically measurable effect on whether children had health insurance. In addition, the program had no effect on the child's health status, the child's need for ongoing care, and the child having an injury within the past month. However, the authors of the 2005 study reported that Head Start had a positive impact on receiving dental care for both cohorts. The differences between the intervention and control groups on access to dental care was statistically significant at the one percent and five percent confidence levels for the three- and four-year-old cohorts, respectively.

Impacts on Parenting Outcomes.   For parenting outcomes, the 2005 study assessed 10 measures for both cohorts. For the three-year-old cohort, access to Head Start failed to produce at least marginally statistically measurable effects at the 10 percent confidence level on six of the 10 outcomes.[114] For the four-year-old cohort, access to Head Start failed to produce at least marginally significant effects on eight of the 10 measures.[115]

For the two measures of parental education activities, access to Head Start yielded consistent marginally beneficial effects for the three-year-old cohort at the 10 percent confidence level, while the effects for the four-year-old cohort were inconsistent.[116] At the marginally statistical significance level of 10 percent, access to the program was associated with an increase in the number of times parents reported to have read to their child for both cohorts. As for exposure to a variety of cultural enrichment activities, access to Head Start for the three-year-old cohort produced a positive impact at the five percent confidence level, while the effect for the four-year-old cohort was statistically insignificant.

For both cohorts, the effects on disciplinary practices reported by parents were inconsistent. Of the four parenting measures, access to Head Start produced positive results that were marginally statistically significant for the three-year-old cohort.[117] Head Start may be linked to reductions in parent-reported child spanking within the last week and the number of times the child was spanked. These reductions were marginally statistically significant at the 10 percent confidence level. Access to the program appears to have had no effect on parent-reported levels of spanking for the four-year-old cohort.[118]

For parent-reported safety practices, access to Head Start for the three-year-old cohort failed to yield statistically significant results on all four outcome measures.[119] The same trend occurred for the four-year-old cohort.[120] Thus, Head Start appears to be ineffective in improving the safety practices of parents.

Kindergarten and First Grade Findings

The 2010 Head Start Impact Study found that Head Start has had little to no effect on cognitive, social-emotional, health, and parenting outcomes of participating children. For the three-year-old cohort, access to Head Start had one (0.9 percent) harmful impact at the one percent confidence level, six (5.4 percent) marginally beneficial impacts at the 10 percent confidence level, and five (4.5 percent) beneficial impacts at the five percent confidence level out of 112 measures. For the four-year-old cohort, access to Head Start had one (0.9 percent) harmful impact at the five percent confidence level, one (0.9 percent) marginally harmful impact at the 10 percent confidence level, four (3.6 percent) marginally beneficial impacts at the 10 percent confidence level, and one beneficial impact at the five percent confidence level out of 112 measures. Table 4.5 presents the findings for the kindergarten and first grade impacts.

Impacts on Cognitive Development.   For cognitive development, the 2010 study assessed 19 kindergarten outcomes and 22 first-grade outcomes for the three-year-old cohort. For kindergarten, access to Head Start had no statistically measurable effects at the five percent significance level on nine measures of language and literacy, two measures of Spanish language and literacy, and three measures of math skills.[121] However, access to the program had a marginally positive impact on the Batería Woodcock-Muñoz (WM) Identificación de letras y palabras (WM Letter-Word identification for Spanish language) at the 10 percent confidence level. The negative effect of Head Start was statistically significant at the one percent significance level for one of the five measures of school performance assessment outcomes: "Kindergarten teachers reported poorer math skills for children in the Head Start group than for those in the control group."[122] Head Start had no statistically measurable impacts on the remaining 4 school assessment outcomes.[123] Otherwise, Head Start appears to have no effect in kindergarten on spelling, English letter-word identification, basic reading skills, and other school performance assessment measures.

For the first grade, access to Head Start for the three-year-old cohort has similarly bleak results. None of the 22 first-grade cognitive outcomes

TABLE 4.5. Findings of Head Start Impact Study, Kindergarten and First Grade Impacts

Cognitive Outcomes	3-Year-Old Cohort Outcomes		4-Year-Old Cohort Outcomes	
	Kinder-garten	First Grade	Kinder-garten	First Grade
Language and Literacy Measures				
Peabody Picture Vocabulary (PPVT)-Adapted	0	0	0	Pos*
Woodcock-Johnson III (WJ III) Letter-Word Identification	0	0	0	0
WJ III Spelling	0	0	0	0
WJ III Oral Comprehension	0	Pos*	0	0
Comprehensive Test of Phonological and Print Processing (CTOPPP) Elison Subtest	0	n/a	0	n/a
Letter Naming	0	n/a	0	n/a
WJ III Pre-Academic Skills	0	0	0	0
WJ III Work Attack	0	0	0	0
WJ III Basic Reading Skills	0	0	0	0
WJ III Academic Applications	n/a	0	n/a	0
WJ III Academic Skills	n/a	0	n/a	0
WJ III Passage Comprehension	n/a	0	n/a	0
WJ III Writing Sample	n/a	0	n/a	0
Spanish Language and Literacy Measures				
Test de Vocabulario en Imagenes Peabody (TVIP)-Adapted	0	0	0	0
Batería Woodcock-Muñoz (WM) Identificación de letras y palabras	Pos*	0	0	0
Math Skills Measures				
WJ III Applied Problems	0	0	0	0
WJ III Quantitative Concepts	0	0	0	0
WJ III Math Reasoning	0	0	0	0
WJ III Calculation	n/a	0	n/a	0
School Performance Assessment Measures				
School accomplishments	0	0	0	0
Promotion	0	0	0	0
Language and literacy ability	0	0	0	0
Math ability	Neg***	0	0	0
Social studies and science ability	0	0	0	0

(continued)

TABLE 4.5. (Continued)

Cognitive Outcomes	3-Year-Old Cohort Outcomes		4-Year-Old Cohort Outcomes	
	Kinder-garten	First Grade	Kinder-garten	First Grade
Social-Emotional Outcomes				
Parent-Reported Measures				
Aggressive behavior	0	0	0	0
Hyperactive behavior	Pos**	0	0	0
Withdrawn behavior	0	0	0	Pos*
Total Problem behavior	0	0	0	0
Social competencies	0	0	0	0
Social skills and positive approaches to learning	Pos*	0	0	0
Closeness	0	Pos**	0	0
Conflict	0	0	0	0
Positive relationships	0	Pos*	0	0
Teacher-Reported Measures				
Adjustment Scales for Pre-school Intervention (ASPI)-Aggressive	0	0	0	0
ASPI-Inattentive/Hyperactive	0	0	0	0
ASPI-Withdrawn/Low Energy	0	0	0	0
ASPI-Oppositional	0	0	0	0
ASPI-Problems with Peer Interaction	0	0	0	0
ASPI-Shy/Socially Reticent	0	0	0	Neg**
ASPI-Problems with Structured Learning	0	0	0	0
ASPI-Problems with Teacher Interaction	0	0	0	Neg*
Closeness	0	0	0	0
Conflict	0	0	0	0
Positive relationships	0	0	0	0
Health Outcomes				
Parent-Reported Measures				
Child received dental care	0	0	0	0
Child has health insurance coverage	Pos**	0	Pos*	Pos**
Child's overall health status is excellent/good	0	0	Pos*	0
Child needs ongoing care	0	0	0	0
Child had care for injury last month	0	0	0	0
Parenting Outcomes				
Parent-Reported Measures				
Parent spanked child in last week	Pos*	0	0	0
Parent used time out in last week	Pos**	Pos*	0	0
Parent read to child in last week	0	0	0	0

TABLE 4.5.   (Continued)

Cognitive Outcomes	3-Year-Old Cohort Outcomes		4-Year-Old Cohort Outcomes	
	Kinder-garten	First Grade	Kinder-garten	First Grade
Parental safety practices scale	0	n/a	0	n/a
Family cultural enrichment Scale	0	0	0	0
Parenting style: Authoritarian	0	Pos**	0	0
Parenting style: Authoritative	0	0	0	0
Parenting style: Neglectful	0	0	0	0
Parenting Style: Permissive	0	0	0	0
Teacher-Reported Measures				
School contact and communication	0	0	0	0
Parent participation	0	0	0	0

Key: 0 Finding was not statistically significant
   Pos Positive or beneficial impact
   Neg Negative or harmful impact
   *   Statistically significant at the 10 percent confidence level ($p \leq 0.10$)
   **   Statistically significant at the 5 percent confidence level ($p \leq 0.05$)
   ***   Statistically significant at the 1 percent confidence level ($p \leq 0.01$)
   n/a No measure was assessed or reported
   †   No statistically significance test was performed
Sources: U.S. Department of Health and Human Services, Administration for Children and Families. *Head Start Impact Study: Final Report* (Washington, DC, January 2010), Exhibit 4.2, 4-11 to 4-13; Exhibit 4.5, 4-23 to 4-25; Exhibit 5.1, 5-4 to 5-6; Exhibit 5.2, 5-9 to 5-11; Exhibit 6.1, 6-3 to 6-4; Exhibit 6.2, 6-7; Exhibit 7.1, 7-4 to 7-6; Exhibit 7.2, 7-9 to 7-10.

showed a statistically measurable impact at the five percent significance level.[124] The authors reported a small positive and marginally statistically significant positive outcome at the 10 percent significance level for the Woodcock-Johnson (WJ) III Oral Comprehension outcome measure. By the first grade, there was little to no effect on cognitive outcomes. Thus, for all 41 outcome measures for kindergarten and first grade, Head Start failed to have a positive measurable impact, at least at the standard five per-cent level of statistical significance. The exception is the harmful impact on teacher-assessed math ability in kindergarten.

For the cognitive development of the four-year-old cohort, the 2010 study assessed 19 kindergarten outcomes and 22 first-grade outcomes. For kindergarten, access to Head Start had no statistically measurable effect on nine measures of language and literacy, two measures of Spanish lan-guage and literacy, three measures of math skills, and five measures of school performance assessment at the five percent confidence level.[125]

For first grade, access to Head Start for the four-year-old cohort had similarly dismal results. None of the 22 first-grade cognitive outcomes showed a statistically measurable impact at the five percent significance level.[126] However, the authors reported a very small positive and marginally statistically significant positive outcome for the Peabody Picture Vocabulary Test (PPTV Adapted) outcome measure, which measures receptive vocabulary like listening comprehension for spoken words,[127] at the less rigorous 10 percent significance level. Hence, there may be some suggestive evidence that Head Start slightly increased the receptive vocabulary of children. However, for all 41 outcome measures for kindergarten and first grade, Head Start failed to produce measurable impacts at the standard five percent level of statistical significance.

Impacts on Social-Emotional Development.   For social-emotional development, the 2010 study assessed 20 kindergarten outcomes and 20 first-grade outcomes for the three-year-old cohort. For kindergarten, access to Head Start had no statistically measurable effect on the 11 teacher-reported measures and seven of nine parent-reported measures.[128] However, parents of children with access to Head Start reported less hyperactive behavior than parents of children in the control group. This finding was significant at the five percent level. The authors also reported that Head Start had a marginally positive impact on improving social skills and approaches to learning at the 10 percent significance level.

For first grade, access to Head Start for the three-year-old cohort had similarly ineffective results. Head Start had no statistically measurable impact on the 11 teacher-reported measures and seven of the nine first-grade parent-reported outcomes. Head Start appears to have had a positive impact on parent reports of closeness with their child at the five percent significance level. In addition, the authors reported that Head Start had a positive impact on improving parents' positive relationships with their children. However, this finding is statistically significant at the less rigorous 10 percent confidence level.[129]

For social-emotional development of the four-year-old cohort, the 2010 study assessed 20 kindergarten outcomes and 20 first-grade outcomes. For kindergarten, access to Head Start had no statistically measurable effect on nine parent-reported measures and 11 teacher-reported measures.[130]

For first grade, access to Head Start for the four-year-old cohort had similarly underwhelming results, having no statistically measurable impact on eight of the nine first-grade parent-reported outcomes.[131] At the less rigorous 10 percent significance level, the authors reported that the parents of children in the Head Start group perceived their children to be less likely to display withdrawn behavior. One of the 11 teacher-reported measures showed a statistically significant harmful outcome at the five percent significance level. According to the authors, "Teachers reported that Head Start group children were more shy or socially reticent than the control group children."[132] In addition, the authors reported that teachers perceived that they had more interaction problems with Head Start students than the students in the control group. This harmful impact was marginally statistically significant at the 10 percent confidence level. As a consequence, when assessed in the first grade, access to Head Start appears to be more harmful than beneficial on social-emotional development for four-year-olds.

Impacts on Child Health Outcomes.   For parent-reported child health, the 2010 study assessed five kindergarten outcomes and five first-grade outcomes for the three-year-old cohort. For kindergarten, access to Head Start had no statistically measurable effect on four of the five health measures. Access to Head Start showed a small positive effect for health insurance coverage at the five percent significance level. By kindergarten, for example, access to the program failed to influence the receipt of dental care and the health status of children. For first grade, access to Head Start failed to affect the five parent-reported health outcomes.[133]

Similarly unimpressive, the 2010 study assessed the same health outcomes for the four-year-old cohort. For kindergarten, access to Head Start had no statistically measurable effect on three measures: dental care, ongoing care needs, and received care for an injury within the past month.[134] The authors reported that Head Start had small positive impacts on insurance coverage and on parents' perception of the overall health status of their child, but these findings are marginally statistically significant at the 10 percent significance level.

For first grade, access to Head Start failed to affect four of the five parent-reported health outcomes for the four-year-old cohort.[135] While access to Head Start had no effect on dental care, overall health status, ongoing care needs, and received care for an injury within the past month, Head Start had a small positive effect on health insurance coverage at the five percent significance level.

Impacts on Parenting Outcomes.   For parenting outcomes, the 2010 study assessed 11 kindergarten measures and 10 first-grade measures for both cohorts. For kindergarten, access to Head Start had no statistically measurable effect on seven of the nine measures reported by parents and the two measures reported by teachers for the three-year-old cohort.[136] However, parents of children with access to Head Start were less likely to use a "time out" in the past week. The positive effect of this outcome was small but statistically significant at the five percent significance level. The authors reported that access to Head Start had a small negative impact on parents spanking their children at the less rigorous 10 percent confidence level.

For first grade, access to Head Start failed to have an impact on six of the eight parent-reported measures of parenting.[137] Parents of children with access to Head Start were less likely to report using an authoritarian parenting style. The beneficial effect of this outcome was small but statistically significant at the five percent significance level. The authors reported that parents of children with access to Head Start were less likely to use a "time out" within the past week. However, this finding is marginally statistically significant at only the 10 percent confidence level. On the two measures of teacher-reported perceptions of parenting, access to Head Start failed to have statistically measurable impacts.

For parenting outcomes for the four-year-old cohort, the 2010 study assessed 11 kindergarten measures and 10 first-grade measures. For kindergarten, access to Head Start had no statistically measurable effect on the nine measures reported by parents and the two measures reported by teachers. The trend of no statistically measurable impact continued in first grade, with access to Head Start failing to have statistically measurable impacts.[138]

The results of the 2010 Head Start Impact Study demonstrate that the initial modestly positive effects of Head Start nearly faded away by kindergarten and first grade. Thinking about probability, the 2010 Head Start Impact Study would have likely found, by chance alone, nearly six (5.6) outcomes of the 112 measures to be statistically significant at the five percent confidence level for each cohort. For the three-year-old cohort, six outcomes were statistically significant at least at the five percent confidence level, and one of these findings was a harmful impact at the one percent confidence level. For the four-year-old cohort, only two outcomes, including a harmful impact, were statistically significant at the five percent confidence level. Thus, we can reasonably conclude that all of these findings are likely the result of chance and not caused by the program.

The Long-Delayed Third-Grade Impact Study.   The Head Start Impact Study follows students' performance through the end of third grade. On December 21, 2012, the Friday before Christmas, the Department of Health and Human Services (HHS) released the findings of the Third-Grade Head Start Impact Study without a press release to notify the public.[139] HHS withheld this study for approximately 4.5 years after the final data were collected.

The results of the third-grade impact evaluation shed further light on the infectiveness of Head Start. The third-grade study found that Head Start has had little to no effect on cognitive, social-emotional, health, and parenting outcomes of participating children.

There appears to be a pattern of withholding the results of experimental evaluations at HHS. There is reason to believe that the 2010 study of first-grade students was neither completed nor published in a timely fashion.[140] According to the report, data collection for the kindergarten and first-grade evaluation was completed in 2006—nearly four years before its results were made public. For the national impact evaluation of third-grade students, data collection was conducted during the springs of 2007 and 2008.[141] HHS behaved the same way with the third-grade study. Maybe the Obama administration did not want to be a further purveyor of bad news, while the president, on the campaign trail, was scaring voters about the harm that will be done if future spending increases on Head Start are not as high as he wants. Table 4.6 presents the findings for the third-grade impacts.

Impacts on Cognitive Development.   For cognitive development, the third-grade study assessed 11 outcomes for the three- and four-year-old cohorts. Access to Head Start for the three-year-old cohort had no statistically measurable effects on all measures of cognitive ability, including numerous measures of reading, language, and math ability.[142] For the four-year-old cohort, access to Head Start failed to have statistically measureable effects on 10 out of 11 cognitive outcomes.[143] Except for one measure, access to Head Start for the four-year-old cohort had no impact on several measures of vocabulary, language, and math ability. The exception was reading ability, as measured by the ECLS-K Reading test. The four-year-old cohort with access to Head Start has slightly higher scores on reading ability, compared to their counterparts in the control group. However, this beneficial impact was only statistically significant at the less rigorous 10 percent confidence level. Overall, access to Head Start failed to yield statistically significant impacts at least at the five percent confidence level on all cognitive outcomes.

TABLE 4.6. Findings of Head Start Impact Study, Third Grade Impacts

	3-Year-Old Cohort Outcomes	4-Year-Old Cohort Outcomes
Cognitive Outcomes		
Language and Literacy Measures		
Early Childhood Longitudinal Study-Kindergarten (ECLS-K) Reading	0	Pos*
Peabody Picture Vocabulary (PPVT)-Adapted	0	0
Woodcock-Johnson III (WJ III) Letter-Word Identification	0	0
Spanish Language and Literacy Measures		
Batería Woodcock-Muñoz (WM) Identificación de letras y palabras (WM Letter-Word Identification)	0	0
Math Skills Measures		
WJIII Applied Problems	0	0
WJIII Calculation	0	0
School Performance Assessment Measures		
Promotion	0	0
Language and literacy ability	0	0
Math ability	0	0
Reading/language arts skills	0	0
Math skills	0	0
Social-Emotional Outcomes		
Parent-Reported Measures		
Aggressive behavior	0	Pos**
Hyperactive behavior	0	0
Withdrawn behavior	0	0
Total problem behavior	0	Pos*
Social skills and positive approaches to learning	Pos**	0
Teacher-Reported Measures		
Conduct problems	0	0
Emotional symptoms	0	Neg***
Hyperactivity	0	0
Peer problems	0	0
Pro-social behavior	0	0
Total difficulties	0	0
Closeness with teacher	0	Neg*
Conflict with teacher	0	0
Positive teacher-child relationships	0	Neg*
Social competency	0	0
Child-Reported Measures		
Externalizing	0	0

TABLE 4.6.   (Continued)

	3-Year-Old Cohort Outcomes	4-Year-Old Cohort Outcomes
Internalizing	0	0
Peer relations	0	Neg**
School	0	0
Health Outcomes		
Parent-Reported Measures		
Child received dental care	0	0
Child has health insurance coverage	0	0
Child's overall health status is excellent/good	0	0
Child needs ongoing care	0	0
Child had care for injury last month	0	0
Parenting Practices Outcomes		
Parent-Reported Measures		
Parent spanked child in last week	0	0
Parenting style: Authoritarian	0	0
Parenting style: Authoritative	Pos**	0
Parenting style: Neglectful	0	0
Parenting style: Permissive	0	0
Supportive school environment	0	0
Effect of parenting on parent's life	0	0
Doing things together	0	0
Time spent with child	0	Pos***
Parent perception of school services	0	0
Teacher-Reported Measures		
School contact and communication	0	0
Parent participation	0	0

Key: 0 Finding was not statistically significant

Pos Positive or beneficial impact

Neg Negative or harmful impact

*   Statistically significant at the 10 percent confidence level ($p \leq 0.10$)

**   Statistically significant at the 5 percent confidence level ($p \leq 0.05$)

***   Statistically significant at the 1 percent confidence level ($p \leq 0.01$)

n/a   No measure was assessed or reported

†   No statistically significance test was performed

Sources: Mike Puma, Stephen Bell, Ronna Cook, Camilla Heid, Pam Broene, Frank Jenkins, Andrew Mashburn, and Jason Downer. *Third Grade Follow-Up to the Head Start Impact Study Final Report* (Washington, DC: Office of Planning, Research and Evaluation, Administration for Children and Families, U.S. Department of Health and Human Services, October 2012), Exhibit 4.1, 77; Exhibit 4.2, 78; Exhibit 4.3, 81–82; Exhibit 4.4, 83–84; Exhibit 4.5, 85; Exhibit 4.6, 86; Exhibit 4.7, 87; and Exhibit 4.8, 88.

Impacts on Social-Emotional Development.   For social-emotional development, the third-grade study assessed 19 outcomes for each cohort. For five measures of parent-reported social-emotional outcomes, access to

Head Start for the three-year-old cohort failed to affect four of the five measures.[144] For this cohort, Head Start failed to affect parental-reported problem behaviors. However, at the five percent confidence level, access to Head Start yielded a slight beneficial impact on children displaying better social skills and positive approaches to learning. For the four-year-old cohort, access to Head Start failed to affect three of the five parent-reported social-emotional outcomes.[145] For the four-year-old cohort, access to Head Start is associated with a small decrease in aggressive behavior. This finding is statistically significant at the five percent confidence level. There is suggestive evidence that access to Head Start for this cohort slightly reduced total problem behavior as reported by parents. This finding is statistically significant at the less rigorous 10 percent confidence level.

For third grade, access to Head Start had no statistically measurable effect on the 10 teacher-reported measures of social-emotional development for the three-year-old cohort.[146] However, access to Head Start for the four-year-old cohort appears to have a few harmful effects. Out of 10 measures, access to Head Start is associated with one harmful impact at the one percent confidence level and two suggestive harmful impacts at the 10 percent confidence level.[147] Teachers reported "strong evidence of an unfavorable impact on the incidence of children's emotional symptoms" that was highly statistically significant at the one percent confidence level.[148] In addition, there was suggestive evidence of small harmful impacts on closeness with teacher and positive teacher-child relationships at the less rigorous 10 percent confidence level.

For child-reported measures of social-emotional outcomes, access to Head Start had no statistically measurable effect on the four outcomes for the three-year-old cohort.[149] However, access to Head Start for the four-year-old cohort appears to have had one harmful impact. For the four-year-old cohort, children in the third grade with access to Head Start reported worse peer relations than their counterparts.[150] This harmful impact was statistically significant at the five percent confidence level.

Impacts on Child Health Outcomes.   For parent-reported child health, the study assessed five third-grade outcomes for each cohort. Access to Head Start had no statistically measurable effect on all five health measures for each cohort.[151]

Impacts on Parenting Outcomes.   For parenting outcomes, the third-grade study assessed 10 measures for both cohorts. Access to Head Start had no statistically measurable effect on nine of the 10 measures reported by parents and the two measures reported by teachers for the three-year-old cohort.[152] However, parents of children in the three-year-old cohort with access to Head Start self-reported improved authoritative parenting style (i.e., high control and high warmth), compared to their counterparts. This beneficial finding was statistically significant at the five percent confidence level. Similarly, access to Head Start had no statistically measurable effect on nine of the 10 measures reported by parents and the two measures reported by teachers for the four-year-old cohort.[153] Differing from the three-year-old cohort, parents of children in the four-year-old cohort reported to have spent more time with their children than their counterparts in the control group. This beneficial finding is statistically significant at the one percent confidence level.

Attempts to Undercut the Head Start Impact Findings.   Some may argue that other research that directly assessed Head Start performance shows that the program is effective. Research based on the Head Start Family and Child Experiences Survey (FACES) found that Head Start children made gains in vocabulary, math, and writing skills during the Head Start program year.[154] However, the research design of FACES is inadequate for determining the program's effectiveness.

Without a control group, FACES assesses the academic skills of Head Start children at the start and end of the program year. In the scientific literature, this evaluation design is called the one-group pretest-posttest design. This design has poor internal validity because of its inability to rule out rival hypotheses that may have caused the gains.[155] FACES has three specific threats to internal validity.

First, the changes in the outcome measures may be the result of factors acting independently between the pretest and posttest. The gains could be a result of some parents more actively teaching their children at home. In the scientific literature, this threat to internal validity is called history.

Second, the FACES design cannot rule out the fact that the cognitive abilities of children naturally evolve with age. This internal validity threat, called maturation, means that the observed gains found in the FACES research are also likely to be strongly influenced by the natural biological and psychological developmental process of children. Without a control group, the FACES design cannot separate the effect of maturation in the measured outcomes.

Third, the FACES design is susceptible to the internal validity threat of testing. The testing threat occurs when the effect of initially taking a pretest influences the results of the posttest. After the initial student assessment at the start of the Head Start year, children may adapt and learn how to perform better on the year-end test. In essence, the lack of a control group means that FACES research cannot determine whether the children became better test takers by themselves or the program actually helped them to improve their academic skills.

On the other hand, the experimental design of the reports resulting from the Head Start Impact Study rules out the influences of history, maturation, and testing. The use of random assignment and a control group equally distributes the potential influences of these threats between the intervention group and control group. Therefore, these potential threats to internal validity should not affect the results of the Head Start Impact Study.

Another argument offered to undercut the Head Start Impact Study's kindergarten, first-grade, and third-grade findings is that the program produces gains, but those gains fade due to Head Start students attending poorly performing elementary and middle schools. This assumption is based on research by Professors Valerie E. Lee of the University of Michigan and Susanna Loeb of Stanford University. They used the National Education Longitudinal Study (NELS) of 1988 to assess the quality of middle schools attended by eighth graders who attended Head Start, attended other preschool programs, or did not attend preschool.[156] Using a nationally representative sample of all eighth graders, Lee and Loeb found that former Head Start participants attended lower-quality schools compared to the schools attended by students who had attended other preschool programs or did not attend preschool programs. However, the finding that Head Start students go on to attend worse schools is not surprising. Children living in impoverished, socially disorganized neighborhoods are more likely than children in wealthier neighborhoods to attend lower-performing schools.

The potential suggestion that this finding explains why the Head Start Impact Study found almost no effect on kindergarten, first-grade, and third-grade academic achievement is dubious. The fact that former Head Start students attend poorly performing schools should not affect the results of the experimental evaluation because the evaluation assembled similarly situated children and randomly assigned them to intervention and control groups. Random assignment establishes equivalency on preexisting differences between the intervention and control groups (e.g., the groups have similar socioeconomic backgrounds). Because the intervention and control groups are equal on pre-existing differences, it is highly unlikely that the schools attended by the intervention group after participation in Head Start were systematically worse than the schools attended by the control group. For this argument to hold any credence, one must assume that children in the intervention group were systematically sorted into worse schools than members of the similarly situated control group. If this sorting is in fact a reality, such a negative result for the intervention group would be attributable to attending Head Start.

Last, some will argue that a few studies have found that Head Start produces long-term benefits by the time participants reach adulthood. This proposition begs the question: If Head Start has little to no effect when participants are children, how can the program suddenly become effective in adulthood? These arguments are based on studies that use significantly weaker evaluation designs than the experimental methodology of the Head Start Impact Study. Two frequently referenced studies use national surveys, which of the many questions posed asked whether the respondents attended Head Start when they were younger.[157] In essence, these types of studies are based on retrospective questions about Head Start attendance of people who have reached adulthood. The degree of misreporting is unknown. While these types of studies often exploit sophisticated econometric techniques, the authors of one study acknowledge that their "study is no substitute for a national randomized trial."[158]

Taxpayers are spending considerable sums on Head Start and other early childhood education programs. Policymakers should be basing their decisions about Head Start and other preschool programs on the most useful and up-to-date empirical evidence.

Even Start Family Literacy Program

Created in 1989, the Even Start Family Literacy Program, hereinafter referred to as Even Start, is intended to meet the basic educational needs of parents and children from birth to age seven for low-income families.[159] In general, Even Start provides "(1) adult basic or secondary education and English language instruction for parents, (2) assistance for parents to promote their children's educational development, and (3) early childhood education for children."[160] Since its creation, Even Start has been reformed by Congress at least five times.[161] Even Start is anticipated to have direct and indirect effects on adults and children.[162] The program is directly expected to increase the literacy and parenting skills of adults, while also improving the literacy skills of children. These beneficial effects are assumed to be observable after one year of program participation. Indirectly, the program is expected to improve the economic self-sufficiency of adults within two or more years.

Then, the economic self-sufficiency benefits accrued by the parents are expected to enhance the already increasing literacy skills of children.

The Third National Even Start Evaluation assessed the effectiveness of Even Start in 18 locations with a total of 309 intervention and 154 control group families.[163] The prior national evaluations were more concerned with assessing the operation of Even Start, rather than the program's effectiveness. The third evaluation was restricted to programs operating during the 1999–2000 or 2000–2001 program years.

Even Start sites that were believed to provide high-intensity and moderate-intensity service levels were selected for the evaluation.[164] Thus, sites offering only minimal services were excluded from the evaluation. In addition, the early childhood education classrooms of 18 sites were comparable in overall quality to Head Start classrooms.[165] The 18 sites were located in 14 states:

- Decatur, Alabama
- Phoenix, Arizona
- Montclair, California
- Carrollton, Georgia
- Godfrey, Illinois
- Wichita, Kansas
- Kansas City, Kansas
- Shelbyville, Kentucky
- Bloomington, Minnesota
- Mountain Grove, Missouri
- Syracuse, New York
- Oklahoma City, Oklahoma
- Reading, Pennsylvania
- Austin, Texas (2 sites)
- Houston, Texas
- San Angelo, Texas
- Norfolk, Virginia[166]

The majority of the sites operated in urban areas. While 46 percent of the families served by all Even Start sites are Hispanic, 75 percent of the families participating in the 18 evaluation sites were Hispanic.[167] Unfortunately, participation in the evaluation for program sites was voluntary, so many sites refused to participate.

The first report of the Third National Even Start Evaluation assessed the differences of pretest and posttest (nine months after pretest) comparisons between the intervention and control groups.[168] The final report presents the findings of an assessment of outcomes about nine months after the original posttest data was collected for the first report.[169] Thus, the final report assesses program impacts about 18 months after initial entry into Even Start. According to the final report authors:

> Collecting follow-up data nine months after posttesting gave those families the opportunity to participate in Even Start for a second school year, possibly leading to positive effects under the assumption that a greater amount of exposure to Even Start would lead to larger literacy gains and to statistically significant program impacts.[170]

First-Year Impacts

Table 4.7 summarizes the selected findings for the first-year and 18-month follow-up reports. The first-year report measured the impact of Even Start on 41 outcomes. Of these outcomes, only three (seven percent) impacts were marginally statistically significant at the 10 percent confidence level.[171] However, two of these impacts offer suggestive evidence of harmful impacts due to Even Start.

Impact on Child Outcomes.   While all 13 of the child outcome measures failed to yield impacts that were statistically significant at the traditional five percent confidence level, three measures were marginally statistically significant at the 10 percent confidence level.[172] The marginally harmful impacts were the ability to analyze and solve practical mathematic problems (Woodcock-Johnson Psycho-Educational Battery-Revised: Applied Problems) and to identify tape-recorded words with missing phonemes (Woodcock-Johnson Psycho-Educational Battery–Revised: Incomplete Words). The single impact that was marginally beneficial was the measures of problem behavior assessed by elementary school teachers (Social Skills Rating System: Problem Behaviors–Elementary). Otherwise, Even Start failed to improve academic and behavioral outcomes of children participants. Thus, Even Start had no impact on nine of 12 child outcome measures, possibly harmful impacts on two outcomes, and perhaps a beneficial impact on a single outcome.

TABLE 4.7. Selected Findings of Third National Even Start Evaluation

Child Outcomes	First-Year Follow-Up	18-Month Follow-Up
Peabody Picture Vocabulary Test	0	0
Woodcock-Johnson Psycho-Educational Battery (Revised) Letter-Word Identification	0	0
Woodcock-Johnson Psycho-Educational Battery (Revised)–Diction	0	0
Woodcock-Johnson Psycho-Educational Battery (Revised)–Applied Problems	Neg*	0
Woodcock-Johnson Psycho-Educational Battery (Revised)–Incomplete Words	Neg*	0
Woodcock-Johnson Psycho-Educational Battery (Revised)–Sound Blending	0	0
Woodcock-Johnson Psycho-Educational Battery (Revised)–Early Development	0	0
Story and Print Concepts	0	0
Social Skills Rating System: Social Skills–Preschool	0	0
Social Skills Rating System: Social Skills–Elementary	0	0
Social Skills Rating System: Problem Behavior–Preschool	0	0
Social Skills Rating System: Problem Behavior–Elementary	Pos*	0
Vinland Adaptive Behavior Scales–Communication Domain	0	0
School Record Outcomes–Preschool		
Percent days attended	n/a	0
Percent days absent	n/a	0
Child ever tardy	n/a	0
Child in special education	n/a	0
School Record Outcomes–Elementary		
Percent days attended	n/a	0
Percent days absent	n/a	0
Child ever tardy	n/a	0
Child in special education	n/a	0
Parent Report of Child Literacy		
Child knows alphabet	0	0
Child counts to 100	0	0
Child knows colors	0	0
Extent child reads (<2.6 years old)	0	0
Extent child reads (>2.6 years old)	0	Pos*
Age-appropriate writing	0	Pos*
Child knows print concepts	0	0
Parent Outcomes		
Woodcock-Johnson Psycho-Educational Battery (Revised)–Letter-Word	0	0

TABLE 4.7. (Continued)

Child Outcomes	First-Year Follow-Up	18-Month Follow-Up
Woodcock-Johnson Psycho-Educational Battery (Revised)–Passage Comprehension	0	0
Woodcock-Johnson Psycho-Educational Battery (Revised)–Word Attack	0	Pos*
Woodcock-Johnson Psycho-Educational Battery (Revised)–Reading Vocabulary	0	0
Woodcock-Johnson Psycho-Educational Battery (Revised)–Reading Comprehension	0	0
Woodcock-Johnson Psycho-Educational Battery (Revised)–Basic Reading Skills	0	0
Parent education	0	n/a
Parent GED attainment	0	Pos*
Parent employment	0	0
Annual household income	0	0
Parent Report of Parent Literacy at Home		
Variety of parent reading	0	0
Variety of parent writing	0	0
Parenting Outcomes		
Parent reads to child daily	0	0
Amount of reading to child	0	0
Variety of reading to child	0	0
Quality of reading to child	0	0
Parent Report of Literacy Resources at Home		
Number of books Child has	0	0
Variety of non-print resources	0	0
Variety of print resources	0	0
Parent Report of Parent Support of Child's School		
Parent participation in school	0	0
Parent opinion about school	0	0

Key: 0 Finding was not statistically significant
   Pos Positive or beneficial impact
   Neg Negative or harmful impact
   *   Statistically significant at the 10 percent confidence level ($p \leq 0.10$)
   ** Statistically significant at the 5 percent confidence level ($p \leq 0.05$)
   *** Statistically significant at the 1 percent confidence level ($p \leq 0.01$)
   n/a No measure was assessed or reported
   †   No statistically significance test was performed

Sources: Robert St. Pierre, Anne Ricciuti, Fumiyo Tao, Cindy Creps, Janet Swartz, Wang Lee, Amanda Parsad, and Tracy Rimdzius, *Third National Even Start Evaluation: Program Impacts and Implications for Improvement* (Cambridge, MA: Abt Associates Inc., 2003), Exhibit 6.13, 180; Anna E. Ricciuti, Robert G. St.Pierre, Wang Lee, Amanda Parsad, and Tracy Rimdzius, *Third National Even Start Evaluation: Follow-Up Findings from the Experimental Design Study* (Washington, DC: U.S. Department of Education, Institute of Education Sciences, National Center for Education Evaluation and Regional Assistance, 2004), Table 4.2, 38.

Impact on Parent Report of Child Literacy.   Participation in Even Start was unsuccessful at increasing seven measures of parental perceptions of child literacy.[173] For example, the program failed to affect parental assessments of their children knowing the alphabet, counting to 100, knowing colors, and the extent to which the child can read.

Impact Parent Outcomes.   On all 10 measures of parental outcomes, Even Start failed to yield even marginally statistically significant results.[174] Parents participating in Even Start fared no better or worse than control parents on such measures as letter-word identification, mathematical problem solving, reading ability, educational attainment, and household income.

Impact on Parent Report of Parent Literacy at Home Outcomes.   On two measures of self-reported parental literacy at home, Even Start failed to yield even marginally statistically significant results.[175] The differences in the variety of reading and writing by parents in the intervention and control groups were statistically indistinguishable from zero.

Impact on Parent Report of Literacy Resources at Home Outcomes.   On three measures of self-reported literacy resources at home, Even Start also failed to yield even marginally statistically significant results.[176] The differences in the number of books available to children by nonprint and print resources in the intervention and control groups were statistically indistinguishable from zero.

After nine months of participating in Even Start, there is suggestive evidence that the program produces more harm than good. However, the evidence for both the harmful and beneficial impacts is weak. "Because of the large number of outcomes assessed and because of the mix in direction of results," the authors of the first-year report concluded, "we do not assign any meaning to these findings."[177]

18-Month Impacts

The 18-month follow-up report assessed the impact of Even Start on 48 outcomes nine months after the posttest was administered for the first-year report. Of these outcomes, only four (eight percent) impacts were marginally statistically significant at the 10 percent confidence level.[178] In contrast to the findings of the first-year report, all of these impacts were beneficial outcomes. These results are also presented in Table 4.6.

Impact on Child Outcomes.   For the 18-month follow-up, all of the 13 child outcome measures failed to yield impacts that were statistically significant.[179] The marginal impacts that occurred in the first-year report faded away. In the longer term, Even Start had no beneficial or harmful impacts on child academic and behavior outcomes.

Impact on School Record Outcomes for Preschool and Elementary School.   Based on official school records, participation in Even Start for the extended follow-up period failed to yield any statistically measurable impacts on eight outcome measures.[180] Regardless of whether the Even Start children were in preschool or elementary school, their school attendance and tardiness were no different when compared to members of the control group. Further, program participation had no effect on whether a child was involved in special education.

Impact on Parent Report of Child Literacy.   At the time of the extended follow-up, participation in Even Start was unsuccessful at increasing five out of seven measures of parental perceptions of child literacy.[181] However, the two beneficial impacts were only marginally statistically significant at the 10 percent confidence level. According to parent self-reports, Even Start children were more likely to read when older than 2.6 years and more likely able to engage in age-appropriate writing. Just like in the first-year report, the program failed to affect parental assessments of their children knowing the alphabet, counting to 100, knowing colors, and the extent to which the child could read when under 2.6 years of age.

Impact on Parent Outcomes.   On all 10 measures of parental outcomes for the extended follow-up, Even Start failed to yield even marginally statistically significant results for even outcomes.[182] Parents participating in Even Start fared no better or worse than control parents on such measures as letter-word identification, mathematical problem solving, reading ability, and household income. At the less rigorous level of statistical significance, participation in Even Start produced suggestive indications that the program may help parents apply phonic and structural analysis skills to the pronunciation of unfamiliar printed words (Woodcock-Johnson Psycho-Educational Battery-Revised: Word Attack) and earning a GED. Less than 10 percent of Even Start parents earned a

GED, compared to 2.5 percent for control group parents—a difference of 7.38 percent.

Impact on Parent Report of Parent Literacy at Home Outcomes.   On two measures of self-reported parental literacy at home for the extended follow-up, Even Start failed to yield even marginally statistically significant results.[183] The differences in the variety of reading and writing by parents in the intervention and control groups were statistically indistinguishable from zero.

Impact on Parent Report of Literacy Resources at Home Outcomes.   On three measures of self-reported literacy resources at home for the extended follow-up, Even Start also failed to yield even marginally statistically significant results.[184] The differences in the number of books available to children by nonprint and print resources in the intervention and control groups were statistically indistinguishable from zero.

Thinking about probability, the first-year and follow-up reports should have by pure chance alone found at a minimum two findings each of statistical significance at the five percent levelfive percent level of confidence. The fact that both reports founds a few impacts at the marginal 10 percent level of statistical significance means that the Even Start programs, despite being thought of as delivering high- and medium-intensity services, are ineffective.

21st Century Community Learning Centers

The role of the federal government in funding after-school programs increased substantially after passage of the Improving America's School Act of 1994, which created the 21st Century Community Learning Centers program. Congress wanted to open up local schools so that their communities could use them more extensively beyond normal hours by.[185] The social program was intended to "support continuing education and lifelong learning opportunities to children and adults to help keep the country's workforce competitive for the 21st century."[186] In 1998, the social program was altered to provide activities in public schools during afterschool hours.[187] Accordingly, "The goal of the program is to help students meet local and state academic standards in core subjects, such as reading and mathematics."[188]

In 1999, the U.S. Department of Education commissioned a multisite experimental impact evaluation of the 21st Century Community Learning Centers program. The evaluation assessed the effectiveness of 21st Century programs operating in 12 schools and 26 afterschool centers. The 21st Century programs were located in eight states and primarily served urban areas.[189] The majority of students participating in the 21st Century programs under evaluation were black and eligible for free or reduced price lunches.[190] The experimental evaluation focused on elementary school students. For the evaluation, 2,308 eligible students were randomly assigned to intervention or control groups.[191] The selected findings for the impact of 21st Century programs two years after random assignment are summarized in Table 4.8.

The authors of the evaluation concluded:

> The study's findings are consistent with a mixed picture of effects of after-school programs. The 21st Century programs that participated in the study improved some outcomes such as feelings of safety, did not affect a wide range of other outcomes including academic ones, and had some negative effects on behaviors.[192]

TABLE 4.8. Selected Findings for the 21st Century Community Learning Centers Programs, Elementary School Students, Year 2 Findings

Homework Outcomes	Overall Impact
Percentage of students in the following activities after school at least one day in prior week, according to student reports:	
Homework	0
Tutoring	0
Percentage of students in the following activities after school at least one day in prior week, according to parent reports:	
Homework	0
Tutoring	Pos***
Percentage of students who report that they "often" or "always" complete the homework teachers assign	0
Percentage of students whose parents report doing the following:	
Helped their child with homework at least three times last week	0
Checked on their child's homework	0
Asked their child about things they were doing in class at least even times last month	0

(continued)

TABLE 4.8. (Continued)

Homework Outcomes	Overall Impact
Percentage of students who report that their parent "often" or "always" does the following:	
Asks if homework is complete	0
Looks at homework to see if it is complete	0
Looks at homework to see if it is correct	0
Explains homework in a way that is easy to understand	0
Percentage of students who report that an adult who is not their parent "often" or "always" does the following:	
Asks if homework is complete	0
Looks at homework to see if it is complete	0
Looks at homework to see if it is correct	0
Explains homework in a way that is easy to understand	0
Percentage of students who report that their parent or an adult who is not their parent "often" or "always" does the following:	
Asks if homework is complete	0
Looks at homework to see if it is complete	0
Looks at homework to see if it is correct	0
Percentage of students who report the following individual asked the child to correct homework	
Parent	0
An adult who is not their parent	0
A parent or an adult who is not their parent	0
Academic Outcomes	
Mean grade	
Math	0
English/language arts	0
Science	0
Social studies/history	Neg*
Mean reading test score	0
Percentage of students whose teachers report the following:	
"Agree" or "strongly agree" that student completes assignments to teacher's satisfaction	0
Student achieves at "above-average" or "very high" level	Neg**
"Agree" or "strongly agree" that student comes to school prepared and ready to learn	0
Student "usually tries hard" in reading or English	Neg**
Student "often" performs at or above his or her ability	0
Level of effort composite based on teacher assessment of student's effort, performance at ability level, attentiveness, participation, and volunteering	0

TABLE 4.8.   (Continued)

Homework Outcomes	Overall Impact
Behavioral Outcomes	
Mean number of days student was	
Absent	0
Late	0
Percentage of students whose teachers report doing the following "two or more times":	
Disciplining the child for misbehaving	0
Sending the child to office for misbehaving	0
Giving child detention	0
Calling parents about child's behavior	Neg**
Percentage of students who report the following happens "some" or "a lot":	
Student has to miss recess or sit in hall	Neg**
Parents have to come to school about problem	Neg**
Student-reported discipline problem composite (mean)	Neg**
Teacher-reported discipline problem composite (mean)	Neg**
Negative behavior composite (mean)	0
Percentage of students who were suspended during most recent school year	Neg**
Safety Outcomes	
Percentage of students who report feeling the following levels of safety after school up until 6 p.m.:	
Very safe	0
Somewhat safe	0
Not at all safe	Pos***

Key: 0 Finding was not statistically significant
    Pos Positive or beneficial impact
    Neg Negative or harmful impact
    *   Statistically significant at the 10 percent confidence level ($p \leq 0.10$)
    **   Statistically significant at the 5 percent confidence level ($p \leq 0.05$)
    *** Statistically significant at the 1 percent confidence level ($p \leq 0.01$)
    n/a No measure was assessed or reported
    †   No statistically significance test was performed
Source: Susanne James-Burdumy, Mark Dynarski, and John Deke, "When Elementary Schools Stay Open Late: Results from the National Evaluation of the 21st Century Community Learning Centers Program," *Educational Evaluation and Policy Analysis* 29, no. 4 (December 2007): 296–318, Table 3, 306–307; Table 4, 308; Table 5, 309; Table 6, 310.

Impacts on Homework Outcomes

From the perspectives of students and parents, the evaluation assessed the effectiveness of 21st Century programs based on 22 outcome measures.[193]

Only one outcome measure yielded a statistically significant result. According to parent reports, 27.5 percent students in the intervention group engaged in afterschool tutoring activities, compared to 16.1 percent for control group students—a statistically significant beneficial impact of 11.4 percent at the one percent confidence level. Otherwise, 21st Century programs appear to have no effect on parent-reported measures, including several measures of parental homework assistance, and several student-reported measures, such as assessments on how much parents help students with their homework.

Impacts on Academic Outcomes

Eleven academic outcomes were assessed. Only two of these measures yielded statistically significant results at the five percent confidence level, while one measure was marginally statistically significant at the 10 percent confidence level.[194] These three outcomes point to harmful impacts of participating in 21st Century programs.

Participation in 21st Century programs appears to have no impact on math, English/language arts, and science grades.[195] For example, the average math grade for the intervention group was 79.9 percent, compared to 80.6 percent for the control group. While the intervention group had a slightly lower math grade, on average, the difference from the control group's average math grade is statistically insignificant. There is, however, suggestive evidence that 21st Century programs may negatively affect social studies/history grades. The average social studies/history grade for the intervention group was 81.2 percent, compared to 82.2 percent for the control group—a marginally statistically significant effect of 1.0 percent at the less rigorous 10 percent confidence level. In addition, there appears to be no difference between the reading test scores of the intervention and control groups, suggesting that the 21st Century programs do little to improve reading skills.

Teachers were asked to assess student effort in the classroom. Based on teacher reports, students in the intervention group fared no better or worse on assessments regarding completing assignments to teacher's satisfaction, class preparation and readiness to learn, and performing at or above the student's ability.[196] However, 21st Century programs appear to have harmful impacts on teacher assessments involving whether the student is achieving at an "above-average" or "very high" level and whether the student "usually tries hard" in reading or English class. Teachers reported that 22.2 percent of intervention group students were achieving at an "above-average" or "very high" level, compared to 28.1 percent for the control group—a statistically significant difference of 5.9 percent at the five percent confidence level. In addition, teachers conveyed that 46.7 percent of the intervention group usually tried hard in reading or English classes, compared to 52.4 percent for the control group—a statistically significant difference of 5.7 percent at the five percent confidence level. Last, a level of effort composite test consisting of teacher assessments regarding student effort, performance, attentiveness, participation, and volunteering found that intervention group students were no different from control group students.

Impacts on Behavioral Outcomes

Of the 12 behavioral outcomes that were assessed, six measures indicate that 21st Century programs produced more harm than good.[197] Participation in the afterschool program had no apparent effect on the number of days students were absent from or late to school. On teacher-reported measures of disciplining students for misbehavior, sending students to the office for misbehaving, and giving students detention, participation in 21st Century programs failed to produce statistically significant results. Yet teachers reported that they had to call parents about misbehavior problems for 28.1 percent of the intervention group and 23.1 percent of the control group—a statistically significant harmful difference of 5.1 percent at the five percent confidence level.

At the five percent level of confidence, 21st Century students were more likely to report having to miss recess or sit in the hall for behavior problems.[198] At the same confidence level, students in the afterschool program were more likely to report their parents coming to school to address problem behavior. In spite of these negative results, a student-reported composite test consisting of students' assessments of their misbehavior found that intervention group students were no different from control group students. Contrarily, the teacher-reported composite test of students' misbehavior found that the intervention group's behavior was more problematic than the behavior of the control group students. The difference was statistically significant at the five percent confidence level.

A very important indicator of student behavior is the level of suspensions. For this measure, 11.5 percent of the intervention group was suspended during the most recent school year, compared to 7.5 percent for the control group—a statistically significant harmful difference of 4.1 percent at the five percent confidence level.

Impacts on Safety Perceptions

Of the three safety outcomes that were assessed, two of the measures indicate that 21st Century programs have no effect on students' perceived safety.[199]

The differences between the percentages of intervention and control students reporting to be "very safe" or "somewhat safe" after school up to 6 p.m. were statistically indistinguishable. Despite this lack of impact, 2.5 percent of the intervention group reported that they did not feel safe at all, compared to 7.1 percent of the control group—a statistically significant beneficial impact at the one percent confidence level.

The findings from the 21st Century impact evaluation strongly suggest that the program is a failure.

Abstinence Education

When Congress passed the Personal Responsibility and Work Opportunity Reconciliation Act of 1996, they not only reformed the nation's welfare system, but also created a new abstinence formula grant program. According to Ron Haskins and Isabel V. Sawhill of the Brookings Institution, "The legislation contained a strict definition of abstinence education, which, along with subsequent rules issued by the Department of Health and Human Services (HHS), prohibited programs from including education about contraception or advocacy for the use of contraception."[200] Programs funded under these grants are required to engaging the following activities:

- Have as its exclusive purpose teaching the social, psychological, and health gains to be realized by abstaining from sexual activity;
- Teach abstinence from sexual activity outside marriage as the expected standard for all school-age children;
- Teach that abstinence from sexual activity is the only certain way to avoid out-of wedlock pregnancy, sexually transmitted diseases, and other associated health problems;
- Teach that a mutually faithful, monogamous relationship in the context of marriage is the expected standard of sexual activity;
- Teach that sexual activity outside the context of marriage is likely to have harmful psychological and physical effects;
- Teach that bearing children out-of-wedlock is likely to have harmful consequences for the child, the child's parents, and society;
- Teach young people how to reject sexual advances and how alcohol and drug use increases vulnerability to sexual advances; and
- Teach the importance of attaining self-sufficiency before engaging in sexual activity.[201]

Whether abstinence education programs are effective has been a hotly contested issue. The Balanced Budget Act of 1997 authorized an experimental evaluation of federally funded abstinence education program. Until the publication of the congressionally mandated evaluation, most evaluations of abstinence education programs were of such poor methodological quality that the effectiveness of these programs is unknown. The experimental evaluation, performed by Mathematica Policy Research, "was based on four of the best abstinence education programs in the country."[202] The four highly regarded abstinence education programs operated in Powhatan, Virginia; Miami, Florida; Clarksville, Mississippi; and Milwaukee, Wisconsin.[203] The ages of the students at the time of enrolling in the programs ranged from eight to 14 or older.[204] Across the four sites, a total of 2,502 students were assigned to the intervention and control groups.[205]

The abstinence education evaluation assessed the impact of the programs one year and three years after random assignment. Table 4.9 summarizes the selected findings of the reports. The first-year evaluation focused

TABLE 4.9.   Selected Findings of Abstinence Education Programs

A. Intermediate Outcomes (First Year Findings)	Outcomes
Views on Abstinence, Teen Sex, and Marriage	
Very supportive of abstinence	Pos***
Views unsupportive of teen sex	Pos***
Views supportive of marriage	0
Peer Influences	
Friends' support for abstinence	0
Self-Concept and Communication with Parents	
Self-efficacy, -esteem, and -control	0
Communication with parents	0
Perceived Consequences of Teen Sex	
General consequences of teen sex	Pos***
Personal consequences of teen sex	Pos***

B. Primary Findings (Fifth Year Findings)	
Sexual Activity	
Remained abstinent (always)	0
Abstinent last 12 months	0
Number of sexual partners (percent)	
Remained abstinent	0
One partner	0

(continued)

TABLE 4.9. (Continued)

B. Primary Findings (Fifth Year Findings)	Outcomes
Two partners	0
Three partners	0
Four or more partners	0
Expect to abstain through high school	0
Expect to abstain as a teenager	0
Expect to abstain until marriage	0
Unprotected sex at first intercourse	
Remained abstinent	0
Had sex with condom	0
Had sex without condom	0
Unprotected sex within last 12 months	
Remained abstinent	0
Had sex, always used condom	0
Had sex, sometimes used condom	0
Had sex, never used condom	0
Other forms of birth control use within last 12 months	
Remained abstinent	0
Had sex, always used birth control	0
Had sex, sometimes used birth control	0
Had sex, never used birth control	0
Consequences of teen sex	
Ever been pregnant	0
Ever had a baby	0
Ever had a (reported) sexually transmitted disease	0
Other risk behaviors	
Smoked cigarettes within past month	Pos*
Drank alcohol within past month	0
Ever used marijuana	0

Key: 0 Finding was not statistically significant
   Pos Positive or beneficial impact
   Neg Negative or harmful impact
   *   Statistically significant at the 10 percent confidence level ($p \leq 0.10$)
   **   Statistically significant at the 5 percent confidence level ($p \leq 0.05$)
   *** Statistically significant at the 1 percent confidence level ($p \leq 0.01$)
   n/a No measure was assessed or reported
   †   No statistically significance test was performed

Sources: Rebecca A. Maynard, Christopher Trenholm, Barbara Devaney, Amy Johnson, Melissa A. Clark, John Homrighausen, and Ece Kalay, *First-Year Impacts of Four Title V, Section 510 Abstinence Education Programs* (Princeton, NJ: Mathematica Policy Research, June 2005), Table V.1, 60; Table V.2, 61; Table V.3, 63; Table V.4, 64; Christopher Trenholm, Barbara Devaney, Ken Fortson, Lisa Quay, Justin Wheeler, and Melissa Clark, *Impacts of Four Title V, Section 510 Abstinence Education Programs: Final Report* (Mathematica Policy Research, April 2007), Table IV.1, 30; Figure IV.1, 31; Table IV.2, 32; Figure IV.2, 33; Figure IV.3, 34; Figure IV.4, 35; Table IV.3, 36; and Table IV.4, 37.

intermediate outcomes that assessed changes in attitudes about engaging sexual activities, while the final report focused on primary outcomes such as abstaining from sex. On average, the data from the second study reports findings five years after the youth enrolled in the study sample.[206] The youth had an average age of 16 during the second and final follow-up survey.[207]

Impacts on Views of Abstinence, Teen Sex, and Marriage

Overall, participation in abstinence education programs was associated with increased support for abstinence and decreased support for engaging in teen sex, while the programs had no effect on supportive views of marriage.[208] On a four-point scale (zero = least supportive to three = most supportive), members of the intervention and control group were asked about their level of support for abstaining from sex. The intervention group had an average score of 1.86, while the control group averaged 1.78. The difference of 0.08 was statistically significant at the one percent confidence level. On a different four-point scale (zero = least unsupportive to three = most unsupportive), respondents were asked whether their views were unsupportive of teen sex. Members of the intervention and control groups averaged 2.23 and 2.16, respectively. The difference of 0.07 was statistically significant at the one percent confidence level. Despite these positive changes, the difference between the intervention and control groups' views regarding the support of marriage was statistically indistinguishable from zero.

Impact on Peer Influences

All four of the abstinence programs were assessed on a measure of friends' support for abstinence.[209] Respondents were asked to rate their friends' support for abstinence on a six-point scale, with zero equaling least supportive and five equaling most supportive. Compared to the average score of the control group of 3.44, the average score for the intervention group was 3.50. The difference between these average scores was statistically insignificant, suggesting the abstinence education had no effect on the perceived support for abstinence by friends.

Impacts on Self-Concept and Communication with Parents

For the measure of self-concept, abstinence education had no effect on changing youths' perceptions about themselves.[210] In addition, program participation failed to influence the ability of the youths to communicate with their parents.

Impacts on Perceived Consequences of Teen Sex

Abstinence education was more successful at helping youths develop an understanding of the consequences of teen sex.[211] Respondents were asked to rate their views on the general consequences of engaging in teen sex, based on four-point scale, with zero equaling no adverse consequences and three equaling many adverse consequences. Compared to the average score of the control group of 1.89, the average score for the intervention group was 1.99. The difference between these average scores was statistically significant at the one percent confidence level. Using a similar scale (zero = no adverse consequences to two = many adverse consequences), respondents were asked about the personal consequences—immediately affecting themselves—of the consequences of engaging in teen sex. The intervention group averaged 1.09, while the control group averaged 1.00—a statistically significant difference of 0.09 at the one percent confidence level.

Thus, abstinence education appears to be positively effective at changing personal attitudes about engaging in sexual activities for four of the eight intermediate outcomes measures. Do these positive changes result in youths abstaining from sex?

Impact on Sexual Activity and Other Risk Behaviors

Participation in federally funded abstinence education programs failed to affect all of the 24 sexual activity outcomes presented in Table 4.8. The authors conclude:

> Findings indicate that, despite the effects seen after the first year, programs had no statistically significant impact on eventual behavior. Based on data from the final follow-up survey, youth in the program group were no more likely to abstain from sex than their control group counterparts; among those who reported having sex, program and control group youth had similar numbers of sexual partners and had initiated sex at the same mean age. Youth in the program group, however, were no more likely to have engaged in unprotected sex than their control group counterparts.[212]

Five years, on average, after first enrolling in the evaluation, a minority of youths in the intervention and control groups reported that they had always been abstinent.[213] Forty-nine percent of both groups reported always being abstinent. Thus, the majority of youth in both groups admitted to engaging in sex. For remaining abstinent in the last 12 months, 56 percent of the intervention group reported in the affirmative, compared to 55 percent of the control group—a difference of one percent that is statistically indistinguishable from zero.

While the federally funded abstinence education program failed to affect its primary goal, maybe the program affected the number of sexual partners. Youths in the intervention group were no more or less likely to have sex with one or more partners.[214] Sixteen percent of both groups reported having at least one partner, while 11 percent of both groups reported having two partners. Similarly, eight percent of both groups reported having three partners. A slight difference, while statistically insignificant, occurred for those reporting to have four or more partners. For the intervention group, 17 percent reported having four or more partners, while the figure for their counterparts was 16 percent.

While abstinence education programs failed to influence sexual activity and the number of sexual partners, the programs may have influenced future expectations regarding sex. When asked whether they expected to abstain from sex through high school, 60 percent of the intervention group reported in the affirmative, compared to 58 percent of the control group—a statistically insignificant difference of two percent.[215] When asked whether they expected to abstain from sex throughout their teenage years, 45 percent and 44 percent of the intervention and control groups reported in the affirmative, respectively. The difference of one percent was statistically indistinguishable from zero.

Federally funded abstinence education programs had no impact on whether participants had unprotected sex at the time of first intercourse.[216] Forty-four percent of the intervention group reported using a condom, while the figure for the control group was 43 percent—a statistically insignificant difference of one percent. For those reporting not using a condom when having sex for the first time, seven percent and eight percent of the intervention and control group members, respectively, reported in the affirmative—a statistically indistinguishable difference of one1 percent.

While majorities of both groups reported remaining abstinent during the past 12 months, 23 percent of both groups reported that they always used a condom when having sex.[217] Seventeen percent of both groups reported sometimes using condoms while having sex, while four percent of both groups reported never using condoms. The lack of impact continued for the use of other forms of birth control within the last 12 months.[218] Twenty-nine percent of both groups reported always using birth control, while 13 percent and 14 percent of the intervention and control groups, respectively, reported sometime using birth control. The difference of one percent was statistically insignificant. For those reporting to have never used birth control within the last 12 months, two percent reported in the affirmative for both groups.

The trend in ineffectiveness continued for the consequences of having sex. Federally funded abstinence programs appear to have no impact on preventing pregnancies, having a child, and catching a sexually transmitted disease (STD).[219] For pregnancies, 10 percent of both groups reported having ever been pregnant. For both groups, five percent of the youths reported ever having a baby. While five percent of the intervention group reported having caught an STD, the figure for the control group was four percent—a statistically insignificant difference of one percent.

The only bright spot for federally funded abstinence education programs is that they may slightly reduce cigarette smoking in the past month— 16 percent and 19 percent of the intervention and control group members, respectively, reported having smoked cigarettes within the past month,[220] However, this difference of three percent is only marginally statistically significant at the 10 percent confidence level. In addition, participation in abstinence education programs appears to have no effect on drinking alcohol in the past month or ever using marijuana.

Supporters of federally funded abstinence education programs often assert that these social programs are effective based on quasi-experimental evaluation designs that suffer from significant threats to internal validity.[221] However, these supporters also like to trot out the findings of a small single-site experimental evaluation of an abstinence education program that served black students in sixth and seventh grades.[222] While abstinence education supporters make the broad generalization that this particular evaluation proves that federally funded abstinence education works, the authors warn that "The results of this trial should not be taken to mean that all abstinence-only interventions are efficacious."[223] Further, and perhaps most important for federal policy, "This trial tested a theory-based abstinence-only intervention that would not have meet federal criteria for abstinence programs . . . It was not moralistic and did not criticize the use of condoms."[224] Apparently, this particular social program is not preachy enough to qualify for federal funding.

Upward Bound

Upward Bound was created in 1965 and is an original War on Poverty social program. Through the provision of supplemental academic and support services and activities, Upward Bound is intended to help economically disadvantaged students successfully complete high school and attend college.[225] Specifically, the program is supposed to offer rigorous academic, tutoring, and counseling services to 13- to 19-year-olds in grades nine to 12. Upward Bound sites are required to provide weekly services during the school year and five to eight weeks of services during the summer. Summer activities are typically intended to replicate a college experience and frequently entail living on a college campus. The principle academic activities during the summer are coursework in English, math, and science.[226] Nonacademic activities include college preparation, counseling, tutoring, and the development of studying skills. Those applying to participate in the program are disproportionately young females and blacks.[227]

"By using a probability sample of projects and random assignment of students to a treatment and control group," the national evaluation of Upward Bound "provides both strong external and internal validity."[228] The intervention and control groups were comprised of eligible youth applying to the program during the 1992–1993 and 1993–1994 school years at 67 project sites.[229] The intervention group included 1,481 students and the control group included 1,266 students.[230]

For the Upward Bound evaluation, the median length of time participating in Upward bound for the intervention group was 19 months.[231] Not only were members of the intervention group more likely to receive precollege services, but these services appeared to be more intense.[232] Students were interviewed during several follow-up surveys. Follow-up surveys of all intervention and control group members were conducted in during the following school years: 1994–1995, 1996–1997, 1998–1999, 2001–2002, and 2003–2004. The early follow-up surveys occurred while many of the students were still attending high school. Because the program is expected to increase college attendance, the results presented in this chapter focus on reports based on when the students would be of college age: about two years and seven to nine years after expected high school graduation. In addition, the results will concentrate on the findings for all students and those with higher and lower expectations of attending college. The selected results of the Upward Bound evaluation are summarized in Tables 4.10 (two years after expected high school graduation) and 4.11 (seven to nine years after expected high school graduation).

The final report based on the Upward Bound evaluation assessed the impact of the program seven to nine years after the study participants were scheduled to graduate from high school.[233]

TABLE 4.10. Selected Findings of Upward Bound Evaluation Two Years after Expected High School Graduation

High School Credits, Grades, and Graduation	Two Years after Expected High School Graduation		
	All Students	Higher Expectations	Lower Expectations
Credits			
Total	0	0	Pos*
Total core	0	0	Pos**
Math	Pos**	0	Pos**
Science	0	0	0
English	0	0	0
Social studies	0	0	0
Foreign language	0	0	Pos*
Computer science	0	0	Pos*
Vocational	0	0	0
Advanced Placement and Honor Credits			
Total	0	0	Pos*
Total core	0	0	Pos*
Math	0	0	Pos**
Science	0	0	Pos*
English	0	0	0
Social studies	0	0	0
Foreign language	0	0	0
Overall Grade Point Average	0	0	0
High School Status			
Graduated	0	0	0
Still in high school	0	0	0
Dropped out	0	Neg*	0
GED	0	0	0
Postsecondary Enrollment and Credits, Excluding Unverified Self-Reported Enrollment			
Postsecondary School Status			
Any postsecondary school	0	0	0
4-year college	0	0	Pos**
2-year college	0	0	0
Vocational school	0	0	0
Credits Earned			
All postsecondary schools	0	0	Pos**
Nonremedial	0	0	0
Remedial	0	0	0
Other	0	0	0

TABLE 4.10.   (Continued)

High School Credits, Grades, and Graduation	Two Years after Expected High School Graduation		
	All Students	Higher Expectations	Lower Expectations
4-year colleges	0	0	Pos***
Nonremedial	0	0	Pos***
Remedial	0	0	0
Other	0	0	0
2-year colleges	0	0	0
Nonremedial	0	0	0
Remedial	0	0	0
Other	0	0	0
Vocational schools	0	0	0
Nonremedial	0	0	0
Remedial	0	0	0
Other	0	0	0

Key: 0 Finding was not statistically significant
Pos Positive or beneficial impact
Neg Negative or harmful impact
*   Statistically significant at the 10 percent confidence level ($p \leq 0.10$)
**   Statistically significant at the 5 percent confidence level ($p \leq 0.05$)
***   Statistically significant at the 1 percent confidence level ($p \leq 0.01$)
n/a No measure was assessed or reported
†   No statistically significance test was performed
Sources: U.S. Department of Education, Office of the Under Secretary, Policy and Program Studies Service, *The Impacts of Regular Upward Bound: Results from the Third-Follow-Up Data Collection* (Washington, DC, April 2004), Table II.5, 26; Table II.6, 27; Table III.2, 37; Table III.4, 39.

Impacts on High School Credits, Grades, and Graduation

Two years after expected high school graduation, the effectiveness of Upward Bound was assessed on 21 outcome measures of high school credits, grades, and graduation. For all students, 20 of the 21 outcome measures yielded statistically insignificant results.[234] While participation in the program failed to increase the number of overall credits earned, the intervention group on average earned 3.2 math credits, compared to 3.0 math credits for the control group—a difference of 0.2 credits that is statistically significant at the five percent confidence level. Otherwise, Upward Bound had no statistically measurable effect on credits earned in science, English, social studies, foreign language, computer science, and vocational education. Further, the program failed to affect the attainment of Advanced

TABLE 4.11.   Selected Findings of Upward Bound Evaluation Seven to Nine Years after High School Graduation

Postsecondary Outcomes	Seven to Nine Years after High School Graduation		
	All Students	Higher Expectations	Lower Expectations
Postsecondary Enrollment			
Any postsecondary enrollment	0	Pos***	Pos*
Highest level of schooling attended			
Four-year college or university	0	0	0
Two—year college	0	0	0
Vocational institution	0	0	Pos**
Highly selective Four-year institution	0	0	0
Postsecondary Completion			
Any degree, certificate, or license	0	0	Pos**
Highest degree, certificate, or license			
Bachelor's degree or higher	0	0	0
Associate's degree	0	Neg**	0
Certificate or license	Pos*	0	0

Key: 0 Finding was not statistically significant
Pos Positive or beneficial impact
Neg Negative or harmful impact
*   Statistically significant at the 10 percent confidence level ($p \leq 0.10$)
**   Statistically significant at the 5 percent confidence level ($p \leq 0.05$)
***   Statistically significant at the 1 percent confidence level ($p \leq 0.01$)
n/a No measure was assessed or reported
†   No statistically significance test was performed
Sources: Neil S. Seftor, Arif Mamun, and Allen Schirm, *The Impacts of Regular Upward Bound on Postsecondary Outcomes 7–9 Years after Scheduled High School Graduation: Final Report* (Princeton, NJ: Mathematica Policy Research, January 2009), Table III.1, 41; Table IV.2, 59.

Placement and honors credits in high school. Based on the two years after expected high school graduation follow-up, Upward Bound had no statistically measurable impact on overall grade point averages, graduating from high school with a diploma, dropping out, or earning a GED.

The results for the two years after expected high school graduation are more interesting when the data are parsed by students with higher and lower expectations of attending college. For those with high expectations of attending college before random assignment, the program failed to have statistically measurable impacts on 20 of 21 outcome measures.[235] A suggestive harmful impact was for dropping out of high school. For students with higher college attendance expectations, four percent of the intervention group dropped out of high school, while three percent of the control group dropped out—a marginally statistically significant difference of one percent at the 10 percent confidence level.

Impacts on Postsecondary Enrollment, Credits, and Completion

Two years after expected high school graduation, the evaluators also examined the students' postsecondary education experiences. According to the authors of the third follow-up evaluation, "The ultimate goal of Upward Bound is to increase the chances that high school students from low-income families or families in which neither parent has completed a bachelor's degree will attend and graduate from institutions of higher education."[236] The evaluators asked students if they had attended college. However, due to the likelihood that "some of them reported attending postsecondary institutions that they never actually attended," the evaluators verified the reported information with postsecondary institutions.[237] Therefore, we will concentrate on the postsecondary outcomes that were verified.

For postsecondary school status two years after expected high school graduation, the evaluators asked students whether they attended any postsecondary school, four-year college, two-year college, or vocational school. Of the 4 outcome measures, Upward Bound failed to have statistically measurable impacts.[238] For example, 65 percent and 62 percent of the intervention and control groups attended any postsecondary school, respectively. The difference of three percent was statistically indistinguishable from zero. Upward Bound also failed to affect the number and types of postsecondary credits earned. Regardless of whether the credit outcome measures were related to any postsecondary schools, four-year colleges, two-colleges, or vocational schools, Upward Bound had no effect on credits earned for 16 outcomes.

Two years after expected high school graduation, results get more interesting when the findings are parsed by expectations of attending college. On all four measures of postsecondary enrollment, Upward Bound failed to have statistically measureable results on attending any postsecondary school, four-year college, two-year college, or vocational school for students with higher expectations of attending college at the time of random assignment.[239] For students with lower expectations of attending college, Upward Bound failed to have statistically measureable impacts on three out of four outcome measures. While the program had no impact on enrolling in any postsecondary school, two-year college, or vocational school, 35 percent of the intervention group with lower expectations attended a four-year college, while the attendance rate for similar control group members was 14 percent—a statistically significant difference of 21 percent at the five percent confidence level.

A similar pattern was found for postsecondary credits earned by the time of the two years after expected high school graduation follow-up survey. On all 16 credit outcome measures, Upward Bound was ineffective for students with higher college expectations.[240] For students with lower expectations, Upward Bound had statistically significant impacts on three out of 16 measures. The program was associated with increasing the overall number of postsecondary credits earned. On average, members of the intervention group with lower expectations earned an additional 9.2 credits from any postsecondary school, compared to similar counterparts. The gain of 9.2 credits is statistically significant at the five percent confidence level. This same group of students also earned more credits from four-year colleges. On average, they earned 13.0 more four-year college credits than similar members of the control group—a highly statistically significant impact at the one percent confidence level. This same group of Upward Bound students was also more likely to earn four-year college credits that were nonremedial. Despite these positive findings, no statistically measurable effects were found for credits earned at two-year colleges and vocational schools.

What happened seven to nine years after expected high school graduation? On all five outcome measures of postsecondary enrollment for all students, Upward Bound failed to yield statistically measurable results.[241] Upward Bound was ineffective at increasing attendance at any postsecondary institutions, including four-year colleges, two-year colleges, and vocational institutions. Also, the program appears to have no effect on the ability of students to attend highly selective four-year colleges. The selected results of the Upward Bound impacts for two years after expected high school graduation are summarized in Table 4.11.

Interestingly, Upward Bound was associated with increased attendance at any postsecondary institution for those who, at the time of random assignment, had higher expectations of attending college.[242] For those with higher expectations, 85.99 percent of the intervention group and 82.74 percent of the control group were enrolled in any postsecondary institution seven to nine years after their expected high school graduation—a statistically significant difference of 3.25 percent at the one percent confidence level. Nevertheless, when the results are parsed by type of postsecondary institution, the differences between the intervention and control groups are statistically insignificant. Thus, we are unable to identify what types of school the intervention students were more likely to be enrolled in. Further, the program appears to have no impact on the ability of intervention students with higher expectations to attend highly selective four-year colleges.

For students with lower expectations, Upward Bound had a positive but marginally statistically significant effect.[243] For any postsecondary enrollment, 75.48 percent of the intervention group and 69.93 percent of the control group reported in the affirmative. The difference of 5.56 percent is marginally statistically significant at the less rigorous 10 percent confidence level. However, this marginally significant effect appears to be driven by the fact that students with lower expectations who had the opportunity to participate in Upward Bound were more likely to be enrolled at vocational institutions. For vocational institution enrollment, 11.12 percent of the intervention group and 4.69 percent of the control group reported being enrolled in these institutions—a statistically significant difference of 6.43 percent at the five percent confidence level. Otherwise, Upward Bound does not appear to affect the enrollment of lower-expectation students at two- and four-year colleges. In addition, lower-expectation students with the opportunity to participate in Upward Bound were just as likely to attend highly selective four-year colleges, compared to similar control group members.

Assessing the situation seven to nine years after their expected high school graduation, did the opportunity to participate in Upward Bound help students earn postsecondary degrees? For all students, Upward Bound appears to have had no effect on earning any degree, certificate, or license.[244] For earning any degree, certificate, or license, 37.03 percent and 34.77 percent of the intervention and control groups, respectively, reported in the affirmative. The difference of 2.26 percent was statistically insignificant. While Upward Bound appears to have no effect on whether students earn associate's degrees and bachelor's degrees or higher, there is suggestive evidence that the program may help students earn certificates or licenses. On this measure, 8.62 percent of the intervention group earned certificates or licenses, compared to 4.08 percent of the control group—a marginally statistically significant difference of 4.54 percent at the 10 percent confidence level.

Seven to nine years after their expected high school graduation, Upward Bound appears to have no effect on whether students with high expectation of attending college earned any degree, certificate, or license.[245] However, the results change when the analysis is broken down by type of postsecondary completion. While Upward Bound appears to have no effect on attaining bachelor's degrees, certificates, or licenses, the program has a harmful impact on attaining associate's degrees. For higher-expectation students, 5.85 percent and 9.75 percent of the intervention and control groups, respectively, earned associate's degrees—a statistically significant difference of 3.89 percent at the five percent confidence level. In contrast to the results for students with higher expectations, Upward Bound appears to provide more help for lower-expectation students to complete any postsecondary degree, certificate, or license. For these students, 39.31 percent of the intervention group earned any degree, certificate, or license, compared to 27.29 percent for similar control group members. The difference of 12.02 percent is statistically significant at the five percent confidence level. Despite this positive finding, the analysis was unable to statistically detect what type of postsecondary degree, certificate, or license the intervention group students with lower expectations were more likely to earn.

Based on rigorous scientific evidence, Upward Bound appears to be another failed Great Society program. Yet like its siblings, the social program has survived for decades.

SNAP Employment and Training Program

The Department of Agriculture's Supplemental Nutrition Assistance Program (SNAP), formerly known as the Food Stamp program, was created in 1961. SNAP has been in the news in the past year due to the explosive growth in the number of Americans receiving food stamps. As of August 2012, almost 45 million people were receiving food stamps.[246] In addition to providing cash transfers to welfare recipients to be used for the purchase of food, SNAP operates an employment assistance training program, called the SNAP Employment and Training Program, which was created in 1986.

According to the Government Accountability Office (GAO), officials at SNAP did not track any outcome measures for their employment and training program in fiscal year (FY) 2009.[247] For example, SNAP official failed to track how many program participants entered employment, experienced wage gains, attained credentials or education, and other obvious outcomes.[248] Despite the program's lack of concern with performance, in FY 2009, Congress appropriated almost $401 million for the program, which served 934,231 people.[249] There may be a good reason SNAP bureaucrats do not want to assess program effectiveness.

In the late 1980s, the Department of Agriculture sponsored a large-scale, multisite experimental evaluation of what was at the time called the Food Stamp Employment and Training Program.[250] During FY 1988, over 13,000 study participants at the 53 separate local food stamp agencies from 23 states were randomly assigned to intervention and control groups.[251] Similar to job-training and welfare-to-work programs of today, participants were required to engage in job search activities, job search training, welfare and work experience activities, and educational and vocational skills training.[252] Study participants were followed quarterly for one year. Overall, the program "was found to have no effect on participants' employment and earnings, and only a relatively small effect on average food stamp benefits."[253] The finds are summarized in Table 4.12.

TABLE 4.12.   Findings for the National Evaluation of the Food Stamp Employment and Training Program

Employment and Earnings Outcomes	Impact
Employment Status	
First quarter	0
Second quarter	0
Third quarter	0
Fourth quarter	0
Entire year	0
Days Worked	
First quarter	0
Second quarter	0
Third quarter	0
Fourth quarter	0
Entire year	0
Hourly Wage at Current or Most Current Job for Participants Who Were Working	
First quarter	0
Second quarter	0
Third quarter	0
Fourth quarter	0
Entire year	0
Total Earnings of All Participants	
First quarter	0
Second quarter	0
Third quarter	0
Fourth quarter	0
Entire year	0
Welfare Dependency	
Level of Welfare Cash Assistance Received	
First quarter	0
Second quarter	0
Third quarter	0

(continued)

TABLE 4.12.   (Continued)

Employment and Earnings Outcomes	Impact
Fourth quarter	0
Entire year	0
Level of Food Stamp Benefits Received	
First quarter	0
Second quarter	Pos*
Third quarter	Pos*
Fourth quarter	0
Entire year	Pos**

Key: 0 Finding was not statistically significant
      Pos Positive or beneficial impact
      Neg Negative or harmful impact
      *   Statistically significant at the 10 percent confidence level ($p \le 0.10$)
      **   Statistically significant at the 5 percent confidence level ($p \le 0.05$)
      ***   Statistically significant at the 1 percent confidence level ($p \le 0.01$)
      n/a No measure was assessed or reported
      †   No statistically significance test was performed
Source: Michael J. Puma and Nancy R. Burstein, "The National Evaluation of the Food Stamp Employ-ment and Training Program," *Journal of Policy Analysis and Management* 13, 2 (1994): Table 2, 322; Table 3, 322; Table 4, 323; Table 5, 323; Table 6, 324, Table 7, 325.

Impacts on Employment and Earnings

Of the 20 measures of employment and earnings, the Food Stamp Employment and Training Program was found to be ineffective.[254] The program had no statistically measurable impact on the ability of the intervention group to find employment by quarter and year.[255] For example, 54.5 percent of the control group found employment during the first year, compared to 51.6 percent of the intervention group. The difference was statistically indistinguishable from no impact at all.

By quarter and year, the program also had no effect on the number of days worked by the intervention group and the hourly wages of their current or most recent jobs.[256] In addition, the program had no effect on the total earnings of participants.[257] For example, the average yearly earnings for the intervention group were $2,475.15, while the control group averaged $2,542.60. The difference of $67.45 in lower earnings for the intervention group failed to be statistically significant.

Impacts on Welfare Dependency

Of the 10 measures of welfare dependency, the Food Stamp Employment and Training Program was found to have only one impact that was statistically significant at the five percent confidence level.[258] Participation in the employment and training program failed to reduce the overall receipt of welfare cash assistance such as benefits received from AFDC and other welfare programs. However, a slight impact on reducing the amount of food stamp benefits received over the course of a year was found. For the year follow-up, the intervention group averaged $920 in food stamp benefits, while the control group averaged $985—a statistically significant beneficial difference of $65 at the five percent confidence level. This positive finding appears to be driven by two suggestive findings for the second and fourth quarters that the intervention group averaged $23 and $24 fewer in benefits compared to the control group. These two differences were marginally statistically significant at the 10 percent confidence level.

While the Food Stamp Employment and Training Program failed on all measures of employment, earnings, and general welfare cash assistance, it appears to have had a minute effect on reducing food stamp benefit level.

Welfare-to-Work

When Congress passed the Family Support Act of 1988, the Aid to Families with Dependent Children (AFDC) program was altered to provide education, employment, and support services to AFDC recipients.[259] As a result, most AFDC single parents with children ages three to five were expected to participate in welfare-to-work programs.[260] States had the option of requiring AFDC single parents with children ages one to five to participate in welfare-to-work programs.

In 1996, Congress passed the Personal Responsibility and Work Opportunity reconciliation Act (PRWORA), which replaced AFDC with Temporary Assistance for Needy Families (TANF). TANF established lifetime limits on most families' receipt of federally funded TANF benefits and created financial incentives for states to operate mandatory, work-focused, welfare-to-work programs.[261] Under TANF, the receipt of benefits was no longer an entitlement.

Of all the social programs reviewed in this book, welfare-to-work strategies have the most remarkable results, relatively speaking. In 1989, the Department of Health and Human Services (HHS), with the assistance of the Department of Education, funded the National Evaluation of Welfare-to-Work Strategies (NEWWS). NEWWS assessed the long-term effects of 11 mandatory welfare-to-work programs operating at seven sites during the late 1980s and 1990s.[262] The seven sites were:

- Atlanta, Georgia
- Columbus, Ohio

- Detroit, Michigan
- Grand Rapids, Michigan
- Oklahoma City, Oklahoma
- Portland, Oregon
- Riverside, California[263]

Employment-focused programs were implemented in Atlanta, Grand Rapids, Riverside, and Portland. Atlanta, Grand Rapids, and Riverside also operated education-focused programs, as did Columbus (two programs), Detroit, and Oklahoma City.

At three of the sites, NEWWS compared two general types of pre-employment strategies: labor force attachment (LFA) and human capital development (HCD). The LFA approach used employment-focused activities that emphasized short-term job search strategies to encourage welfare recipients to quickly find employment.[264] In contrast, the HCD approach emphasized longer-term skill building activities such as basic education.[265] The HCD approach can be considered an education-focused approach.

Followed for five years, over 55,000 welfare recipients were randomly assigned to intervention and control groups.[266] The intervention group received either employment- or education-focused services, while people in the control group were not required to engage in employment or educational activities. Depending on the particular sites, the five-year follow-up period ended between 1991 and 1999.[267]

Overall, NEWWS found that "the HCD approach did not produce added economic benefits relative to the LFA approach."[268] Further, "the LFA approach moved welfare recipients into jobs more quickly than did the HCD approach—a clear advantage when federally funded welfare months are time-limited."[269] When the NEWWS results for the 11 programs are divided by employment-focused and education-focused approaches, the employment-focused programs generally had larger beneficial impacts on employment, earnings, and welfare receipt than the education-focused approach.[270] However, the evaluation authors concluded that of the 11 programs, the one operating in Portland, while considered employment-focused, used a "mixed" approach that blended both employment search and education or training, might be the most effective.[271]

Impact on Employment and Earnings

Table 4.13 summarizes the five-year NEWWS findings by site and approach. The impact of the sites by approach had inconsistent effects on

TABLE 4.13. Selected Findings for the National Evaluation of Welfare-to-Work Strategies, Years 1 to 5

	Atlanta		Grand Rapids		Riverside		Columbus		Detroit	Oklahoma City	Portland
	LFA	HCD	LFA	HCD	LFA	HCD	Integrated	Traditional			
Employment and Earnings											
Ever employed (%)	Pos**	0	0	0	Pos***	Pos***	Pos**	0	Pos**	0	Pos**
Average number of quarters employed	Pos***	Pos**	Pos***	Pos*	Pos***	Pos***	Pos**	Pos*	0	0	Pos***
Average total earnings	Pos***	Pos**	Pos*	0	Pos***	Pos*	Pos***	Pos*	Pos*	0	Pos***
Welfare Dependency											
Average number of months of welfare receipt	Pos***	Pos***	Pos***	Pos***	Pos***	Pos***	Pos***	Pos***	Pos***	n/a	Pos***
Average total welfare payment	Pos***	Pos***	Pos***	Pos***	Pos***	Pos***	Pos***	Pos***	Pos**	n/a	Pos***
Average number of months of food stamp receipt	Pos**	Pos**	Pos***	Pos***	Pos***	Pos***	Pos***	Pos***	Pos***	n/a	Pos***

(continued)

TABLE 4.13. (Continued)

	Atlanta		Grand Rapids		Riverside		Columbus		Detroit	Oklahoma City	Portland
	LFA	HCD	LFA	HCD	LFA	HCD	Integrated	Traditional			
Average total food stamp benefits	Pos**	0	Pos***	Pos***	Pos***	Pos***	Pos***	Pos***	Pos**	n/a	Pos**
Combined Income											
Earnings as a percentage of combined income, including welfare and food stamp benefits	Pos***	Pos***	Pos***	Pos**	0	Pos***	Pos***	Pos***	Pos***	n/a	Pos***

Key: 0 Finding was not statistically significant

Pos Positive or beneficial impact

Neg Negative or harmful impact

*   Statistically significant at the 10 percent confidence level ($p \le 0.10$)

**   Statistically significant at the 5 percent confidence level ($p \le 0.05$)

*** Statistically significant at the 1 percent confidence level ($p \le 0.01$)

n/a No measure was assessed or reported

†   No statistically significance test was performed

Source: Gayle Hamilton, Stephen Freedman, Lisa Gennetian, Charles Michalopoulos, Johanna Walter, Diana Adams-Ciardullo, Anna Gassman-Pines, Sharon McGroder, Martha Zaslow, Jennifer Brooks, Surjeet Ahluwalia, Electra Small, and Bryan Ricchetti, *National Evaluation of Welfare-to-Work Strategies: How Effective Are Different Welfare-to-Work Approaches? Five-Year Adult and Child Impacts for Eleven Programs* (Washington, DC: U.S. Department of Health and Human Services, Administration for Children and Families and Office of the Assistant Secretary for Planning and Evaluation; and U.S. Department of Education, 2001), Table 4.1, 86–87; Table 5.1, 111; Table 5.2, 120; Table 6.1, 127.

welfare recipients ever being employed over the course of five years.[272] Of the four employment-based approaches (Atlanta LFA, Grand Rapids LFA, Riverside LFA, and Portland), three programs yield statistically significant results at the five percent or one percent confidence levels. The biggest difference in ever being employed for the employment-focused approach occurred in the Riverside LFA, with 74.5 percent of the intervention group reported to have ever been employed, compared to 66.1 percent for the control group. The difference of 8.4 percent was statistically significant at the one percent confidence level. For the seven employment-focused approaches (Atlanta HCD, Grand Rapids HCD, Riverside HCD, Columbus Integrated and Traditional, Detroit, and Oklahoma City), only three sites had impacts on being ever employed that were statistically significant at the five percent or one percent confidence levels. The largest impact for this approach occurred in the Riverside HCD, with 66.9 percent of the intervention group reporting having ever worked, compared to 61.1 percent for the control group. The difference of 5.8 percent is statistically significant at the one percent level of confidence.

The employment-focused approach was consistently associated with increases in the number of quarters that welfare recipients were employed over five years.[273] The beneficial impacts for all four employment-focused programs were highly statistically significant at the one percent confidence level. The program with the largest impact was Portland, with the intervention group averaging 9.4 quarters of employment and the control group averaging 7.8 quarters—a statistically significant difference of 1.6 quarters at the one percent confidence level. In other words, the Portland intervention group was employed for 47.0 percent of the five-year period, compared to 39.0 percent for the control group. As for the employment-focused programs, the results were less consistent. Only three (Atlanta HCD, Riverside HCD, and Columbus Integrated) of the seven programs had statistically significant positive impacts at the five percent or one percent confidence levels. Riverside HCD had the largest impact with the intervention group averaging 5.5 quarters of employment, compared to 4.7 quarters for the control group—a statistically significant difference of 0.8 quarters at the one percent confidence level. The Riverside HCD intervention group was employed for 27.5 percent of the 5-year period, compared to 23.5 percent for the control group. There were suggestive positive findings at the marginally significant 10 percent confidence level for Grand Rapids HCD and Columbus Traditional. There was no effect in Detroit and Oklahoma City.

Similar to the previous employment outcomes, the employment-focused programs generally fared better on average total earnings over five years.[274] Three of these programs yielded positive earnings impacts at the one percent level of confidence, while the Grand Rapids LFA had a marginally positive impact at the 10 percent confidence level. The largest impact occurred in Portland, with the intervention group averaging $26,041 and the control group averaging $20,891—a statistically significant difference of $5,150 at the one percent confidence level. For the education-focused programs only, the Atlanta HCD and Columbus Integrated programs produced positive results that were statistically significant at the five percent or one percent confidence levels, respectively. The Riverside HCD, Columbus Traditional, and Detroit programs yielded marginally positive impacts on earnings at the 10 percent confidence level, while there were no statistically measurable impacts in the Grand Rapids HCD and Oklahoma City programs.

Impact on Welfare Dependency

Except for the Oklahoma City program, where welfare dependency was not assessed, the other 10 programs were associated with decreasing the number of months of receiving welfare (AFDC/TANF) over five years.[275] For each of the 10 programs, the intervention groups averaged fewer months on welfare than the averages for the control groups. In addition, all of these differences were statistically significant at the one percent confidence level. For the employment-focused programs, Portland had the greatest impact. On average, the intervention and control groups in Portland spend 19.8 and 25.3 months on welfare, respectively—a difference of 5.6 months. In other words, the intervention group, on average, spent 33.0 percent of the 5-year time span on welfare, while the control group spent, on average, 42.2 percent of the five-year time period on welfare. For education-focused programs, the Columbus Integrated program had the largest impact. For this program, the intervention group averaged 23.3 months on welfare over five years, while the control group averaged 27.2 months—a difference of 3.9 months. The Columbus Integrated intervention group spent 38.8 percent of the five-year period on welfare, compared to 45.3 percent for the control group.

A similar trend was found for the assessment of average total welfare (AFDC/TANF) payments received over five years. All of the beneficial impacts for the 10 programs were statistically significant at the one percent confidence level, expect for Detroit, which was significant at the five percent confidence level.[276] For the employment-focused programs, Portland had the largest impact, with the intervention group averaging $8,940 over five years, compared to $11,686 for the control group—a difference of $2,746. The largest average dollar decrease in welfare payments for the education-focused programs occurred at the Riverside HCD. The intervention group averaged $17,176 in welfare payments, compared to $20,126 for the control group—a difference of $2,949.

Likewise, the intervention groups from each of the 10 programs spent less time, on average, participating in the Food Stamps program, compared to the control groups.[277] Further, all of these impacts were statistically significant at the one percent confidence level, expect for both Atlanta programs, which were significant at the five percent level. For the employment-focused programs, Riverside LFA had the greatest impact. On average, the intervention and control groups spent 25.3 and 29.0 months, respectively, on food stamps—a statistically significant difference of 3.6 months at the one percent confidence level. In other words, the intervention group, on average, spent 42.2 percent of the five-year time span on food stamps, while the control group spent, on average, 48.3 percent of the five-year time span on food stamps. For education-focused programs, the Riverside HCD program had the largest impact on the total months on food stamps. For the Riverside HCD program, the intervention group averaged 27.4 months on welfare over five years, while the control group averaged 31.2 months—a difference of 3.8 months. The Riverside HCD intervention group spent 45.7 percent of the five-year period on food stamps, compared to 52.0 percent for the control group.

The intervention groups from nine of the 10 programs received, on average, lower dollar amounts of food stamps over five years, compared to the control groups.[278] The program that failed to have a statistically measurable impact was the Atlanta HCD program. All of the beneficial impacts for the nine programs were statistically significant at either the five percent or one percent confidence levels. For the employment-focused programs, Riverside LFA had the largest impact, with the intervention group averaging $4,981 over five years, compared to $5,870 for the control group—a statistically significant difference of $888 at the one percent confidence level. The largest average dollar decrease in food stamp benefits for the education-focused group occurred at the Riverside HCD program. The intervention group averaged $5,492 in welfare payments, compared to $6,504 for the control group—a statistically significant difference of $1,013 at the one percent confidence level.

Impact on Earnings as a Share of Total Income

How did the welfare-to-work programs affect the ability of welfare recipients to become self-sufficient? Overall, the employment-focused and education-focused approaches had small but statistically significant impacts on increasing the share of employment earnings as a percentage of all income, including welfare payments, food stamps, and estimated Earned Income Tax Credits less estimated payroll taxes.[279] Of the employment-focused programs, the difference between the intervention and control groups in Portland was the largest. The Portland intervention group's share of total incomes from earnings averaged 45.5 percent, while the control group's share averaged 38.7 percent—a statistically significant difference of 6.8 percent at the one percent confidence level. For the education-focused programs, the greatest difference occurred at the Columbus Integrated program. For this program, the intervention group's earnings share averaged 48.6 percent, compared to 44.3 percent for the control group—a statistically significant difference of 4.3 percent at the one percent confidence level. While both approaches yielded beneficial outcomes on this measure, none of the intervention groups were able to have a majority of their income come from the fruits of their labor. Despite following the intervention groups for five years, NEWWS welfare-to-work programs, on average, were unsuccessful at moving welfare participants to self-sufficiency.

While many beneficial results were found, neither the employment-focused or education-focused approaches moved welfare participants into full-time employment over the five-year follow-up period.

Employment Retention and Advancement (ERA) Project

Compared to the evaluations of federal social programs in this review so far, NEWWS demonstrated that welfare-to-work programs can have consistent beneficial impacts. While the five-year study period of NEWWS indicates that welfare recipients still remain overly dependent on welfare programs, many did find jobs. Despite this limited success, many welfare recipients found jobs that were low-paying and unstable, so the Department of Health and Human Services and Department of Labor funded the Employment Retention and Advancement (ERA) project.[280] Initiated in 1998, the ERA project assessed the effectiveness of 12 different employment retention and advancement programs across the nation. The goal of ERA "was to identify and rigorously test a diverse set of innovative models designed to promote employment stability and wage or earnings progression among current or former welfare recipients or other low-income groups."[281] Further, the social programs evaluated were "'real world' interventions initiated by practitioners and not ones set up and funded for solely for research purposes."[282]

The individual ERA programs were implemented in the following locations:

- Texas (Corpus Christi, Fort Worth, Houston)
- Los Angles Enhanced Job Club (EJC), California
- Los Angeles Reach for Success (RFS), California
- Salem, Oregon
- Chicago, Illinois
- Riverside Training Focused, California
- Riverside Work Plus
- Riverside Post-Assistance Self-Sufficiency (PASS)
- Cleveland, Ohio
- Eugene, Oregon
- Medford, Oregon
- South Carolina[283]

The ERA programs sought to develop partnerships between welfare agency staff and staff from other organizations that may provide assistance such as community colleges and Workforce Investment Act (WIA) one-stop centers (discussed in Chapter 5).[284] In addition, the ERA programs sought to develop linkages with employers to assist in finding higher-paying jobs for ERA participants.[285] For those employed, in an attempt to help ERA participants retain and advance in their jobs, ERA programs offered counseling services related to on-the-job issues, and advice on handling personal and family matters that could affect job performance.[286]

The ERA programs can be categorized by the types of clients they served.[287] The Texas, Los Angeles EJC, and Salem programs served unemployed TANF recipients, while the Chicago, Los Angeles RFS, Riverside Training Focused, and Riverside Works Plus programs concentrated on servicing employed TANF recipients. The Cleveland, Eugene, Medford, Riverside PASS, and South Carolina programs attended to employed individuals not receiving TANF benefits.

From 2000 to 2004, over 27,000 single parents were randomly assigned to intervention and control groups.[288] The services provided to the control group were usually the normal welfare-to-work programs established under PRWORA.[289] Therefore, the effects for the intervention groups represent the added value of the ERA services beyond the normal welfare-to-work services.

Unemployed TANF Recipients

The ERA programs that targeted unemployed TANF recipients attempted to improve job placement and job retention above the levels that would have been achieved through regular TANF services.[290] The selected findings for these programs are summarized in Table 4.14. The Texas ERA programs (Corpus Christi, Fort Worth, and Houston) provided a $200-per-month stipend to participants who had left TANF and were working at least 30 hours per week.[291] The stipend was also available for those working a minimum of 15 hours per week combined with participation in education and training activities. Twelve stipends was the maximum number that participants could receive. Outcomes for the Texas ERA programs were tracked over four years.

The Los Angeles EJC program attempted to increase the employment retention and career advancement of unemployed TANF participants though an "enhanced" job club that provided basic job search assistance, career planning, and career searches that targeted each participant's most desired field of interest.[292] The development of the Los Angeles EJC program was influenced by the successful results of the Portland welfare-to-work program found in the NEWWS.[293] According to the evaluation authors, Los Angeles EJC was based on a "proven" program.[294] Beyond helping participants find employment, the Salem ERA program provided additional services once the individual found employment. The program attempted to help unemployed TANF recipients find employment in their fields of interest.[295] Services were provided at WIA one-stop centers rather than local welfare agencies.

TABLE 4.14. Selected Findings for ERA Programs Targeting Unemployed TANF Recipients

	Corpus Christi (Years 1 to 4)	Fort Worth (Years 1 to 4)	Houston (Years 1 to 4)	Los Angeles EJC (Years 1 to 3)	Salem (Years 1 to 3)
Employment Measures					
Ever employed	0	0	0	0	0
Average quarterly employment	Pos**	0	0	0	0
Had employment spell of at least 4 quarters	Pos***	0	0	0	0

TABLE 4.14.   (Continued)

	Corpus Christi (Years 1 to 4)	Fort Worth (Years 1 to 4)	Houston (Years 1 to 4)	Los Angeles EJC (Years 1 to 3)	Salem (Years 1 to 3)
Length of longest employment spell, in quarters	Pos**	0	0	0	0
Length of longest unemployment spell, in quarters	Pos*	0	0	0	0
Earnings					
Average annual earnings	Pos***	0	0	0	0
Quarters with earnings of $3,500 or more	Pos**	0	0	0	0
Welfare Dependency					
Average annual TANF benefits received	0	0	Neg**	0	Neg***
Average annual food stamps received	Pos**	Neg**	0	0	0

Key: 0 Finding was not statistically significant

Pos Positive or beneficial impact

Neg Negative or harmful impact

*   Statistically significant at the 10 percent confidence level ($p \leq 0.10$)

**   Statistically significant at the 5 percent confidence level ($p \leq 0.05$)

***   Statistically significant at the 1 percent confidence level ($p \leq 0.01$)

n/a No measure was assessed or reported

†   No statistically significance test was performed

Source: Richard Hendra, Keri-Nicole Dillman, Gayle Hamilton, Erik Lundquist, Karin Martinson, Melissa Wavelet, Aaron Hill, Sonya Williams, *How Effective are Different Approaches Aiming to Increase Employment Retention and Advancement? Final Impacts for Twelve Models*, MDRC, April 2010, Table 3.3, pp. 56; Table 3.4, pp. 58-59; Table 3.5, pp. 60-61; Table 3.7, pp. 85-86; and Table 3.8, pp. 96-97.

Impacts on Employment.   Overall, the ERA programs serving unemployed TANF recipients had no effect on the participants ever being employed over the three- or four-year follow-up period.[296] For the average quarterly employment rate, four out of the five sites failed to produce statistically measurable impacts. The exception was Corpus Christi. The Corpus Christi intervention group had an average quarterly employment rate of 51.7 percent, compared to 48.0 percent for the control group—a statistically significant difference of 3.7 percent at the five percent confidence level. The trend of Corpus Christi being the only program to produce at least marginally statistically significant results on employment outcomes continued for measures of working at least four quarters consecutively and length of longest employment and unemployment spells. Over four years, 63.4 percent of Corpus Christi intervention group members worked at least four consecutive quarters, compared to 58.2 percent of the control group—a statistically significant difference of 6.5 percent at the one percent confidence level. On average, the longest spell of employment for the intervention group was 0.4 quarters longer than the longest working spell for the control group. This difference was statistically significant at the five percent confidence l evel. Marginally statistically significant at the 10 percent confidence level, the longest unemployed spell of Corpus Christi intervention group members was 0.4 quarters less than the longest unemployment spell for the control group.

Impacts on Earnings. On two measures of earnings—average annual earnings and percentage of quarters earning $3,500 or more—Corpus Christi was the only ERA program serving unemployed TANF recipients to yield statistically measurable impacts.[297] Over the 4-year study period, the intervention group had average annual earnings from employment of $5,011, while the control group earned $4,371—a statistically significant difference of $640 at the one percent confidence level. Further, the Corpus Christi program increased the percentage of quarters in which the intervention group earned at least $3,500 by 1.9 percent—12.8 percent for the intervention group and 10.9 percent for the control group. The difference of 1.9 percent was statistically significant at the five percent confidence level.

Impacts on Welfare Dependency. The findings for the ERA programs targeting unemployed TANF recipients contradicted the employment and earnings outcomes. The programs in Corpus Christi, Forth Worth, and Los Angeles had no statistically measurable impact on the dollar amount of TANF benefits received, while the programs in Houston and Salem had harmful impacts.[298] In Houston, the intervention group over four years averaged $759 in TANF benefits per year, while the control group averaged $703—a statistically significant difference of $56 at the five percent confidence level. The harmful effect was greater in Salem. Over three years, the intervention group averaged $1,602 in annual TANF benefits, compared to $1,304 in benefits for the control group. The difference of $298 is statistically significant at the one percent confidence level.

For the average annual dollar amount of food stamps received, three of the five programs failed to have statistically measurable effects.[299]

Participation in the Corpus Christi program was associated with an average annual decrease of $134 in food stamps, while participation in Fort Worth was associated with an average annual increase of $162. Both of these findings are statistically significant at the five percent confidence level.

While past evaluations found that the job club approach replicated in the Los Angeles EJC program was effective, the replicated program "was not found to be effective in helping people retain or advance in jobs."[300] Being based on a "proven" program does not always equal actual effectiveness.

Employed TANF Recipients

Similar to the ERA programs focused on unemployed TANF recipients, the ERA programs that targeted employed TANF recipients attempted to increase job retention and career advancement above levels that would have been achieved through regular TANF services.[301] The career advancement services, the most prominent of the services offered, included career and job development activities that encouraged advancement through job mobility, education and training referrals, and staff counseling.[302] The selected findings for these programs are summarized in Table 4.15.

TABLE 4.15. Selected Findings for ERA Programs Targeting Employed TANF Recipients

	Chicago (Years 1 to 4)	Los Angeles RFS (Years 1 to 3)	Riverside Work Plus (Years 1 to 4)	Riverside Training Focused (Years 1 to 3)
Employment Measures				
Ever employed	0	0	0	0
Average quarterly employment	Pos*	0	0	0
Had employment spell of at least 4 quarters	0	0	0	0
Length of longest employment spell, in quarters	Pos*	0	0	0
Length of longest unemployment spell, in quarters	Pos*	0	0	0
Earnings				
Average annual earnings	Pos*	0	0	0
Quarters with earnings of $3,500 or more	Pos**	0	0	0

(*continued*)

TABLE 4.15.   (Continued)

	Chicago (Years 1 to 4)	Los Angeles RFS (Years 1 to 3)	Riverside Work Plus (Years 1 to 4)	Riverside Training Focused (Years 1 to 3)
Welfare Dependency				
Average annual TANF benefits received	Pos***	0	0	Neg*
Average annual food stamps received	Neg**	0	0	0

Key: 0   Finding was not statistically significant
      Pos   Positive or beneficial impact
      Neg   Negative or harmful impact
      *   Statistically significant at the 10 percent confidence level ($p \leq 0.10$)
      **   Statistically significant at the 5 percent confidence level ($p \leq 0.05$)
      ***   Statistically significant at the 1 percent confidence level ($p \leq 0.01$)
      n/a   No measure was assessed or reported
      †   No statistically significance test was performed
Source: Richard Hendra, Keri-Nicole Dillman, Gayle Hamilton, Erik Lundquist, Karin Martinson, Melissa Wavelet, Aaron Hill, and Sonya Williams, How Effective Are Different Approaches Aiming to Increase Employment Retention and Advancement? Final Impacts for Twelve Models (MDRC, April 2010), Table 4.3, 115–116; Table 4.5, 134–135; Table 4.7, 147–148.

The aim of the Chicago ERA program was to help employed TANF recipients move into higher-paying jobs.[303] As long as the TANF recipients were employed, according to Illinois policy, they were exempt from the 5-year TANF limits. Because of this policy, Illinois sought to reduce its growing number of TANF recipients by encouraging them to advance into higher-paying jobs. The Chicago ERA program required mandatory participation and offered more comprehensive services focused on work retention and career advancement, compared to the less intensive retention-oriented program offered to the control group.

The Los Angeles RFS program was "an intensely marketed, individualized, and flexible advancement program" that tried to move employed TANF recipients into higher-paying jobs with better benefits and career prospects.[304] The respective control group received services that focused on finding any job. The Riverside Work Plus and Training Focused programs differed from each other in that they offered a different combination of services that had different participation requirements.[305] The Work Plus program emphasized work as a way for advancement, while the Training Focused program prioritized education and training.

Impacts on Employment.   Overall, the ERA programs serving employed TANF recipients had no effect on the participants ever being employed over the three- or four-year follow-up period.[306] For the average quarterly employment rate, all sites failed to produce statistically measurable impacts at least at the five percent confidence level. However, the Chicago ERA program had a marginally statistically significant effect on ever being employed four years after random assignment. The Chicago intervention group had an average quarterly employment rate of 55.0 percent, compared to 52.4 percent for the control group—a statistically significant difference of 2.6 percent at the 10 percent confidence level. None of the programs had statistically significant impacts on working at least four quarters consecutively. At the marginally statistically significant confidence level of 10 percent, the Chicago ERA program was the only program to affect length of longest employment and unemployment spells. On average, the longest spell of employment for the intervention group was 0.4 quarters longer than the longest working spell for the control group. The longest unemployed spell of the Chicago intervention group members was 0.4 quarters less than the longest unemployment spell for the control group.

Impacts on Earnings.   On two measures of earnings—average annual earnings and percentage of quarters earning $3,500 or more—Chicago was the only ERA program serving employed TANF recipients to yield marginally statistically measurable impacts.[307] Over the 4-year study period, the intervention group had average annual earnings from employment of $6,967, while the control group earned $6,490—a statistically significant difference of $470 at the less rigorous 10 percent confidence level. Further, the Chicago program increased the percentage of quarters in which the intervention group earned at least $3,500 by 2.6 percent—21.6 percent for the intervention group and 19.0 percent for the control group. The difference of 2.6 percent was statistically significant at the five percent confidence level.

Impact on Welfare Dependency.   The findings for the ERA programs targeting employed TANF recipients were generally inconsistent. The Los Angeles RFS and Riverside Work Plus programs had no statistically measurable impact on the dollar amount of TANF benefits received, while the Chicago and Riverside Training Focused programs had conflicting impacts.[308] In Chicago, the intervention group over four years averaged $778 in TANF benefits per year, while the control group averaged $1,010—a statistically significant reduction of $232 at the one percent confidence level. In contrast, the Riverside Training Focused program had a marginally statistically significant harmful impact. Over three years, the intervention group averaged $2,195 in annual TANF benefits, compared to $2,060 in benefits for the control group. The difference of $175 is statistically significant at the 10 percent confidence level.

For the average annual dollar amount of food stamps received, four of the five programs failed to have statistically measurable effects.[309] However, participation in the Chicago program was associated with an average annual increase of $153 in food stamps. This harmful impact was statistically significant at the five percent confidence level.

Employed Individuals, Not Receiving TANF

Unlike the previous ERA programs that focused on unemployed or employed TANF recipients, the remaining set of ERA programs targeted employed individuals not receiving TANF benefits. For these ERA programs, the goal was to aid in both employment retention and advancement for low-wage workers. The individuals participating at these sites were comprised of a mix of individuals that had previously received TANF benefits and those that had not participated in TANF. All participants were involved in the ERA programs on a voluntary basis. The services offered included reemployment services, staff coaching on job-related matters, career counseling, and education and training referrals.[310] The selected findings for these programs are summarized in Table 4.16.

TABLE 4.16. Selected Findings for ERA Programs Targeting Employed Individuals, not Receiving TANF

	Cleveland (Years 1 to 3)	Eugene RFS (Years 1 to 3)	Medford (Years 1 to 3)	Riverside PASS (Years 1 to 4)	South Carolina (Years 1 to 4)
Employment Measures					
Ever employed	0	Pos*	Neg***	0	0
Average quarterly employment	0	0	0	Pos***	0
Had employment spell of at least 4 quarters	0	0	0	0	0

TABLE 4.16.   (Continued)

	Cleveland (Years 1 to 3)	Eugene RFS (Years 1 to 3)	Medford (Years 1 to 3)	Riverside PASS (Years 1 to 4)	South Carolina (Years 1 to 4)
Length of longest employment spell, in quarters	0	0	0	Pos***	0
Length of longest unemployment spell, in quarters	0	0	0	Pos***	0
Earnings					
Average annual earnings	0	0	0	Pos***	0
Quarters with earnings of $3,500 or more	0	0	0	Pos***	0
Welfare Dependency					
Average annual TANF benefits received	0	0	0	0	0
Average annual food stamps received	0	0	0	0	0

Key: 0 Finding was not statistically significant
    Pos Positive or beneficial impact
    Neg Negative or harmful impact
    *   Statistically significant at the 10 percent confidence level ($p \leq 0.10$)
    **   Statistically significant at the 5 percent confidence level ($p \leq 0.05$)
    ***   Statistically significant at the 1 percent confidence level ($p \leq 0.01$)
    n/a No measure was assessed or reported
    †   No statistically significance test was performed
Source: Richard Hendra, Keri-Nicole Dillman, Gayle Hamilton, Erik Lundquist, Karin Martinson, Melissa Wavelet, Aaron Hill, and Sonya Williams, *How Effective Are Different Approaches Aiming to Increase Employment Retention and Advancement? Final Impacts for Twelve Models* (MDRC, April 2010), Table 5.3, 168–169; Table 5.4, 178–179; Table 5.5, 90–191; Table 5.6, 202–203; Table 5.10, 224–225.

The aim of the Cleveland ERA program was to increase the job retention of low-wage, entry-level workers in the long-term nursing care industry.[311] The Cleveland ERA program was needed to counter the traditionally high turnover rate in this particular industry. The control group consisted of similar workers employed in the same field.

The Eugene ERA program served low-wage workers who had previously received TANF but were not participating in the welfare program.[312] The program aimed to move individuals into more stable employment and higher-paying jobs. Individual assistance, service referrals, and advancement-focused career counseling comprised the intensive retention and advancement provided by a collaboration of welfare and workforce agencies.[313]

In Medford, the ERA program targeted individuals who had left TANF or current participants of other public welfare programs.[314] By providing individualized staff assistance, advancement-focused career counseling, and referrals to postemployment services, the Medford ERA program was expected to increase the long-term employment prospects of participants.[315] The Riverside Post-Assistance Self-Sufficiency (PASS) ERA program targeted recent TANF leavers who were employed.[316] The program offered "job search activities, career development services, referrals to education and training slots, life skills workshops, arrangements for supportive service payments, and referrals to social service programs."[317]

With the goal of helping employed individuals succeed in the labor market, the South Carolina ERA provided modest financial incentives, job search assistance, short-term vocational training, and other support services.[318] The financial incentives included $50 awards for remaining in a new job for a month, three months, and six months.

Impacts on Employment.   On most employment outcome measures, the ERA programs serving employed individuals not receiving TANF benefits had little to no effect. In Cleveland, Riverside PASS, and South Carolina, the ERA programs had no effect on participants ever being employed over the three- or four-year follow-up period.[319] However, the Eugene ERA had a marginally positive impact on ever being employed after random assignment. The Eugene invention group had an ever employed rate of 95.9 percent, compared to 93.7 percent for the control group—a statistically significant difference of 2.2 percent at the less rigorous 10 percent confidence level. The opposite occurred at the Medford ERA. Over three years, participation in the Medford ERA appears to slightly reduce employment. The intervention group had an ever employed rate of 94.8 percent, while the control group's rate was 97.9 percent—a statistically significant difference of 3.1 percent at the one percent confidence level.

For the average quarterly employment rate, four out of the five sites failed to produce statistically measurable impacts at least at the five percent confidence level. However, the Riverside PASS ERA program had a statistically significant effect on average quarterly employment over four years. The Riverside PASS intervention group had an average quarterly employment rate of 59.7 percent, compared to 56.3 percent for the control group—a statistically significant difference of 3.4 percent at the one percent confidence level. None of the programs had statistically significant impacts on working at least four quarters consecutively. For the remaining employment measures of longest employment and unemployment spells, Riverside PASS ERA was the only program to yield statistically significant results. On average, the longest spell of employment for the intervention group was 0.6 quarters longer than the longest working spell for the control group. The longest unemployed spell of the Riverside PASS intervention group members was 0.6 quarters less than the longest unemployment spell for the control group. Both of these impacts were statistically significant at the one percent confidence level.

Impacts on Earnings. On two measures of earnings—average annual earnings and percent of quarters earning $3,500 or more—the Riverside PASS program was the only ERA program to yield statistically measurable impacts.[320] Over the four-year study period, the intervention group had average annual earnings from employment of $9,711, while the control group earned $8,843—a statistically significant difference of $868 at the one percent confidence level. Further, the Riverside PASS program increased the percentage of quarters in which the intervention group earned at least $3,500 by 4.1 percent—33.5 percent for the intervention group and 29.5 percent for the control group. The difference of 4.1 percent was statistically significant at the one percent confidence level.

Impact on Welfare Dependency. The findings for the ERA programs targeting employed individuals not participating in TANF yielded consistent statistically insignificant results.[321] All of these programs failed to affect the dollar amounts of TANF and food stamp benefit received.

Overall, the ERA experimental evaluation strongly indicates that providing additional services on top of the normal TANF work and job search requirements makes little to no difference. That is a whole lot of effort that went to waste.

Healthy Marriage Initiative

Single-parents families have long been seen as a driver of family poverty and other risks for children. Children raised by single parents are more likely to live in poverty and display health, academic, behavioral, and criminal problems than children raised by married biological parents.[322] Reacting to the growing number of children being raised outside of two-parent biological families and the resulting greater risks, the George W. Bush administration sought to alter relevant programs within the Department of Health and

Human Services (HHS) to promote marriage. According to Ron Haskins and Isabel Sawhill, "Given the rather modest response by states to the 1996 welfare reform law's emphasis on marriage, the administration of George W. Bush created a strong federal role in trying to strengthen marriage from its earliest days in office."[323] The reauthorization of PRWORA by Congress in 2005 was an opportunity for the George W. Bush administration to cement into law federal marriage promotion programs that had been previously funded through unobligated funds at the Department of Health and Human Services.[324] Subsequently, the official federal marriage programs were named the Healthy Marriage Initiative. From its earliest stages, Bush's marriage initiative was backed by social conservatives.

Two large-scale multisite experimental evaluations of Healthy Marriage Initiative programs were commissioned, with final and preliminary impact results available. So far, the news is not good. The first evaluation is the Building Strong Families (BSF) demonstration project sponsored by the U.S. Department of Health and Human Services.[325] The Supporting Health Marriage evaluation is the second.[326]

Building Strong Families

Launched in 2002, BSF provides counseling services at 8 sites to unmarried couples who were expecting or had recently had a baby:

- Atlanta, Georgia
- Baltimore, Maryland
- Baton Rouge, Louisiana
- Orange and Broward Counties, Florida
- Houston, Texas
- Allen, Marion, and Lake Counties, Indiana
- Oklahoma City, Oklahoma
- San Angelo, Texas[327]

The marriage program's intent was to steer low-income unmarried couples with or expecting a child toward marriage. BSF is based on three components.[328] First, couples were provided group sessions on relationship skills. The sessions are intended to improve communication conflict management, affection, intimacy, and trust between the couples. The sessions ware further intended to help the transition to parenthood and parent-infant relationships. Second, couples received individual support from program family coordinators. The family coordinators encouraged program participation, reinforced relationship skills, and provided ongoing emotional support. Third, assessment and referral services are provided so that couples can participate in education, employment, mental health, child-care, housing, and legal services programs.

The 8-site demonstration project is undergoing an experimental evaluation by Mathematica Policy Research, a leading research firm that specializes in conducting impact evaluations of government programs. More than 5,000 couples were randomly assigned to a relationship counseling group or a control group that could not participate in the program. To be eligible for random assignment, participants had to meet the following criteria:

- Both members of the couple wanted to partake in the program.
- The couple was engaged in a romantic relationship.
- The couples were expecting or had recently had a baby.
- The couple was unmarried at the moment their baby was conceived.
- Both members of the couple were at least 18 years old.[329]

In 2010, Mathematica released the initial findings from a 15-month follow-up study.[330] The long-term follow-up study reporting results for the couples' children reached the age of three was released in November 2012.[331] At the time of entry into BSF, most couples were in stable relationships and desired to marry their partner.[332] Only 37 percent of both couples had high school diplomas.[333] The majority of participants were black (52 percent), 12 percent were white, and 20 percent were Hispanic.[334] For 38 percent of the couples, their child was born before they applied to participate in BSF.[335]

Impacts on Relationship Status.   The summarized results of the 15- and 36-month follow-up studies are presented in Table 4.17. Overall, the authors of the 15-month follow-up study found that "BSF did not make couples more likely to stay together or get married. In addition, it did not improve couples' relationship quality."[336] For example, 17 percent of all couples participating in the program eventually married, while 18 percent of the couples excluded from the program were married 15 months after random assignment—a statistically indistinguishable difference of one percentage point.[337] For the measures of still being romantically involved and living together (married or unmarried), BSF, in general, failed to have statistically significant effects.

The 36-month follow-up study, concluded: "After three years BSF had no effect on the quality of couple's relationships and did not make couples

TABLE 4.17. Selected Findings for the Building Strong Families Program for Unmarried Couples with or Expecting Children at 15 and 36 Months

Relationship Status	Overall	Atlanta	Baltimore	Baton Rouge	Florida Counties	Houston	Indiana Counties	Oklahoma City	San Angelo
Married									
15 months	0	0	0	0	0	0	Neg*	0	0
36 months	0	0	0	0	0	n/a	0	0	0
Still romantically involved									
15 months	0	0	Neg***	0	0	0	0	Pos*	0
36 months	Neg*	0	0	0	Neg***	n/a	0	0	0
Living together (married or unmarried)									
15 months	0	0	0	0	0	0	Neg*	0	0
36 months	Neg*	0	0	0	Neg***	n/a	0	0	0
Relationship Quality									
Relationship happiness									
15 months	0	0	n/a	0	n/a	0	0	Pos***	0
36 months	0	n/a	n/a	n/a	n/a	n/a	n/a	n/a	n/a
Support and affection									
15 months	0	0	Neg**	0	0	0	0	Pos**	0
36 months	0	0	0	0	0	n/a	0	0	0
Use of constructive conflict behaviors									
15 months	0	Pos**	0	0	0	0	0	Pos***	0
36 months	0	0	0	0	0	n/a	0	0	0

Avoidance of destructive behaviors							
15 months	0	0	0	0	0	0	0
36 months	Neg**	0	0	n/a	0	Pos**	0
Fidelity							
15 months	0	0	0	0	0	Pos*	0
36 months	0	0	0	n/a	0	Pos**	0
Avoidance of Intimate Partner Violence							
Mother reports no severe physical assaults							
15 months	0	Neg*	0	0	0	0	0
36 months	0	n/a	n/a	n/a	n/a	0	n/a
Father reports no severe physical assaults							
15 months	0	0	0	0	0	0	0
36 months	0	n/a	n/a	n/a	n/a	n/a	n/a
Coparenting							
Quality of coparenting relationship							

(continued)

TABLE 4.17. (Continued)

Relationship Status	Overall	Atlanta	Baltimore	Baton Rouge	Florida Counties	Houston	Indiana Counties	Oklahoma City	San Angelo
15 months	0	0	Neg*	0	0	0	0	Pos*	0
36 months	0	0	0	0	Neg*	n/a	0	0	0
Father Involvement									
Lives with child									
15 months	0	0	Neg*	0	0	0	0	Pos*	0
36 months	0	0	0		Neg*	n/a	0	0	0
Spends substantial time with child daily									
15 months	0	0	Neg*	0	0	0	0	0	0
36 months	Neg**	0	Neg*	0	Neg*	n/a	0	0	0
Engagement with child									
15 months	n/a	n/a	n/a	n/a	n/a	n/a	n/a	n/a	n/a
36 months	0	0	0	0	0	n/a	0	0	0
Provides substantial financial support									
15 months	0	0	Neg**	0	0	0	0	Pos***	0
36 months	Neg*	0	0	0	0	n/a	0	0	0
Parental responsiveness (observed)									
15 months	n/a	n/a	n/a	n/a	n/a	n/a	n/a	n/a	n/a
36 months	0	n/a	n/a	n/a	n/a	n/a	n/a	n/a	n/a

Mothers' Parenting Behavior

Engagement in cognitive and social play

0	0	0	0	0	0	0	0	0	0
0	n/a	n/a	n/a	n/a	n/a	n/a	n/a	n/a	n/a

Frequently spanked child in previous month

Pos**	0	0	0	0	0	Pos**	0	0	0
n/a	n/a	n/a	n/a	n/a	n/a	n/a	n/a	n/a	n/a

Parenting stress and aggravation

Pos*	0	0	0	0	0	Pos**	0	0	0
n/a	n/a	n/a	n/a	n/a	n/a	n/a	n/a	n/a	n/a

Parental responsiveness (observed)

n/a	n/a	n/a	n/a	n/a	n/a	n/a	n/a	n/a	n/a
Pos*	n/a	n/a	n/a	n/a	n/a	Pos**	n/a	n/a	n/a

Fathers' Parenting Behavior

Engagement in cognitive and social play

0	Neg**	0	0	0	0	0	0	0	0
0	n/a	n/a	n/a	n/a	n/a	n/a	n/a	n/a	n/a

Frequently spanked child in previous month

179

(continued)

TABLE 4.17. (Continued)

Relationship Status	Overall	Atlanta	Baltimore	Baton Rouge	Florida Counties	Houston	Indiana Counties	Oklahoma City	San Angelo
15 months	0	0	0	0	0	0	0	0	0
36 months		n/a	n/a	n/a	n/a	n/a	n/a	n/a	n/a
Parenting stress and aggravation									
15 months	0	0	0	Pos**	0	0	0	0	0
36 months	n/a	n/a	n/a	n/a	n/a	n/a	n/a	n/a	n/a

Key: 0 Finding was not statistically significant
Pos Positive or beneficial impact
Neg Negative or harmful impact
* Statistically significant at the 10 percent confidence level ($p \leq 0.10$)
** Statistically significant at the 5 percent confidence level ($p \leq 0.05$)
*** Statistically significant at the 1 percent confidence level ($p \leq 0.01$)
n/a No measure was assessed or reported
† No statistically significance test was performed

Source: Robert G. Wood, Sheena McConnell, Quinn Moore, Andrew Clarkwest, and JoAnn Hsueh, *Strengthening Unmarried Parents' Relationships: The Early Impacts of Building Strong Families* (Princeton, NJ: Mathematica Policy Research, May 2010), Table ES.1, xiv; Figure 5, 13; Table 6, 14; Table 10, 21; Figure 7, 21; Table 11, 22 and Robert G. Wood, Quinn Moore, Andrew Clarkwest, Alexandra Killewald, and Shannon Monahan, The Long-Term Effects of Building Strong Families: A Relationship Skills Education Program for Unmarried Parents: Final Report, (Princeton, NJ: Mathematica Policy Research, November 2012), Table A.1a, A.3, Table A.2a, A.5, Table A.3a, A.7, Table A.4a, A.9, Table A.5a, A. 11, Table A.7a, A.14, Table A.8a, A.16, and Table A.9a, A.18.

more likely to stay together or get married."[338] For example, 21 percent of all couples participating in the intervention and control groups eventually married 36 months after random assignment, so BSF had a statistically indistinguishable effect on marriage.[339] However, there is suggestive evidence that BSF had long-term harmful impacts. For the measure of still being romantically involved, 57 percent and 60 percent of the intervention and control couples, respectively, reported in the affirmative—a marginally statistically significant difference of three percent at the 10 percent confidence level. For the last relationship measure, 47 percent and 50 percent of the intervention and control couples, respectively, reported living together 36 months after random assignment—a marginally statistically significant difference of three percent at the 10 percent confidence level.

For the 15-month follow-up, none of the individual sites yielded statistically significant impacts at least at the five percent confidence level.[340] However, there is suggestive evidence that BSF had a harmful impact at the Indiana counties program. In Indiana, 15.4 percent of the BSF intervention group were married 15 months after random assignment, while 21.0 percent of the control group were married—a marginally statistically significant harmful impact at the less rigorous 10 percent confidence level.[341]

Seven of the eight sites failed to yield statistically significant impacts at least at the five percent confidence level for the measure of still being romantically involved 15 months after random assignment. In Baltimore, 59.4 percent and 70.3 percent of the intervention and control group were still romantically involved, respectively.[342] The harmful difference of 10.9 percent is statistically significant at the one percent confidence level. Suggestive evidence of a potential beneficial impact occurred in Oklahoma City. At this location, 81.5 percent of the intervention group was still romantically involved, compared to 76.4 percent for the control group.[343] The difference of 5.1 percent was marginally statistically significant at the less rigorous 10 percent confidence level.

For living together, regardless of marital status, all of the individual sites failed to produce statistically significant impacts at least at the five percent confidence level. However, suggestive evidence of a potential harmful impact occurred in Indiana. At this location, 59.2 percent of the intervention group couples were living together, compared to 67.2 percent for the control group.[344] The difference of 8.0 percent was marginally statistically significant at the less rigorous 10 percent confidence level.

For the 36-month follow-up, the harmful impact in Baltimore and suggestive beneficial impact in Oklahoma City on couples being still romantically involved faded away to no effect at all.[345] In addition, the suggestive harmful impact in the Indiana counties on couples still living together faded away as well.[346] Two harmful impacts emerged in the Florida counties. First, 54.8 percent and 67.4 percent of Florida counties couples in the intervention and control groups, respectively, reported being still romantically involved—a statistically significant harmful impact of 12.7 percent at the one percent confidence level.[347]

Impacts on Relationship Quality.   While the overall effect of BSF on five measures of relationship quality was statistically insignificant in the 15- and 36-month follow-ups, a few of the sites produced statistically significant results. For relationship happiness at the 15-month follow-up, five of the six sites where these outcomes were assessed failed to produce meaningful results. In Oklahoma City, the intervention group had slightly higher reports of relationship happiness than the control group.[348] The beneficial impact was statistically significant at the one percent confidence level.

For levels of support and affection at the 15-month follow-up, six of the eight sites failed to produce meaningful results. In Oklahoma City, the intervention group had slightly higher reports of support and affection than the control group.[349] The beneficial impact was statistically significant at the five percent confidence level. However, in Atlanta, a small harmful impact was found that was statistically significant at the five percent confidence level. For the 36-month follow-up, the results in Oklahoma City and Atlanta became statistically indistinguishable from zero.[350]

For use of constructive conflict behaviors at the 15-month follow-up, six of the eight sites failed to produce statistically significant impacts. In Atlanta and Oklahoma City, the intervention groups had slightly better scores than their respective control groups.[351] These beneficial impacts were statistically significant at the five percent confidence level. However, these effects faded away at the time of the 36-month follow-up.[352]

For the two measures assessing destructive behavior avoidance and fidelity at the 15-month follow-up, seven of the eight sites failed to produce meaningful or suggestive results. In Oklahoma City, the intervention group had slightly better reports of avoiding destructive behaviors than the control group.[353] The beneficial impact was statistically significant at the five percent confidence level. Also in Oklahoma City, a small yet suggestive impact was found for increasing relationship fidelity that was marginally statistically significant at the 10 percent confidence level.[354] However, the statistical significance of the long-term impact that the Oklahoma City program had on fidelity increased to the five percent confidence level. At the time of the 36-month follow-up, the intervention couples in Atlanta were less likely to avoid destructive conflict behaviors compared to their control couple counterparts.[355] The harmful impact is statistically significant at the five percent confidence level.

Impacts on Avoidance of Intimate Partner Violence.   For the 15-month follow-up, all of the individual sites failed to yield statistically significant impacts at least at the five percent confidence level for reports of severe physical violence as reported by mothers and fathers. However, there is suggestive evidence of a harmful impact in Baltimore. While 85.3 percent of the Baltimore intervention group mothers reported to have not suffered from severe assaults from their partner, 90.7 percent of the control group mothers reported the same. The harmful impact of 5.3 percent was marginally statistically significant at the less rigorous 10 percent confidence level.

Impacts on Coparenting.   For quality of coparenting relationships at the time of the 15-month follow-up, the eight sites failed to produce statistically significant results at least at the five percent confidence level. However, there is suggestive, while contradictory, evidence that BSF had beneficial and harmful effects in Oklahoma City and Baltimore, respectively.[356] Both of these findings were marginally statistically significant at the 10 percent confidence level. For the 36-month follow-up, the suggestive impacts in Baltimore and Oklahoma City became statistically insignificant.[357] In the long-term, a suggestive harmful impact on co-parenting relationships in the Florida counties emerged at the marginally statistically significant 10 percent confidence level.[358]

Impacts on Father Involvement.   For the involvement of fathers with their children at the time of the 15-month follow-up, all of the eight sites failed to produce meaningful results at least at the five percent confidence level. However, there is suggestive evidence of harmful and beneficial impacts in Baltimore and Oklahoma City, respectively.[359] In Baltimore, 43.8 percent of the intervention group fathers lived with their child, compared to 51.2 percent for the control group fathers—a marginally statistically significant difference of 7.4 percent at the 10 percent confidence level. In Oklahoma City, 71.2 percent of the intervention group fathers lived with their child, compared to 65.7 of the control group—a marginally statistically significant impact of 5.5 percent at the 10 percent confidence level. For the 36-month follow-up, the suggestive effects in Baltimore and Oklahoma City faded.[360] A suggestive long-term harmful impact on fathers living with their children emerged in the Florida Counties. At the 36-month follow-up, 43.4 percent and 53.3 percent of fathers in the intervention and control groups, respectively, were living with their children—a statistically harmful impact of 9.9 percent at the five percent confidence level.[361]

For fathers spending substantial time with their child daily at the 15-month follow-up, all of the eight sites failed to produce meaningful results at least at the five percent confidence level. In spite of this, there is suggestive evidence of a harmful impact in Baltimore.[362] In Baltimore, 53.1 percent of the intervention group fathers spent substantial time with their child daily, compared to 60.5 percent of the control group fathers—a marginally statistically significant difference of 7.3 percent at the 10 percent confidence level. The harmful effect in Baltimore persisted at the time of the 36-month-follow-up.[363] In Baltimore, 39.4 percent of the intervention group fathers spent substantial time with their child daily, compared to 47.2 percent of the control group fathers—a marginally statistically significant difference of 7.8 percent at the 10 percent confidence level.

For the father's provision of substantial financial child support at the 15-month follow-up, six of the eight sites failed to produce statistically significant results. Nonetheless, there is evidence, again, of harmful and beneficial impacts in Baltimore and Oklahoma City, respectively.[364] In Baltimore, 61.2 percent of the intervention group fathers provided considerable financial support, compared to 70.5 percent of the control group fathers—a statistically significant difference of 9.3 percent at the five percent confidence level. In Oklahoma City, 80.0 percent of the intervention group fathers lived with their child, compared to 72.0 of the control group—a statistically significant impact of eight percent at the one percent confidence level. The effects in Baltimore and Oklahoma City faded away at the time of the 36-month follow-up.[365]

Impacts on Mother's Parenting Behavior.   While none of the sites produced statistically significant impacts on the mother's engagement in cognitive and social play at the 15-month follow-up, BSF appears to have had an overall beneficial impact on reducing spanking by mothers, and the parenting stress and aggravation of mothers.[366] For spanking within the last month, 12.9 percent and 15.4 percent of BSF intervention and control group mothers, respectively, reported to have spanked their child—a statistically significant difference of 2.5 at the five percent confidence level. Despite this beneficial finding, it appears to be primarily driven by the result in Houston. While seven of the sites failed to produce statistically significant effects on this measure, 95.2 percent and 84.5 percent of Houston mothers in the intervention and control groups, respectively, reported to have avoided spanking their child during the previous month.[367] The beneficial difference of 10.7 was statistically significant at the five percent confidence level.

The result for the overall impact of BSF on the mother's parenting stress and aggravation appears to be similarly driven by the Houston program. In general, BSF across the sites produced a small but suggestive impact on the parenting stress self-reported by mothers that was marginally statistically significant at the 10 percent confidence level.[368] While seven of the sites failed to produce statistically significant effects on this measure, the Houston intervention group mothers reported less stress and aggravation than their counterparts in the control group.[369] The beneficial difference was statistically significant at the five percent confidence level.

Impacts on Father's Parenting Behavior.   Overall, BSF had no impact on the father's engagement in cognitive and social play with his child at the 15-month follow-up. However, a harmful statistically significant impact was found in Baltimore.[370] At the five percent confidence level, intervention group fathers were slightly less likely to engage in cognitive and social play than their counterparts in the control group.

While none of the sites produced statistically significant impacts on the father's spanking of his child in the previous month, the Baton Rouge program had a beneficial and statistically significant impact at the five percent confidence level on the father's self-reported parenting stress and aggravation.

Supporting Health Marriage

As part of the federal government's family-strengthening policy agenda, HHS set out to test whether it can successfully provide marriage counseling programs to keep married parents of low-income families together.[371] The Supporting Healthy Marriage (SHM) program model consists of three main components.[372] The first component is based on curriculum-based relationship and marriage education skills workshops conducted in small groups. The second is the offering of supplemental activities, such as educational and social events, intended to provide additional support by encouraging couples to practice the skills learned in the workshops. The third component matches couples with specialized staff members to help them take advantage of all the available services. Marriage counseling under this program costs the taxpayer an average of $9,100 per couple, with a range going from $7,400 in Wichita to $11,500 in Oklahoma City.[373]

From 2007 to 2009, 6,298 married couples meeting SHM's participation criteria in eight sites across the nation were randomly assigned to intervention and control groups. While the control group couples were not allowed to partake in SHM services, they were free to seek similar services elsewhere. A majority of the couples taking part in the SHM evaluation were either Hispanic or black.[374] Only 39.9 percent of both spouses had a high school diploma, while 42.0 percent of the couples had family incomes below the federal poverty level. Overall, 74.9 percent and 70.5 percent of men and women, respectively, reported to be happy or very happy with their marriages. However, 62.9 of men and 64.4 percent of women acknowledged trouble in their marriages. The results of the SHM evaluation impacts 12 months after random assignment are summarized in Table 4.18.

TABLE 4.18.   Selected Findings for the Supporting Healthy Marriage Program for Low-Income Families at 12 Months

Relationship Status	Overall Impact
Married	0
Marital Appraisals	
Couple's average report of relationship happiness	Pos***
Either spouse reports marriage in trouble	Pos***
Warmth and Support in Relationship	
Men's report of warmth and support	Pos***
Women's report of warmth and support	Pos***
Observed men's warmth and support	0
Observed women's warmth and support	0
Positive Communication Skills in Relationship	
Men's report of positive communication skills	Pos***
Women's report of positive communication skills	Pos***
Observed men's positive communication skills	Pos*
Observed men's positive communication skills	Pos*
Negative Interactions in Relationship	
Men's report of negative behavior and emotions	Pos***

TABLE 4.18.   (Continued)

Relationship Status	Overall Impact
Women's report of negative behavior and emotions	Pos***
Men's report of psychological abuse	Pos***
Women's report of psychological abuse	Pos***
Men's report of any physical assault	Pos**
Women's report of any physical assault	0
Men's report of any severe physical assault	0
Women's report of any severe physical assault	0
Observed men's anger and hostility	0
Observed women's anger and hostility	Pos*
Fidelity	
Neither spouse reported infidelity	0
Individual Psychological Distress	
Men's psychological distress	Pos**
Women's psychological distress	Pos***
Coparenting Relationship	
Men's report of cooperative coparenting	0
Women's report of cooperative coparenting	0

Key: 0 Finding was not statistically significant

Pos Positive or beneficial impact

Neg Negative or harmful impact

*   Statistically significant at the 10 percent confidence level ($p \leq 0.10$)

**   Statistically significant at the 5 percent confidence level ($p \leq 0.05$)

***   Statistically significant at the 1 percent confidence level ($p \leq 0.01$)

n/a   No measure was assessed or reported

†   No statistically significance test was performed

Source: JoAnn Hsueh, Desiree Principe Alderson, Erika Lundquist, Charless Michalopoulos, Daniel Gubits, David Fein, and Virginia Knox, *The Supporting Healthy Marriage Evaluation: Early Impacts on Low-Income Families* (Washington, DC: Office of Planning, Research and Evaluation, Administration for Children and Families, U.S. Department of Health and Human Services, 2012), Table 4, 27; Table 5, 29; Table 6, 33; Table 7, 34; Table 8, 35.

Impact on Relationship Status.   Similar to the BSF findings, the SHM program failed to affect the marital status of participants. At the 12-month follow-up, 90.0 percent of the SHM intervention group couples were still married, while 89.3 percent of the control group couples were still married.[375] While this result is a short-term outcome, the SHM program failed to produce statistically meaningful results for its primary outcome of interest. The program was no more likely to keep low-income married couples together than similar counterparts denied access to the federal program.

Despite this major failure, the SHM program did produce beneficial impacts on many outcomes of lesser importance.

Impacts on Marital Appraisals.   Participation in the SHM program was associated with a small beneficial effect on the couples' average report of relationship happiness at the one percent confidence level.[376] For the percentage of either spouse reporting that their marriage is in trouble, 47.7 percent of the intervention group answered in the affirmative, while 52.9 percent of the control group answered in the affirmative—a statistically significant beneficial impact of 5.2 percent at the one percent confidence level.

Impacts on Warmth and Support in Relationship.   Both men and women in the intervention group self-reported small increases in warmth and support in their relationships, compared to members of the control group.[377] Both beneficial impacts are statistically significant at the one percent confidence level. To confirm these results, program staff personally observed the couples' interactions to assess the level of warmth and support in the relationships. The observational assessment of the warmth and support displayed by men and women failed to produce statistically meaningful results.[378] These contradictory results mean that the self-reported findings need to be taken with caution.

Impacts on Positive Communication Skills in Relationship.   Both men and women in the intervention group self-reported minute increases in positive communication skills in their relationships, compared to their counterparts in the control group.[379] Both beneficial impacts are statistically significant at the one percent confidence level. The observational assessments of communication skills indicate at the less rigorous 10 percent confidence level that the SHM program improved communication skills for both men and women.[380] The findings based on observation by program staff are suggestive of beneficial impacts for men and women, and these results do offer support to SHM being effective at improving positive communication skills.

Impacts on Negative Interactions in Relationship.   Both men and women in the intervention group self-reported tiny decreases in negative behavior and emotions with their partners, compared to their counterparts in the control group.[381] Both beneficial impacts are statistically significant at the one percent confidence level. The same beneficial outcomes for men and women occurred for measures of psychosocial abuse.[382]

The effects on being the recipient of any physical assaults were inconsistent. While there was no effect for women, participation in the SHM program appears to be linked to men being less likely to report being victims of physical assaults.[383] This beneficial impact is statistically significant at the five percent confidence level. For the self-reported measure of being a victim of any severe physical assaults, the findings for men and women were statistically insignificant.

The observational assessments of the anger and hostility displayed by the couples yielded inconsistent results.[384] While the assessment by program staff yielded a statistically insignificant result for men, the SHM may have produced a small reduction in the anger and hostility of women observed by program staff. The beneficial difference was marginally statistically significant at the 10 percent confidence level.

Impact on Fidelity.   Similar to the BSF findings, the SHM program failed to affect the marital fidelity of participants. At the 12-month follow-up, 92.4 percent of the SHM intervention group couples reported no cheating in their marriages, compared to 91.2 percent of the control group couples.[385]

Impacts on Individual Psychological Distress.   Both men and women in the intervention group self-reported tiny decreases in psychological distress, compared to their counterparts in the control group.[386] The beneficial impact for men was statistically significant at the five percent confidence level, while the impact for women was statistically significant at the one percent confidence level.

Impact on Coparenting Relationship.   Participation in the SHM program failed to affect the self-reported levels of cooperative parenting for men and women.[387] The program appears to have no effect on how well parents get along with each other and support each other while parenting.

Based on the best available evidence, the Building Strong Families and Supporting Healthy Marriage programs appear to do little to promote marriage—whether getting couples to marry or keeping couples married.

Moving to Opportunity and Section 8 Housing Vouchers

According to William Julius Wilson, a professor of sociology at Harvard University, concentrated poverty—defined as areas where 40 percent or more of residents live in poverty as defined by the federal government—"magnifies the problems associated with poverty in general: joblessness, crime, delinquency, drug trafficking, broken families, and dysfunctional schools."[388] Further, "Neighborhoods of highly concentrated poverty are seen as dangerous, and therefore they become isolated, socially and economically, as people go out of their way to avoid them."[389] Neighborhood conditions, such as crime, broken families, and dysfunctional schools, are thought to have negative effects—independent of individual factors—on individuals residing in concentrated poverty neighborhoods.

For example, neighborhoods characterized by concentrated neighborhood disadvantage display higher levels of legal cynicism, police dissatisfaction, and tolerance of deviance than neighborhoods with less disadvantage.[390] An analysis of 196 Chicago neighborhoods found that collective efficacy helps explain lower rates of crime and observed disorder.[391] Collective efficacy is the notion that social cohesion among neighbors joined with their willingness to intervene on behalf of the common good is linked to fewer occurrences of crime. In short, increased collective efficacy is associated with lower crime rates. The analysis also found that increased concentrated disadvantage was associated with increased physical and social disorder in the neighborhoods. Contrarily, increased collective efficacy was associated with decreased physical and social disorder, and reductions in violent and property crimes.

How widespread is concentrated poverty? From 2006 to 2010, residents living in concentrated poverty census tracts comprised 3.5 percent of the U.S. population and 12.4 percent of all those in poverty.[392] Of residents living in concentrated poverty tracks, 49.0 percent lived in poverty.[393] The residents of these census tracts are more likely to have less than a high school diploma (34.0 percent) than possess a bachelor's degree or higher (12.8 percent), compared to areas of less poverty. The largest share of people living in these census tracts is black (38.1 percent) and Hispanic (29.5 percent).

Conducted in five cities—Baltimore, Boston, Chicago, Los Angeles, and New York—the Moving to Opportunity (MTO) demonstration assessed the impact of offering families with children under 18 living in public housing developments or concentrated poverty areas the opportunity to move out of their neighborhoods.[394] From 1994 to 1998, eligible families were randomly assigned to three groups. The first group received an MTO rental assistance voucher that could be used only in census tracts with poverty rates below 10 percent. The MTO group also received mobility counseling to assist with relocation to stable housing in low-poverty areas. The Section 8 group was offered regular Section 8 vouchers that did not have a neighborhood poverty rate restriction. The control group did not receive vouchers but was eligible to receive public housing assistance. Overall, 4,608 families were randomly assigned to one of the groups.

The MTO evaluation sought to determine whether improved neighborhood environments would cause improvements for adults and children in the following areas: housing; health; delinquent, criminal, and risky behavior; education; employment and earnings; and income and public assistance.[395] Two major reports based on the MTO evaluation were released. The first report presented the interim findings for four to seven years after random assignment.[396] The second report presented the long-term findings 10 to 15 years after random assignment.[397] According to the authors of the interim report on the initial findings of the MTO evaluation:

> Individuals who move to a new community are likely to be affected by the norms and values of that community through peer pressure and community expectations. We would expect these effects to be stronger the more the individual interacts with members of the new community. We would also expect such effects to be stronger if the norms and values of the new community are substantially different from those of the individual's old community.[398]

In addition, the social and physical environment may affect outcomes for the transferred individuals.[399] For example, the social resources of the new community, including better schools, may help improve the academic performance of transferred children. The economic environment may also have effects as well. Improved access to higher-paying jobs with benefits may substantially boost the economic prospects of transferring families.

The families in the MTO, Section 8, and control groups were 97.1 percent minority and 91.6 percent female-headed households with a median of three children.[400] A large majority (72.2 percent) of the household heads were not working at the time of random assignment.

A brief summary of the four- to seven-year follow-up report will be discussed first. Afterward, a more detailed summary of the 10- to 15-year follow-up study will be presented. The interim report concluded that there is "convincing evidence that MTO had real effects on the lives of participating families in the domain of housing conditions and assistance and on the characteristics of schools attended by their children."[401] The MTO and Section 8 groups were less likely to be currently living in public housing than the control group.[402] However, families in the MTO and Section 8 groups were more likely to be receiving public housing assistance four to seven years after random assignment than the control group families.[403] Further, household heads in the MTO and Section 8 groups were more likely to report having trouble making utility payments within the last 12 months than household heads in the control group.[404] Despite these negative findings, both MTO and Section 8 families were more likely to be satisfied with their current housing conditions, and the safety and quality of their neighborhoods[405] For example, both of these groups were more likely to report feeling safe in their neighborhoods during the day and night. There also appear to be a few health-related benefits. While on most measures of adult physical health, the MTO and Section 8 had no effect, the percentage of adults in the MTO group that were obese was 5.1 percent lower than the rate for the control group.[406] As for children ages five to 11 and 12 to 19, being a member of the MTO group or Section 8 group failed to yield beneficial outcomes on all physical health measures.[407]

For all youth aged 15 to 19, there was no statistically meaningful difference in being ever arrested for any crime, arrested for violent crime, or arrested for property crime.[408] However, female youth aged 15 to 19 in the Section 8 group were less likely to be arrested compared to similar female youth in the control group. This finding held for being arrested for a violent crime too. Unexpectedly, male youth age 15 to 19 in the MTO group were more likely to be arrested for property crime than similar members of the control group.

Despite these limited positive findings, "There is no convincing evidence of effects on educational performance; employment and earnings; or household income, food security, and self-sufficiency."[409] While children in the MTO and Section 8 groups were more likely to attend schools with lower percentages of students receiving free school lunches and higher percentages of white students, there were no beneficial impacts on cognitive and academic outcomes.[410] Further, members of the MTO and Section 8 groups fared no better on measures of being currently employed and annual earnings.[411] Based on survey and administrative data, the interim report authors concluded that "Although MTO increased the likelihood of families living in neighborhoods that appear to have better employment opportunities and norms toward work, both data sources indicate no significant overall impacts of MTO on the employment rates or earnings of adults or older youth."[412]

As for welfare dependency, being a member of the MTO and Section 8 groups had no effect on currently receiving AFDC/TANF, Food Stamps, SSI, or Medicaid benefits, compared to the control group.[413] Further, being a member of the MTO and Section 8 groups failed to affect whether adults were working and off of TANF.[414]

Tables 4.19 to 4.23 summarize the selected findings for adults, youth, and children that are based on 10 to 15 years after random assignment.

Long-Term Impacts on Housing, Neighborhood, and Social Networks

Table 4.19 summarizes the selected findings for the impact of MTO and Section 8 on housing, neighborhoods, and social networks. The opportunity

TABLE 4.19. Selected MTO Evaluation Findings for Adult Housing, Neighborhood, and Social Networks Outcomes

	MTO	Section 8
Housing		
Rates current housing as excellent or good	Pos**	Pos**
Currently in public housing	Pos**	Pos**
Currently receiving any housing assistance	0	0
Neighborhood		
Median household income	Pos**	Pos**
Average census tract share of persons who are poor	Pos**	Pos**
Average census tract share minority	Pos**	Pos**
Feels safe or very safe during day	Pos**	Pos**
Feels safe or very safe at night	Pos**	Pos**
Social Network		
Has at least 1 close friend who graduated from college	Pos**	0
Has at least 1 close friend who works full-time	Pos*	0

Key: 0 Finding was not statistically significant
  Pos Positive or beneficial impact
  Neg Negative or harmful impact
  *   Statistically significant at the 10 percent confidence level ($p \leq 0.10$)
  **   Statistically significant at the 5 percent confidence level ($p \leq 0.05$)
  *** Statistically significant at the 1 percent confidence level ($p \leq 0.01$)
  n/a No measure was assessed or reported
  †   No statistically significance test was performed

Source: Lisa Sanbonmatsu, Jens Ludwig, Lawrence F. Katz, Lisa Gennetian, Greg J. Duncan, Ronald C. Kessler, Emma Adam, Thomas W. McDade, Stacy Tessler Lindau, Matthew Sciandra, Fanghua Yang, Ijun Lai, William Congdon, Joe Amick, Ryan Gillette, Michael A. Zabek, Jordon Marvakov, Sabrina Yusuf, and Nicholas A. Potter, *Moving to Opportunity for Fair Housing Demonstration Program: Final Impacts Evaluation* (Washington, DC: U.S. Department of Housing and Urban Development, Office of Policy Development and Research, November 2011), Exhibit 2.4, 55; Exhibit 2.5, 56; Exhibit 2.6, 59; Exhibit 2.10, 63–64; Exhibit 2.11, 65.

to use MTO or Section 8 vouchers was associated with increased satisfaction with current housing conditions.[415] While 57.0 percent of the control group reported their current housing situation as excellent or good, the rates for the MTO and Section 8 groups were 5.3 percent and 10.9 percent higher, respectively. Both of these differences were statistically significant at the five percent confidence level. In addition, the MTO and Section 8 groups were less likely to be currently living in public housing than the control group.[416] Compared to 29.6 percent of the control group living in public housing, the rates for the MTO and Section 8 groups were 10.7 percent and 11.0 percent lower, respectively. These differences were statistically significant at the five percent confidence level. Despite these beneficial outcomes, the differences in the percentages of MTO and Section 8 families receiving housing assistance from the percentage for the control group families were statistically indistinguishable from zero. Overall, 62.0 percent of the control group was currently receiving housing assistance, while 64.6 percent and 57.5 percent of the MTO and Section 8 families were currently receiving housing assistance, respectively.

Overall, being offered MTO or Section 8 vouchers was associated with living in neighborhoods that were less poor and more racially white in composition.[417] On average, the control group lived in census tracts where 39.6 percent of the residents were poor. The differences for the MTO and Section 8 groups were 8.9 percent and 6.9 percent lower, respectively. Both of these differences were statistically significant at the five percent confidence level. While 88.0 percent of the residents of the census tracts where the control group lived were minorities, the minority percentages for the census tract for the MTO and Section 8 groups were 81.9 percent and 86.2 percent respectively. The reductions of 6.1 percent and 1.8 percent were statistically significant at the five percent confidence level. The opportunity to move was also associated with living in communities with higher median household incomes. The median neighborhood house income for the control group was $27,809, while the median figures for the MTO and Section 8 groups' neighborhoods were $9,149 and $5,600 more, respectively. Both of these differences were statistically significant at the five percent confidence level. All dollar values are expressed in 2009 dollars.

The adults in the MTO and Section 8 groups were more likely to perceive their neighborhoods as safer. While 80.4 percent of the control group reported that they felt safe during the day, the percentages for the MTO and Section 8 groups were 84.0 percent and 84.9 percent, respectively.[418] The differences of 3.6 percent for the MTO group and 4.5 percent for the Section 8 group were statistically significant at the five percent confidence level.

For having at least one close friend who graduated from college, 60.3 percent of adults in the MTO group reported in the affirmative, while 53.2 percent of adults in the control group reported in the affirmative.[419] The difference of 7.1 percent was statistically significant at the five percent confidence level. The difference between the control group and Section 8 group was statistically insignificant. Being offered an MTO voucher appears to have a marginally positive effect on adults reporting that they have at least one close friend who works full-time. Of the control group, 74.2 percent had at least one close friend working full-time, while the percentage for the MTO group was 77.5 percent—a statistically significant difference at the less rigorous 10 percent confidence level.

Long-Term Impacts on Adult and Youth Physical and Mental Health Outcomes

Table 4.20 presents a summary of the selected findings for the impact of MTO and Section 8 on physical and mental health outcomes for adults and youth. Youth 10 to 20 years old and adults were asked about their current health status. When asked about their physical health, 56.4 percent of adults in the control group reported that their health was good or better.[420] For adults in the MTO and Section 8 groups, 56.4 percent and 55.9 percent, respectively, reported that their current health status was good or better. For youth aged 10 to 20, 88.8 percent and 88.3 percent of the MTO and Section 8 members reported that their current health status was good or better, respectively.[421] These percentages are not statistically different from the 88.3 percent of control group youth reporting that their health status was good or better. The slight differences for adults and youth were statistically insignificant, indicating that being offered an MTO or Section 8 voucher has no long-term effect on the self-reported health status.

While being offered an MTO or Section 8 voucher had no effect on self-reported asthma conditions, the vouchers appear to have a long-term impact on the obesity of adults and no impact for youth aged 10 to 20.[422] While the measure of being obese with a body mass index (BMI) equal to or greater than 30 yields statistically insignificant results for both adults and youths age 10 to 20 years old, adult members of the MTO and Section 8 groups were statistically less likely to have BMI scores equal to or greater than 35. Of control group adults, 35.1 percent have a BMI equal to or greater than 30.

TABLE 4.20. Selected MTO Evaluation Findings for Adult and Youth Physical and Mental Health Outcomes

	Adult		Youth 10 to 20		Youth 13 to 20	
	MTO	Section 8	MTO	Section 8	MTO	Section 8
Physical Health Outcomes						
Self-reported health currently good or better	0	0	0	0	n/a	n/a
Asthma or wheezing attack	0	0	0	0	n/a	n/a
Obesity						
Currently obese: Body mass index (BMI) ≥ 30	0	0	0	0	n/a	n/a
BMI ≥ 35	Pos**	Pos**	n/a	n/a	n/a	n/a
BMI ≥ 40	Pos**	0	n/a	n/a	n/a	n/a
Diabetes						
Had diabetes or treated for it during the past year	0	Pos**	n/a	n/a	n/a	n/a
HbA1c test detected diabetes	Pos**	0	n/a	n/a	n/a	n/a
Hypertension: Currently has high blood pressure	0	0	n/a	n/a	n/a	n/a
Accidents and injuries requiring medical attention in past year	n/a	n/a	0	0	n/a	n/a
Mental Health Outcomes						
Psychological Distress Index, past month	Pos**	Pos*	n/a	n/a	0	0
Major depression, lifetime	Pos*	Pos**	n/a	n/a	0	0
Any mood disorder	0	0	n/a	n/a	0	0
Generalized anxiety disorder, lifetime	0	0	n/a	n/a	0	Pos*
Any anxiety disorder, lifetime	0	0	n/a	n/a	0	0

Panic attacks, lifetime	0	0	n/a	0	0
Posttraumatic stress disorder, lifetime	0	0	n/a	0	0
Dependence on drugs or alcohol, past month	Neg**	0	n/a	n/a	n/a
Serious behavioral or emotional problems	n/a	Pos*	n/a	n/a	0

Key: 0 Finding was not statistically significant

Pos Positive or beneficial impact

Neg Negative or harmful impact

* Statistically significant at the 10 percent confidence level ($p \leq 0.10$)

** Statistically significant at the 5 percent confidence level ($p \leq 0.05$)

*** Statistically significant at the 1 percent confidence level ($p \leq 0.01$)

n/a No measure was assessed or reported

† No statistically significance test was performed

Source: Lisa Sanbonmatsu, Jens Ludwig, Lawrence F. Katz, Lisa Gennetian, Greg J. Duncan, Ronald C. Kessler, Emma Adam, Thomas W. McDade, Stacy Tessler Lindau, Matthew Sciandra, Fanghua Yang, Jjun Lai, William Congdon, Joe Amick, Ryan Gillette, Michael A. Zabek, Jordon Marvakov, Sabrina Yusuf, and Nicholas A. Potter, *Moving to Opportunity for Fair Housing Demonstration Program: Final Impacts Evaluation* (Washington, DC: U.S. Department of Housing and Urban Development, Office of Policy Development and Research, November 2011), Exhibit 3.2, 90–92; Exhibit 3.4, 95–97; Exhibit 4.2, p. 115; Exhibit 4.3, 121–122; Exhibit 4.4, 124–125; Exhibit 4.5, 126–129; Summary Exhibit 4.6, 130–132.

Of MTO and Section 8 adults, 30.5 percent and 29.8 percent, respectively, had a BMI equal to or greater than 30—statistically significant differences of 4.6 percent and 5.3 percent, respectively, at the five percent confidence level. For the measure of a BMI equal to or greater than 40, the finding for the MTO adults yielded statistically significant results, while there appears to be no impact for Section 8 adults. Compared to adult control group members, with 17.5 percent having a BMI equal to or greater than 40, 13.1 percent of the adult MTO group had a BMI equal to or greater than 40—a statistically significant difference of 3.4 percent at the five percent confidence level.

Being offered MTO vouchers appears to have no effect on adults self-reporting having diabetes or being treated for it during the last year, compared to the control group adults.[423] However, there appears to be a beneficial effect for Section 8 adults, with 9.9 percent reporting in the affirmative, compared to 16.0 percent for control group adults—a statistically significant difference of 6.1 percent at the five percent confidence level. A more accurate measure of determining whether study participants were more or less likely to have diabetes is the HbA1c assessment, which scientifically tests for the presence of diabetes. For this test, 15.2 percent and 19.3 percent of the adult MTO and Section 8 group, respectively, had HbA1c tests indicating diabetes, compared to 20.4 percent for the adult control group. The difference of 5.2 percent for the adult MTO group was statistically significant at the five percent confidence level, while the different of 1.1 percent for the adult Section 8 group was statistically insignificant. In addition, adults were also tested for hypertension (high blood pressure). The results indicated that the opportunity to move through either MTO or Section 8 vouchers has no effect, compared to the results for the control group.

Youth age 10 to 20 were asked if they had had accidents or injuries requiring medical attention within the past year. The responses provided in the MTO and Section 8 groups were statistically indistinguishable from the responses given by similar control group members.[424]

Adults and youth 13 to 20 years old were also assessed on long-term outcomes related to mental health. Being offered MTO vouchers is associated with decreased psychological distress within the past month for adults, but not for youth 13 to 20 years old.[425] There is only suggestive evidence that being offered a Section 8 voucher leads to lower psychological distress. The average psychological distress index score for MTO adults is lower than the average score for adults in the control group. The beneficial impact is statistically significant at the five percent confidence level.

However, the average score for Section 8 adults was marginally lower than the average score for control group adults. The difference was statistically significant at the less rigorous 10 percent confidence level.

For incidences of major depression for adults, there is suggestive evidence that being offered MTO vouchers appears to have an effect, while the offer of Section 8 vouchers appears to reduce major depression over one's lifetime.[426] Of control group adults, 20.3 percent had major depressive episodes during their lifetime, while the finding for Section 8 adults was 15.5 percent—a statistically significant difference of 4.8 percent at the five percent confidence level. Being offered MTO vouchers may marginally reduce major depression over one's lifetime for adults. Of MTO adults, 17.1 percent had at least one major depressive episode over their lifetime. The difference from the control group is statistically significant at the less rigorous 10 percent confidence level. Being offered either an MTO or Section 8 voucher appears to have no influence on episodes of major depression for youth 13 to 20 years old.[427]

For adults and youth 13 to 20 years old, being offered MTO or Section 8 vouchers failed to affect the lifetime presence of any mood disorder, anxiety disorder, panic attacks, and posttraumatic stress disorder (PTSD).[428] While the opportunity to take advantage of a MTO voucher had no statistically meaningful effect on generalized anxiety disorders over one's lifetime, there is suggestive evidence that the offer of Section 8 vouchers is associated with decreased generalized anxiety disorders for youth. Over their lifetimes, 1.9 percent of youth 13 to 20 years old in the control group had generalized anxiety disorders, compared to 0.9 percent of similar MTO youth—a difference of 1.0 percent that is marginally statistically significant at the 10 percent confidence level.

Of control group adults, 5.5 percent were dependent on drugs or alcohol within the past month, while 8.4 percent of MTO adults were dependent.[429] The difference of 2.9 percent is statistically significant at the five percent confidence level.

Youth in families that had the opportunity to use MTO vouchers may have had fewer serious behavioral and emotional problems than similar control group members.[430] Of MTO youth 13 to 20 years old, 8.1 percent had serious behavioral and emotional problems, compared to 10.3 percent for similar control group youth—a marginally statistically significant difference of 2.2 percent at the 10 percent confidence level. There appears to be no effect for the Section 8 youth.

Long-Term Impacts on Economic Self-Sufficiency and Welfare Dependency

Table 4.21 presents a summary of the selected findings for the impact of MTO and Section 8 on economic self-sufficiency and welfare dependency. According to the authors, "Generally, we find no persistent systematic MTO impacts on employment, earnings, income, and other economic outcomes."[431] However, some of the economic self-sufficiency impacts of Section 8 appear to be harmful.

While being offered an MTO voucher had no effect on being employed at the time of the long-term follow-up for adults and grown children, the program appears to have a harmful impact on youth.[432] For youth 15 to 20 years old, 22.0 percent of the MTO group were employed from the fourth quarter of 2007 through the third quarter of 2008, compared to 25.6 percent for similar control group youth—a statistically significant harmful impact of 3.6 percent at the five percent confidence level. A different pattern in the findings occurred for Section 8. Being offered a Section 8 voucher had a harmful impact on currently being employed for adults, but appears to have had no effect for grown children and youth. Compared to similar control group adults with a current employment rate of 52.5 percent, 44.8 percent of the Section 8 group were currently employed—a statistically significant harmful impact of 7.7 percent at the five percent confidence level. Adults were also questioned about their full-time employment status. While being offered MTO vouchers had no effect on adults being currently employed full-time, the offer of Section 8 vouchers had a marginally statistically significant harmful impact on full-time employment. Compared to 36.7 percent of the control group adults being currently employed full-time, 32 percent of Section 8 adults were currently full-time employees—a statistically significant difference of 4.7 percent at the less rigorous 10 percent confidence level.

Adults were asked further about their earnings over the last year and being employed at their current main job for at least one year. The average earnings for the MTO and Section 8 adults were not statistically distinguishable from the average earnings of control group adults.[433] On average, MTO and Section 8 adults earned $12,616 and $11,675 in 2009 dollars, respectively, compared to $12,289 for control group adults. While being offered MTO vouchers had no effect for adults on being employed for at least one year at their main job, the offer of a Section 8 voucher had a harmful effect. Compared to 46.9 percent of similar control group adults, 40.6 percent of Section 8 adults reported being employed for at least one year at their main job—a

TABLE 4.21. Selected MTO Evaluation Findings for Adults, Grown Children, and Youth on Economic Self-Sufficiency and Welfare Dependency

Economic Self-Sufficiency	Adult		Grown Children 21 to 30		Youth 15 to 20	
	MTO	Section 8	MTO	Section 8	MTO	Section 8
Currently employed	0	Neg**	0	0	Neg**	0
Currently employed full time	0	Neg*	n/a	n/a	n/a	n/a
Annual individual earnings (previous calendar year)	0	0	n/a	n/a	n/a	n/a
Employed over 1 year at current main job	0	Neg**	n/a	n/a	n/a	n/a
Currently working and household is not receiving TANF	0	Neg**	n/a	n/a	n/a	n/a
Currently enrolled in school	n/a	n/a	0	0	0	0
Currently idle (neither enrolled in school nor working)	n/a	n/a	0	0	0	0
Employment benefits						
Health insurance	0	0	n/a	n/a	n/a	n/a
Paid sick leave	0	0	n/a	n/a	n/a	n/a
Paid vacation	0	0	n/a	n/a	n/a	n/a
Welfare Dependency						
Currently receiving TANF	0	0	n/a	n/a	n/a	n/a
Currently receiving food stamps	0	0	n/a	n/a	n/a	n/a
Currently receiving Supplemental Security Income	0	0	n/a	n/a	n/a	n/a
Currently receiving Medicaid	0	0	n/a	n/a	n/a	n/a
Fraction of months actively receiving TANF benefits, July 2007 to June 2009	0	0	0	0	n/a	n/a

(continued)

TABLE 4.21. (Continued)

Economic Self-Sufficiency	Adult		Grown Children 21 to 30		Youth 15 to 20	
	MTO	Section 8	MTO	Section 8	MTO	Section 8
Total TANF benefits while active on case, July 2007 to June 2009	0	0	Neg*	0	n/a	n/a
Fraction of months actively receiving food stamp benefits, July 2007 to June 2009	Neg**	0	0	0	n/a	n/a
Total food stamp benefits while active on case, July 2007 to June 2009	Neg**	0	0	0	n/a	n/a

Key: 0 Finding was not statistically significant
Pos Positive or beneficial impact
Neg Negative or harmful impact
* Statistically significant at the 10 percent confidence level ($p \leq 0.10$)
** Statistically significant at the 5 percent confidence level ($p \leq 0.05$)
*** Statistically significant at the 1 percent confidence level ($p \leq 0.01$)
n/a No measure was assessed or reported
† No statistically significance test was performed

Source: Lisa Sanbonmatsu, Jens Ludwig, Lawrence F. Katz, Lisa Gennetian, Greg J. Duncan, Ronald C. Kessler, Emma Adam, Thomas W. McDade, Stacy Tessler Lindau, Matthew Sciandra, Fanghua Yang, Ijun Lai, William Congdon, Joe Amick, Ryan Gillette, Michael A. Zabek, Jordon Marvakov, Sabrina Yusuf, and Nicholas A. Potter, Moving to Opportunity for Fair Housing Demonstration Program: Final Impacts Evaluation (Washington, DC: U.S. Department of Housing and Urban Development, Office of Policy Development and Research, November 2011), Exhibit 5.7, 152; Exhibit 5.8, 154–155; Exhibit 5.10, 156; Exhibit 5.12, p.160; Exhibit 5.13, 161; Supplemental Exhibit 5.5, 171.

statistically significant harmful impact of 6.3 percent at the five percent confidence level. In addition, the offer of MTO and Section 8 vouchers failed to have statistically meaningful impact on health insurance, paid sick leave, and paid vacation employment benefits for adults.[434]

Adults were also asked about whether they were currently working and not receiving TANF benefits. The offer of MTO vouchers failed to influence this measure. On the other hand, the offer of Section 8 vouchers was associated with fewer adults reporting they were currently working and not receiving TANF benefits.[435] Compared to 49.9 percent of similar control group adults, 42.8 percent of Section 8 adults were employed and not receiving TANF benefits —a statistically significant harmful impact of 7.1 percent at the five percent confidence level.

Grown children and youth were assessed on whether they were enrolled in school or currently idle.[436] The offer of MTO and Section 8 vouchers failed to influence current enrollment in school as well as neither being enrolled in school nor working.

The offer of MTO and Section 8 vouchers appears to have no beneficial impact on welfare dependency for adults and grown children.[437] For adults in the MTO and Section 8 groups, the rates of self-reported current participation in TANF, Food Stamps, Supplemental Security Income, and Medicaid were not different from the rates reported by control group adults. However, the results for TANF and Food Stamp participation differed when official administrative data was used. The fraction of months of actively receiving TANF benefits from July 2007 to June 2009 for adults and grown children in the MTO and Section 8 groups did not statistically differ from similar control group members. Nevertheless, grown children in the MTO group, on average, received $368.50 in TANF benefits, compared to the average of $270.13 for similar members of the control group—a marginally statistically significant difference of $98.32 at the 10 percent confidence level. There were no effects on TANF benefits received based on official data for MTO and Section 8 adults, and Section 8 grown children. While the participation in and benefits from the Food Stamps program for grown children in the MTO and Section 8 groups was statistically indistinguishable from the findings for similar control group members, there is evidence of harmful impacts for MTO adults. MTO adults spent 64.0 percent of the months between July 2007 and June 2009 participating in the Food Stamp program, compared to 59.6 percent for adult control group members—a statistically significant difference of 4.6 percent at the five percent confidence level. On average, the control group adults received $3,074.08 in food stamps benefits, while the adult MTO group averaged $3,384.02—a statistically significant difference of $309.94 at the five percent confidence level.

Long-Term Impacts on Risky and Criminal Behavior

Table 4.22 presents a summary of the selected findings for the impact of MTO and Section 8 on risky and criminal behavior. Youth 13 to 20 years old were assessed on their risky behavior. The risky behavior index is composed of self-reported data on smoking, alcohol drinking, marijuana use, and sexual engagement.[438] Overall, the MTO and Section 8 youth did not report higher or lower risk behaviors, compared to similar control group youth. With one exception, this finding persisted with the individual components of the risky behavior index. MTO and Section 8 youth were more likely to report having ever smoked, compared to control group youth. While 31.2 percent of control group youth admitted having ever smoked, the rates for the MTO and Section 8 youth were 35.4 percent and 35.5 percent, respectively. The differences of 4.2 percent and 4.3 percent were statistically significant at the five percent confidence level.

On the behavior problems and delinquency indexes, the self-reported behavior of MTO and Section 8 youth were statistically no different from what was reported by control group youth.[439] For measures of criminal arrests, most of the outcomes found no statistically meaningful differences between the MTO or Section 8 youth and control group youth.[440] By and large, number of arrests for any crime for MTO and Section 8 youth 15 to 20 years old was statistically indistinguishable from the number of arrests for control group youth. This pattern held for the number of specific arrests for violent crimes, general drug crimes, drug distribution, and other types of crime. The exceptions are for property crime and drug possession arrests. MTO youths averaged 0.304 property crime arrests per individual, compared to 0.239 property crime arrests for control group youth—a statistically significant harmful impact of 0.065 additional arrests per individual at the five percent confidence level. The opposite may have occurred for drug possession arrests for Section 8 youth. Section 8 youth averaged 0.083 drug possession arrests per individual, compared to 0.117 drug possession arrests for control group youth—a marginally statistically significant beneficial impact of 0.034 additional arrests per individual at the 10 percent confidence level.

On all measures of crime arrests for grown children 21 to 30 years old, being in either the MT0 or Section 8 group had no impact.[441] In addition

TABLE 4.22. Selected MTO Evaluation Findings for Adults, Grown Children, and Youth on Risky and Criminal Behavior

Risky and Criminal Behavior	Adults		Youth 13 to 20		Youth 15 to 20		Grown Children 21 to 30	
	MTO	Section 8	MTO	Section 8	MTO	Section 8	MTO	Section 8
Risky Behavior								
Risky behavior index	n/a	n/a	0	0	n/a	n/a	n/a	n/a
Ever smoked	n/a	n/a	Neg**	Neg**	n/a	n/a	n/a	n/a
Ever had alcoholic drink	n/a	n/a	0	0	n/a	n/a	n/a	n/a
Ever used marijuana	n/a	n/a	0	0	n/a	n/a	n/a	n/a
Ever had sex	n/a	n/a	0	0	n/a	n/a	n/a	n/a
Behavior problems index	n/a	n/a	0	0	n/a	n/a	n/a	n/a
Delinquency index	n/a	n/a	0	0	n/a	n/a	n/a	n/a
Criminal Behavior								
Number of post-random assignment arrests by crime type								
Any crime arrests	0	0	n/a	n/a	0	0	0	0
Violent crime arrests	0	0	n/a	n/a	0	0	0	0
Property crime arrests	Neg*	0	n/a	n/a	Neg**	0	0	0
Drug crime arrests	0	0	n/a	n/a	0	0	0	0

(continued)

TABLE 4.22. (Continued)

Risky and Criminal Behavior	Adults		Youth 13 to 20		Youth 15 to 20		Grown Children 21 to 30	
	MTO	Section 8	MTO	Section 8	MTO	Section 8	MTO	Section 8
Drug possession arrests	0	0	n/a	n/a	0	Pos*	0	0
Drug distribution arrests	0	0	n/a	n/a	0	0	0	0
Other crime arrests	0	0	n/a	n/a	0	0	0	0
Incarceration: Ever in jail or prison	n/a	n/a	n/a	n/a	n/a	n/a	0	0

Key: 0 Finding was not statistically significant
    Pos Positive or beneficial impact
    Neg Negative or harmful impact
    *   Statistically significant at the 10 percent confidence level ($p \leq 0.10$)
    ** Statistically significant at the 5 percent confidence level ($p \leq 0.05$)
    *** Statistically significant at the 1 percent confidence level ($p \leq 0.01$)
    n/a No measure was assessed or reported
    † No statistically significance test was performed

Source: Lisa Sanbonmatsu, Jens Ludwig, Lawrence F. Katz, Lisa Gennetian, Greg J. Duncan, Ronald C. Kessler, Emma Adam, Thomas W. McDade, Stacy Tessler Lindau, Matthew Sciandra, Fanghua Yang, Ijun Lai, William Congdon, Joe Amick, Ryan Gillette, Michael A. Zabek, Jordon Marvakov, Sabrina Yusuf, and Nicholas A. Potter, *Moving to Opportunity for Fair Housing Demonstration Program: Final Impacts Evaluation* (Washington, DC: U.S. Department of Housing and Urban Development, Office of Policy Development and Research, November 2011), Exhibit 6.5, 196–197; Exhibit 6.6, 198; Exhibit 6.7, 199–200; Exhibit 6.8, 201–202; Exhibit 6.9, 203; Exhibit 6.10, 204; and Supplemental Exhibit 6.1, 206–207.

for this group, the opportunity to participate in MTO and Section 8 vouchers had no statistically measurable impact on incarceration.[442] As for adults, all of the arrest outcomes failed to yield statistically significant results at least at the five percent confidence level.[443] However, there is suggestive evidence that MTO adults had more arrests for property crimes than did similar control group members. On average, MTO adults had 0.176 property crime arrests, compared to 0.133 property crime arrests for control group adults—a marginally statistically significant difference of 0.043 arrests at the 10 percent confidence level.

Long-Term Impacts on School Characteristics and Academic Achievement

Table 4.23 presents a summary of the selected findings for the impact of MTO and Section 8 on school characteristics and academic achievement. The opportunity for families to use MTO and Section 8 vouchers had consistent and long-term beneficial effects on school characteristics.[444] The average schools attended by the 10- to 20-year-old youth in the MTO and Section 8 groups had higher percentages of white students and lower percentages of black and Hispanic students, which is thought to mean the MTO and Section 8 groups attended better schools. Further, the portion of students eligible for free school lunches was lower for the schools attended by MTO and Section 8 youth, compared to the schools attended by control group youth. Perhaps more importantly, the schools attended by MTO and Section 8 youth were more likely to have a state school ranking above the 75th percentile than the schools attended to by the control group. All of the findings for school characteristics were statistically significant at the five percent confidence level. The schools attended by MTO and Section 8 youth did not differ in pupil-teacher ratios compared to the schools attended by youth in the control group.

In spite of the overall beneficial effects on school characteristics, there appear to be few beneficial effects on academic achievement. For youth 13 to 20 years old, the opportunity to participate in MTO and Section 8 vouchers had no statistically measurable impact on reading and math assessments.[445] Further, the opportunity to participate in these programs failed to affect whether these students were educationally on track.

For youth 10 to 20 years old, the opportunity to participate in the MTO and Section 8 programs was associated with a decreased likelihood of taking advanced coursework.[446] For the MTO and Section 8 youths, 86.2 percent

TABLE 4.23. Selected MTO Evaluation Findings for the School Characteristics and Academic Achievement

School Characteristics	Youth 10 to 20		Youth 13 to 20		Youth 15 to 20		Youth 19 to 20		Grown Children 21 to 30	
	MTO	Section 8	MTO	Section 8	MTO	Section 8	MTO	Section 8	MTO	Section 8
Characteristics of the Average School Attended										
Share minority	Pos**	Pos**	n/a	n/a	n/a	n/a	n/a	n/a	n/a	n/a
Share black	Pos**	Pos**	n/a	n/a	n/a	n/a	n/a	n/a	n/a	n/a
Share Hispanic	Pos**	Pos**	n/a	n/a	n/a	n/a	n/a	n/a	n/a	n/a
Share eligible for free lunch	Pos**	Pos**	n/a	n/a	n/a	n/a	n/a	n/a	n/a	n/a
Pupil-teacher ratio	0	0	n/a	n/a	n/a	n/a	n/a	n/a	n/a	n/a
Share school ranking above 75th percentile	Pos**	Pos**	n/a	n/a	n/a	n/a	n/a	n/a	n/a	n/a
Academic Achievement										
Reading assessment score	n/a	n/a	0	0	n/a	n/a	n/a	n/a	n/a	n/a
Math assessment score	n/a	n/a	0	0	n/a	n/a	n/a	n/a	n/a	n/a
Educationally on-track	n/a	n/a	0	0	n/a	n/a	n/a	n/a	n/a	n/a
Earned high school diploma	n/a	n/a	n/a	n/a	n/a	n/a	Neg*	0	n/a	n/a
Advanced coursework	Neg**	Neg**	n/a	n/a	n/a	n/a	n/a	n/a	n/a	n/a
Ever repeated a grade	0	Neg**	n/a	n/a	n/a	n/a	n/a	n/a	n/a	n/a
Took SAT/ACT	n/a	n/a	n/a	n/a	0	Neg*	n/a	n/a	n/a	n/a
Currently Enrolled in Secondary Schooling										
Currently enrolled in secondary school	n/a	n/a	n/a	n/a	n/a	n/a	n/a	n/a	0	0
Has high school diploma	n/a	n/a	n/a	n/a	n/a	n/a	n/a	n/a	0	0

								Pos**
Has high school diploma or GED	n/a	n/a	n/a	n/a	n/a	n/a	n/a	0
College Attendance since 2007								
Any college	n/a	n/a	0	0	n/a	n/a	0	0
2-year college	n/a	n/a	0	0	n/a	n/a	0	0
4-year college	n/a	n/a	0	0	n/a	n/a	0	0

Key: 0 Finding was not statistically significant

Pos Positive or beneficial impact

Neg Negative or harmful impact

* Statistically significant at the 10 percent confidence level ($p \leq 0.10$)

** Statistically significant at the 5 percent confidence level ($p \leq 0.05$)

*** Statistically significant at the 1 percent confidence level ($p \leq 0.01$)

n/a No measure was assessed or reported

† No statistically significance test was performed

Source: Lisa Sanbonmatsu, Jens Ludwig, Lawrence F. Katz, Lisa Gennetian, Greg J. Duncan, Ronald C. Kessler, Emma Adam, Thomas W. McDade, Stacy Tessler Lindau, Matthew Sciandra, Fanghua Yang, Jjun Lai, William Congdon, Joe Amick, Ryan Gillette, Michael A. Zabek, Jordon Marvakov, Sabrina Yusuf, and Nicholas A. Potter, *Moving to Opportunity for Fair Housing Demonstration Program: Final Impacts Evaluation* (Washington, DC: U.S. Department of Housing and Urban Development, Office of Policy Development and Research, November 2011), Exhibit 7.3, 225–227; Exhibit 7.6, 230; Exhibit 7.7, 231–232; Exhibit 7.8, 233–234; Exhibit 7.9, 235–237.

and 84.8 percent, respectively, partook in advanced coursework, while 88.9 percent of the control group youth did the same. The differences of 2.7 percent and 4.1 percent were statistically significant at the five percent confidence level. The opportunity to participate in MTO vouchers had no effect on taking the Scholastic Assessment Test (SAT) or American College Testing (ACT) exam, while there is only suggestive evidence that the opportunity to participate in Section 8 vouchers decreased the likelihood of taking these exams. Less than half (47.8 percent) of the Section 8 youth 15 to 20 years old took one of these exams, compared to 51.8 percent for similar control group youth. However, this difference of four percent is only marginally statistically significant at the less rigorous 10 percent confidence level. On top of these harmful impacts, Section 8 youth were more likely to have repeated a grade than their counterparts in the control group. Of the control group youth, 37.7 percent repeated a grade, compared to 42.5 percent of Section 8 youth—a statistically significant difference of 4.8 percent at the five percent confidence level.

Grown children 21 to 30 years old were assessed on their secondary schooling. The opportunity of grown children to participate in the MTO and Section 8 programs failed to influence current secondary school enrollment and possessing a high school diploma.[447] Compared to the findings for their counterparts in the control group, the MTO grown children were no more likely to possess either a high school degree or GED. In contrast, the Section 8 grown children were more likely to have earned either credential. While 70.7 percent of the control grown children possessed either credential, 76.2 percent of the Section 8 grown children had either credential—a statistically significant difference of 5.5 percent at the five percent confidence level. The evaluation also assessed whether youth 19 to 20 years old had earned high school diplomas. For these youth, 62.2 percent of the control group earned high school diplomas, compared to 54.9 percent for the MTO youth—a marginally significant difference of 7.3 percent at the 10 percent confidence level. There was no meaningful difference for the Section 8 youth.

For attending college since 2007, the opportunities to participate in MTO and Section 8 vouchers failed to impact attending any college, 2-year colleges, and 4-year colleges for youth 15 to 20 years old and grown adults 21 to 30 years old.[448]

According to the authors of the long-term follow-up study, "The MTO findings suggest that housing mobility programs alone are unlikely to be a panacea for the schooling problems and labor market difficulties faced by disadvantaged families living in public housing projects and other high-poverty, inner-city neighborhoods."[449]

Summary

With few exceptions, federal social engineering, whether liberal or conservative, does not work when it comes to attempting to make children and families better. Federal social programs largely fail at improving the academic and cognitive abilities of infants, toddlers, and older children. Overall, these programs do little to move people out of poverty. And forget about becoming economically self-sufficient. These same social programs fail to stop kids from having sex, get couples married, or keep marriages together.

The most notable exception is work-to-welfare. While NEWWS found many beneficial results, neither the employment-focused nor the education-focused approach moved welfare participants into full-time employment over the 5-year follow-up period. While both welfare-to-work approaches yielded beneficial outcomes, on average, the intervention group members were unable to have a majority of their income come from the fruits of their own labor; instead, 5 years after random assignment, they were still heavily dependent on government income transfers.

Chapter 5

Workers

The federal government has dedicated decades to trying to improve the earnings of low-income individuals through various employment and training programs. During fiscal year (FY) 2009, the Government Accountability Office (GAO) identified 47 employment and training programs administered by nine departments of the federal government.[1] Further complicating the matter, the GAO has concluded that there is little evidence that these programs are effective.

In the name of progress, federal employment and training programs have gone through a procession of changes over the years. Originally created during the 1930s, employment and training programs were intended to provide relief from the hardships of capitalism through work initiatives. The programs include the Wagner-Peyser Employment Service (ES), Works Progress Administration (WPA), and Civilian Conservation Corps (CCC).[2] The Wagner-Peyser Act of 1933 created the federal grant-in-aid program that funds state employment services and the ES.[3] Despite the fact that civilian unemployment just prior to World War II was about the same as it was when the ES, WPA, and CCC were created, support for employment and training programs continued to build after the war.[4]

During the 1960s, the federal government established new employment and training programs for people who were unemployed and economically disadvantaged. These programs provided a combination of remedial education, vocational training, on-the-job training, subsidized work experience, basic life-skills training, and job search assistance. Programs funded under the Manpower Development and Training Act (MDTA) of 1962 were originally intended to retrain workers dislocated by technological advances, but the MDTA was converted into a job-training program for economically disadvantaged persons without employable skills.[5]

Created by the Economic Opportunity Act of 1964, the Job Corps is a residential job-training program that serves disadvantaged youths aged 16 to 24 at 125 sites across the nation. While the federal government has overhauled adult employment and training programs about every decade, Job Corps has consistently offered basic education and vocational training to participants over the years.

In 1973, MDTA programs were superseded by the Comprehensive Employment and Training Act (CETA), which was designed to decentralize control of federally sponsored job-training programs.[6] Increased decentralization and improved flexibility of federal employment and training programs, as we will see, is a constant theme of reform. Under CETA, public and nonprofit organizations were responsible for the delivery of services.[7] The most notable aspect of CETA was its Public Service Employment (PSE) program—a political patronage "job creation" program that was a boon to big city mayors. PSE funding allowed big city mayors to dish out jobs to constituents without regard to the value of the work performed. In 1978, PSE provided 725,000 public service jobs.[8] PSE was not only important to the mayors, but the program provided critical support to community organizations that advocated the progressive expansion of government.[9] According to the GAO, few PSE participants acquired permanent, unsubsidized jobs.[10] Instead of using PSE funds to hire the unemployed, "Many of the participants did not come from the rolls of the unemployed but from predecessor programs."[11] The most serious threat to the ability of PSE to create new jobs was "maintenance of effort" violations that occurred when federal funds paid for jobs that would have normally been financed with state and local government funds.[12] Maintenance of effort violations included such practices as using PSE participants to fill vacant full-time, part-time, or temporary positions; to rehire laid-off, former employees; and to fill positions normally contracted out.[13] These violations meant that federal funds were being used to supplant local funds, meaning that the PSE program was not being used to create new jobs, but to fund current jobs. While most PSE participants hoped to find permanent employment, relatively few found jobs not propped up by federal funds.[14] Nearly a decade after CETA's passage, charges of corruption and mismanagement contributed to Congress's decision to replace CETA with the Job Training Partnership Act of 1982 (JTPA).[15]

Passed in 1982, JTPA eliminated PSE and decentralized the administrative structure of CETA to make implementation more flexible. In addition, training under JTPA would be privatized by allowing for-profit vocational schools to receive funding.[16] By introducing federal funding to the private sector, supporters of JTPA thought more effective services would be provided. In addition, JTPA created Private Industry Councils (PICs) that were given the responsibility for planning the employment and training services to be provided in communities.[17] Instead of CETA's government-planned services, JTPA required PICs to be dominated by business leaders—a policy preference that continues today.[18]

According to testimony at congressional hearings, JTPA was intended to help alleviate the shortage of skilled workers that were needed by industry.[19] This "skills gap" has been used for decades to justify the need for federal employment and training programs.[20] Despite claims of a skills gap, the federal government does not systematically collect data on the causes of job vacancies, so the actual number of unfilled positions due to shortages of skilled labor is unknown.[21] If the skills gap is real and caused by a lack of individuals with high-tech skills, then one would assume that employment and training programs as currently implemented should be oriented toward filling the gap.

Continuing the theme of reinventing employment and training programs by increasing flexibility, Congress passed the Workforce Investment Act (WIA) in 1998, which superseded the JTPA. During the signing ceremony, President Bill Clinton asserted that "This is the crowning jewel of a lifetime learning agenda, the Workforce Investment Act to give all our workers opportunities for growth and advancement."[22] In contrast to the JTPA, the WIA emphasizes a "one-stop" approach in which most federally funded employment and training programs provided in an area are located in a single location.[23] The one-stop centers serve as central locations where those seeking job assistance can find referrals for various services, including those not administered by the Labor Department. Approximately, 1,850 one-stop centers operate across the nation.[24] While WIA programs are administered differently, these supposedly new programs offer virtually the same services provided by the JTPA.[25] Despite the asserted need to provide training for "high skilled" jobs, employers primarily use one-stop centers to fill low-skill positions.[26] As such, employers view the labor available from these centers as being predominantly low skilled.[27]

WIA's most significant departure from JTPA is that the act allows for adults to use Individual Training Accounts (ITAs) to obtain employment and training services. Similar to vouchers, ITAs are intended to allow participants to apply consumer choice that will introduce competition to employment and training service providers. Under most circumstances, WIA mandates that adults and dislocated workers eligible for training services must be provided with ITAs that allow them to select their training provider from a list approved by local WIA administrators.[28]

While ITAs are not true vouchers, these accounts increase participant choice compared to previous federal job-training systems. Burt S. Barnow of George Washington University identified four factors that prevent ITAs from becoming true vouchers:

> First, states are required to establish an eligible training provider (ETP) list that includes training programs that meet state requirements for placement rates and wage rates for WIA and all customers. Second, programs are required to fund training for occupations in high demand, and many states restrict training to occupations with high projected growth by federal, state, or local occupational projections. Third, local programs were permitted to establish cost and time limits for their customers using ITAs. Finally, local programs were permitted to use "guided choice" in permitting customers to make use of their ITAs.[29]

Local programs tend to use the guided choice strategy, where customers had the option of choosing between approved training providers.[30] To select their training options, ITA participants use Eligible Training Provider (ETP) lists of state-approved job-training providers that were created by workforce boards.[31] ETPs are comprised of training providers that fulfill reporting requirements (e.g., job placement rates) intended to enhance the decision process of job-training seekers. In addition, ETPs are intended to screen out programs considered ineffective at placing participants in new jobs or that do not provide training for occupations in demand in the local area.[32]

While WIA intended ITAs to be used under most circumstances, local administrators have the option of using different methods for providing training services.[33] However, individuals can receive customized and on-the-job training without the use of ITAs.[34]

According to an analysis of program year (PY) 2001 WIA Standardized Record Data, there appears to be a divergence between workforce boards that extensively use ITAs and those that use the accounts very little.[35] Approximately 20 percent of workforce boards used ITAs for fewer than 20 percent of their trainees, while 40 percent used ITAs heavily, or even exclusively.[36]

Even though ITAs are being used, Gordon Lafer, an associate professor at the University of Oregon's Labor Education and Research Center, contends that adult WIA participants are receiving the same job search assistance, classroom training, on-the-job training, and other services as adults who were involved in the programs that performed inadequately under

JTPA. In addition, WIA requires that state and local governments collect performance data to demonstrate the effectiveness of the programs. Training providers that receive ITA funds for providing services to WIA participants are required to have an established history of positive outcomes that meet or surpass each state's performance criteria.[37] Further, "WIA required states to establish eligible training provider lists (ETPLs) of providers and approved training course offerings that have met and continue to meet the state's performance criteria."[38] By requiring collection of performance measures, Congress anticipated that the Labor Department would hold states responsible for their use of WIA funds. Failing to meet expected performance levels may lead to reduced state funding allocations. Conversely, states that exceed performance expectations may be awarded additional funding.

WIA programs are divided into three block grant programs: WIA Dislocated Workers, WIA Adults, and WIA Youth. Both the WIA Dislocated Workers and Adults programs aim to increase the employment, retention, earnings, and occupational skill attainment of participants.[39] The WIA Dislocated Workers program is reserved for individuals who have lost their jobs as a result of plant closings or mass layoffs, and their return to the same type of occupation or industry is unlikely.

The WIA Adults block grant program is designated for all adults 18 years of age or older. When funding is limited, states are to give priority to those receiving public assistance and individuals considered to have low incomes.[40]

Originally, there were three levels of service for WIA Dislocated Workers and Adults programs. First, the initial core services included brief skills assessment and job search assistance.[41] The services initiated at this stage were generally self-service, meaning that participants were offered information on the local job market, but they were required to take their own initiative in finding employment.[42] Second, if the core services were not successful, then intensive services were provided.[43] Intensive services include detailed skills assessment, training in punctuality, interviewing skills, and case management. Third, remedial education, occupational skills training, and "job readiness" instruction were offered only after the individual has participated in the first two levels of service.[44] In addition, state and local governments were given authority to tailor the content of job-training programs to meet their specific needs. However, the Department of Labor no longer requires job seekers to progress through the sequence of services.[45]

The WIA Youth block grant program is intended to endow young workers with the necessary knowledge and skills to become productive citizens and meet the needs of employers.[46] The WIA Youth program provides funding for such services as tutoring, summer employment, and occupational skills training.

The Workforce Investment Act of 1998 mandated a large-scale, multisite evaluation of the Department of Labor's job-training programs and required the department to report the results by September 2005. Despite this mandate and deadline, the Department of Labor under the William J. Clinton and George W. Bush administrations procrastinated over performing the evaluation.[47] In November 2007, nine years after the passage of the WIA and more than two years after the deadline, the department finally submitted a request for proposals for the evaluation.[48] The contract for the experimental evaluation was awarded in June 2008, almost four years after the deadline.[49] According to the GAO, the evaluation will not be completed until June 2015—nearly 10 years after its original due date and 17 years after Congress mandated the evaluation.[50]

The delay in conducting the large-scale, multisite experimental evaluation means that Congress faces considerable uncertainty about the effectiveness of WIA programs. The absence of rigorous scientific results means that there has been no reliable assessment of WIA, the system of "one-stop" employment service centers it created, and the ITAs. This is especially important because the House of Representatives Committee on Education and the Workforce in June 2012 reported out of committee the Workforce Investment Improvement Act of 2012 (H.R. 4297). In the Senate, the Committee on Health, Education, Labor, and Pensions has drafted reauthorization legislation but has not reported the legislation out of committee at the time the writing of the manuscript for this book was completed. Without being able to identify what works with WIA, Congress's attempts to reauthorize WIA require legislating in the dark.

This point brings us to the issue of repeated efforts by Congress to reform federal employment and training programs. For decades, members of Congress have claimed to have reformed the previously flawed federal job-training system with new legislation. This bravado continues today. Commenting on passage of the Workforce Investment Improvement Act of 2012 (H.R. 4297) out of the House of Representatives Committee on Education and the Workforce, Chairman John Kline (R-MN) asserted, "I am pleased the committee has taken definitive action to fix the nation's broken job training system and help more Americans attain the skills and education they need to find a job."[51]

During an April 2012 hearing on H.R. 4297, Chairman Kline stated, "The legislation will provide a more dynamic, effective, and accountable workforce development system."[52] According to hearing witness Norma Noble of the Oklahoma Governor's Council for Workforce and Economic Development, "Without bold reforms to WIA, such as program and funding consolidation, our workforce system will fall further and further behind in our ability to equip American workers with the skills necessary to remain competitive in the global economy."[53] "In closing," Noble concluded, "the Workforce Investment Act, at its core, is about jobs. If there was ever a time for a 'must pass' piece of legislation, now would be that time to fix America's workforce system and get America back to work."[54]

Even more optimistic, Representative Howard "Buck" McKeon (R-CA) professed:

> I consider the reauthorization of WIA to be one of the most pressing items on the committee's agenda and see it as an integral step to rebuilding our changing economy and getting Americans back to work. American workers looking to sharpen their skills and keep up with the changing economy don't see WIA as a partisan, political issue. They see WIA as an opportunity to protect their livelihoods. House Republicans understand the urgency and are working to reauthorize the law in the 112th Congress.[55]

Despite these confident proclamations, are Department of Labor employment and training programs effective? One would naturally think so based on these statements. However, numerous large-scale multisite experimental evaluations strongly suggest that federal job-training programs are mostly ineffective. Before we cover the evaluation literature, we need to understand WIA's performance monitoring system because it is often used to assert that WIA programs are effective.

WIA Performance Monitoring System

As a management tool, performance monitoring systems monitor the implementation of programs on a real-time basis.[56] While WIA's performance monitoring system may collect some useful information, "it suffers from shortcomings," according to Diane Blank of the GAO and her coauthors, "that may limit its usefulness in understanding the full reach of the system and may lead to disincentives to serve those who may most need services."[57] Furthermore, "little is known about what the system is achieving."[58] The dilemma facing the performance monitoring system is how to reward local WIA administrators for successful outcomes without establishing an incentive for administrators to help only job seekers that are the most likely to succeed.[59] WIA participants that receive only self-service and informational services are not included in the performance measure system.[60] A large majority of WIA participants do not receive any assistance beyond self-service and informational services. Therefore, only a small share of participants that are offered more advanced services are included in the performance monitoring system.

First, performance monitoring does not measure program impacts. WIA mandated the collection of before and after earning data to estimate the change in income for performance measurement.[61] Thus, the U.S. Department of Labor created the Workforce Investment Act Standardized Record Data (WIASRD) system to monitor the performance of local programs.

When it comes to the performance measures already established by the Department of Labor, the data indicate "outcomes" only of participants in job-training programs. Thus, these outcomes should not be confused with program "impacts." Program impacts are assessed by comparing outcomes for program participants with estimates of what the outcomes would have been had the participants not partaken in the program. Instead of using a control group, the Department of Labor's assessment is made by comparing the before-and-after intervention incomes of job training participants. The resulting change in income is often considered an outcome of job training participation. However, using such performance monitoring data to conclude that the changes in income are the result of job training participation has low internal validity.

Did, in fact, the job training make a difference in this specific instance? To establish internal validity, some kind of control condition is required in order to determine what would have happened to the intervention group had they not received the intervention. The lack of a control group means that internal validity is a hazard to the ability of performance monitoring being used to make causal inferences about the impact of job training participation.

Second, the likelihood of a "pre-program dip" is another problem that complicates the usefulness of job-training performance monitoring systems when pre–job-training income is compared to post–job-training income. This problem occurs because individuals frequently undergo a pre–job-training dip in income before seeking assistance. A loss of income leads people to seek job training. This preprogram dip in income may cause any comparisons without a valid control group to overstate the effectiveness of job training.

Consider the following example. In $year_{t-1}$, potential job-training participants may have experienced temporary declines in income that caused them to seek services. After participating in job-training activities, the participants' incomes in $year_t$ may have increased; however, their income at $year_t$ may have returned to the income levels of $year_{t-2}$ before the temporary dip. Comparing incomes from $year_t$ and $year_{t-1}$ will lead the performance monitoring system to make false conclusions about the impact of job training on the incomes of participants.

Third, the process of setting standards for the WIA performance monitoring system is flawed. Under the current system, standards are set for state and local areas through negotiations with the Department of Labor, rather than the regression modeling that was used previously under JTPA.[62] Because the WIA performance standards are not adjusted by a regression model that controls for local demographics and conditions, programs are not held harmless for the populations they serve.[63] Thus, serving less disadvantaged individuals (or those most likely to succeed) may be preferred by local administrators to increase the likelihood of passing performance standards. In effect, this system provides an incentive for "cream skimming."

Fourth, the effect of cream skimming can make the results of the performance monitoring system to overstate the effectiveness of WIA programs. Through gaming the system, local administrators can engage in strategic decision making by officially enrolling WIA participants after the participants have found employment.[64] Burt S. Barnow and Jeffrey A. Smith, a professor of economics at the University of Michigan, found that local JTPA administrators engaged in strategic behavior by manipulating whether participants were formally enrolled and thus recorded in the performance monitoring system.[65] Under the JTPA performance system, only individuals officially enrolled in JTPA programs were counted toward performance standards.[66] For instance, some local administrators increased reported performance by providing job search assistance without officially registering those engaged in job search assistance. If an unregistered participant gained employment, the individual would then be officially enrolled and counted as a success.

The dilemma facing the performance monitoring system is how to reward local WIA administrators for successful outcomes without establishing an incentive for administrators to help only job seekers that the most likely to succeed.[67] Performance management systems can cause local program administrators to select job-training participants based on their perceived likelihood of success on performance measures.[68] WIA participants that receive only self-service and informational services are not included in the performance measure system.[69] A large majority of WIA participants do not receive any assistance beyond self-service and informational services. Therefore, only a small share of participants, those who are offered more advanced services, are included in the performance monitoring system.

Does the presence of a performance monitoring system influence job-training program impacts? Data from the national Job Training Partnership Act (JTPA) evaluation have been used to test the relationship between performance measures and actual program impacts. One study found that short-term performance measures were poor indicators of long-term earning impact.[70]

The literature on performance monitoring with regard to federal job-training programs indicates two potential problems for how local administrators respond to performance standards. First, performance monitoring affects who gets provided services because of the incentive for cream skimming. Second, local administrators can respond to performance monitoring by gaming the system.

Under JTPA, local administrators had robust incentives to select individuals most likely to have positive labor market results, regardless of whether those results were due to JTPA participation.[71] Barnow and Smith argue that even with the requirement that before-and-after performance measures be collected, WIA's performance standards still provide local administrators with the incentive to carefully select participants based on anticipated positive employment outcomes.[72] Because of the non–regression-adjusted performance standards, local WIA administrators may have even more of an incentive to serve those most likely to appear to benefit from job-training services.[73]

According to the GAO, the performance data from the vast majority of individuals participating in services provided at one-stop service centers are not recorded in the WIASRD system.[74] In addition, the GAO found local program administrators often decide to record in the WIASRD system only those who can help them meet their performance targets.[75]

Under JTPA, Kathryn Anderson, a professor of economics at Vanderbilt University, and her colleagues found evidence of cream skimming.[76] They found that the placement rate of participants into jobs in Tennessee of

70.7 percent would drop to 61.6 percent if JTPA job-training participants were randomly selected from the economically disadvantaged eligible for participation.[77] This finding is a result of the underrepresentation of women, blacks, high school dropouts, Supplemental Security Income recipients, urban residents, and older workers.

Barnow and Smith concluded that the "literature provides modest evidence that program staff responded to the incentives provided by the JTPA performance standards system to choose participants likely to improve their measured performance whether or not they benefited from program services."[78]

The Effectiveness of ITAs

According to Christopher King of the University of Texas at Austin and Burt S. Barnow, the evidence for vouchers benefiting disadvantaged populations is mixed.[79] For example, consider the Seattle-Denver Income Maintenance Experiments (SIME/DIME) that were conducted from 1970 to 1977.[80] SIME/DIME was a negative income tax (NIT) program that assessed a variety of income guarantees and tax rates on a host of outcome measures for low-income households. SIME/DIME underwent an experimental evaluation to determine the projects' effectiveness.

Demonstrating the law of unintended consequences, the NIT was found to reduce the employment and marriage rates of participants.[81] While SIME/DIME is mainly known as a NIT experiment, the project also provided career counseling and job training to low-income households. Participants were randomly divided into four counseling/training groups:

1. No counseling or training (control group)
2. Free, nondirected, vocational counseling provided by community colleges
3. Free, nondirected, vocational counseling plus 50 percent tuition subsidy at any institution chosen by the participant
4. Free, nondirected, vocational counseling plus a 100 percent tuition subsidy at any institution chosen by the participant[82]

The education and training subsidies provided for groups three and four can be considered vouchers.[83] The subsidies could be used for any education or training course that was intended to prepare the participants for an occupation or career.[84] The liberal use of the subsidies led to participants seeking a broad array of services, including courses for education degrees (GED, associate, bachelor, and graduate degrees), registered nursing degrees, skills upgrades, trade apprentices, and occupational licenses.[85]

Over half the participants sought education and training from community colleges.[86]

The impact of the counseling and training was tracked up to six years after random assignment. The experimental evaluation found that compared to the control group, the counseling-only, 50 percent tuition subsidy, and 100 percent tuition subsidy treatment groups failed to experience increases in earnings and hours worked.[87] However, the evaluations did not disentangle the effect of the NIT rates from the counseling/training effects, so the true impact of training vouchers is difficult to obtain.

As previously mentioned, there are no published scientifically rigorous experimental impact evaluations indicating that WIA programs, including ITAs, are effective at improving employment outcomes. Instead of performing the congressionally mandated experimental evaluation of WIA, the Department of Labor did perform two less rigorous evaluations that shed some light on the performance of WIA. The first evaluation, by Mathematica Policy Research, was a randomized experiment comparing the outcomes for three ITA approaches without a true control group serving as a counterfactual condition.[88] The evaluation took place at seven sites:

- Phoenix, Arizona
- Maricopa County, Arizona
- Bridgeport, Connecticut
- Jacksonville, Florida
- Atlanta, Georgia
- Northeast Georgia
- North Cook County, Illinois[89]

ITA participants were randomly divided into three groups that were offered varying degrees of service. However, the evaluation did not use a control group that did not receive any WIA services. Thus, the evaluation does not provide policymakers with valid estimates of the effectiveness of WIA. The absence of a control group means that this evaluation has no scientific value in determining the actual effectiveness of ITAs.

The first group received the "Structured Consumer Choice" approach, where participants underwent intensive career counseling and were steered toward training programs thought by workforce boards to yield high returns.[90] While participants had some control over the selection of training options, local administrators could veto the participants' choice. The dollar amount of ITAs was the highest for the first approach and could be as high as $8,000 at most sites. The average dollar value for this ITA approach was $4,647.[91] However, local administrators were reluctant to veto participant choices when the individual selected programs not considered having high enough yielding returns.

The second group received the "Guided Customer Choice" approach, where participants were provided counseling that was less intensive than under the first approach.[92] A local administrator could not reject the training program selected by an individual as long as the program was listed as a state-approved provider. ITAs under the second approach were fixed between $3,000 and $5,000, with an average of $3,608.[93]

For the third approach, "Maximum Customer Choice," counseling by local administrators was not required, and a local administrator could not reject the training program selected by an individual as long as the program was listed as a state-approved provider.[94] ITAs under the third approach were fixed between $3,000 and $5,000, with an average of $3,579.[95]

Participants were tracked over 15 months. Compared to each other, the three ITA approaches had few statistically significant effects on employment rates, weeks worked, and earnings.[96] For example, in quarter 1, Structured Choice participants had an employment rate of 32 percent, compared to a 27 percent employment rate for Maximum Choice participants—a statistically significant difference of five percent at the one percent confidence level.[97] However, employment rates for the Structured Choice and Maximum Choice participants were statistically indistinguishable from each other in quarters two through five and for the overall employment rate from the combined period of quarters one through five. When employment rates were measured using state Unemployment Insurance records, the results for three ITA approach comparisons were even less favorable.[98]

The ITA evaluation collected earnings outcomes based on survey data and state Unemployment Insurance wage records. Based on standard levels of statistical significance and survey data, the three ITA approaches failed to yield higher earnings, compared to each other, during the entire 15-month (five quarters) follow-up period.[99] However, the authors of the evaluation reported a statistically significant outcome at the less rigorous 10 percent significance level for the comparison between Structured Choice and Maximum Choice participants. Structured Choice participants earned $1,308 more than those in the Maximum Choice group.[100]

The earnings outcomes based on state Unemployment Insurance wage records produced different results. Based on standard levels of statistical significance, Guided Choice participants earned $1,207 more in earnings over the 15-month follow-up period compared to the earnings of Maximum Choice participants.[101] The other differences between the approaches failed to be statistically different from no impact.

Compared to each other, the three approaches did not have any statistically significant impacts on the percentage of individuals receiving Unemployment Insurance (UI) benefits and the number of weeks of UI benefits received.[102] However, Maximum Choice participants received, on average, $217 more in UI benefits than Structured Choice participants.[103] This finding is statistically significant at the five percent confidence level. The other comparisons failed to yield statistically significant differences.

ITA participants appear to be satisfied with their training options and services received. For the Structured Choice ITAs, 72 percent of participants reported being "satisfied" with the training options offered.[104] For the Guided Choice and Maximum Choice ITAs, 71 percent and 66 percent of participants reported being "satisfied" with the training options offered, respectively.[105]

Large majorities of individuals participating in the three ITA approaches reported being satisfied with the training services provided to them. For the Structured Choice ITAs, 82 percent of participants reported being "very satisfied" or "satisfied" with the training services provided.[106] For the Guided Choice and Maximum Choice ITAs, 81 percent of participants in both groups reported being "very satisfied" or "satisfied" with the training services provided.[107]

Mathematica Policy Research performed a long-term follow-up survey that analyzed the ITA outcomes six to eight years after random assignment.[108] Compared to each other, the three ITA approaches did not affect labor force participation rates, how much participants worked, and average hours worked per quarter over the long-term follow-up period.[109] There appears to be some difficulty in matching ITA participants to occupations they trained for. For the long-term follow-up period, only 42 percent of Structured Choice participants, 38 percent of Guided Choice participants, and 42 percent of Maximum Choice participants were employed in the field relevant to the training they received.[110] Thus, a solid majority of trainees failed to find jobs in the occupations they trained for. However, the average quarterly earnings of Structured Choice participants of $6,592 were statistically greater than the average quarterly earnings of Guided Choice participants at $6,152—a statistically significant difference of $440 at the five percent confidence level.[111] Other comparisons yielded differences that were statistically indistinguishable from zero. When UI administrative records were used, none of the ITA approaches yielded statistically significant differences in quarterly earnings.[112]

The ITA approach had little to no effect on the receipt of UI and welfare benefits. Differences in the receipt of UI benefits were statistically indistinguishable from zero.[113] In general, there were no differences in the receipt of food stamps or other types of welfare-related cash assistance, with one exception. Maximum Choice participants reported that their households received cash assistance benefits for 0.3 months longer than Guided Choice participants.[114] This difference was statistically significant at the less rigorous 10 percent confidence level.

The second WIA evaluation, by Impaq International, used a nonexperimental design that employed a propensity score analysis to estimate the effects of participating in WIA over 16 quarters (four years).[115] The Impaq International evaluation estimated the overall effect of participating in WIA, so the analysis did not estimate the impact of ITAs. However, most WIA participants that received training used ITAs.[116] Overall, both females and males participating in any WIA service (core, intensive, or training services) provided by the Adult and Dislocated Workers Programs experienced increases in earnings compared to the comparison groups. However, the results were not consistent for WIA training participants.

In particular, the Impaq International evaluation compared the earnings outcomes of WIA training participants, most of whom used ITAs, to WIA Core/Intensive services participants. Females participating in the Adult Program experienced consistently higher quarterly earnings than their counterparts.[117] By the end of the 10th quarter, female WIA training participants were earning $800 more than their counterparts—a statistically significant difference at the five percent confidence level.[118] For males, the earnings increases were lower and less consistent.[119] However, by the end of 10 quarters, male WIA training participants were earning about $600 more than their counterparts—a statistically significant difference at the five percent confidence level.[120]

The estimated earnings impacts for females and males participating in the Dislocated Workers Program found no positive effect on earnings over 16 quarters.[121] Dislocated females and males participating in WIA training failed to have earnings that were statistically distinguishable from their comparison groups, suggesting that training had no effect.[122]

Given the Department of Labor's reluctance to use experimental evaluation designs that use control groups to determine the effectiveness of

WIA programs, the results of the Mathematica Policy Research ITA evaluation without a control group and the Impaq International propensity score evaluation need to be interpreted with caution. Without a control group, the Mathematica study has little scientific value for determining the actual effectiveness of ITA. The authors offer the following acknowledgement:

> Because the customers who entered training are not a random sample of all customers—and, in particular, entering training at all may be affected by which model a customer was assigned—we cannot interpret differences across models in the outcomes of this group as the "impact" of the model. We call these differences *conditional*—since they are conditional on an outcome measure—and do not interpret the results as implying a causal relationship.[123]

While the propensity score analysis used by Impaq International may be stronger than many other quasi-experimental evaluation designs, the results may still be biased toward finding positive effects when none actually exist. The authors acknowledge that they cannot rule out the possibility that the pattern of positive findings "results from selection into the program, in which counselors admit applications who have better job prospects, or selection into training, whereby those with immediate job opportunities forgo training. In this case, earnings impact estimates would not reflect program effects but rather selection by counselors or participants."[124] The forthcoming experimental impact evaluation of WIA should yield more valid results than these less rigorous studies.

The following sections will review the findings of five large-scale, multisite experimental evaluations of federal job-training programs and two smaller multisite evaluations of demonstration programs. Demonstrations are usually new programs thought to be innovative that are evaluated before adoption on a wider scale. Employment and training programs focused on both adults and youth will be covered first. Afterward, programs focusing solely on adults will be covered. Last, programs that serve youth and young adults will be reviewed.

Combined Adult and Youth Employment and Training Evaluation

The National JTPA Study

Conducted at 16 sites across the nation during the late 1980s and early 1990s, the Job Training Partnership Act (JTPA) evaluation tracked program effects for over 20,000 adult men and women, and male and female out-of-school youths, over the course of 30 months (five years).[125] This evaluation is truly a large-scale, multisite experimental evaluation that assesses the effectiveness of federal employment and training programs on a national scale.

Three types of job-training activities were examined. The first, classroom training, consisted mainly of occupational skills instruction and basic education.[126] The second intervention was a combination of on-the-job training and job-search assistance.[127] The third type of training, "other services," offered different services to participants on the basis of their age.

Adults mainly received job-search assistance, customized occupational-skills training, and on-the-job training.[128] Youths were enrolled in basic education courses along with "tryout employment," where participants were hired on a probationary status to learn the job, and "job shadowing," where they observed regular employees during the workday.[129]

Table 5.1 summarizes the selected findings of the JTPA evaluation. While the JTPA evaluation assessed program impact on numerous outcomes, the most important findings are summarized in Table 5.1 and discussed in the following text. The effects of JTPA are indicated with the following classifications:

- 0   Finding was not statistically significant
- Pos   Positive or beneficial impact
- Neg   Negative or harmful impact
- *   Marginally statistically significant at the 10 percent confidence level $(p \leq 0.10)$
- **   Statistically significant at the five percent confidence level $(p \leq 0.05)$
- ***   Statistically significant at the one percent confidence level $(p \leq 0.01)$
- n/a   No measure was assessed or reported
- †   No statistical significance test was performed

A indicator of 0 means that the program failed to have a statistically measurable impact on a particular outcome measure. A Pos** indicator means that the program had a statistically significant impact at the five percent confidence level, which is considered to be a beneficial result. A Neg*** indicates a harmful finding at the one percent confidence level. Subsequent tables use the same format.

Effect on Education.   Participation in JTPA programs appears to be associated with obtaining a GED or high school diploma for adult women, while training had no effect on educational attainment of adult men. At the

TABLE 5.1. The Effectiveness of JTPA: Selected Findings

Outcome	Adult Women	Adult Men	Female Youths	Male Youth Nonarrestees	Male Youth Arrestees
Education					
GED or high school diploma 30 months after random assignment	Pos**	0	Pos*	0	0
Welfare Dependency					
Receipt of AFDC benefits 30 months after random assignment	0	Neg**	0	0	0
Receipt of food stamp benefits 30 months after random assignment	0	0	0	0	0
Income					
Months 1 to 6	Pos*	0	0	0	n/a
Months 7 to 18	Pos***	0	0	0	n/a
Months 19 to 30	Pos***	Pos**	0	0	n/a
Total	Pos***	Pos*	0	0	Neg**
Income by Training Type					
Classroom Training					
Months 1 to 6	0	0	Neg*	0	n/a
Months 7 to 18	0	0	0	0	n/a
Months 19 to 30	0	0	0	0	n/a
Total	0	0	0	0	n/a
OJT/JSA					
Months 1 to 6	Pos***	0	Pos**	0	n/a
Months 7 to 18	Pos*	0	0	0	n/a

(continued)

TABLE 5.1. (Continued)

Outcome	Adult Women	Adult Men	Female Youths	Male Youth Nonarrestees	Male Youth Arrestees
Months 19 to 30	Pos*	Pos*	0	0	n/a
Total	Pos**	0	0	0	n/a
Other Services					
Months 1 to 6	Pos**	0	0	0	n/a
Months 7 to 18	Pos***	0	0	0	n/a
Months 19 to 30	Pos***	0	0	0	n/a
Total	Pos***	0	0	0	n/a
Hours Worked					
Hours worked, 30 months	Pos***	0	n/a	n/a	n/a
Criminal Activity					
Arrested, 21 months	n/a	n/a	0	Neg**	0
Arrested, 36 months	n/a	n/a	0	Neg**	0

Key: 0 Finding was not statistically significant
Pos Positive or beneficial impact
Neg Negative or harmful impact
*   Statistically significant at the 10 percent confidence level ($p \leq 0.10$)
**   Statistically significant at the 5 percent confidence level ($p \leq 0.05$)
*** Statistically significant at the 1 percent confidence level ($p \leq 0.01$)
n/a No measure was assessed or reported
†   No statistically significance test was performed

Source: Larry L. Orr, Howard S. Bloom, Stephen H. Bell, Fred Doolittle, Winston Lin, and George Cave, *Does Training for the Disadvantaged Work?* (Washington, DC: Urban Institute Press, 1996), Exhibit 4.8, 111; Exhibit 4.18, 127; Exhibit 4.9, 112; Exhibit 129; Exhibit 4.10, 113; Exhibit 4.20, 130; Exhibit 4.4, 103; Exhibit 4.15, 121; Exhibit 5.7, 153; Exhibit 5.17, 178; Exhibit 4.22, 132.

30-month mark, 32 percent of adult female participants earned a GED or high school diploma, compared to 20.4 percent for adult female control group members.[130] The positive impact of 11.6 percent was statistically significant at the five percent confidence level. Adult male participants had a rate of 24.2 percent, while the rate for similar control group members was 16.3 percent.[131] The difference of 7.9 percent was statistically indistinguishable from zero.

The education findings for youths were reported for female youths, male youth nonarrestees (no history of arrest before random assignment), and male youth arrestees (a history of arrest prior to random assignment). Participation in JTPA may have increased the educational attainment of female youth, and may have failed to affect the educational attainment of male youth nonarrestees and arrestees. At the 30-month mark, 39.4 percent of the female youth JTPA participants earned a GED or high school diploma, compared to 31.7 percent for the female youth members of the control group.[132] The beneficial impact of 7.7 percent was marginally statistically significant at the 10 percent confidence level. Participation in JTPA failed to have statistically significant impacts on the receipt of GEDs or high school diplomas for male youth nonarrestees and arrestees.

Effect on Welfare Dependency.   While participation in JTPA appears to have had no effect on the welfare dependency of adult women, JTPA is associated with the increased dependency of adult men. The following findings are based on the 30-month follow-up period and include individuals who received no benefits during the period. Adult women averaged $1,972 in AFDC benefits, while adult women control group members averaged $2,049—a statistically indistinguishable difference of $77.[133] Participation in JTPA for adult men had an average impact of an additional $100 of AFDC benefits, with intervention and control group members averaging $258 and $158, respectively.[134] The difference of $100 is statistically significant at the five percent confidence level. For the receipt of food stamps, participation in JTPA had no effect on the level of benefits received for adult women and men.[135]

For female youths, male youth nonarrestees, and male youth arrestees, participation in JTPA had no effect on the level of AFDC or food stamp benefits received over the 30-month follow-up period.[136]

Effect on Income.   Members of the intervention and control groups were tracked over 30 months, and results were reported for three periods:

months one to six, months seven to 18, and months 19 to 30.[137] In addition to these three periods, the effects for the entire 30-month period are reported as well. Women tended to fare better than men. During months one to six, adult women JTPA participants earned $2,060, while adult women control group members earned $1,951—a marginally statistically significant increase of $109 at the confidence level of 10 percent.[138] For months seven to 18 and 19 to 30, adult women participants averaged $525 and $542 more in income, compared to adult women control group members, respectively.[139] These differences were statistically significant at the one percent confidence level. Over the entire 30-month period, adult female participants earned a total income of $13,417, compared to $12,241 for adult female control group members.[140] Thus, the participation of adult females in JTPA training programs was associated with an increase of $1,176, which was statistically significant at the one percent confidence level. If this finding was parceled out of 30 months, then adult female JTPA participants earned about $39 more per month than adult female control group members.

While the effects for women were, at best, small, the findings for men were even less impressive. During months one to six, adult male JTPA participants earned $3,351, while adult male control group members earned $3,226—an increase of $125 that is statistically indistinguishable from zero.[141] For months seven to 18 and 19 to 30, adult male participants averaged $329 and $524 more in income, compared to adult male control group members, respectively.[142] The difference of $329 for months seven to 18 was statistically insignificant, while the difference of $524 during months 19 to 30 was statistically significant at the five percent confidence level. Over the entire 30-month period, adult male participants earned a total income of $19,474, compared to $18,496 for adult male control group members.[143] Thus, the participation of adult males in JTPA training programs was associated with an increase of $978 that was statistically significant at the less rigorous 10 percent confidence level. If this finding was parceled out of 30 months, then adult male JTPA participants earned $33 more per month than adult male control group members.

Over the course of the three follow-up periods of one to 6, seven to 18, and 19 to 30 months, participation in JTPA failed to have a statistically significant impact on the incomes of female youths and male youth nonarrestees.[144] However, participation in JTPA did have a negative impact on the incomes of male youth arrestees. Male youth arrestees in the intervention group averaged $14,633 in income over the 30-month period, while similar members of the control group averaged $18,842—a statistically significant decrease of $4,209 at the five percent confidence level.[145]

In addition, the JTPA evaluation broke down the results by type of training received—classroom training, on-the-job training/job search assistance, and "other services." Classroom training for adult men and women failed to raise the incomes of participants over the course of 30 months, and the other JTPA interventions—on-the-job training and other services—failed to raise the incomes of adult male participants.[146]

Although, initially, the incomes of adult women participating in on-the-job training/job search assistance increased by an average of $484 (about $81 per month) and was statistically significant at the one percent confidence level, this impact was fleeting.[147] During the subsequent measurement periods of months seven to 18 and 19 to 30, the incomes of the women who received this type of training increased by $787 and $1,021, respectively. However, these findings are marginally statistically significant at the 10 percent confidence level. Over the 30-month follow-up period, adult women JTPA participants earned $2,292 more than the earnings of similarly situated control group members—a difference that is statistically significant at the five percent confidence level. Thus, adult women JTPA participants earned about $76 more per month compared to their counterparts.

Only the effect on the income of women in the "other services" category was positive and lasting. Women participants earned, on average, $478 more than nonparticipants during the first six months (statistically significant at the five percent confidence level), while the impact increased to over $1,700 during the two subsequent time periods (statistically significant at the one percent confidence level).[148] Over the 30-month follow-up period, adult women JTPA participants in "other services" earned $3,949 more than similarly situated control group members—a difference that is statistically significant at the one percent confidence level. Thus, adult women JTPA partaking in "other services" earned about $132 more per month compared to their counterparts.

As for adult males, participation in any form of training failed to have an effect on earnings during the various follow-up periods, except for one case. Adult males participating in on-the-job training/job search assistance experienced an increase in earnings of $1,125 during the months seven to 18 follow-up period, compared to their counterparts.[149] However, this finding is statistically significant at the less rigorous 10 percent confidence level.

In general, JTPA training by type had no significant positive impact on the incomes of female and male youths. Of the three intervention types, female youths participating in classroom training and on-the-job training/job search assistance experienced income increases during the first six months.[150] Statistically significant at the five percent confidence level, the average income increase of $762 during the first time period faded away during the remaining 24-month follow-up period.[151] The finding for classroom training of an additional $762 was marginally statistically significant at the confidence level of 10 percent. For male youth nonarrestees, the three types of intervention had no impact on income.[152] The results for male youth arrestees were not presented.

In sum, JTPA programs were largely ineffective in raising the incomes of adult males as well as male and female youths. Only the "other services" elements appear to have had a sustainable impact on adult women.

JTPA's Effect on Hourly Wages.

A program's effect on participants' hourly wages is an important indicator in any evaluation of job-training programs. Human capital theory suggests that if job-training programs do, in fact, increase the skills of participants, then employers would be willing to pay program graduates higher hourly wages in return for increased productivity. The JTPA programs had a negligible effect on the wages of adult men and women (hourly wages of youths were not measured).[153] Over the 30-month period, the hourly wages of adult men and women increased by 2.2 percent and 2.7 percent, respectively. However, the authors of the evaluation downplay the finding because the wage analysis does not include unemployed individuals.[154] The small increase may reflect the characteristics of participants who were already more likely to succeed, rather than being a result of JTPA programs. If the wage results include unemployed individuals with a zero for their hourly wages, then the outcome would have been considerable smaller. Nevertheless, this small finding indicates that, in the opinion of employers, JTPA did little to increase the skills of participants.

A question may arise regarding how the incomes of some adult women in certain programs increased in comparison to the control group if their wages barely increased. This contradiction may be explained by the fact that adult women participants worked more hours than adult women in the control group.[155] For adult women and men, JTPA appears to be ineffective in boosting the skills of participants to a level that would allow them to secure higher-paying jobs.

Impact on Arrest Rates.   To measure the impact of JTPA participation on criminality, the arrest rates for the intervention and control group members were taken at approximately 21 months and 36 months after random assignment.[156] During the 21-month follow-up period, participation in JTPA had no effect on the arrest rates for female youths and male youth arrestees. However, participation in JTPA is associated with an increase in criminality for male youth nonarrestees. During this time period, male youth nonarrestees in the intervention group had an arrest rate of 14.1 percent, compared to the 9.6 percent arrest rate for similarly situated control group members.[157] The increase of 4.5 percent is statistically significant at the five percent confidence level. This result is an important reminder that social programs can produce harmful effects.

The same pattern held for the 36-month follow-up period. Participation in JTPA had no effect on the arrest rates of female youths and male youth arrestees, while the program appears to have increased the criminality of male youth nonarrestees. Male youth nonarrestees in the intervention group had an arrest rate of 25.8 percent, compared to the 18.7 percent arrest rate for similarly situated control group members.[158] The increase of 7.1 percent is statistically significant at the five percent confidence level.

Overall, the performance of JTPA programs is widely considered to be a failure. While the effects for adult females had several positive outcomes, the results were generally not large enough to be considered very meaningful. Further, JTPA programs were largely ineffective in raising the incomes of adult males or male and female youths. In some cases, JTPA programs produced harmful effects. For JTPA participants, male youth nonarrestees were more likely to be arrested, and male youth arrestees experienced a decline in income.

Adult Employment and Training Evaluation

The multisite experimental impact evaluation of employment and training programs specifically targeting adults are the Unemployment Insurance (UI) Self-Employment Demonstrations and Project GATE (Growing America through Entrepreneurship).

Unemployment Insurance (UI) Self-Employment Demonstrations

Enacted in 1993, the North American Free Trade Agreement (NAFTA) Implementation Act authorized states to create self-employment assistance (SEA) programs for unemployed workers. To assess the effectiveness of these SEA programs, the U.S. Department of Labor sponsored the Unemployment Insurance (UI) Self-Employment Demonstrations. These demonstrations consisted of two experimental impact evaluations of the Washington State Self-Employment and Enterprise Development (SEED) Project, operating at six sites, and the Massachusetts Enterprise Project, operating at seven sites.[159] For the Washington SEED demonstration, 755 new UI claimants were assigned to the intervention group, and 752 new claimants were assigned to the control group. As for the Massachusetts Enterprise Project, 614 and 608 new UI claimants were assigned to the intervention and control groups, respectively.

Both of these demonstration evaluations occurred in single, yet separate, states. While these dual evaluations do not fully meet the criteria for being considered large-scale evaluations, the programs are included because they were conducted at multiple sites within their respective states. In addition, these demonstration programs are included because their results are more positive relative to the other evaluations of employment and training programs reviewed in this chapter.

For each state, eligible unemployed individuals were randomly assigned to intervention and control groups. All members of the intervention and control groups were eligible for regular UI benefits. In contrast to the Washington program, the Massachusetts program was reserved for UI participants judged most likely to exhaust their UI benefits.[160]

In addition to their regular UI benefits, participants in both programs were eligible to receive periodic self-employment assistance payments.[161] As the participants in the Washington State program developed their businesses, they were eligible to receive their remaining available UI benefits in a single lump-sum payment as an incentive to quickly find employment.[162]

The training services provided to the intervention groups included business start-up and financial assistance to aid participants in becoming self-employed.[163] Under the Massachusetts Enterprise Project, participants attended a one-day training seminar provided by business experts. Over the course of a few weeks, they were also required to attend an individualized counseling session and several workshops on varying business topics. While participants were trying to become entrepreneurs, they were not required to perform the required job-search requirements of normal UI beneficiaries. In contrast, the Washington State SEED Project participants received all of their four counseling sessions over the course of one week. If SEED Project participants achieved five milestones, then they were eligible to receive a lump-sum payment equal to their remaining UI benefits. These milestones were:

- Training session completion
- Development of an satisfactory business plan
- Creation of a business bank account
- Complying with all licensing requirements
- Acquiring adequate financing[164]

Impacts were assessed over two observation periods through follow-up surveys.[165] The first follow-up survey for Washington was administered 21 months after random assignment, while the first follow-up survey for Massachusetts was administered 19 months after random assignment. The second follow-up surveys were administered approximately 31 and 33 months after random assignment in Massachusetts and Washington, respectively. In addition, the Massachusetts results are reported in two groups. The first group includes cohorts one and two, while the second group consists of only cohort three.[166] The results for cohort three were measured only for the first follow-up period.

Washington State SEED Project Impact on Employment.   The results of the Washington SEED Project are summarized in Table 5.2. During the first follow-up survey at 21 months after random assignment, 57 percent of Washington SEED Project participants reported being self-employed at some point, compared to the 32 percent figure for members of the control group—a statistically significant difference of 25 percent at the one percent confidence level.[167] Over the course of the entire 33-month study (second follow-up survey), 63 percent and 41 percent of SEED Project participants and control group members reported being self-employed at least once, respectively. This difference of 22 percent is statistically significant at the one percent confidence level.

While SEED Project participants were more likely to report being self-employed, how long were these periods of self-employment compared to the experience of the control group members? For the first follow-up survey, SEED Project participants reported being self-employed for an average of 3.2 months per year over the 21-month follow-up period, while the figure for the control group was 1.0 month.[168] The difference of 2.2 months per year is statistically significant at the one percent confidence level. To put this finding in perspective, SEED Project participants had an annual self-employment rate of 26.7 percent over the 21-month period, while control group members had an annual self-employment rate of 8.3 percent. For the entire 33-month period, SEED Project participants and control group members averaged 3.0 and 1.0 months per year of self-employment,

TABLE 5.2. The Effectiveness Washington SEED: Selected Findings

Outcome	Result
Self Employment	
Self-Employed at Some Point	
21-month	Pos***
33-month	Pos***
Time in Self Employment	
21-month	Pos***
33-month	Pos***
Currently Self Employed	
21-month	Pos***
33-month	Pos***
Earnings	
21-month	Pos**
33-month	Pos***
Wage and Salary Employment	
Wage and Salary Employment at Some Point	
21-month	Neg***
33-month	Neg***
Time in Wage and Salary Employment	
21-month	Neg**
33-month	Neg**
Currently Employed in a Wage and Salary Position	
21-month	Neg**
33-month	0
Earnings	
21-month	0
33-month	Neg*
Combined Employment Experiences	
Employed at Some Point	
21-month	Pos***
33-month	0
Time Employed	
21-month	Pos***
33-month	Pos***
Currently Employed	
21-month	0
33-month	Pos**
Earnings	
21-month	0
33-month	0
Gross Business Income	
1990	Pos**

TABLE 5.2.   (Continued)

Outcome	Result
1991	Pos***
1992	Pos***
Earnings in UI-Covered Employment	
Quarter 1	Neg**
Quarter 2	Neg**
Quarter 3	Neg*
Quarter 4	Neg**
Quarter 5	0
Quarter 6	0
Quarter 7	0
Quarter 8	0
Quarter 9	0
Unemployment Insurance, Initial Benefit Year	
Length of First UI Spell	Pos***
Benefit Amount, First Spell	Pos***
Benefit Amount, Full Initial Benefit Year	Pos***
Benefit Amount, Full Benefit Year, Including Lump Sum	Neg***
Subsequent Unemployment Insurance Payments	
Received UI Benefits after SEED	0
Benefit Amount, After SEED Year	0
Total UI Benefits Received	Neg***

Key: 0   Finding was not statistically significant
   Pos   Positive or beneficial impact
   Neg   Negative or harmful impact
   *   Statistically significant at the 10 percent confidence level ($p \leq 0.10$)
   **   Statistically significant at the 5 percent confidence level ($p \leq 0.05$)
   ***   Statistically significant at the 1 percent confidence level ($p \leq 0.01$)
   n/a   No measure was assessed or reported
   †   No statistically significance test was performed
Source: Jacob M. Benus, Terry R. Johnson, Michelle Wood, Neelima Grover, and Theodore Shen, "Self-Employment Programs: A New Reemployment Strategy: Final Impact Analysis of the Washington and Massachusetts Self-Employment Demonstrations," *Unemployment Insurance Occasional Paper No. 95-4* (Washington, DC: U.S. Department of Labor, December 1995), Table 7.1, 85; Table 7.2, 87;Table 7.3, 90; Table 7.4, 91; Table 7.5, 93; Table 7.6, 94, Table 7.7, 95; Table 7.8, 96; Table 7.9, 97; Table 7.10, 98; Table 7.11, 99; Table 7.14, 104; Table 7.21, 114; Table 7.25, 120; Table 7.16, 107; Table 7.17, 108; Table 7.18, 110.

respectively—a statistically significant difference of 2.0 months per year at the one percent confidence level. To put this finding in perspective, SEED Project participants had an annual self-employment rate of 25.0 percent over the 33-month period, while control group members had an annual self-employment rate of 3.0 percent.

When the 21-month follow-up survey was administered, 37 percent of SEED Project participants and 21 percent of control group members reported being currently self-employed, respectively—a statistically significant difference of 16 percent at the one percent confidence level.[169] For the 33-month follow-up period, these figures were 38 percent and 25 percent for SEED Project participants and control group members, respectively. The difference of 13 percent is statistically significant at the one percent confidence level.

Despite appearing to increase the likelihood of being self-employed, what was the effect of the SEED Project on earnings? The following dollar values are expressed in 1990 dollars. For the 21-month follow-up period, SEED Project participants averaged $2,382 in annual self-employment income, while the control group averaged $695 in annual self-employment income.[170] Thus, SEED Project participants earned $1,687 in additional income, compared to the control group. This difference is statistically significant at the five percent confidence level. Using the findings for months of employment, we can estimate monthly self-employment income. The SEED Project participants averaged $744 per month, while the control group averaged $695 per month. The same trend held for the 33-month follow-up period. SEED Project participants earned an average of $2,350 per year in self-employment income, compared to $576 for the control group—a statistically significant difference at the one percent confidence level. Thus, the SEED Project participants averaged $783 per month, while the control group averaged $576 per month. While the self-employment earnings findings are positive results, the program does not appear to move individuals into full-time self-employment on an annual basis.

While the SEED Project appears to have had a somewhat positive effect on self-employment, the program appears to have reduced wage and salary employment. Twenty-one months after random assignment, 73 percent and 80 percent of the SEED Project participants and control group members, respectively, reported have at least one wage and salary job.[171] The difference of seven percent is statistically significant at the one percent confidence level. Over the course of the entire 33-month study, 81 percent and 87 percent of SEED Project participants and control group members reported being employed at least once in a wage and salary job, respectively. This difference of six percent is statistically significant at the one percent confidence level. If SEED Project participants were less likely to be employed in wage and salary jobs because they were fully self-employed, this result would be a beneficial impact. However, as was previously indicated, program participants appear to have been unable for become fully self-employed.

For the first follow-up survey, SEED Project participants reported being employed in wage or salary jobs for an average of 4.1 months per year over the 21-month follow-up period, while the figure for the control group was 4.7 months.[172] The difference of 0.6 months per year is statistically significant at the five percent confidence level. Thus, to put this finding in perspective, SEED Project participants had an annual wage and salary employment rate of 34.2 percent over the 21-month period, while control group members had an annual wage and salary employment rate of 39.2 percent. For the entire 33-month period, SEED Project participants and control group members averaged 4.5 and 5.2 months per year of wage and salary employment, respectively—a statistically significant difference of 0.7 months per year at the five percent confidence level. To put this finding in perspective, SEED Project participants had an annual wage and salary employment rate of 37.5 percent over the 33-month period, while control group members had an annual wage and salary employment rate of 43.3 percent.

When the 21-month follow-up survey was administered, 53 percent of SEED Project participants and 60 percent of control group members reported being currently employed in wage and salary jobs, respectively—a statistically significant difference of seven percent at the five percent confidence level.[173] For the 33-month follow-up, these figures were 57 percent and 61 percent for SEED Project participants and control group members, respectively. The difference of four percent is not statistically distinguishable from zero.

Despite appearing to decrease the likelihood of being employed in wage and salary jobs, what was the effect of the SEED Project on earnings? The following dollar values are expressed in 1990 dollars. For the 21-month follow-up period, SEED Project participants averaged $8,029 in annual wage and salary employment income, while the control group averaged $9,231 in annual wage and salary employment income.[174] While SEED Project participants earned $1,202 less than the control group, this difference is statistically indistinguishable from zero. Using the findings for the months of employment, we can estimate monthly self-employment income. The SEED Project participants averaged $669 per month, while the control group averaged $769 per month. The same trend held for the 33-month follow-up period. SEED Project participants earned an average of $8,414 per year in self-employment income, compared to $9,920 for the control group—a statistically significant reduction of $1,506 at the less rigorous 10 percent confidence level. The SEED Project participants averaged $701 per month, while the control group averaged $827 per month. In spite of receiving training to become self-employed entrepreneurs, intervention group members earned considerably more in wage and salary income than self-employment income.

What was the SEED Project's impact on overall employment? Twenty-one months after random assignment, 96 percent and 92 percent of the SEED Project participants and control group members, respectively, reported having at least one incidence of either self-employment or wage and salary employment.[175] The difference of four percent is statistically significant at the one percent confidence level. Over the course of the entire 33-month study, 98 percent and 97 percent of SEED Project participants and control group members reported being self-employed at least once, respectively. This difference of one percent is not statistically significant.

For the first follow-up survey, SEED Project participants reported being employed in any type of job for an average of 7.1 months per year over the 21-month follow-up period, while the figure for the control group was 5.9 months.[176] The difference of 1.2 months per year is statistically significant at the one percent confidence level. To put this finding in perspective, SEED Project participants had an annual overall employment rate of 59.2 percent over the 21-month period, while control group members had an overall employment rate of 49.2 percent. Over the entire 33-month period, SEED Project participants and control group members averaged 7.5 and 6.4 months per year of overall employment, respectively—a statistically significant difference of 1.1 months per year at the one percent confidence level. To put this finding in perspective, SEED Project participants had an annual overall employment rate of 62.5 percent over the 33-month period, while control group members had an annual overall employment rate of 53.3 percent. The SEED Project appears to have done little to move participants into full-time employment, regardless of whether it was self-employment or wage and salary employment.

When the 21-month follow-up survey was administered, 78 percent of SEED Project participants and 75 percent of control group members reported being currently employed in any type of employment, respectively—a statistically indistinguishable difference of three percent.[177] For the 33-month follow-up period, these figures were 84 percent and 78 percent for SEED Project participants and control group members, respectively. The difference of six percent is statistically significant at the five percent confidence level.

What was the effect of the SEED Project on earnings for overall employment? For the 21-month follow-up period, SEED Project participants averaged $11,477 in annual total employment income, while the control group averaged $10,499 in annual total employment income.[178] While SEED Project participants earned $978 more than the control group, this difference is statistically indistinguishable from zero. Using the findings for the months of employment, we can estimate monthly self-employment income. The SEED Project participants averaged $956 per month, while the control group averaged $875 per month. The same trend held for the 33-month follow-up period. SEED Project participants earned an average of $12,585 per year in self-employment income, compared to $11,590 for the control group—a statistically indistinguishable difference of $995. The SEED Project participants averaged $1,049 per month, while the control group averaged $966 per month.

In addition to the surveys used to collect self-reported data, the authors of the evaluation used gross business income data reported to the Washington State Department of Revenue. While the data are reported on an annual basis and are somewhat different from the survey data, they are another useful indicator of the performance of the SEED Project. In 1990, program participants earned an average of $4,135 in gross business income, while the figure for the control group members was $1,935.[179] The difference of $2,200 is statistically significant at the five percent confidence level. In 1991 and 1992, SEED Project participants had gross incomes that averaged $6,438 and $7,685 more than the gross business incomes of the control group—differences that are statistically significant at the one percent confidence level.

While the impact of the SEED Project on gross business income is considerable, the results did not carry over when the outcome measure is earnings from wages and employment covered by the UI system. Based on nine quarters of data, participation in the SEED Project failed to increase earnings from covered wages and employment. For the first and second quarters, program participants earned, on average, $330 and $383 less than the control group—statistically significant differences at the five percent confidence level.[180] While the program group averaged earning $271 less that the control group, this difference is marginally statistically significant at the 10 percent confidence level. For the fourth quarter, program participants earned $371 less than the control group—a statistically significant difference at the five percent confidence level. Afterward, the negative impact of the SEED Project faded way. The differences in earnings from the fifth quarter through the ninth quarter failed to be statistically distinguishable from zero.

Participation in the SEED Project appears to have reduced the amount of time spent collecting UI benefits. For the first spell or bout of UI receipt,

SEED Project participants averaged 11.4 weeks, while the control group members averaged 17.5—a statistically significant difference of 6.1 weeks at the one percent confidence level.[181] According to the authors of the evaluation, however, "The large reduction in length of first spell is primarily due to treatment group members completing their five milestones to receive their lump-sum payment and then no longer drawing regular UI payments."[182]

The results for the amount of UI benefits received during initial benefit year need to be taken with caution because the lump-sum payments for SEED Project participants are excluded from the analysis.[183] While the lump-sum payments were drawn from a source other than UI benefits, the average payment was $4,225.[184] For the first spell of UI benefits, SEED Project participants averaged $2,086, while the control group averaged $3,368—a statistically significant difference of $1,282 at the one percent confidence level.[185] The trend in SEED Project participants receiving a lesser amount of UI benefits continued over a full year. SEED Project participants and control group members averaged $2,333 and $3,792 in full-year benefits—a statistically significant reduction of $1,459 at the one percent confidence level. However, when the lump-sum awards are included in the analysis, the SEED Project becomes more costly. For the combined UI and lumps-sum measure, SEED Project participants were awarded an average of $4,857, while the control group averaged $3,792—a statistically significant difference of $1,065 at the one percent confidence level. Consequently, the SEED project, in fact, did not reduce costs, but increased them.

How did the SEED Project affect claims for new UI benefits? Thirty-one percent of SEED Project participants filed for new claims after participation in the program, compared to 31.8 percent for the control group.[186] The difference of 0.8 percent is statistically indistinguishable from zero. For the amount of UI benefits received, program participants and control group members averaged $1,214 and $1,296—a statistically insignificant difference of $82. Combining the period of participation in the SEED Project and the subsequent period after, program participants received an average of $6,071 in UI benefits, including the lump-sum payments, while the control group averaged $5,088. The difference of $983 is statistically significant at the one percent confidence level. Thus, the SEED Project appears to have had no affect on claims for new benefits; rather, it increased the amount of money received by participants.

Massachusetts Enterprise Project.   Table 5.3 summarizes the results of the Massachusetts Enterprise Project evaluation. During the first

TABLE 5.3. The Effectiveness of the Massachusetts Enterprise Project: Selected Findings

	Results	
Outcome	Cohorts 1 and 2	Cohort 3
Self Employment		
Self-Employed at Some Point		
19-month	Pos***	Pos***
31-month	Pos**	n/a
Time in Self Employment		
19-month	Pos***	Pos***
31-month	Pos**	n/a
Currently Self Employed		
19-month	Pos**	Pos***
31-month	0	n/a
Earnings		
19-month	0	Pos**
31-month	0	n/a
Wage and Salary Employment		
Wage and Salary Employment at Some Point		
19-month	0	Neg*
31-month	0	n/a
Time in Wage and Salary Employment		
19-month	0	0
31-month	0	n/a
Currently Employed in a Wage and Salary Position		
19-month	0	Neg**
31-month	0	n/a
Earnings		
19-month	0	Neg**
31-month	0	n/a
Combined Employment Experiences		
Employed at Some Point		
19-month	Pos***	Pos**
31-month	Pos**	n/a
Time Employed		
19-month	Pos***	Pos***
31-month	Pos***	n/a
Currently Employed		
19-month	Pos***	Pos**
31-month	0	n/a
Earnings		

(*continued*)

TABLE 5.3.   (Continued)

	Results	
Outcome	Cohorts 1 and 2	Cohort 3
19-month	Pos**	0
31-month	Pos**	n/a
Unemployment Insurance		
Length of First UI Spell	Pos***	0
Benefit Amount, Year 1 (Months 1 to 12)	Pos***	0
Benefit Amount, Year 2 (Months 13 to 24)	0	n/a
Benefit Amount, Year 3 (Months 25 to 31)	0	n/a
Benefit Amount, Total (Months 1 to 31)	Pos***	n/a

Key: 0 Finding was not statistically significant
    Pos Positive or beneficial impact
    Neg Negative or harmful impact
    * Statistically significant at the 10 percent confidence level ($p \leq 0.10$)
    ** Statistically significant at the 5 percent confidence level ($p \leq 0.05$)
    *** Statistically significant at the 1 percent confidence level ($p \leq 0.01$)
    n/a No measure was assessed or reported
    † No statistically significance test was performed
Source: Jacob M. Benus, Terry R. Johnson, Michelle Wood, Neelima Grover, and Theodore Shen, "Self-Employment Programs: A New Reemployment Strategy: Final Impact Analysis of the Washington and Massachusetts Self-Employment Demonstrations," *Unemployment Insurance Occasional Paper No. 95-4* (Washington, DC: U.S. Department of Labor, December 1995), Table 8.1, 131; Table 8.2, 133; Table

follow-up survey at 19 months after random assignment for cohorts one and two, 52 percent of Enterprise Project participants reported being self-employed at some point, compared to the 35 percent figure for members of the control group—a statistically significant difference of 17 percent at the one percent confidence level.[187] Over the course of the entire 31-month study (second follow-up survey), 58 percent and 47 percent of Enterprise Project participants and control group members reported being self-employed at least once, respectively. This difference of 11 percent is statistically significant at the five percent confidence level.

Similar results were reported for cohort three. Sixty-five percent of Enterprise Project participants reported being self-employed sometime during the 19-month follow-up period, compared to 45 percent for the control group—a statistically significant difference of 20 percent at the one percent confidence level.[188]

While Enterprise Project participants were more likely to report being self-employed, how long were these periods of self-employment compared to the experience of the control group members? For the first follow-up survey for cohorts one and two, Enterprise Project participants reported being self-employed for an average of 2.5 months per year over the 19-month follow-up period, while the figure for the control group was 1.4 months.[189] The difference of 1.1 months per year is statistically significant at the one percent confidence level. To put this finding in perspective, Enterprise Project participants had an annual self-employment rate of 20.8 percent over the 19-month period, while control group members had an annual self-employment rate of 11.7 percent. For the entire 31-month period, Enterprise Project participants and control group members averaged 2.6 and 1.7 months per year of self-employment, respectively—a statistically significant difference of 0.9 months per year at the five percent confidence level. To put this finding in perspective, Enterprise Project participants had an annual self-employment rate of 21.7 percent over the 31-month period, while control group members had an annual self-employment rate of 14.2 percent.

Similar results were reported for cohort three. For the first follow-up survey for cohort three, Enterprise Project participants reported being self-employed for an average of 3.8 months per year over the 19-month follow-up period, while the figure for the control group was 1.7 months.[190] The difference of 2.1 months per year is statistically significant at the one percent confidence level. To put this finding in perspective, Enterprise Project participants had an annual self-employment rate of 31.7 percent over the 19-month period, while control group members had an annual self-employment rate of 14.2 percent. Clearly, the intervention did not move participants into full-time, year-round self-employment.

For cohorts one and two, when the 19-month follow-up survey was administered, 40 percent of Enterprise Project participants and 29 percent of control group members reported being currently self-employed, respectively—a statistically significant difference of 11 percent at the five percent confidence level.[191] For the 31-month follow-up, these figures were 43 percent and 38 percent for Enterprise Project participants and control group members, respectively. The difference of five percent is statistically indistinguishable from zero, suggesting that the initial positive effect of the Enterprise Project on self-employment faded.

Comparable results were reported for cohort three. For cohort three, when the 19-month follow-up survey was administered, 57 percent of Enterprise Project participants and 36 percent of control group members reported being currently self-employed, respectively—a statistically significant difference of 21 percent at the one percent confidence level.[192]

Despite appearing to increase the likelihood of being self-employed, what was the effect of the Enterprise Project on earnings? The following dollar values are expressed in 1990 dollars. For the 19-month follow-up period, Enterprise Project participants averaged $2,916 in annual self-employment income, while the control group averaged $1,404 in annual self-employment income—a statistically insignificant difference of $1,512.[193] Using the findings for the months of employment, we can estimate monthly self-employment income. The Enterprise Project participants averaged $1,166 per month, while the control group averaged $1,003 per month. The same trends held for the 31-month follow-up period. Enterprise Project participants earned an average of $2,627 per year in self-employment income, compared to $1,439 for the control group—a statistically insignificant difference of $1,188. The Enterprise Project participants averaged $1,010 per month, while the control group averaged $846 per month.

Similar results were reported for cohort three. For the 19-month follow-up period for cohort three, Enterprise Project participants averaged $3,243 in annual self-employment income, while the control group averaged $1,336 in annual self-employment income—a statistically insignificant difference of $1,907 at the five percent confidence level.[194] The Enterprise Project participants averaged $853 per month, while the control group averaged $786 per month. The same trends held for the 19-month follow-up period.

While the Enterprise Project appears to have had a somewhat positive effect on self-employment, the program appears to have reduced wage and salary employment. For cohorts one and two, 19 months after random assignment, 65 percent and 64 percent of the Enterprise Project participants and control group members reported have at least one wage and salary job, respectively.[195] The difference of one percent is statistically indistinguishable from zero. Over the course of the entire 31-month study, 71 percent and 75 percent of Enterprise Project participants and control group members reported being self-employed at least once, respectively. This reduction of four percent is statistically insignificant.

For cohort three, 19 months after random assignment, 54 percent and 64 percent of the Enterprise Project participants and control group members, respectively, reported having at least one wage and salary job.[196] The difference of 10 percent is statistically significant at the less rigorous 10 percent confidence level.

For the first follow-up survey for cohorts one and two, Enterprise Project participants reported being employed in wage or salary jobs for an average of 3.8 months per year over the 19-month follow-up period, while the figure for the control group was 3.2 months.[197] The difference of 0.6 months per year is statistically indistinguishable from zero. Putting this finding in perspective, Enterprise Project participants had an annual wage and salary employment rate of 31.7 percent over the 21-month period, while control group members had an annual wage and salary employment rate of 26.7 percent. For the entire 31-month period, Enterprise Project participants and control group members averaged 4.4 and 4.1 months per year of wage and salary employment, respectively. This difference of 0.3 months is statistically indistinguishable from zero. Based on this finding, Enterprise Project participants had an annual wage and salary employment rate of 36.7 percent over the 31-month period, while control group members had an annual wage and salary employment rate of 34.2 percent.

For the first follow-up survey for cohort three, Enterprise Project participants reported being employed in wage or salary jobs for an average of 3.0 months per year over the 19-month follow-up period, while the figure for the control group was 3.4 months.[198] The difference of 0.4 months is statistically indistinguishable from zero.

When the 19-month follow-up survey was administered for cohorts one and two, 52 percent of Enterprise Project participants and 46 percent of control group members reported being currently employed in wage and salary jobs, respectively—a statistically indistinguishable difference of six percent.[199] For the 31-month follow-up period, these figures were 56 percent and 54 percent for Enterprise Project participants and control group members, respectively. The difference of two percent is not statistically distinguishable from zero.

When the 19-month follow-up survey was administered for cohort 3, 40 percent of Enterprise Project participants and 52 percent of control group members reported being currently employed in wage and salary jobs, respectively—a statistically significant difference of 12 percent at the five percent confidence level.[200]

Despite appearing to have no beneficial effect on being employed in wage and salary jobs, what was the effect of the Enterprise Project on earnings? The following dollar values are expressed in 1990 dollars. For the 19-month follow-up period for cohorts one and two, Enterprise Project participants averaged $9,311 in annual wage and salary employment income, while the control group averaged $6,613 in annual wage and salary income—a statistically significant difference of $2,698 at the five percent confidence level.[201] The Enterprise Project participants averaged $2,450 per month, while the control group averaged $2,067 per month. The same pattern held for the 31-month follow-up period. Enterprise Project participants earned an average of $10,119 per year in wage and salary income, compared to $7,797 for the control group—a marginally statistically significant difference of $2,333 at the 10 percent confidence level. The Enterprise Project participants averaged $2,300 per month, while the control group averaged $1,902 per month.

For the 19-month follow-up period for cohort three, Enterprise Project participants averaged $5,827 in annual wage and salary employment income, while the control group averaged $8,385 in annual self-employment income—a statistically significant difference of $2,558 at the five percent confidence level.[202] The Enterprise Project participants averaged $1,942 per month, while the control group averaged $2,466 per month.

What was the Enterprise Project's impact on overall employment? Nineteen months after random assignment for cohorts one and two, 93 percent and 82 percent of the Enterprise Project participants and control group members, respectively, reported having at least one incidence of either self-employment or wage and salary employment.[203] The difference of 11 percent is statistically significant at the one percent confidence level. Over the course of the entire 31-month study, 97 percent and 92 percent of Enterprise Project participants and control group members reported being self-employed at least once, respectively. This difference of five percent is statistically significant at the five percent confidence level.

Nineteen months after random assignment for cohort 3, 96 percent and 89 percent of the Enterprise Project participants and control group members, respectively, reported having at least one incidence of either self-employment or wage and salary employment.[204] The difference of seven percent is statistically significant at the five percent confidence level.

For the first follow-up survey for cohorts one and two, Enterprise Project participants reported being employed in any type of job for an average of 6.5 months per year over the 19-month follow-up period, while the figure for the control group was 4.5 months.[205] The difference of 2.0 months per year is statistically significant at the one percent confidence level. Accordingly, Enterprise Project participants had an annual overall employment rate of 54.2 percent over the 19-month period, while control group members had an overall employment rate of 37.5 percent. Over the entire 31-month period, Enterprise Project participants and control group members averaged 7.4 and 5.8 months per year of overall employment, respectively—a statistically significant difference of 1.6 months per year at the one percent confidence level. To put this finding in perspective,

Enterprise Project participants had an annual overall employment rate of 61.7 percent over the 31-month period, while control group members had an annual overall employment rate of 48.3 percent.

For the first follow-up survey for cohort three, Enterprise Project participants reported being employed in any type of job for an average of 7.1 months per year over the 19-month follow-up period, while the figure for the control group was 5.3 months.[206] The difference of 1.8 months per year is statistically significant at the one percent confidence level. Consequently, Enterprise Project participants had an annual overall employment rate of 59.2 percent over the 19-month period, while control group members had an overall employment rate of 44.2 percent.

When the 19-month follow-up survey was administered for cohorts one and two, 81 percent of Enterprise Project participants and 68 percent of control group members reported being currently employed in any type of employment, respectively—a statistically significant difference of 13 percent at the one percent confidence level.[207] For the 31-month follow-up period, these figures were 87 percent and 81 percent for Enterprise Project participants and control group members, respectively. The difference of six percent is statistically indistinguishable from zero, suggesting that the program failed to have a long-term impact.

When the 19-month follow-up survey was administered for cohort three, 88 percent of Enterprise Project participants and 79 percent of control group members reported being currently employed in any type of employment, respectively—a statistically significant difference of nine percent at the five percent confidence level.[208]

What was the effect of the Enterprise Project on earnings from overall employment? For the 19-month follow-up period for cohorts one and two, Enterprise Project participants averaged $13,151 in annual total employment income, while the control group averaged $8,483 in annual total employment income.[209] Enterprise Project participants earned $4,668 more than the control group. This difference is statistically significant at the five percent confidence level. The Enterprise Project participants averaged $2,023 per month, while the control group averaged $1,885 per month. The same trend held for the 31-month follow-up period. Enterprise Project participants earned an average of $14,664 per year in self-employment income, compared to $10,056 for the control group—a statistically significant difference of $4,608 at the five percent confidence level. The Enterprise Project participants averaged $1,982 per month, while the control group averaged $1,734 per month.

For the 19-month follow-up period for cohort three, Enterprise Project participants averaged $10,358 in annual total employment income, while the control group averaged $10,493 in annual total employment income.[210] Enterprise Project participants earned $135 less than the control group. However, this difference is statistically indistinguishable from zero. The Enterprise Project participants averaged $1,459 per month, while the control group averaged $1,980 per month.

Participation in the Enterprise Project appears to have slightly reduced the amount of time spent collecting UI benefits. For the first spell of UI receipt for cohorts one and two, Enterprise Project participants averaged 24.5 weeks, while the control group members averaged 26.5—a statistically significant difference of 2.0 weeks at the one percent confidence level.[211] This reduction represents a 7.5 percent decrease in time receiving UI benefits.

For cohort three, the average lengths of the first spell of receiving UI was 24.4 weeks and 23.7 weeks for program participants and control group members, respectively.[212] The difference of 0.7 weeks is statistically indistinguishable from zero.

In year one of the observation period for cohorts one and two, Enterprise Project participants averaged $6,120 in UI benefits, while the control group averaged $6,845—a statistically significant difference of $725 at the one percent confidence level.[213] In year two, Enterprise Project participants and control group member averaged $307 and $410 in full-year benefits—a difference of $103 that is statistically indistinguishable from zero. In the remaining seven months of the study (coined "year three" by the author), program participants and control group members received $141 and $140, respectively—a statistically indistinguishable difference of $1. Over the course of the 31-month follow-up period, program participants received $6,567 in UI benefits, while the control group received $7,400—a statistically significant reduction of $833 at the one percent confidence level.

In year one of the observation period for cohort three, Enterprise Project participants averaged $6,517 in UI benefits, while the control group averaged $6,250—a statistically indistinguishable difference of $267.[214]

Washington Project SEED and the Massachusetts Enterprise Project indicate the self-employment assistance programs can increase the rate of self-employment, but the effects on overall employment and income are certainly less promising. While both of these programs operated only within their respective states, the programs were implemented in several locations. Nevertheless, the ability of these programs to have similar effects on a larger scale is unknown.

Project GATE (Growing America through Entrepreneurship)

In an attempt to help Americans start businesses, the Department of Labor teamed with the Small Business Administration (SBA) to create an employment program to assistant people in creating or expanding their own business enterprises.[215] Begun in 2003, Project GATE operated in Philadelphia, Pennsylvania; Pittsburgh, Pennsylvania; Northeast Minnesota (including Duluth and Virginia); Minneapolis and St. Paul, Minnesota; and Portland, Lewiston, and Bangor, Maine. Of the 4,198 individuals in the study, 2,095 were assigned to the intervention group, and 2,103 were allocated to the control group.

Project GATE participants "were offered assessments, classroom training and one-on-one technical assistance in developing their business and applying for an SBA Microloan or other source of business finance."[216] Classroom training and technical assistance was provided by Nonprofit Community-Based Organizations (CBOs) and the SBA's Small Business Development Centers (SBDCs).[217] All of the program services were provided free to participants.[218]

Participants were recruited from those seeking employment and training services at the Department of Labor's one-stop centers.[219] Created as a nationwide network by the Workforce Investment Act of 1998, these centers serve as focal points for those seeking services from state and federal government employment and training programs. Twenty one-stop centers from the previously mentioned program sites participated in Project GATE.[220]

To assess the impact of Project GATE, two data collection methods were used. The first method was a three-wave survey administered six, 18 and 60 months after the initial random assignment. The second method used information obtained from UI administrative data.

Project GATE participants received about 16 weeks of program services.[221] In general, the training courses were in how to start a business.[222] Participants with existing businesses were offered one-on-one technical assistance to deal with business issues.[223] Those needing business loans were provided assistance with the application process.[224]

According to the authors of the process evaluation of Project GATE, the program was implemented as planned (implementation fidelity), and the program could be replicated on a wider scale because it was implemented at sites with very different communities that varied by urbanization, local economic conditions, and socioeconomic population characteristics.[225] In other words, the results of this evaluation, according to the authors, should have high external validity.

Impact on Business Ownership

The selected results of the Project GATE evaluation are summarized in Table 5.4. At the time of random assignment, 21 percent of Project GATE participants and 20 percent of control group members owned businesses—a

TABLE 5.4.   The Effectiveness of Project GATE: Selected Findings

		Results	
Outcome	Full Sample	Receiving UI at Time of Random Assignment	Not Receiving UI at Time of Random Assignment
Business Ownership			
Business Ownership Rate			
6-month	Pos***	n/a	n/a
18-month	0	n/a	n/a
60-month	0	n/a	n/a
Business Ownership Rate			
Quarter 1	Pos*	0	0
Quarter 2	Pos***	Pos**	0
Quarter 3	Pos***	Pos***	0
Quarter 4	Pos*	Pos*	0
Quarter 5	0	Pos**	0
Quarter 6	0	Pos*	0
Quarter 7	0	0	0
Quarter 8	0	Pos*	0
Quarter 9	0	0	0
Quarter 10	0	0	0
Quarter 11	0	0	0
Quarter 12	0	0	0
Quarter 13	0	0	0
Quarter 14	0	0	0
Quarter 15	0	0	0
Quarter 16	0	0	0
Business Openings			
6-month	Pos***	n/a	n/a

TABLE 5.4. (Continued)

Outcome	Full Sample	Results Receiving UI at Time of Random Assignment	Not Receiving UI at Time of Random Assignment
18-month	Pos**	n/a	n/a
60-month	0	n/a	n/a
Business Closures			
6-month	0	n/a	n/a
18-month	0	n/a	n/a
60-month	0	n/a	n/a
Business Has any Employees			
6-month	0	n/a	n/a
18-month	0	n/a	n/a
60-month	0	n/a	n/a
Business Has Full-Time Employees			
6-month	0	n/a	n/a
18-month	0	n/a	n/a
60-month	0	n/a	n/a
Business Has Part-Time Employees			
6-month	0	n/a	n/a
18-month	0	n/a	n/a
60-month	0	n/a	n/a
Sales Exceed Expenses			
6-month	0	n/a	n/a
18-month	0	n/a	n/a
60-month	0	n/a	n/a
Time to Start of First Business	Pos**	n/a	n/a
Longevity of Business	Pos*	n/a	n/a
Impact on Earnings			
Quarter 1	0	n/a	n/a
Quarter 2	0	n/a	n/a
Quarter 3	0	n/a	n/a
Quarter 4	0	n/a	n/a
Quarter 5	0	n/a	n/a
Quarter 6	0	n/a	n/a
Quarter 7	0	n/a	n/a
Quarter 8	0	n/a	n/a
Quarter 9	0	n/a	n/a
Quarter 10	0	n/a	n/a
Quarter 11	0	n/a	n/a

(continued)

TABLE 5.4. (Continued)

| | | Results | |
Outcome	Full Sample	Receiving UI at Time of Random Assignment	Not Receiving UI at Time of Random Assignment
Quarter 12	0	n/a	n/a
Quarter 13	0	n/a	n/a
Quarter 14	0	n/a	n/a
Quarter 15	0	n/a	n/a
Quarter 16	0	n/a	n/a
Self-Employment Rate			
Quarter 1	Pos*	0	n/a
Quarter 2	Pos***	Pos***	n/a
Quarter 3	Pos***	Pos**	n/a
Quarter 4	Pos*	Pos**	n/a
Quarter 5	0	Pos*	n/a
Quarter 6	0	0	n/a
Quarter 7	0	0	n/a
Quarter 8	0	0	n/a
Quarter 9	0	0	n/a
Quarter 10	0	0	n/a
Quarter 11	0	0	n/a
Quarter 12	0	0	n/a
Quarter 13	0	0	n/a
Quarter 14	0	0	n/a
Quarter 15	0	0	n/a
Quarter 16	0	0	n/a
Wage and Salary Employment Rate			
Quarter 1	Neg*	Neg***	n/a
Quarter 2	Neg*	Neg**	n/a
Quarter 3	0	Neg*	n/a
Quarter 4	0	Neg***	n/a
Quarter 5	Neg**	Neg***	n/a
Quarter 6	Neg*	0	n/a
Quarter 7	0	0	n/a
Quarter 8	0	0	n/a
Quarter 9	Neg*	0	n/a
Quarter 10	0	0	n/a
Quarter 11	0	0	n/a
Quarter 12	0	0	n/a
Quarter 13	Neg*	0	n/a
Quarter 14	Neg**	0	n/a

TABLE 5.4. (Continued)

Outcome	Full Sample	Receiving UI at Time of Random Assignment	Not Receiving UI at Time of Random Assignment
		Results	
Quarter 15	Neg**	0	n/a
Quarter 16	Neg**	0	n/a
Overall Employment Rate			
Quarter 1	0	0	n/a
Quarter 2	0	0	n/a
Quarter 3	0	0	n/a
Quarter 4	0	0	n/a
Quarter 5	0	0	n/a
Quarter 6	0	0	n/a
Quarter 7	Pos*	Pos*	n/a
Quarter 8	0	0	n/a
Quarter 9	0	0	n/a
Quarter 10	0	0	n/a
Quarter 11	0	0	n/a
Quarter 12	0	0	n/a
Quarter 13	0	0	n/a
Quarter 14	0	0	n/a
Quarter 15	0	0	n/a
Quarter 16	0	0	n/a
Hours Worked at Self-Employment			
Quarter 1	0	n/a	n/a
Quarter 2	Pos**	n/a	n/a
Quarter 3	Pos**	n/a	n/a
Quarter 4	Pos**	n/a	n/a
Quarter 5	Pos***	n/a	n/a
Quarter 6	Pos***	n/a	n/a
Quarter 7	0	n/a	n/a
Quarter 8	0	n/a	n/a
Quarter 9	0	n/a	n/a
Quarter 10	0	n/a	n/a
Quarter 11	0	n/a	n/a
Quarter 12	0	n/a	n/a
Quarter 13	0	n/a	n/a
Quarter 14	0	n/a	n/a
Quarter 15	0	n/a	n/a
Quarter 16	0	n/a	n/a

(continued)

TABLE 5.4. (Continued)

Outcome	Full Sample	Results Receiving UI at Time of Random Assignment	Not Receiving UI at Time of Random Assignment
Hours Worked at Wage and Salary Jobs			
Quarter 1	Neg**	n/a	n/a
Quarter 2	Neg***	n/a	n/a
Quarter 3	Neg*	n/a	n/a
Quarter 4	0	n/a	n/a
Quarter 5	Neg**	n/a	n/a
Quarter 6	Neg**	n/a	n/a
Quarter 7	0	n/a	n/a
Quarter 8	0	n/a	n/a
Quarter 9	0	n/a	n/a
Quarter 10	Neg*	n/a	n/a
Quarter 11	0	n/a	n/a
Quarter 12	0	n/a	n/a
Quarter 13	Neg**	n/a	n/a
Quarter 14	Neg**	n/a	n/a
Quarter 15	Neg**	n/a	n/a
Quarter 16	Neg**	n/a	n/a
Total Hours Worked at Wage and Salary Jobs and Self-Employment			
Quarter 1	0	n/a	n/a
Quarter 2	0	n/a	n/a
Quarter 3	0	n/a	n/a
Quarter 4	0	n/a	n/a
Quarter 5	0	n/a	n/a
Quarter 6	0	n/a	n/a
Quarter 7	0	n/a	n/a
Quarter 8	0	n/a	n/a
Quarter 9	0	n/a	n/a
Quarter 10	0	n/a	n/a
Quarter 11	0	n/a	n/a
Quarter 12	0	n/a	n/a
Quarter 13	0	n/a	n/a
Quarter 14	0	n/a	n/a
Quarter 15	0	n/a	n/a
Quarter 16	0	n/a	n/a

TABLE 5.4. (Continued)

		Results	
		Receiving	Not Receiving
		UI at Time	UI at Time
	Full	of Random	of Random
Outcome	Sample	Assignment	Assignment
Self-Employment Salary Earnings			
Quarter 1	0	0	n/a
Quarter 2	0	0	n/a
Quarter 3	0	0	n/a
Quarter 4	0	0	n/a
Quarter 5	0	0	n/a
Quarter 6	0	0	n/a
Quarter 7	0	0	n/a
Quarter 8	0	0	n/a
Quarter 9	0	0	n/a
Quarter 10	0	0	n/a
Quarter 11	0	0	n/a
Quarter 12	0	0	n/a
Quarter 13	0	0	n/a
Quarter 14	0	0	n/a
Quarter 15	0	0	n/a
Quarter 16	0	0	n/a
Wage and Salary Earnings			
Quarter 1	0	0	n/a
Quarter 2	0	0	n/a
Quarter 3	0	0	n/a
Quarter 4	0	0	n/a
Quarter 5	0	0	n/a
Quarter 6	0	0	n/a
Quarter 7	0	0	n/a
Quarter 8	0	0	n/a
Quarter 9	0	0	n/a
Quarter 10	0	0	n/a
Quarter 11	0	0	n/a
Quarter 12	0	0	n/a
Quarter 13	0	0	n/a
Quarter 14	0	0	n/a
Quarter 15	0	0	n/a
Quarter 16	0	0	n/a
Total Earnings			
Quarter 1	Neg**	Neg***	n/a

(continued)

TABLE 5.4. (Continued)

		Results	
Outcome	Full Sample	Receiving UI at Time of Random Assignment	Not Receiving UI at Time of Random Assignment
Quarter 2	Neg**	Neg**	n/a
Quarter 3	0	0	n/a
Quarter 4	0	0	n/a
Quarter 5	0	0	n/a
Quarter 6	0	0	n/a
Quarter 7	0	0	n/a
Quarter 8	0	0	n/a
Quarter 9	0	0	n/a
Quarter 10	0	0	n/a
Quarter 11	0	0	n/a
Quarter 12	0	0	n/a
Quarter 13	0	0	n/a
Quarter 14	0	0	n/a
Quarter 15	0	0	n/a
Quarter 16	0	0	n/a
Hourly Wage of Most Current Job	0		
Self-Sufficiency			
Received UI, TRA, TAA Benefits	0	n/a	n/a
Weeks of UI Received			
6-month	Neg**	n/a	n/a
18-month	Neg**	n/a	n/a
60-month	0	n/a	n/a
Amount of UI, TRA, TAA Benefits Received			
6-month	Neg*	n/a	n/a
18-month	0	n/a	n/a
60-month	0	n/a	n/a

Key: 0 Finding was not statistically significant

Pos Positive or beneficial impact

Neg Negative or harmful impact

* Statistically significant at the 10 percent confidence level ($p \leq 0.10$)

** Statistically significant at the 5 percent confidence level ($p \leq 0.05$)

*** Statistically significant at the 1 percent confidence level ($p \leq 0.01$)

n/a No measure was assessed

† No statistically significance test was performed

Source: Jacob Benus, Theodore Shen, Sisi Zhang, Marc Chan, and Benjamin Hansen, *Growing America through Entrepreneurship: Final Evaluation of Project GATE* (Columbia, MD: Impaq International, December 2009), Figure V.1, 60; Figure V.2, 62; Figure V.4, 67; Figure V.5, 72; Figure V.6, 73; Table V.3, 76; Table V.4, 78; Table V.5, 79; Table V.6, 81; Table V.7, 84; Figure VI.1, 97; Figure VI.2, 98; Figure VI.3, 99; Figure VI.4, 100; Figure VI.5, 102; Figure VI.6, 103; Figure VI.7, 104; Figure VI.8, 105; Figure VI.9, 106; Figure VI.10, 111; Figure VI.11, 112; Figure VI.12, 113; Figure VI.13, 114; Figure VI.14, 115; Figure VI.15, 116; Table VI.4, 120; Table VII.1, 126.

statistically indistinguishable difference of one percent.[226] Six months after random assignment, 44 percent of Project GATE participants and 38 percent of control group members reported being business owners—a statistically significant difference of six percent at the one percent confidence level.[227] Eighteen months later, 44 percent of Project GATE participants were business owners, while 41 percent of control group members were business owners.[228] After 60 months, 38 percent of both groups reported owning their own businesses.[229] The findings for the 18- and 60-month intervals were statistically insignificant, indicating that the positive effect of Project GATE on businesses ownership quickly faded. When assessed over the course of 16 quarters, Project GATE had initial, yet small, positive impacts on business ownership.[230] In the first quarter, the intervention group had a business ownership rate of 37 percent, compared to 34 percent for the control group—a marginally statistically significant difference of three percent at the 10 percent confidence level. By the second and third quarters, the business ownership rates of the intervention group were five percent higher than the ownership rates for the control group. These differences were statistically significant at the one percent confidence level. By the fourth quarter, the difference of four percent was still in favor of the intervention group, but it was marginally statistically significant at the 10 percent confidence level. From the fifth through sixteenth quarters, Project GATE has no statistically significant impact on business ownership. Similar findings were found when the Unemployment Insurance administrative data was analyzed.[231]

Despite having no lasting effect on overall business ownership, Project GATE participants and control group members receiving UI benefits at the time of random assignment responded differently to Project GATE than participants and control group members not receiving UI benefits. When the impacts were limited to those receiving UI benefits, Project GATE participants were more likely to report owning their own businesses during the first few quarters after random assignment.[232] During the second and third quarters, Project GATE participants had self-reported ownership rates that were 8.7 percent and 8.9 percent higher, respectively, than the ownership rates reported by control group members.[233] These differences were statistically significant at the five percent confidence level. At the less rigorous 10 percent confidence level, Project GATE participants receiving UI benefits had an ownership rate during the fourth quarter that was 5.1 percent higher than the control group members receiving UI benefits.[234] During the fifth quarter, the difference was 6.3 percent in favor of Project GATE participants and was statistically significant at the five percent confidence level.[235] Thereafter, the gains from Project GATE faded to differences that were marginally statistically significant at the 10 percent confidence level and then decreased to differences that were statistically indistinguishable from zero.

Project Gate had an initial impact on business starts-up, while the program had no impact on business closures. At the time of random assignment and the 6-month follow-up, 20 percent of Project GATE participants and 14 percent of control group members reported starting a new business—a statistically significant difference of six percent at the five percent confidence level.[236] Between the six-month and 18-month follow-ups, 33 percent of Project GATE participants and 28 percent of control group members reported starting new businesses—a statistically significant difference of five percent at the one percent confidence level.[237] Between the 18-month and 60-month follow-up periods, the effect of Project GATE faded. Forty-four percent of Project GATE participants and 41 percent of control group members reported starting new businesses—a statistically indistinguishable difference of three percent.[238] Project GATE did not have any impact on business foreclosures during the three follow-up periods.[239] This finding means that participation in Project GATE had no effect on decreasing or increasing business foreclosures.

Further, compared to members of the control group, the businesses operated by Project GATE participants did not differ in having full- or part-time employees other than the owners.[240] In addition, participation in the program failed to lead to monthly sales exceeding monthly expenses, compared to the control group.[241]

Over the course of the 60-month follow-up period, Project GATE participants and control group members averaged 11.0 and 13.1 months, respectively, from random assignment to start their first business—a statistically significant difference of 2.1 percent at the five percent confidence level.[242] On average, businesses started by Project GATE participants lasted 32.5 months until closure, compared to 30 months for the control group.[243] This difference of 2.5 months is statistically significant at the less rigorous 10 percent confidence level.[244] However, the authors warn that "This observed difference may reflect the fact that program group members started their businesses sooner than control group members and the truncation of the observation period at approximately five years."[245]

Impact on Employment and Earnings

Despite some of the positive findings, increased business ownership and start-ups among Project GATE participants failed to increase earnings. Over the entire 60-month follow-up period, program participants earned $10,870 in average wages and salary from self-employment, while the average for the control group was $9,906.[246] However, the difference of $963 is statistically indistinguishable from zero, strongly indicating that Project GATE had no impact on self-employment earnings. On a quarterly basis over 16 periods, self-employment earnings of program participants failed to be statistically different from the earnings of the control group.[247]

Project GATE's impact on self-employment was short-lived. During the first quarter after random assignment, 37 percent and 34 percent, respectively, of program participants and control group members reported being self-employed.[248] The difference of three percent was statistically significant at the less rigorous 10 percent confidence level. The impact of Project GATE increased to five percent during the second and third quarters after random assignment.[249] For both quarters, 42 percent and 37 percent of program participants and control group members, respectively, reported being self-employed. These differences were statistically significant at the five percent confidence level. During the fourth quarter, the difference decreased to four percent—42 percent for the program group and 38 percent for the control group. The difference is statistically significant at the 10 percent confidence level. From the fifth through sixteenth quarters, participation in Project GATE failed to be statistically different from zero—suggesting that the program had no lasting impact. A similar trend was found when members of the project and control groups were limited to UI recipients.[250]

According to the authors, "Project GATE reduced the likelihood of wage and salary employment in about half the quarters following random assignment."[251] When the impacts were limited to those receiving UI benefits, Project GATE participants were less likely to find employment in wage and salary jobs for the first five quarters after random assignment.[252] In four of these quarters, the difference was statistically significant at the five percent confidence level, while in a single quarter, the difference was significant at the less rigorous 10 percent level. Afterward, the differences were not statistically significant.

However, Project GATE had almost no effect when the outcome measure is overall employment rate. Through 16 quarters, the differences between the overall employment rates of the program and control groups were statistically significant for only the seventh quarter.[253] The overall employment rate for the intervention group was 80 percent, while the rate was 77 percent for the control group—a statistically significant difference of three percent at the less rigorous 10 percent confidence level. This general trend of no effect was also found when the analysis·was limited to those receiving UI benefits.[254] The overall employment rates for UI recipients of the intervention and control groups were statistically indistinguishable from zero, except for the seventh quarter. The overall employment rate for the intervention group UI recipients was 85 percent, while the rate was 80 percent for the control group UI recipients—a marginally statistically significant difference of five percent at the 10 percent confidence level.

Despite the lack of impact on overall employment rates, Project GATE participants were more likely to report working longer self-employment hours per quarter than the control group members. Project GATE failed to have an impact on the number of self-employment hours worked during the first quarter. However, program participants worked an additional 23 to 40 hours of self-employment per quarter during the second through sixth quarters, compared to the control group.[255] These differences during the second through sixth quarters were statistically significant at the one percent and five percent confidence levels. Program participation had no impact on hours worked from the seventh through sixteenth quarters. However, participation in Project GATE was associated with fewer hours worked for wage and salary employment.[256] In eight of the 16 quarters, program participation was associated with reduced hours worked that were statistically significant at the five percent confidence level. In the third quarter, the negative effect of Project GATE on participants was marginally statistically significant at the 10 percent confidence level.

While Project GATE had an initial positive effect on self-employment hours worked and a negative impact on wage and salary employment hours, the program had no effect on total employment hours worked in self-employment and wage and salary jobs through 16 quarters.[257]

While Project GATE participants initially worked more self-employment hours, the increased hours had no effect on self-employed salary earnings over 16 quarters.[258] The extra time put into self-employment failed to increase self-employment earnings. As for wage and salary earnings from employment, program participation had no effect as well.[259] The same patterns of no effect for self-employment and employment earnings held when the analysis was limited to UI recipients.[260]

For total earnings, participation in Project GATE was associated with statistically significant reductions in income at the five percent level of confidence for the first and second quarters after random assignment.[261] For example, program participants earned $456 less, on average, than the control group during the second quarter. In subsequent quarters, the differences in total earnings were statistically insignificant, meaning that the initial negative impact of the program faded. The same pattern held when the analysis was limited to UI recipients.[262]

How did Project GATE affect hourly wages and benefits? The authors measured these outcomes during the 60-month follow-up survey. Program participation had no effect on hourly wages. Participants earned an average of $18.10 per hour, while the control group averaged $18.59 per hour—a statistically insignificant difference of $0.49.[263] Participation in the program failed to increase the likelihood of having paid sick leave, paid vacation, and paid holidays. In addition, program participation had no effect on the likelihood of having retirement, pension, 401(k) plans, and life insurance.

Impact on Self-Sufficiency

How did the Project GATE participants compare to control group members on measures of self-sufficiency? For UI, Trade Readjustment Allowances (TRA), or Trade Adjustment Assistance (TAA) benefits, Project GATE, over the 60-month follow-up period, had no impact on the likelihood of benefit receipt, number of weeks of benefits, or the amount of benefits received.[264] However, when the analysis was limited to UI benefits, program participation was associated with a small, yet statistically significant, increase in the number of weeks on UI between random assignment and the six-month follow-up, and between the six-month follow-up and the 18-month follow-up.[265] For example, the program participants averaged seven weeks of UI benefits, compared to an average of six weeks for the control group—a statistically significant difference of one week at the five percent confidence level.

Initially, program participation lead to an average increase in the total amount of UI, TRA, and TAA benefits of $289 during the period between random assignment and the 6-month follow-up.[266] However, this difference was statistically significant at the less rigorous 10 percent confidence level. Project GATE's impact on benefit income levels was statistically indistinguishable from zero for the later reporting periods.

Overall, Project GATE had an initial impact on business ownership that quickly fades. The same pattern held for the self-employment rate. Most important, Project GATE failed to increase the self-employment earning of participants and temporarily reduced the total earnings of participants.

Youth Employment and Training Evaluations

The multisite experimental evaluations of employment and training programs specifically targeting youth are Job Corps, JOBSTART, Center for Employment Training (CET) Replication, and Quantum Opportunity Program (QOP).

The National Job Corps Study

Created in 1964, Job Corps is a residential job-training program that serves disadvantaged youths aged 16 to 24 in 125 sites across the nation. Before the U.S. Senate Committee on Appropriations, Subcommittee on Labor, Health and Human Services, Education, and Related Agencies in 2011, Secretary of Labor Hilda L. Solis testified that the "Job Corps program has a long history of preparing disadvantaged youth for a successful transition into the workforce."[267] Also in 2011, Ray Uhalde, vice president of Workforce and Education Policy at Jobs for the Future, testified before the U.S. House of Representatives Committee on Appropriations, Subcommittee on Labor, Health and Human Services, Education, and Related Agencies:

> Job Corps—you know, Job Corps is the one national program that we have that has been evaluated rigorously for use that's been able to demonstrate a statistically significant improvement of about 12 percent in earnings up to three or four years for all the students and for the older students even more.[268]

Is Job Corps an effective program? Its primary hypothesis relating to employment and earnings is that "youth who obtain Job Corps education and training will become more productive and, hence, will have greater employment opportunities and higher earnings than those who do not."[269]

To monitor Job Corps' performance, the program tracks 58 metrics that include the number of graduates and the average wages of graduates.[270] In 2011, the Department of Labor Office of Inspector General (OIG) found serious deficiencies with 22 of the 58 metrics (37.9 percent), including 10 with multiple deficiencies.[271] Specifically:

- Nine metrics reported inaccurate results
- Job Corps did not report results and/or establish performance targets for four metrics
- 19 metrics were not published and made publically available[272]

Most noteworthy of these deficiencies are performance metrics related to job-training matches and cost efficiency. Job-training matches are calculated by the number of Job Corps participants that found employment after leaving the program. The OIG examined data from two time periods: program year 2009 (July 1, 2009 to June 30, 2010) and the month of October 2010. For these time periods, Job Corps reported 17,787 participants found employment.[273] However, the OIG found that Job Corps overstated 7,517 (42.3 percent) of these matches.[274] Of these overstated matches, 3,226 either failed to relate to the vocational training received, such as trainees in office administration being placed in fast food restaurants.[275] Another 4,291 matches were for enrollments in postsecondary education and training, and were for 513 for military enlistments, regardless of the relevancy to the training received while at Job Corps.[276] In addition, 1,569 placements were for "jobs that required little or no previous work-related skills, knowledge, or experience, such as fast food cooks and cashiers, janitors, and dishwashers that potentially could have been obtained without Job Corps training."[277]

According to Job Corps, the cost of the program per participant in program year 2009 was $26,551.[278] This estimate excludes program administration expenses, so it undercounts the true cost of the program on a per participant basis. The OIG estimates that the actual cost per participant is $37,880—a difference of $11,329.[279] Perhaps a more important performance metric is the cost per successful job placement. For this measure, the OIG estimates that each Job Corps participant who is successfully placed into any job costs taxpayers $76,574.[280]

Even if these deficiencies in the performance metrics were corrected, they ultimately cannot tell us about the effectiveness of Job Corps. These performance metrics do not include a counterfactual condition, which is vital to determining effectiveness. No matter which cost-efficiency measure is used, Job Corps is an expensive program. However, we are fortunate because Job Corps has undergone a rigorous large-scale, multisite experimental impact evaluation. In 2001, the National Job Corps Study was published. The experimental evaluation was based on a nationally representative sample of Job Corps participants, with over 11,000 individuals assigned to the intervention and control groups.[281] The selected findings for the National Job Corps Study are summarized in Table 5.5.

Impact on Education. Participation in Job Corps was linked to a greater likelihood of earning a GED or high school diploma. After completion of the 48-month follow-up period, 47.3 percent of Job Corps participants

TABLE 5.5.   The Effectiveness of Job Corps: Selected Findings

Outcome Measure	Results
Education (48 months)	
Earned GED or high school diploma	Pos***
Earned GED	Pos***
High school diploma	Neg***
Vocational, technical, or trade certificate	Pos***
College degree	0
Employment (48 months)	
Average percentage of weeks employed	Neg***
Average hours employed per week	Neg**
Earnings	
Average weekly earnings	
Year 1	Neg***
Year 2	0
Year 3	Pos***
Year 4	Pos***
Years 1 to 4	0
Year 4 average weekly earnings by group	
Age 16 to 17	Pos**
Age 18 to 19	0
Age 20 to 24	Pos**
White, non-Hispanic	Pos**
Black, non-Hispanic	Pos**
Hispanic	0
Other	0
Never arrested	Pos**
Nonserious arrest only	0
Serious arrest (murder, assault, robbery, burglary)	0
Hourly wages	
Quarter 10	Pos***
Quarter 16	Pos***
Criminal activity	
Arrested	
Year 1	Pos***

TABLE 5.5. (Continued)

Outcome Measure	Results
Year 2	0
Year 3	0
Year 4	0
Years 1 to 4	Pos***
Arrest charge	
Murder	0
Assault	0
Robbery	0
Burglary	0
Larceny	0
Drug law violations	0
Convicted	Pos***
Most serious conviction	
Murder	0
Assault	0
Robbery	0
Burglary	0
Larceny	0
Drug law violations	0
All convictions	
Murder	0
Assault	0
Robbery	Pos*
Burglary	0
Larceny	0
Drug law violations	0
Corrections	
Percentage incarcerated	Pos***
Average time incarcerated	0
Percentage ever put on parole or probation	Pos*
Welfare dependency	
Percentage received welfare benefits, any program	
Year 1	Pos***
Year 2	Pos***
Year 3	Pos***
Year 4	0
Years 1 to 4	Pos***
Amount of welfare benefits received, any program	
Year 1	Pos**
Year 2	Pos***

(continued)

TABLE 5.5.   (Continued)

Outcome Measure	Results
Year 3	Pos***
Year 4	Pos**
Years 1 to 4	Pos***
Percentage received AFDC/TANF benefits	
Year 1	0
Year 2	Pos*
Year 3	0
Year 4	0
Years 1 to 4	0
Amount of AFDC/TANF benefits received	
Year 1	0
Year 2	0
Year 3	0
Year 4	0
Years 1 to 4	Pos*
Percentage received food stamp benefits	
Year 1	0
Year 2	0
Year 3	Pos**
Year 4	0
Years 1 to 4	Pos***
Amount of food stamp benefits received	
Year 1	0
Year 2	0
Year 3	0
Year 4	0
Years 1 to 4	0

Key: 0 Finding was not statistically significant

　　Pos Positive or beneficial impact

　　Neg Negative or harmful impact

　　*　　Statistically significant at the 10 percent confidence level ($p \leq 0.10$)

　　**　　Statistically significant at the 5 percent confidence level ($p \leq 0.05$)

　　***　Statistically significant at the 1 percent confidence level ($p \leq 0.01$)

　　n/a No measure was assessed

　　†　　No statistically significance test was performed

Source: Peter Z. Schochet, John Burghardt, and Steven Glazerman, *National Job Corps Study: The Impacts of Job Corps on Participants' Employment and Related Outcomes* (Princeton, NJ: Mathematica Policy Research, Inc., June 2001), Table V.7, 104; Table VI.2, 126; Table VI.3, 127; Figure VI.14, 170; Table VII.6, p207-208; Table VII.8, 212; Table VII.9, 215; Table VII.10, 218; Table VII.1, 184; Table VII.2, 189; Table VII.3, 191.

earned a GED or high school diploma, while the rate for control group members was 34.4 percent—a statistically significant difference of 12.9 percent at the one percent confidence level.[282] This difference in educational attainment appears to be because Job Corps is a GED mill. Job Corps participants are more likely to earn a GED, while they are less likely to earn a high school degree. For the GED-only outcome, 41.6 percent of participants earned certificates, while 26.6 percent of the control group earned certificates—a statistically significant difference of 15 percent at the one percent confidence level.[283] For the high school degree outcome, 5.3 percent of participants earned diplomas, while 7.5 percent of control group members earned diplomas—a statistically significant difference of 2.2 percent at the one percent confidence level.[284] While Job Corps increased the likelihood of obtaining a GED, it slightly decreased the likelihood of earning a high school diploma.

At the statistically significant confidence level of one percent, the difference between earning vocational, technical, or trade certificates was 22.3 percent in favor of program participants—37.5 for Job Corps participants and 15.2 percent for control group members.[285] Participation in Job Corps had no effect on earning two- or four-year college degrees. If Job Corps participants are more likely to earn vocational or trade certificates, does this impact affect employment and earnings?

Impact on Employment.   Over the course of the 48-month study period, Job Corps participants actually worked less than the control group. Measured in the number of weeks employed over the course of the study, Job Corps participants were employed 45.2 percent of the time, while nonparticipants were employed 46.9 percent of the time—a statistically significant difference of 1.7 percent at the one percent confidence level.[286] The study revealed that Job Corps also had little impact on increasing the number of hours worked per week. Over the 48-month follow-up period, Job Corps participants averaged working only 20.5 hours per week, while the control group averaged 21.1 hours per week—a statistically significant difference of 0.5 hours at the five percent confidence level.[287] During the course of the study, the average time participants spent working each week never rose above 28.1 hours.[288] Participants never averaged working more than two hours per week more than the control group.[289] Despite being enrolled in Job Corps, participants failed even to put in a full year's worth of work or come close to working, on average, 40 hours per week.

Impact on Earnings.   While Job Corps was started to raise the incomes of participants, its limited impact has not justified its continued existence. The dollar values reported in this discussion are expressed in 1995 dollars. In the first year after random assignment, the average weekly earnings of Job Corps participants and control group members were $67.60 and $89.60, respectively—a statistically significant reduction of $22.10 at the one percent confidence level.[290] In year two, Job Corps participants averaged $132.20 per week, while control group members averaged $133.30. The difference of $1.10 is statistically indistinguishable from zero. In year three, Job Corps participants and control group members averaged $178.60 and $165.20 per week, respectively. For year three, Job Corps was associated with a statistically significant increase in average weekly earnings of $13.40 at the one percent confidence level. For year 4, Job Corps was associated with an average weekly income increase of $15.90 at the one percent confidence level. Job Corps participants averaged $211.40, while the control group averaged $195.40. Over the total 48-month follow-up period, the difference between average weekly incomes of Job Corps participants and control group members was statistically indistinguishable from zero. When measured on a quarterly basis, the estimated average increase in the weekly incomes of participants was never more than $18.10.[291]

Participants responded to Job Corps differently by age, race, and ethnicity. The authors of the Job Corps evaluation reported findings for these groups for year 4. Job Corps participants aged 16 to 17 experienced an average weekly earnings increase of $17.20, compared to similar control group members.[292] This increase is statistically significant at the five percent confidence level. Job Corps did not increase the earnings of 18- and 19-year-olds, who represent 32 percent of the population served by the program. On average, 18- and 19-year-old Job Corps participants experienced an average weekly income increase of $5.60 that was statistically insignificant. Job Corps participants aged 20 to 24 experienced an average weekly earnings increase of $50.20, compared to similar control group members. This increase is statistically significant at the five percent confidence level.

During the fourth year of the follow-up period, whites and blacks experienced small increases in average earnings per week, while Job Corps had no impact on income for Hispanics and other minorities.[293] For whites, participation in Job Corps was associated with $46.20 in additional weekly earnings, compared to the weekly earnings of similar control group members. This difference is statistically significant at the five percent confidence level. For blacks, the increase in earnings was a statistically significant $22.80 per week at the five percent confidence level. There was no effect for Hispanics. This finding is alarming, given that Hispanics comprise 18 percent of all youths served by the program.

In the fourth year, Job Corps participants without criminal arrest histories before random assignment earned, on average, $21.10 more per week than similar members of the control group.[294] This increase was statistically significant at the five percent confidence level. For Job Corps participants with nonserious and serious arrest records, participating in the program had no effect on weekly income.

Impact of Job Corps on Hourly Wages.   The best way to determine whether Job Corps raises the skills of its participants is to look at its graduates' hourly wages. If Job Corps is effective in improving the skills of its participants, then it should have substantially raised the hourly wages they received. The National Job Corps Study measured hourly wages during two time periods. During the tenth quarter, Job Corps participants earned $0.24 more per hour than nonparticipants—$6.77 per hour for Job Corps participants compared to $6.53 per hour for the control group.[295] The difference of $0.24 is statistically significant at the one percent confidence level. By the sixteenth quarter, this difference had decreased to $0.22 per hour ($7.55 per hour for Job Corps participants and $7.33 per hour for control group members).[296] This difference is statistically significant at the one percent confidence level.

Impact on Crime.   Compared to control group members, Job Corps participants were slightly less likely to be arrested. Over the entire 48-month follow-up period, Job Corps participants had an arrest rate of 28.8 percent, as opposed to the 32.6 percent arrest rate for control group members.[297] This difference of 3.7 percent is statistically significant at the one percent confidence level. Nevertheless, this finding appears to be driven by lower arrest rates during the first year after random assignment. During year one, Job Corps participants and control group members had arrest rates of 11.1 percent and 14.1 percent, respectively. This difference of 3.0 percent is statistically significant at the one percent confidence level. In the remaining years, the differences were statistically indistinguishable from zero. Thus, the minor initial impact of Job Corps on arrests quickly faded. In general, participation in Job Corps had no effect on the type of crime (e.g., murder, assault, robbery, burglary, larceny, drug law violations) participants were arrested for.[298]

Over the course of the 48-month follow-up period, 22.1 percent of Job Corps participants and 25.2 percent of control group members were convicted of a crime—a statistically significant reduction of 3.1 percent at the one percent confidence level.[299] Dissimilar to the arrest findings, the conviction results are not broken down by year. Job Corps participants and control group members did not differ in the most serious charge (e.g., murder, assault, robbery, burglary, larceny, drug law violations) for which they were convicted. However, when the analysis of convictions is based on all convictions, not just the most serious, then Job Corps participants were less slightly less likely to be convicted of robbery. Of Job Corps participants, 1.4 percent were convicted of robbery, while 1.8 percent of the control group had the same conviction. The difference of 0.4 percent is marginally statistically significant at the 10 percent confidence level. There was no effect on convictions for murder, assault, burglary, larceny, and drug law violations.

The slightly lower conviction rate appears to have influenced the results for the incarceration outcome measure. During the 48-month follow-up period, 15.8 percent of Job Corps participants and 17.9 percent of control group members served time in jail—a statistically significant reduction of 2.1 percent at the one percent confidence level.[300] The incarceration results were not broken down by year. However, Job Corps had no effect on the total number of months incarcerated and average time served. Despite this finding, Job Corps participants were slightly less likely to be placed on probation or parole. Of Job Corps participants, 13.5 percent were placed on probation or parole, while 14.6 percent of control group members had similar fates—a statistically significant reduction of 1.2 percent at the less rigorous 10 percent confidence level.

Impact on Welfare Dependency.   Job Corps participants were slightly less likely to receive AFDC/TANF; food stamps; Supplemental Security Income (SSI); Social Security Retirement, Disability, or Survivor benefits (SSA); or general assistance (GA) benefits. In the first year after random assignment, 40.2 percent of Job Corps participants and 42.8 percent of the control group received welfare benefits—a statistically significant reduction of 2.5 percent at the one percent confidence level.[301] In years two and three, the differences were a statistically significant difference of 3.0 percent at the one percent confidence level in favor of Job Corps participants. However, the impact of Job Corps faded. In year 4, 21.7 percent of Job Corps participants and 22.8 percent of control group members received welfare benefits—a statistically indistinguishable difference of one percent. Over the entire four years, 54.5 percent of Job Corps participants received welfare benefits, while 57.5 percent of control group members received welfare benefits—a statistically significant reduction of 3.0 percent at the one percent confidence level.

These slightly lower welfare participation rates for Job Corps participants translated into somewhat lower dollar amounts of welfare benefits received. In the first year after random assignment, Job Corps participants received, on average, $1,109.80 in benefits, while the control group averaged $1,225.90 in benefits—a statistically significant reduction of $116.20 at the five percent confidence level.[302] In years two and three, the differences were $122.90 and $108 in favor of Job Corps participants. These differences were statistically significant at the one percent confidence level. While the difference was statistically significant at the five percent confidence level in year 4, the difference in favor of Job Corps participants fell to only $80.10, on average. Over the course of the entire 48-month follow-up period, Job Corps participants averaged $3,696 in welfare benefits, while the control group averaged $4,155.70 in benefits—a statistically significant reduction of $459.80 at the one percent confidence level.

How did Job Corps impact participation in specific welfare programs? Over the course of the 48-month follow-up period, Job Corps participants were just as likely to receive AFDC/TANF benefits, compared to members of the control group. During this entire period, 33.2 percent of Job Corps participants received AFDC/TANF, while 33.5 percent of the control group did—a statistically indistinguishable difference of 0.3 percent.[303] In years one, three, and four, the differences were statistically indistinguishable as well. The only year there was a difference was year two. For this year, 18.2 percent of Job Corps participants and 19.6 percent of control group members received AFDC/TANF benefits—a marginally statistically significant difference of 1.4 percent at the 10 percent confidence level.

As for the amount of AFDC/TANF dollars received, Job Corps participants received an average of $1,484.70 over the entire 48-month follow-up period, while the control group averaged $1,607.70—a statistically significant difference of $123 at the less rigorous 10 percent confidence level.[304] When the average amounts of AFDC/TANF benefits received are broken down by year, the differences are statistically indistinguishable from zero.

Over the course of the 48-month follow-up period, Job Corps participants were slightly less likely to receive food stamp benefits, compared to members of the control group. During this entire period, 45.7 percent of Job Corps participants received food stamps, while 48.3 percent of the control group received them—a statistically significant reduction of 2.7 percent at the one percent confidence level.[305] However, when the data is analyzed by year, the previous findings appear to be driven by only one of the four years. In year three, 20.3 percent of Job Corps participants received food stamps, compared to 22.2 percent of control group members—a statistically significant reduction of 1.9 percent at the five percent confidence level. In the other years, the differences were statistically indistinguishable from zero. Despite this small effect on the receipt of food stamps, participation had no effect on the average dollar amount of food stamps received.

Is the Job Corps Worth Its High Cost?   Those who did benefit from the Job Corps experienced only slight gains in income. Job Corps appears to be incapable of providing the necessary skills and training to substantially raise the wages of participants. Despite costing taxpayers $76,574 per participant successfully placed into a job, the program has failed to move a significant number of participants into full-time employment.

A second evaluation, the 2001 National Job Corps Study: The Benefits and Costs of Job Corps ("2001 cost-benefit study"), found small increases in income and other benefits due to Job Corps participation that outweighed the costs of the program to society.[306] Hence, Job Corps was deemed a "highly successful" program.[307]

A third evaluation, the National Job Corps Study: Findings Using Administrative Earnings Records Data ("2003 study"), was published in 2003, but the Labor Department withheld it from the general public until 2006.[308] Overall, the 2003 study found that Job Corps participation did not increase employment and earnings. Searching for something positive to report, the 2003 study concluded that "There is some evidence, however, of positive earnings gains for those ages 20 to 24."[309]

Why withhold the 2003 study? Based on survey data, the 2001 cost-benefit study assumed that the gains in income for participants would last indefinitely, a notion unsupported by the literature on job training.[310] But included in the 2003 study is a cost-benefit analysis that directly contradicts the positive findings of the 2001 cost-benefit study.

The 2003 study used official government data, instead of self-reported data, and used the more reasonable assumption that benefits decay, rather than last indefinitely.[311] Contradicting the 2001 cost-benefit study, the 2003 study's analysis of official government data found that the benefits of Job Corps do not outweigh the program's costs. Even more damaging, the 2003 study re-estimated the 2001 cost-benefit study with the original survey data, using the realistic assumption that benefits decay over time. According to this analysis, the program's costs again outweighed its benefits.

Is Job Corps worth $1.8 billion per year?[312] Some argue that Job Corps is worth its cost to taxpayers because there is "some evidence" of positive income gains for those aged 20 to 24.[313] This belief is based on findings that these participants had consistently higher annual incomes from 1998 to 2001 than nonparticipants of similar age.[314] But this conclusion is questionable. In 1998, participants aged 20 to 24 experienced an average increase in annual income of $476 that, by traditional scientific standards, is statistically significant based on the five percent confidence level, meaning that the income gains are very likely attributable to Job Corps. For the remaining years, the income gains were positive, ranging from $429 to $375, but statistically insignificant, meaning that the findings cannot be attributed to participation in Job Corps. Thus, it cannot be concluded that Job Corps consistently raised the incomes of participants aged 20 to 24.

By the logic of the 2003 study, a stronger case can be made that Job Corps consistently reduced the incomes of female participants without children. In 1998 and 1999, childless female participants earned $1,243 and $1,401 *less*, respectively, than similar nonparticipants.[315] These findings are statistically significant at the five percent confidence level, suggesting that Job Corps had a harmful effect. In 2000 and 2001, the earnings of childless female participants were still beneath those of their counterparts, but the differences are statistically insignificant, indicating that the declines in income are not attributable to Job Corps—just like most of the income gains for participants aged 20 to 24 in the 2003 study. The 2003 study's findings are not surprising because the 2001 outcome study found Job Corps ineffective at substantially increasing participants' wages and moving them into full-time employment.[316]

The 2001 outcome study revealed that Job Corps had little impact on the number of hours worked per week. During the course of the study, the average time participants spent working each week never rose above 28.1 hours.[317] On average, participants never worked more than two hours per week more than those in the control group.[318]

If Job Corps actually improves the skills of its participants, then it should have substantially raised their hourly wages. The 2001 study found participants earned $0.24 more per hour than nonparticipants.[319] Six months later, this difference had decreased to $0.22 per hour.[320] Job Corps does not provide the skills and training necessary to substantially raise the wages of participants. One is certainly within reason to question whether the program is a waste of taxpayers' dollars as it costs $76,574 per participant placed in any job with an average participation period of eight months.

JOBSTART

Implemented at 13 sites across the nation between 1985 and 1988, the JOBSTART Demonstration evaluated the impact of job-training programs offered by community-based organizations, schools, and Job Corps.[321] The 13 sites were job-training programs operated in the following locations:

- Buffalo, New York
- Atlanta, Georgia
- New York, New York
- Harford, Connecticut
- San Jose, California
- Chicago, Illinois
- Pittsburgh, Pennsylvania
- Monterey, California
- Dallas, Texas
- Denver, Colorado
- Los Angeles, California
- Phoenix, Arizona
- Corpus Christi, Texas

With funding from the Department of Labor, the targets of JOBSTART were 17- to 21-year-old "economically disadvantaged" school dropouts with poor reading skills.[322] Intended to alleviate the problem of youth unemployment, JOBSTART was a combination of education, occupational skills training, child and transportation support services, and job placement assistance.[323] Based on random assignment, 1,163 individuals were allocated to the intervention (JOBSTART) group, and 1,149 were allocated to the control group.[324] The evaluation used follow-up surveys to assess program impact at 12-, 24-, and 48-month intervals.[325]

Impact on Education and Training.   The findings of the JOBSTART evaluation are summarized in Table 5.6. Over the course of 48 months, JOBSTART participants were more likely to have received education and training, compared to members of the control group.[326] For example, 94.0 percent of JOBSTART participants received education or training, while 56.1 percent of the control group had similar experiences—a statistically significant difference of 37.9 percent at the one percent confidence level.[327] Over the same time period, JOBSTART participants received an average of 799.6 hours of education and training, while members of the control group

TABLE 5.6. The Effectiveness of JOBSTART: Selected Findings

Outcome Measure	Full Sample	Men	Men not Arrested between age 16 and random assignment	Men Arrested between age 16 and random assignment	Women Living with Own Children	Women Living without Children
Education or Training (48 months)						
Ever received any education or training	Pos***	n/a	n/a	n/a	n/a	n/a
Hours of education or training received	Pos***	n/a	n/a	n/a	n/a	n/a
Received GED	Pos***	n/a	n/a	n/a	n/a	n/a
Received GED or high school diploma	Pos***	n/a	n/a	n/a	n/a	n/a
Received trade certificate or license	Pos***	n/a	n/a	n/a	n/a	n/a
Received associate's or 2-year college degree	0	n/a	n/a	n/a	n/a	n/a
Received bachelor's or 4-year college degree	0	n/a	n/a	n/a	n/a	n/a
Earnings						
Income						
Year 1	Neg***	Neg***	n/a	n/a	0	0
Year 2	0	0	n/a	n/a	0	0
Year 3	0	0	n/a	n/a	0	0
Year 4	0	0	n/a	n/a	0	0
Years 1 to 4	0	0	n/a	n/a	0	0
Hourly wages						
Year 1	n/a	0	n/a	n/a	0	Neg*

(continued)

TABLE 5.6. (Continued)

Outcome Measure	Full Sample	Men	Men not Arrested between age 16 and random assignment	Men Arrested between age 16 and random assignment	Women Living with Own Children	Women Living without Children
Year 2	n/a	0	n/a	n/a	0	0
Year 3	n/a	0	n/a	n/a	0	0
Year 4	n/a	0	n/a	n/a	0	0
Years 1 to 4	n/a	0	n/a	n/a	0	Pos***
Welfare dependency						
Ever received AFDC						
Year 1	0	0	n/a	n/a	0	0
Year 2	0	0	n/a	n/a	0	Pos**
Year 3	0	0	n/a	n/a	0	Pos**
Year 4	0	0	n/a	n/a	0	Pos*
Years 1 to 4	0	0	n/a	n/a	0	0
AFDC income						
Year 1	0	0	n/a	n/a	0	0
Year 2	0	0	n/a	n/a	0	0
Year 3	0	0	n/a	n/a	0	Pos*
Year 4	0	0	n/a	n/a	0	0
Years 1 to 4	0	0	n/a	n/a	0	0
Ever received food stamps						
Year 1	0	0	n/a	n/a	0	0
Year 2	0	0	n/a	n/a	Pos*	0
Year 3	0	0	n/a	n/a	Pos*	0
Year 4	0	0	n/a	n/a	0	0

Years 1 to 4	0	0	n/a	0	0
Food stamp income					
Year 1	0	0	n/a	n/a	0	0
Year 2	0	0	n/a	n/a	0	0
Year 3	0	0	n/a	n/a	0	0
Year 4	0	0	n/a	n/a	0	0
Years 1 to 4	0	0	n/a	n/a	0	0
Criminal Activity					
Ever arrested					
Year 1	Pos*	Pos*	0	0	0
Years 1 to 4	0	0	0	0	0

Key: 0 Finding was not statistically significant

Pos Positive or beneficial impact

Neg Negative or harmful impact

* Statistically significant at the 10 percent confidence level ($p \leq 0.10$)

** Statistically significant at the 5 percent confidence level ($p \leq 0.05$)

*** Statistically significant at the 1 percent confidence level ($p \leq 0.01$)

n/a No measure was assessed or reported

† No statistically significance test was performed

Source: George Cave, Hans Bos, Fred Doolittle, Cyril Toussaint, *JOBSTART: Final Report on a Program for School Dropouts.* Manpower Demonstration Research Corporation, October 1993, Table 4.1, p. 95; Table 4.2, p. 97; Table 4.5, p. 109; Table 5.1, p. 119Table; 5.2, p. 120; Table 5.9, 156–159; Table 5.8, 153–154; Table 6.1, 180–181; Table 6.2, 183–184; Table 6.3, 186–187; Table 6.4, 188–189; Table 6.7, 195–196.

received 432.4 hours—a statistically significant difference of 367.2 hours at the one percent confidence level.[328]

Participation in JOBSTART was also associated with being more likely to obtain a GED or high school diploma over the 48-month follow-up period.[329] For instance, 37.6 percent of JOBSTART participants earned a GED, compared to 21.1 percent of the control group—a statistically significant difference of 16.5 percent at the one percent confidence level.[330] Over the same time period, 33.1 percent of JOBSTART participants earned a trade certificate or license, compared to 17.3 percent of the control group—a statistically significant difference of 15.8 percent at the one percent confidence level.[331] Despite these beneficial outcomes, JOBSTART participation failed to have an impact on the receipt of an associate's or bachelor's degree.[332]

Impact on Earnings.   While JOBSTART participants were more likely to earn GEDs, high school diplomas, or trade certificates, this positive impact appears to have done little to increase the earnings of participants. The difference in total earnings over 48 months (four years) between JOBSTART participants and members of the control group was statistically indistinguishable from zero, meaning the program failed to raise participants' incomes.[333] Total earnings for JOBSTART participants and control group members averaged $17,010 and $16,796, respectively—a statistically insignificant difference of $214. When earnings were analyzed by year, the results were not better. In year one, participants earned an average of $2,097, while the control group averaged $2,569—a statistically significant reduction of $499 at the one percent confidence level. In years two through four, the differences were statistically indistinguishable from zero.

During the four-year time period, JOBSTART participation failed to raise incomes when the findings were analyzed by the following subgroups: men, women living with own children, and woman not living with children.[334] For men, participation in JOBSTART was associated with an average earnings decrease of $812 in year one—a statistically significant reduction at the one percent confidence level. The impacts of JOBSTART for men were statistically indistinguishable from zero in years two through four. For the two categories for women, participation in JOBSTART failed to have statistically significant impacts, negative or positive, by year and total years. In addition, JOBSTART failed to have an impact on total income over the four-year follow-up period when the results were analyzed by race and ethnicity.[335]

Impact on Wages.   For men and woman living with their own children, participation in JOBSTART had no effect on raising the hourly wages of participants in each year of the annual follow-up periods over four years.[336] The same pattern generally held for held for women not living with their own children.

In year one for women not living with their children, the average hourly wages for the intervention and control group were $4.14 and $4.43, respectively. The reduction of $0.29 was statistically significant at the less rigorous 10 percent confidence level. In years two and three, the differences were statistically insignificant. During the fourth year, however, female JOBSTART participants not living with children had hourly wages that averaged $0.77 more than their counterparts.[337] This difference was statistically significant at the one percent confidence level. In the view of employers, JOBSTART appears to have done little to increase productivity of participants that would have been recognized through higher hourly wages.

Impact on Welfare Dependency.   In addition to education and income measures, the JOBSTART evaluation measured the level of participation in welfare programs. For example, participation in JOBSTART failed to raise or lower participation in the Aid to Families with Dependent Children (AFDC) and Food Stamp programs in each year after random assignment and over the entire 48-month follow-up period.[338]

For women not living with children at the time of random assignment, participation in JOBSTART had no effect on ever receiving AFDC one year after random assignment.[339] In years two and three, female participants with children at the time of random assignment were less likely to have received AFDC payments, compared to control group members.[340] The differences, statistically significant at the five percent confidence level, in years two and three were 8.0 percent and 9.1 one percent. These decreases in AFDC receipt did not persist into the fourth year at the same level of statistical significance. In year four, the difference was 8.6 percent, with a marginal statistical significance at the 10 percent confidence level.

In general, participation in JOBSTART had no effect on the amount of AFDC income received by women not living with children, except for year two. In this year, these women in the intervention group received, on average, $1,001 in AFDC payments, compared to $1,311 for similar control group members—a statistically significant reduction of $310 at the less rigorous 10 percent confidence level.[341] For food stamp involvement, women participants without children at the time of random assignment were no more or less likely to participate in the Food Stamp program by year and over the entire 48-month follow-up period.[342]

For women living with their own children at the time of random assignment, participation in JOBSTART failed to have an impact on AFDC participation and total AFDC income received, negatively or positively, by year and over the entire 48-month follow-up period.[343] As for food stamps, the differences in participation rates were statistically significant only at the less rigorous 10 percent confidence level for years two and three. During these years, women living with their own children had participation rates that were 6.1 percent and 7.0 percent lower. However, this reduction in food stamp participation did not translate into lower amounts of food stamp income by year and over the entire 48-month follow-up period.

By year and entire 48-month follow-up period, participation in JOBSTART failed to have effects, negatively or positively, on participation in and income received from AFDC and food stamps.[344]

Impact on Crime.　Participation in JOBSTART appeared to have little measurable impact on arrest rates for the full sample.[345] At the year-one follow-up period, 10.1 percent of JOBSTART participants had been arrested at least once, while the rate for control group members was 12.6 percent—a marginally statistically significant difference of 2.6 percent at the 10 percent confidence level.[346] Over the entire four-year follow-up period, the arrest rates were nearly identical at 29.0 percent for the intervention group and 29.3 percent for the control group. This minute difference was statistically insignificant.

There was a pattern of no impact for men arrested between age 16 and random assignment, women living with children at random assignment, and women not living with children at random assignment.[347] However, participation in JOBSTART appears to have lowered the arrest rates of male participants who had not been arrested between age 16 and random assignment. During the first year after random assignment, 11.2 percent of men without previous arrest records between the age of 16 and random assignment were arrested, compared to 17.6 percent for similar control group members—a statistically significant difference of 6.4 percent.[348] The difference between arrests rates over the entire 48-month follow-up period was statistically indistinguishable.

The JOBSTART evaluation assessed drug use only during the fourth year after random assignment. The overwhelming majority of the differences in drug use between JOBSTART participants and control group members, even for the subgroups (men, men with arrest records before random assignment, and women), were statistically indistinguishable at the five percent confidence level.[349] However, JOBSTART men arrested between age 16 and random assignment had lower levels of using any drug other than marijuana during the fourth year—3.7 percent for the JOBSTART group and 10.5 percent for the control group.[350] This difference of 6.9 percent was statistically significant at the five percent confidence level. In addition, for the full sample, 4.1 percent of JOBSTART participants and 5.8 percent of control group members reported using any drug, except marijuana, during year four—a statistically significant difference of 1.7 percent at the less rigorous 10 percent confidence level.

JOBSTART Impacts by Site.   Over the course of the 48-month follow-up period, total earnings for JOBSTART participants failed to be statistically different from members of the control group at 12 of 13 sites, suggesting that the overwhelming majority of JOBSTART sites were ineffective at raising the incomes of participants.[351] One of the sites—Center for Employment Training (CET) in San Jose, California—had a positive impact on earnings. In San Jose over the course of 48 months, job-training participants had an average total income of $29,600, and the control group participants averaged $22,252 in total income—a statistically significant impact of an additional $7,342 at the one percent confidence level.[352] Thus, at a single site, CET appears to have been effective at raising the incomes of participants. For policymakers, the important question is: Can these results be replicated at different sites and for different populations?

Overall, JOBSTART certainly had significant effects on increasing the receipt of GEDs and training, while the program failed to increase obtaining associate's or bachelor's degrees. However, the increased likelihood of obtaining GEDs and training appears to have had no positive effects on earnings. In fact, participation in JOBSTART was associated with a decrease in earnings during the first year after random assignment for all participants, and for men in particular.

CET Replication

Based on the JOBSTART evaluation results for the Center for Employment Training (CET) in San Jose, California, the U.S. Department of

Labor, in 1992, sought to replicate the program at 16 other sites. Twelve of the sites were evaluated:

- New York, New York
- Newark, New Jersey
- Camden, New Jersey
- Reidsville, North Carolina
- Orlando, Florida
- Chicago, Illinois
- Reno, Nevada
- San Francisco, California
- El Centro, California
- Oxnard, California
- Riverside, California
- Santa Maria, California

From 1995 to 1999, the job-training sites randomly assigned 1,485 out-of-school, 16- to 21-year-old youth to the intervention and control groups.[353] Both members of the job-training and control groups were tracked over 48 months after random assignment.

The key elements of the CET model include a full-time commitment to participate in employment and training services in work-like settings.[354] In addition, employers were involved in designing and delivering services.[355]

Impact on Education and Training.   Table 5.7 summarizes the selected findings of the CET evaluation. Over the course of 48 months, the CET participants were more likely to receive training credentials, compared to members of the control group.[356] For example, at the 48-month follow-up period, 52.7 percent of CET participants had earned training credentials, while 41.5percent of control group had earned similar credentials—a statistically significant difference of 11.2 percent at the one percent confidence level.[357] However, the differences between the percentages of CET participants and control group members in obtaining high school diplomas and GEDs were statistically indistinguishable, strongly indicating that the program had no impact on these outcomes.[358]

Impact on Employment and Earnings.   While CET participants were more likely to obtain credentials, this attainment failed entirely to translate into increased employment and earnings. In annual follow-up periods over

TABLE 5.7. The Effectiveness of CET Replication: Selected Findings

| | | | | | High-Fidelity Sites | | | |
Outcome Measure	Full Sample	High-Fidelity Sites	Men	Women	16 to 18 Years Old	19 Years Old and Older	High School Diploma or GED	Without High School Diploma or GED
Education or Training								
Received training certificate by								
Month 1	Pos**	0	0	0	0	0	0	0
Month 12	Pos***	Pos***	Pos***	Pos***	Pos*	Pos***	Pos***	Pos***
Month 24	Pos***	Pos***	0	Pos***	Pos**	Pos***	Pos***	Pos***
Month 36	Pos***	Pos***	0	Pos***	Pos**	Pos***	Pos***	Pos***
Month 48	Pos***	Pos***	0	Pos***	Pos**	Pos***	Pos***	Pos***
Received high school diploma by								
Month 1	0	0	0	0	0	0	n/a	0
Month 12	0	0	0	0	0	0	n/a	0
Month 24	0	0	0	0	0	0	n/a	0
Month 36	0	0	0	0	0	0	n/a	Neg*
Month 48	0	0	0	0	0	0	n/a	Neg*
Received GED by								
Month 1	0	0	0	0	0	0	n/a	0
Month 12	0	0	0	0	0	0	n/a	0
Month 24	0	0	0	0	0	0	n/a	0

(continued)

TABLE 5.7. (Continued)

Outcome Measure	Full Sample	High-Fidelity Sites	High-Fidelity Sites					
			Men	Women	16 to 18 Years Old	19 Years Old and Older	High School Diploma or GED	Without High School Diploma or GED
Month 36	0	0	0	0	0	0	n/a	0
Month 48	0	0	0	0	0	0	n/a	0
Received GED or high school diploma by								
Month 1	0	0	0	Pos*	0	0	n/a	n/a
Month 12	0	0	0	0	0	0	n/a	n/a
Month 24	0	0	0	0	0	0	n/a	n/a
Month 36	0	0	0	0	0	0	n/a	n/a
Month 48	0	0	0	0	0	0	n/a	n/a
Employment and Earnings								
Ever worked								
Year 1	0	0	0	0	0	0	0	0
Year 2	0	0	0	Pos**	0	0	0	0
Year 3	0	0	Neg**	0	0	0	0	0
Year 4	0	0	0	0	0	0	0	0
Year 5	0	0	0	0	0	0	0	0
Number of months worked								
Year 1	0	0	0	0	0	0	Neg**	0
Year 2	0	0	0	0	0	0	Neg**	0
Year 3	0	0	Neg**	0	0	0	0	0

Year 4	0	0	0	0	0	0
Year 5	0	0	0	0	0	0
Earnings						
Year 1	0	0	0	0	Neg**	0
Year 2	0	0	0	0	Neg**	0
Year 3	Neg**	0	0	0	Neg***	0
Year 4	0	0	Pos*	0	0	0
Year 5	0	0	Pos***	0	0	0
Benefits provided for most recent job						
Health insurance	Neg**	0	0	Neg**	Neg**	0
Paid sick days	0	0	0	0	0	0
Paid vacation days	0	0	0	Neg*	0	0

Key: 0 Finding was not statistically significant
Pos Positive or beneficial impact
Neg Negative or harmful impact
*   Statistically significant at the 10 percent confidence level ($p \leq 0.10$)
**   Statistically significant at the 5 percent confidence level ($p \leq 0.05$)
***   Statistically significant at the 1 percent confidence level ($p \leq 0.01$)
n/a   No measure was assessed or reported
†   No statistically significance test was performed

Source: Cynthia Miller, Johannes M. Ros, Kristen E. Porter, Fannie M. Tseng, and Yasuyo Abe, *The Challenge of Replicating Success in a Changing World: Final Report on the Center for Employment Training Replication Cites* (Manpower Demonstration Research Corporation, September 2005), Table 2.3, 32; Table 2.5, 37–38; Table 2.7, 42–43; Table 2.9, 46–47; Table 2.11, 51–52; Table 3.2, 64; Table 3.4, 67; Table 3.5, 69–70; Table 3.6, 72–73; Table 3.8, 81–82; Table 3.9, 83–84; Table 3.10, 85–86; Table 3.11, 88–89; and Table 3.12, 90–91.

five years, the differences in the percentage of CET participants and control group participants that reported ever working were statistically indistinguishable.[359] Similarly, the number of months worked per year over the 5-year follow-up period for CET participants was statistically indistinguishable from the number of months worked by the control group.[360] The services provided by CET appear to be so ineffective that participants never worked more that 7.7 months per year.[361] During the same 5-year follow-up period, the differences in annual incomes between CET and control group participants were statistically indistinguishable from zero.[362] In year 5, for example, CET participants earned an average income of $12,857, while the control group averaged $13,002—a statistically insignificant difference of $145. In addition, CET participants were no more likely to obtain jobs that offered health insurance, paid sick days, and paid vacation days than the jobs obtained by members of the control group.[363] For the characteristics of their most recent job, for example, 39.5percent of CET participants and 40.4 percent of control group members reported having health insurance—a statistically indistinguishable difference of 0.9 percent. Thus, participation in CET appears to have no effect on ever working, the number of months employed per year, income, and benefits.

High-Fidelity Sites.   Next, the outcomes for the high-fidelity sites were compared to the outcomes for the medium-to-low fidelity sites. Of the 12 CET replication sites, only four sites (El Centro, Oxnard, Riverside, and Santa Maria) were considered to consistently implement the original CET model as intended.[364] These sites are considered to be high-fidelity sites and, presumably, should produce greater positive impacts than the lower-fidelity sites.

At the high-fidelity sites, the intervention group was more likely to earn training certificates 12 months to 48 months after random assignment, than the control group.[365] These positive impacts were highly statistically significant at the one percent confidence level. Nevertheless, participation at the high-fidelity sites had no effect on earning high school diplomas or GEDs.

Regardless of fidelity type, participation in CET appears to have no effect on ever working, the number of months employed per year, and income.[366] However, there was a difference in employment benefits provided, with participation at high-fidelity sites having a negative effect on the receipt of health insurance benefits. At high-fidelity sites, 36.6 percent of CET participants reported that their most recent job provided health insurance, while 47.7 percent of control group participants reported that their most recent job provided health insurance—a statistically significant difference of 11.1 percent at the five percent confidence level.[367] Otherwise, there were no differences in the provision of benefits, such as paid sick and vacation days, when the outcomes were separated by implementation fidelity.

High-Fidelity Sites by Gender.   The evaluation also assessed outcomes at the high-fidelity sites by gender. Female high-fidelity CET participants were more likely to earn training certificates 12 to 48 months after random assignment.[368] These differences were highly statistically significant at the one percent confidence level. The results for men were less consistent. Twelve months after random assignment, male CET participants at high-fidelity sites were more likely to earn training certificates. The positive impact was statistically significant at the one percent confidence level. After this time, this positive impact faded away to no effect at all.

Female high-fidelity CET participants were more likely to report ever working during the 30-month follow up period compared to female members of the control group. Of female high-fidelity CET participants, 91.8 percent reported ever working, compared to 80.3 percent of female control group members—a statistically significant difference of 11.5 percent at the five percent confidence level.[369] However, the difference in the reporting of ever working between the female high-fidelity CET and control group participants was statistically indistinguishable at the 54-month follow-up period.[370]

In the annual follow-up periods over five years, the differences in the percentage of female high-fidelity CET and control group participants that reported ever working were statistically indistinguishable for all years, except for year two. In year two, 84.0 percent of female high-fidelity CET participants reported ever working, while 67.3 percent of female control group members reported ever working—a statistically significant difference of 16.7 percent at the five percent confidence level.[371]

The number of months worked per year over the five-year follow-up periods for the female high-fidelity CET participants were statistically indistinguishable from the number of months worked by members of the control group.[372] The services provided by CET appear to be so ineffective that female high-fidelity CET participants never worked more that 8.7 months per year.[373] Further, there was no measurable impact on the receipt of health insurance, paid sick days, and paid vacation days.[374] During the same five-year follow-up period, the differences in annual incomes for female high-fidelity CET and control group participants were statistically indistinguishable.[375]

The outcomes for men participating in the high-fidelity CET sites were even more disappointing. Male high-fidelity CET participants were less likely to report ever working during the 30-month follow up period compared to male members of the control group. Of male high-fidelity CET participants, 93.3 percent reported ever working, compared to 99.4 percent of male control group members—a statistically significant difference of 6.2 percent at the five percent confidence level.[376] However, the negative impact of CET did not carry over into the 54-month follow-up period.[377]

In annual follow-up periods over five years, the differences in the percentage of male high-fidelity CET and control group participants that reported ever working were statistically indistinguishable for all years, except for year three, for which there was a negative impact. In year three, 84.7 percent of male high-fidelity CET participants reported ever working, while 96.4 percent of male control group members reported ever working—a statistically significant difference of 11.7 percent at the five percent confidence level.[378]

The number of months worked per year over the five-year follow-up period for the male high-fidelity CET participants, except for one year, were statistically indistinguishable from the number of months worked by the control group.[379] During the third-year follow-up, male high-fidelity CET participants averaged only 8.4 months of work compared to the 9.8 months of work reported by the control group—a statistically significant difference of 1.4 months at the five percent confidence level.[380] The services provided by CET appear to be so ineffective that male high-fidelity participants never worked more that 9.8 months per year.[381] Further, there was no measurable impact on the receipt of health insurance, paid sick days, and paid vacation days.[382]

During the same five-year follow-up period, the differences in annual incomes for male high-fidelity CET and control group participants for four out of the five years were statistically indistinguishable.[383] In year three, male high-fidelity CET participants had statistically lower annual incomes than the male control group. On average during the third year, male high-fidelity CET participants earned over $3,400 less than their counterparts.[384] This finding was statistically significant at the five percent confidence level.

High-Fidelity Sites by Age.   The CET Replication also assessed the program's impact at high-fidelity sites by two age groups: 16 to 18 years old at program entry and age 19 and older at program entry. From 12 to 28 months after random assignment, participation at high-fidelity sites was associated with obtaining training certificates for both age groups.[385] These impacts had levels of statistical significance that ranged from the 10 percent to one percent confidence levels.

For both age groups, participation at high-fidelity CET sites failed to have an impact on all the ever worked and number of months worked outcomes.[386] On the other hand, there appears to be a limited effect on annual earnings. While there was no effect during years one through three, there appears to have been an effect for years four and five. In year four, 16- to 18-year-old participants earned $16,630, on average, while similar control group members earned $12,226—a statistically significant difference of $4,403.50 at the less rigorous 10 percent confidence level. In year five, these participants experienced an average increase in income of over $5,620, compared to their counterparts ($16,181 versus $12,226).[387] This positive impact is statistically significant at the five percent confidence level.

The results for the age 19 and older participants were less encouraging. Participating at high-fidelity CET sites appears to have had no statistically measurable impact on annual incomes in years one through five.[388]

Further, there was no measurable impact on the receipt of employment benefits of health insurance, paid sick days, and paid vacation days for participants aged 16 to 18. However, high-fidelity CET participants age 19 and older were less likely to obtain jobs that provided health insurance than their counterparts. Of participants age 19 and older, 36.5 percent acquired employment-related health insurance compared to 49.8 percent of the control group—a statistically significant difference of 13.3 percent at the five percent confidence level.[389] For paid vacation days, 42.3 percent of age 19 and older participants and 54.2 percent of similar control group members received this benefit. The difference of 11.9 percent was statistically significant at the less rigorous 10 percent confidence level. Participation at high-fidelity CET sites failed to affect the receipt of paid vacation days for this subgroup.

High-Fidelity Sites by Education.   When the outcomes for the high-fidelity CET sites are analyzed by whether the participants held high school diplomas or GEDs at the time of entry into the study, similarly disappointing results occurred. Both education groups that participated at high-fidelity sites were more likely to obtain training certificates than their counterparts 12 to 48 months after random assignment. These impacts were statistically significant at the one percent confidence level.

For those without high school diplomas or GEDs, participating at the high-fidelity CET sites failed to have impacts on ever worked, months worked, and income outcomes.[390] While participation at high-fidelity CET sites did not lead to participants being more likely to obtain jobs that provided paid sick days and paid vacation days, they were significantly less likely to obtain jobs that provided health insurance. Out of the participant group, 27.1 percent obtained health insurance through their jobs, while 41.8 percent of the control group obtained employer-provided health insurance—a statistically significant difference of 14.7 percent at the five percent confidence level.[391]

For those who had already obtained high school diplomas or GEDs, participating at high-fidelity CET sites had negative outcomes. While participation failed to impact ever worked outcomes, participants with high school diplomas or GEDs experienced decreases in months worked per year and annual income. These participants worked two fewer months per year during the first and second years after participating in the program.[392] These differences were statistically significant at the five percent confidence level. Further, these participants experienced substantial annual income declines of $2,611, $3,704, and $4,620 during follow-up years one through three.[393] In years one and two, the differences were statistically significant at the five percent level, while in year three, the difference was statistically significant at the one percent confidence level. Further, participation at high-fidelity CET sites by this group failed to have an impact on obtaining paid sick days, paid vacation days, and health insurance.[394]

Medium-to-Low Fidelity Sites.   Next, the outcomes for the high-fidelity sites were compared to the outcomes for the medium-to-low fidelity sites. Regardless of fidelity type, participation in CET appears to have had no effect on ever working, the number of months employed per year, and income.[395] However, there was a difference in benefits provided. At high-fidelity sites, 36.6 percent of CET participants reported that their most recent job provided health insurance, while 47.7 percent of control group participants reported that their most recent job provided health insurance—a statistically significant difference of 11.1 percent at the five percent confidence level.[396] Otherwise, there were no differences in the provision of benefits when the outcomes were separated by implementation fidelity.

In conclusion, the CET model had little to no effect on short-term and long-term employment and earnings outcomes. However, the findings for female participants were a little more encouraging than the findings for male participants. The multisite experimental evaluation of CET, according to its authors, "shows, that even in sites that best implemented the model, CET had no overall employment and earnings effects for youth in the program, even though it increased participants' hours of training and receipt of credentials."[397]

The Quantum Opportunity Program Demonstration

The Quantum Opportunity Program (QOP) demonstration, operated by the U.S. Department of Labor and the Ford Foundation from 1995 to 2001, offered intensive and comprehensive services with the intention of helping at-risk youth graduate from high school and enroll in postsecondary education or training.[398] As an afterschool program, QOP provided case management and mentoring, additional education, developmental and community service activities, supportive services, and financial incentives.[399] QOP provided services to participants year-round for five years. The results of the QOP demonstration are particularly important because the program included several features of WIA's youth programs' funding stream.[400] Thus, the findings from the QOP experimental evaluation, according to its authors, provide some insight about the effectiveness of WIA youth programs.[401]

The QOP demonstration was implemented at seven sites across the nation. Five sites—in Cleveland, Fort Worth, Houston, Memphis, and Washington, DC—were funded by the Department of Labor, while the remaining two sites—in Philadelphia and Yakima, Washington—were funded by the Ford Foundation.[402] The total cost per participant for the Labor-funded sites was $18,000 to $22,000, while the cost per participant in the Ford-funded sites was $23,000 in Yakima and $49,000 in Philadelphia.[403]

Through the acquisition of human capital by completing high school and obtaining postsecondary education or training, QOP is intended enhance the career prospects and earnings potential of youth participants.[404] In addition, QOP attempts to help participants develop the skills to avoid risky behaviors that are barriers to success.[405]

Youth entering ninth grade who met the following criteria were eligible to participate:

- Entered ninth grade at a high school selected for the QOP evaluation
- Were not repeating the ninth grade
- Were not physically or learning disabled so as to make participation inappropriate
- Had a grade point average below the 67th percentile among students eligible under the first three criteria[406]

Once the participants were selected, they engaged in several educational, developmental, and community service activities. Educational activities were intended to enhance academic achievement and, thus, increase the likelihood of graduating from high school and attending college or postsecondary training.[407] To reduce risky behaviors and prepare youths for retaining employment, QOP provided training in life and employment-readiness skills.[408] To develop a sense of civic responsibility, participants did voluntary work at local nursing homes and food banks.[409]

QOP has many similarities with WIA youth programs, including:

- Case management and mentoring by adult staff
- Basic education and study skills tutoring
- Community service training
- Year-round services, including summer jobs
- An assortment of support services, including transportation, childcare, food, and emergency financial assistance
- Technical assistance to local service providers[410]

According to the authors of the QOP evaluation:

These similarities between QOP and WIA youth programs suggest that the findings from the evaluation of the QOP demonstration might reveal some of the implementation challenges that WIA youth programs might encounter and *indicate whether WIA youth programs are likely to be effective* [emphasis added].[411]

The evaluation included 580 QOP and 489 control group participants.[412] During the first four years of the QOP demonstration, enrollees spent an average of 174 hours per year on educational, developmental, and community service activities.[413] Annual participation was substantially less than the program's goal of 750 hours of participation per year.[414]

Impact on High School Completion and Performance

Table 5.8 summarizes the selected findings of the QOP evaluation. For the initial postintervention impacts, participation in QOP failed to increase the likelihood of graduating from high school by earning a diploma—60 percent of QOP participants and 64 percent of the control group members received high school diplomas.[415] This difference of four percent is statistically indistinguishable from zero. When the outcome measure was the receipt of either a high school diploma or GED, QOP failed to increase education attainment—76 percent of both the QOP and control groups earned their diploma or GED.[416] At the six-year follow up, participation in QOP failed to have an effect on graduating high school with a diploma and/or earning a GED.[417]

Further, participation in QOP failed to affect academic performance in high school. Specifically, QOP participation failed to influence mathematics and reading achievement, cumulative grade point averages, total credits earned, and being suspended or expelled.[418] For example, the mean cumulative grade point averages for the intervention and control groups, respectively, were 2.13 and 2.19—a statistically indistinguishable difference of 0.06.

Impact on Postsecondary Education or Training

How did QOP affect postsecondary educational attainment? For almost all of the initial postintervention outcomes measures, the differences between the QOP participants and members of the control group failed to be statistically significant at the five percent confidence level. For example, on the ever attended or currently attending a four-year college measure, 15 percent of the QOP participants reported in the affirmative, while 12 percent of the control group reported in the affirmative—a statistically indistinguishable difference of three percent.[419] Similar findings were reported for completing at least one quarter at a four-year college, completing at least one year at a four-year college, and completing at least two years at a four-year college.[420]

However, the authors reported some positive and statistically significant findings at the less rigorous 10 percent significance level when the outcome measures combined two- and four-year college attendance. On the ever attended or currently attending a two- or four-year college measure, 37 percent of the QOP participants reported in the affirmative, while 30 of the control group reported in the affirmative—a marginally statistically distinguishable difference of seven percent at the 10 percent confidence level.[421] A similar

TABLE 5.8. The Effectiveness of QOP: Selected Findings

Outcome Measure	Initial Post-intervention Follow-Up	6-Year Follow-Up
Education		
Received high school diploma	0	0
Received high school diploma or GED	0	0
Mathematics achievement	0	
Reading achievement	0	
Cumulative GPA	0	
Total credit earned	0	
Ever expelled or suspended	0	
Postsecondary Education or Training		
Ever attended or currently attending a 4-year college	0	0
Completed at least 1 quarter at a 4-year college	0	n/a
Completed at least 1 year at a 4-year college	0	0
Completed at least 2 years at a 4-year college	0	0
Earned a bachelor's degree	n/a	0
Ever attended or currently attending a 2- or 4-year college	Pos*	0
Completed at least 1 quarter at a 2- or 4-year college	Pos*	n/a
Completed at least 1 year at a 2- or 4-year college	0	0
Completed at least 2 years at a 2- or 4-year college	0	0
Earned a bachelor's or associate's degree	n/a	0
Ever in college, vocational./technical. school, apprenticeship, or military	Pos**	0
Completed 2 years of college, vocational/technical school, an apprenticeship, or in the military	0	0
Employment		
Has a job	Neg*	
Currently employed	n/a	0
Currently unemployed	n/a	0
Currently out of labor force	n/a	0
Currently employed or in college, voc/tech school, an apprenticeship, or the military	n/a	0
Ever employed	n/a	0
Employed in past 12 months	n/a	0
Percentage of weeks employed in past 12 months	n/a	0
Number of jobs in past 12 months	n/a	0
Tenure at current job (months)	n/a	0
Usual number of hours worked per week in all current jobs	n/a	0
Works at least 35 hours per week at main job	n/a	0

TABLE 5.8. (Continued)

Outcome Measure	Initial Post-intervention Follow-Up	6-Year Follow-Up
Total earnings in past 12 months	n/a	0
Has a job with health insurance	Neg**	0
Has a job with paid time off	n/a	0
Has a job with a pension or retirement benefits	n/a	0
Risky Behaviors and Family Life		
Smoked cigarettes or used other tobacco in past month	n/a	0
Smoked cigarettes or used other tobacco daily in past month	n/a	0
Binge drinking in past month	0	0
Binge drinking on 8 or more days in past month	0	0
Used an illegal drug in past month	n/a	0
Used an illegal drug in past 3 months	Pos**	n/a
Committed a crime in past 3 months	0	Neg*
Committed a crime in past 2 years	n/a	0
Arrested or charged in past 3 months	0	n/a
Arrested or charged in past 2 years	n/a	Neg**
Convicted or pled guilty in past 2 years	n/a	0
Served time in jail, prison, or detention home in past 2 years	n/a	0
Had first child before age 18	n/a	0
Currently living with natural children, but no spouse	n/a	0
Has children with whom not currently living	n/a	0
Currently receiving welfare	n/a	0
Currently receiving food stamps	n/a	0
Currently receiving welfare or food stamps	n/a	0

Key: 0 Finding was not statistically significant

Pos Positive or beneficial impact

Neg Negative or harmful impact

*   Statistically significant at the 10 percent confidence level ($p \leq 0.10$)

**   Statistically significant at the 5 percent confidence level ($p \leq 0.05$)

***   Statistically significant at the 1 percent confidence level ($p \leq 0.01$)

n/a No measure was assessed or reported

†   No statistically significance test was performed

Source: Allen Schirm and Nuria Rodriguez, *The Quantum Opportunity Program Demonstration: Initial Post Intervention Impacts* (Princeton, NJ: Mathematica Policy Research, June 2004), Table 1, 17; Table 2, 22; Table 3, 23; Table 4, 26; Allen Schirm, Elizabeth Stuart, and Allison McKie, *The Quantum Opportunity Program Demonstration: Final Impacts* (Princeton, NJ: Mathematica Policy Research, July 2006), Table 3, 20; Table 6, 30; Table 4, 24; Table 8, 32; Table 5, 27.

finding was reported for completing at least one quarter at a two- or four-year college.[422] However, the findings for completing at least one year at a two- or four-year college and completing at least two years at a two- or four-year college were statistically insignificant at the five percent and 10 percent significance levels, respectively.[423]

Overall, 62 percent of the QOP participants and 53 percent of the control group participants reported ever being in college, vocational/technical school, or the military.[424] This difference of nine percent was statistically significant at the five percent confidence level.[425] However, when the measure was completing two years of college, completing vocational/technical school or an apprenticeship, or being in the military, participation in QOP failed to have a statistically significant effect.[426]

For the six-year follow-up, participation in QOP failed to have an effect on all postsecondary educational attainment measures.[427] Specifically, QOP participation had no effect on attending or graduating from two- and four-year colleges, apprenticeships, or vocational/technical schools.

Impacts on Current Activities

For the initial postintervention impacts, participation in QOP appears to have had little to no impact on the current activities of participants. QOP participants were not more or less likely to be currently attending a two- or four-year college, in apprenticeship, or in the military than members of the control group.[428] Further, participation in QOP appears to have had no effect on obtaining a job with health insurance benefits, a job paying $10 or more per hour, a full-time job paying $10 or more per hour, or a full-time job with health insurance paying $10 or more per hour.[429]

On the other hand, participation in QOP appears to have had a few negative impacts. At the less rigorous 10 percent significance level, QOP participants were less likely to be employed (65percent) than control group members (72 percent)—a difference of seven percent that is statistically significant at the less rigorous 10 percent confidence level.[430] For having a job that provides health insurance benefits, 45 percent of QOP participants reported in the affirmative, while 56 percent of the control group reported in the affirmative—a difference of 11 percent that is statistically significant at the one percent level.[431] QOP participants were also less likely to report currently having a full-time job with health insurance benefits—31 percent for QOP participants and 38 percent for the control group.[432] This difference of seven percent is statistically significant at the five percent level.

Impacts on Risky Behaviors and Family Life

Except for one of the initial postintervention measures, QOP failed to have statistically significant effects on alcohol and illegal drug use. QOP participants were less likely to report illegal drug use in the past month—12 percent for QOP participants and 18 percent for the control group—for a statistically significant difference of six percent at the five percent confidence level.[433]

Participation in QOP failed to have an effect on committing a crime and being arrested or charged in the past three months.[434] QOP failed to have impacts on having a child before age 18; currently living with natural children, but without a spouse; and having a child that does not live with them.[435] Participation in QOP also failed to have an effect on currently receiving welfare and food stamps.[436]

For the six-year follow-up, participation in QOP failed to affect cigarette or tobacco use, binge drinking, and illegal drug use.[437] Five percent of QOP participants and two percent of the control group reported committing a crime in the past three months—a statistically significant difference of three percent at the less rigorous 10 percent confidence level.[438] When asked if they had committed a crime, convicted or plead guilty, or served time in jail or prison within the past two years, the differences between QOP participants and control group members were statistically indistinguishable.[439] However, when asked if they had been arrested for or charged with a crime within the past two years, 11 percent of QOP participants and five percent of control group members reported in the affirmative—a statically significant difference of six percent at the five percent confidence level.[440]

For family life matters during the six-year follow-up, QOP failed to have impacts on having a child before age 18; currently living with natural children, but without a spouse; and having a child hat does not live with them.[441] Participation in QOP also failed to have an effect on currently receiving welfare and food stamps.[442]

Impact on Employment and Earnings

The impact of QOP participation on employment and earnings was measured about six years after the participants' scheduled high school graduation.

At the time of the six-year follow-up, 67 percent of QOP participants and 68 percent of control group members reported being currently employed—a statistically indistinguishable difference of one percent.[443] Other current employment-related measures—such as being unemployed, out of the labor force, or employed; attending college, vocational/technical school, apprenticeships; or being in the military—yielded similarly ineffective results.[444]

For the measure of ever being employed, 96 percent of QOP participants reported in the affirmative, while 95 percent of the control group reported in the affirmative—a statistically indistinguishable difference of one percent.[445] Over the past 12 months, QOP participation failed to affect being employed, amount of weeks employed, and number of past jobs.[446] Participation in QOP also failed to affect tenure at current job, number of hours worked, and working at least 35 hours per week at main job.[447]

As for total earnings in the last 12 months, QOP participants and control group members reported average earnings of $12,676 and $13,198, respectively.[448] While the difference in earnings was statistically indistinguishable from zero, QOP participants earned an average of $522 less than control group members.[449] QOP participants had an average hourly wage of $7.93, while the control group average was $9.14 per hour.[450] This difference of $1.21 was statistically insignificant, suggesting that QOP did not have a negative impact on hourly wages.[451]

For employee benefits, participation in QOP failed to have statistically significant effects on jobs with health insurance, paid time off, and pension or retirement benefits.[452]

According to the authors of the evaluation, QOP failed in achieving its primary and secondary objectives of increasing the likelihood of graduating from high school and engaging in postsecondary education or training.[453] Further, QOP failed to improve participants' employment-related outcomes.[454]

Conclusion

Taken as a whole, the performance of federal employment and training programs is certainly underwhelming. While there are occasional positive outcomes, these benefits tend to be concentrated among the receipt of training, GEDs, and trade-related certifications. Unfortunately, the receipt of these credentials too frequently fails to translate into increased earnings and wages. The bright spot, if we can call it that, appears to be that adult females appear to be most likely, relatively speaking, to benefit from federal employment and training programs. The results for youths appear to have no silver underlining. On a national scale, employment and training programs for this population appear to be a complete failure. While the CET appears to have worked in San Jose, California, the Department of Labor was unable to even replicate a fraction of the positive results.

Last, we must not forget that these programs sometimes appear to do harm. For example, participation in JOBSTART is associated with a decrease in earnings during the first year after random assignment for all participants and for men, in particular. CET participants with a high school degree or GED experienced diminished earnings after participating in training. Male youth with a history of arrest before random assignment in JTPA programs experienced a reduction in earnings. Surprisingly, male youths without a history of arrest at the time of random assignment experienced increased arrest rates after participating in JTPA.

Chapter 6

The Way Forward

The introduction to this book began with a simple question: Do federal social programs work? Based on the scientifically rigorous multisite experimental evaluations reviewed, the answer certainly cannot be in the affirmative. Despite the best social engineering efforts, the evidence overwhelmingly points to the conclusion that federal social programs are ineffective. Is it just a coincidence that the findings of scientifically rigorous experimental evaluations support this conclusion? Ameliorating such problems as low academic achievement and cognitive ability, poverty, joblessness, low wages, sex outside of marriage, and marital difficulties appears to be out of reach for federal social programs. Once upon a time, these problems were personal in nature and did not require federal government action.

Our nation faces a severe debt crisis that threatens our very future. The current debt crisis was not brought about by a world war, like the massive debt that was accumulated fighting World War II. The United States quickly paid down that debt to manageable levels. Today, we need to reduce a debt that was accumulated primarily by an overreliance on government. Americans should not fear eliminating social programs. Once upon a time, President Barack Obama declared that he was willing to eliminate "government programs shown to be wasteful or ineffective."[1] Further, he asserted that "there will be no sacred cows, and no pet projects. All across America, families are making hard choices, and it's time their government did the same."[2] Now is the time for deep budget cuts to federal social programs. President Obama was correct to call for placing wasteful and ineffective programs on the chopping block. However, he has not lived up to his words. Others in his administration have not either.

Obama's first director of the Office of Management and Budget (OMB), Peter R. Orszag, argued that empirical evidence is the foundation of policymaking in the Obama administration.[3] Orszag asserts that the Obama administration "has been clear that it places a very significant emphasis on making policy conclusions based on what the evidence suggests."[4]

Orszag's replacement, OMB acting director Jeffrey Zients, also supports the notion that empirical evidence should drive policymaking. In 2010, he stated that "too many important programs have never been formally evaluated. And when they have, the results of those evaluations have not been fully taken into the decision-making process, at the level of either budgetary decisions or management practices."[5]

To demonstrate how the Obama administration is using empirical evidence to guide decision making, Orszag used the examples of Head Start and Early Head Start:

> Head Start and Early Head Start also both have documented very strong suggestive evidence that they pay off over the medium and long term, both in terms of narrow indicators and broader social indicators for society as a whole. These evaluations demonstrated progress against important program goals and provided documentation necessary to justify increases in funding in the president's budget to . . . further expand access, in the cases of Head Start and Early Head Start.[6]

Of particular interest are Orszag's comments on Head Start. Orszag cites the 2010 Head Start Impact Study as evidence that the number of children participating in Head Start needs to be expanded.[7] Unwittingly, Orszag also justifies the proposed termination of Even Start based on its first-year follow-up study's findings because the program "has been evaluated rigorously three times" and "out of forty-one measurable outcomes, the program demonstrated no measured difference between those enrolled in the program and those not on thirty-eight of the outcomes."[8] Recall that the first-year follow-up study found that Even Start had two marginally statistically significant harmful impacts and one marginally statistically significant beneficial impact on child cognitive abilities. Due to the program being a failure, the Obama administration has decided that Even Start should be terminated. However, no money will be saved for paying down the debt. Instead, the Obama administration plans to devote the funding that would have been spent on Even Start to other "programs that seek to promote improvement of reading, writing, and language arts instruction for students."[9]

However, Orszag's logic does not hold for Head Start and Early Head Start. While the first-year follow-up evaluation found Even Start to have no effect on 38 out of 41 outcome measures, Head Start's performance is even worse. Overall, the 2010 Head Start Impact Study that assessed findings for kindergarten and first grade found that Head Start failed to have an effect on 110 out of 112 outcome measures at the five percent confidence level for the four-year-old group, with one harmful and one beneficial impact. For the three-year-old group, Head Start failed to have an impact on 106 out of 112 measures at the five percent confidence level, with five beneficial impacts and one harmful impact. As for Early Head Start, the initial benefits produced by the program are limited to a minority of participants, and these benefits quickly fade.

Orszag concludes that "the highest level of integrity must be maintained in the process of using science to inform public policy. Sound data are not sufficient to guarantee sound policy decisions, but they are necessary."[10] Indeed, sound data are not a sufficient guarantee for sound policy decisions. Dealing with the data forthrightly is necessary as well.

In no way does the 2010 Head Start Impact Study demonstrate "very strong suggestive evidence" that Head Start "pay[s] off over the medium and long term."[11] Placing more children into an already failed program does not represent placing "significant emphasis on making policy conclusions based on what the evidence suggests."[12] In addition to Head Start being a highly ineffective program, the Government Accountability Office found that Head Start centers across the nation committed fraud by actively enrolling children from families not qualified to participate in the early education program.[13]

Let's hope that Zients was more serious than Orszag about using empirical evidence to inform policymaking when he wrote, "Finding out if a program works is common sense, and the basis upon which we can decide which programs should continue and which need to be fixed or terminated."[14] However, the word "terminated" as used by the Obama administration appears not to mean using the funds of eliminated programs to pay down the debt. Instead, funding will be recycled into new social programs.

Instead of acknowledging failure and eliminating Head Start, the Obama administration wants the program expanded to serve more children. It is as if they never read the Head Start Impact Study. Head Start is truly a sacred cow. Despite the Obama administration's talk of fiscal responsibility and holding social programs accountable, the federal government continues to waste hundreds of billions of dollars each year on ineffective social programs.

The fiscal irresponsibility of the Obama administration, previous administrations, and Congress is a product of deep changes in our politics and understanding of human nature. Our current debt crisis is a direct result of the progressive transformation of America. As a whole, we abandoned our Founding principles. Instead of government securing our natural rights, the role of government is to make people effectively free—to reach their full potential as human beings. While entitlement spending is the primary driver of our nation's debt, the growth in social program spending has far exceeded the pace of inflation, population growth, and the expansion of our economy.

The progressives replaced the Founders' notion of formal freedom with a new positive or effective freedom that required government to assist individuals in achieving their full potential as human beings. Despite this transformation coming from the left, many on the right have embraced federal social engineering. Take federal abstinence education and marriage promotion programs as an example. Some conservatives argue that these social engineering programs are required to undo the damage done by other federal social programs. The standard reasoning is that the welfare state has encouraged out-of-wedlock births and the break-up or nonformation of families. To rectify these problems, we need new social programs, on top of the old ones, to promote marriage among the poor and abstinence for the unmarried. What is baffling is that proponents of these marriage and abstinence programs have faith in the effectiveness of federal social programs, when they often blame federal social programs for causing the underlying problems in the first place.

During the George W. Bush administration, Wade Horn, while serving as the Assistant Secretary for Children and Families within the U.S. Department of Health and Human Services, asserted that the Healthy Marriage Initiative

> would actually wind up doing in the long run is to reduce the need for government to be involved in family life, because helping couples on a voluntary basis access services where they can build strong and healthy marriages, you have less marital breakdown. When you have less marital breakdown you have less need for government to interfere in the daily activities of people's lives.[15]

The message is that social engineering works when the right values are advocated.

So far, offering up more failing social programs on top of older, failed social programs is supposed to decrease the need for government interventions in our lives. What mental state comes to mind when doing the same thing over and over again while expecting different results?

On the left, early child education programs, including early care programs, are believed to be an astonishing success that no reasonable person can doubt. The evidence is so strong that these social programs are effective at providing for children's long-term success, the federal government must continue Early Head Start and Head Start and create similar new programs. Supporters claim that these programs cause increased academic achievement, increased high school graduation rates, increased employment and earnings, and reduced criminality.[16] Just consider the following quote by President Obama:

> By the time many inner-city children reach the school system, they're already behind—unable to identify basic numbers, colors, or letters in the alphabet, unaccustomed to sitting still or participating in a structured environment, and often burdened by undiagnosed health problems. They're unprepared not because they're unloved but because their mothers don't know how to provide what they need. Well-structured government programs—parental counseling, access to regular pediatric care, parenting programs, and quality early-childhood education programs—have a proven ability to help fill the void.[17]

However, Amy E. Lowenstein of New York University notes that the assumption about the effectiveness of early care and child education programs is based on the results of a small set of social programs for low-income children begun decades ago.[18] Lowenstein notes, "A close examination of research on the developmental effects of ECE [Early Care and Education programs], however, suggests that there is a gap between what the research says and what the public believes about ECE's effectiveness."[19] The primary experimental evaluations mentioned by advocates are the High/Scope Perry Preschool program and the Carolina Abecedarian Project. The evaluation of the High/Scope Perry Preschool program began in 1962 and focused on a small sample of black three- and four-year-old children. The Carolina Abecedarian Project, begun in 1972, provided preschool education services to infants growing up in high-risk environments.

Lowenstein offers three cautionary notes that should be acknowledged before generalizing the results of the High/Scope Perry Preschool program and the Carolina Abecedarian Project to other early child education programs. First, the demographic changes in the nation over the last 40 years, including increased maternal employment, have made the counterfactual conditions (control groups) used for High/Scope Perry Preschool and the Carolina Abecedarian Project evaluations irrelevant.[20] The counterfactual conditions used for these studies were largely children at home with their mothers. Lowenstein argues that children of today are much more likely to be in some form of nonmaternal care than during the 1960 s and 1970s. In essence, these studies are outdated.

Second, the generalizability of the High/Scope Perry Preschool and the Carolina Abecedarian Project evaluations is questionable on the following grounds: (1) the evaluations were based on very small samples of children (123 and 111, respectively), (2) the sample children consisted almost entirely of low-income blacks, (3) the findings are not generalizable to other locations, and (4) the beneficial impacts of these programs appear be restricted to females in the treatment group.[21] Third, the Perry and Abecedarian programs were "carefully constructed, high quality, expensive programs" that "do not reflect the assortment of scaled-up ECE programs available to most low-income families with young children today."[22] The Perry and Abecedarian programs "represent the exception rather than the rule."[23] Thus, Lowenstein concludes that the claims of advocates are "somewhat misleading."[24]

Lowenstein is not the only social scientist willing to critically examine the evidence. Robinson G. Hollister of Swarthmore College has pointed out that while the Perry evaluation was initially supposed to be based on random assignment, "the researchers made several nonrandom adjustments to the assignment, for instance, moving siblings so that they would be together in the treatment or control group, or moving all children of working mothers to the control group."[25] As a result, 20 percent of the sample used to make inferences about the effectiveness of the programs was not randomly assigned.[26] For Hollister, the failure to carry out the experimental design "greatly undermine[s] one's ability to take estimates of the 'impacts' as sound."[27] The bottom line is that the Perry evaluation is not really based on a true experimental design, and, thus, it does not benefit from the strong internal validity of true experimental designs.

According to Hollister,

Further doubts about the reliability of the estimates arise from the fact that the estimated impacts in given areas, for example, academic achievement test scores, vary sharply over time (age of the child). For instance, the crime data suddenly show big differences in favor of the program in the age 27 data. The estimated impacts on crime play a large role in the overall high benefit-cost ratios that have been highly touted.[28]

Suddenly, the benefits of the program are prevalent long after the individuals participated in the program. What is most disturbing to Hollister is that the Perry program has never been replicated and rigorously evaluated in other settings, while the program is so frequently mentioned as proof that early child education programs are effective.

While Isabel Sawhill and Ron Haskins, both of the Brookings Institution, advocate for a new universal federal preschool program, they do admit that the Perry and Abecedarian evaluation results have major generalization limitations. Undeterred by these limitations, Sawhill and Hawkins declare that these "results are exactly what is needed from a national preschool program for children from low-income and minority families, and virtually all the children in these three studies were low-income and black or Hispanic."[29] Further, "If results like these could be achieved on a broad scale, a huge investment of tens of billions of dollars, or more, would be justified . . ."[30] Given the record of federal early childhood education programs, most notably Early Head Start and Head Start, their optimism, while exuberant, needs to be taken with caution.

The unfounded optimism that federal social engineering can be effective appears to be unwavering. Despite all the evidence that so few social programs work, the authors of the long-term evaluation of housing mobility programs MTO and Section 8 assert, "Policies to increase skills and directly address other individual barriers to work remain essential if we are to improve the long-term life chances and economic self-sufficiency of disadvantaged families living in high-poverty areas."[31] Irrational exuberance appears to be a common characteristic of federal social engineering advocates.

When it comes to the potential of federal social programs to solve social problems, advocates, policy experts, and politicians need to exercise some humility. "Though almost any reasonable-sounding program will probably work under some conditions," Jim Manzi of the Manhattan Institute writes, "most fail most of the time. The burden of proof should always be on those who claim that some new program is worth the investment."[32] Indeed, the burden of proof must be placed on those calling for new or expanded social engineering programs.

Doing Harm

Politicians and policy experts also need to recognize that federal social programs often produce harm. Just consider the evidence reviewed in earlier chapters. All of the following harmful impacts were statistically significant at least at the five percent confidence level, which means the likelihood of these harmful impacts occurring by chance is very unlikely.

Early Head Start increased the parent-child dysfunctional interactions for whites and increased the parental reliance on AFDC/TANF for Hispanics. The longest job spells of mothers participating in Enhanced Early Head Start were significantly shorter than the job spells of mothers in the control group. For the three-year-old cohort of the Head Start Impact Study, kindergarten teachers reported that math abilities were worse than similar children not given access to the program. For the four-year-old cohort, teachers reported that Head Start children in the first grade were more likely to be shy or socially reticent than their peers. By the third grade, teachers reported that the four-year-old cohort with access to Head Start displayed a higher degree of unfavorable emotional symptoms than similar children without access to the program. Further, children in the four-year-old cohort self-reported poorer peer relations with fellow children than their counterparts in the control group.

The 21st Century Community Learning Centers Programs had a whole host of harmful effects. Overall, teachers found participating students to have disciplinary problems that were confirmed by student-reported data. According to their teachers, participating students were less likely to achieve at above average or high levels in class and were less likely to put effort into reading or English classes. These students were also more likely to have behavior problems in school than their counterparts. Teachers were more likely to have to call the parents of participating students about misbehavior. Participating students were also more likely to be miss recess or be placed in the hall for disciplinary reasons, while also having parents come to school more often to address behavior problems. 21st Century students were also more likely to be suspended from school than similar students. Upward Bound participants with high expectations to earn a college degree were less likely than their counterparts to earn associate's degrees, while being no more or less likely to attain any other college degree.

Employment Retention and Advancement (ERA) programs targeting unemployed TANF recipients experienced in Houston, Texas, and Salem, Oregon, caused participants to be more dependent on the receipt of TANF benefits, while the program in Fort Worth, Texas, was associated with increased dependence on food stamps. The Chicago ERA program targeting employed TANF recipients was associated with increased dependence on food stamps, while the Medford, Oregon, ERA program targeting employed individuals not on TANF was associated with decreased employment.

While having no effect on the marital status of participants, the Building Strong Families (BSF) marriage promotion program had an overall harmful long-term impact on fathers regularly spending time with their children. BSF had long-term harmful impact in specific sites too. In Atlanta, BSF led to a long-term decrease in the ability of participants to avoid destructive conflict behaviors. The long-term harmful impacts in Florida counties were more numerous. BSF caused Florida participants to be less likely to be romantically involved and living together. In addition, Florida fathers participating in the program were less likely to regularly spend time with their children.

In the short term, BSF produced several harmful impacts in Baltimore. In Baltimore, compared to couples in the control group, unmarried couples participating in the program were less likely to still be romantically involved. In addition, Baltimore couples in the program reported less support and affection in their relationships, and fathers were less likely to provide financial support for their children and less likely to engage in cognitive and social play with their children. However, these short-term harmful impacts did not persist in the long-term.

For adults and children with access to Moving to Opportunity (MTO) or Section 8 vouchers, several harmful impacts were produced. Access to a MTO voucher was associated with increased dependence on drugs and alcohol for adults. Also, MTO adults had higher participation rates in food stamps and received more food stamp benefits than their similar counterparts not given access to MTO or Section 8 vouchers. Youth from families given access to MTO vouchers were less likely to be employed and more likely to have smoked than their peers. These youth were also more likely to be arrested for property crimes. As for Section 8, adults offered access were less likely to be currently employed and less likely to have employment spells with the same job for at least a year. In addition, Section 8 adults were less likely to be currently working and not receiving TANF than their counterparts. Section 8 youth were more likely to have smoked than their peers in the control group.

Adult men participating in Job Training Partnership Act (JTPA) programs were more likely to be dependent on AFDC benefits than similar men not given access to the training. Increasing criminality appears to be a common effect of federal job-training programs. Male youths with no criminal arrest record at the time of random assignment were more likely to be arrested after participating in federal job-training programs, while male youth with histories of arrest experienced long-term declines in income. Youth participating in the Quantum Opportunity Program (QOP) were more likely to be arrested. In addition, these youth were less likely to find jobs that provided health insurance benefits.

Based on the JOBSTART evaluation results for the Center for Employment Training (CET) program in San Jose, California, the U.S. Department of Labor attempted to replicate the program at 16 other sites. In a classic example of not being able to replicate the results of a "proven" social program, participation in the CET Replication job-training programs was associated with several harmful outcomes. Men experienced declines in employment, earnings, and number of months worked. Individual participants who possessed a high school diploma or GED at the time of random assignment experienced declines in the number of months worked and earnings. In addition, participants in the high-fidelity sites were less likely to find jobs that provided health insurance. Also, those older than 18 and those with high school degrees or GEDs at the time of random assignment were less likely to have jobs that provided health insurance.

After receiving entrepreneurship training, Project GATE participants spent more time collecting Unemployment Insurance benefits than their counterparts that were not taught how to be entrepreneurs. While Project GATE had no effect on the self-employment income of participants, participation in the program decreased wages and salaries earned from employment. Job Corps is another federal training program that has negative effects. Youth participating in Job Corps worked fewer weeks and worked fewer hours per week than similar youth.

In sum, federal social programs that harm their participants are not uncommon. This fact is all too often ignored by social engineering advocates.

What Congress Should Do

While Congress should abolish as many federal social programs as possible, it needs to take the lead in making sure that the social programs it still funds are evaluated. For example, the Department of Education's Pell grant program subsidizes the postsecondary education of low-income students. Congress appropriated over $41 billion in Pell grants in fiscal year 2011.[33]

Despite such a huge investment of taxpayer dollars, the program has never undergone a multisite experimental evaluation to determine effectiveness. Neither has the Department of Education's Adult Literacy and Education Program. Within the Department of Labor, the Employment Service—a nationwide system of state employment and training programs—has been around since the New Deal but has never been rigorously evaluated. Other Department of Labor programs that have never undergone multisite experimental evaluations are the National Dislocated Workers Grants, Youth Build Program, Trade Adjustment Assistance (TAA) training programs, and TAA college grants. These programs are just a small sample of hundreds of social programs funded by Congress that have never undergone multisite experimental evaluations.

Congress can take several steps to ensure that federal social programs are properly assessed using experimental evaluations. The appendix presents model legislative language that Congress could use to mandate experimental evaluation of the social programs that it authorizes and funds.

Step #1: When authorizing a new program or reauthorizing an existing program, Congress should specifically mandate multisite experimental evaluation of the program.

Congressional mandates are necessary because federal agencies often resist performing experimental evaluations. Local recipients of federal funding may also resist participating in experimental evaluations for a variety of reasons. They may not want to deny services to members of the control group or may not want the final results to reflect negatively on the program. For example, many jurisdictions receiving funding through the Job Training Partnership Act and Job Opportunities and Basic Skills programs refused to cooperate with large-scale experimental evaluations of these programs.[34]

Interest groups and some members of Congress may also oppose experiments. For example, Upward Bound is a program intended to help disadvantaged high school students prepare for college. Many Upward Bound centers and the Council for Opportunity in Education (COE), which lobbies on behalf of Upward Bound centers, opposed Department of Education efforts under the George W. Bush administration to conduct an experimental evaluation of Upward Bound.[35] As discussed in Chapter 4, a previous experimental evaluation found that Upward Bound had no impact on whether most participants attended college.

Research suggests that Upward Bound serves a population that, while viewed as disadvantaged, is already very likely to attend college. However, participants who originally had no expectation of attending college were more likely to enroll in college. In response to these findings, the Bush administration wanted to focus Upward Bound on students with low academic expectations, where the program appeared to be effective, and conduct a new experimental evaluation of the revised program's effectiveness.

However, many Upward Bound centers opposed the policy change and the additional evaluation that would use random assignment to assess the revised program's effectiveness. COE president Arnold L. Mitchem compared the use of random assignment, which would ultimately deny some eligible students access to Upward Bound, to the infamous Tuskegee syphilis experiments, in which medical treatment was withheld from black men so that government scientists could learn about the negative effects of the disease.[36] In the end, a rider barring the Department of Education from using funds to perform the proposed evaluation was attached to the fiscal year 2008 omnibus appropriations law.[37]

As previously mentioned, Congress has the moral imperative to ensure that it allocates taxpayer dollars effectively. Experimental evaluations are the only way to determine to a high degree of certainty the effectiveness of social programs. Congress should not cave in to interest groups that are opposed to rigorous evaluation of their programs. Congress should mandate that all recipients of federal funding, if selected for participation, must cooperate with evaluations in order to receive future funding.

Step #2: The experimental evaluations should be large-scale, nationally representative, multisite studies.

When Congress creates social programs, the funded activities are implemented in multiple cities or towns. Federal social programs are intended to be spread out across the nation. For this reason, Congress should require nationally representative, multisite experimental evaluations of these programs. For multisite evaluations, the selection of the sites to be evaluated should be representative of the population of interest for the program. When program sites and sample participants are randomly selected, the resulting evaluation findings will have high external validity.

While individual programs funded by federal grants may undergo experimental evaluations, these small-scale, single-site evaluations do not inform policymakers of the general effectiveness of national programs. Small-scale evaluations assess the impact on only a small fraction of people served by federal social programs. The success of a single program that serves a particular jurisdiction or population does not necessarily mean that the same program will achieve similar success in other jurisdictions or among different populations. Thus, small-scale evaluations are poor substitutes for large-scale evaluations.

In addition, a multisite experimental evaluation that examines the performance of a particular program in numerous and diverse settings can potentially produce results that are more persuasive to policymakers than results from a single locality.[38]

Remember the example of police departments performing mandatory arrests in domestic violence incidents based on a single site evaluation of the Minneapolis, Minnesota, policy discussed in Chapter 3? Follow-up evaluations conducted in other cities found that what worked in Minneapolis did not always work in other locations. In some cities, the policy was associated with long-term increases in domestic violence.

The BSF social program is a more recent example. While the eight-site experimental evaluation found that BSF did not make couples more likely to stay together or get married, the program had mixed results by site. In Baltimore and the Florida counties, the statistically significant outcomes indicate that BSF has harmful outcomes, and the opposite occurred in Oklahoma City. While unmarried couples in the program were no more likely to marry than were the control group couples, Oklahoma participants reported improvements in relationship happiness, support and affection, use of constructive conflict behaviors, and avoidance of destructive conflict behaviors. Additionally, fathers participating in the program were more likely to provide financial support for their children than were their counterparts in the control group.

If Baltimore and the Florida counties were the only sites evaluated, then the results would indicate that federally sponsored marriage counseling for unmarried couples with children has harmful effects. The somewhat positive Oklahoma City results would have led to the opposite conclusion.

Contradictory results from evaluations of similar social programs implemented in different settings are a product not only of implementation fidelity, but also of the enormous complexity of the social context in which these programs are implemented. Jim Manzi uses the conflicting results of experimental evaluations to explain the influence of "causal density" on the social sciences.[39] "Casual density," a term coined by Manzi, is "the number and complexity of potential causes of the outcomes of interest."[40] Manzi postulates that as causal density rises, social scientists will find greater difficulty in identifying all of the factors that cause the outcome of interest.

Just as with the contradictory effects of mandatory arrest policies by location, the confounding influence of causal density may have contributed to the conflicting BSF findings in Baltimore and Oklahoma City. For this reason, experimental evaluations of federal social programs should be conducted at multiple sites.

Step #3: Congress should specify the types of outcome measures to be used to assess effectiveness.

A federal social program that is intended to ameliorate a particular social problem should be assessed on its impact on that particular social problem. For example, when assessing the impact of prisoner reentry programs, the most important outcome measure is recidivism. Some have questioned the emphasis on recidivism as a measure of effectiveness compared to other measures that assess adjustment or reintegration of former prisoners into society,[41] but while intermediate measures, such as finding employment and housing, are important, these outcomes are not the ultimate goal of reentry programs. If former prisoners continue to commit crimes after going through reentry programs, then any intermediate outcomes are irrelevant to judging whether the programs are effective.

Impact evaluations that rely solely on intermediate outcomes tell little about the effectiveness of federal social programs in ameliorating the targeted social problems. While federal social programs should be assessed on intermediate outcomes, these measures should never substitute for primary outcomes.

Step #4: Congress should institute procedures that encourage government agencies to carry out congressionally mandated evaluations, despite any entrenched biases against experimental evaluations.

Simply mandating an experimental evaluation does not necessarily guarantee that the evaluation will actually be made. The Department of Labor, for example, has a poor track record of implementing and disseminating experimental evaluations mandated by Congress.

The Workforce Investment Act (WIA) of 1998 mandated a large-scale, multisite evaluation of the Department of Labor's job-training programs; however, as discussed in Chapter 5, the Department of Labor procrastinated. Now, while Congress tries to reauthorize WIA, it has no idea about the effectiveness of these programs. The Government Accountability Office has reported that the evaluation will not be completed until June 2015— nearly 10 years after its original due date and 17 years after Congress mandated the evaluation.

Congress needs to take steps to ensure that evaluations are completed in a timely manner. One recommended method is to require department heads, such as the attorney general or secretary of labor, to submit annual progress reports, with the first report to be submitted no later than one year after Congress mandates the evaluation. The progress reports would go to the appropriations and oversight committees of both chambers of Congress. For example, the Department of Labor would be required to submit the report to the Senate and House Committees on Appropriations; the Senate Committee on Health, Education, Labor and Pensions; and the House Committee on Education and the Workforce. Thirty days after the report is submitted to Congress, it should be posted on the department's Web site.

Step #5: Congress should require that congressionally mandated evaluations be submitted to the relevant congressional committees in a timely manner after completion.

Thirty days after any evaluation is submitted to Congress, the evaluation should be made available on the Web site of the federal government agency responsible for the evaluation. Requiring that Congress and the public be informed of evaluation results is important because government agencies are quick to release positive results but sometimes reluctant to release negative results.

For example, a cost-benefit analysis of Job Corps that found that the program costs outweighed the benefits was finalized in 2003, but the Department of Labor withheld it from the public until 2006. The Government Accountability Office has criticized the Department of Labor for its history of delaying the release of its research findings. Similarly, the Department of Health and Human Services has noticeably delayed the release of reports based on the Head Start Impact Study that reported underwhelming results. Congress needs to be vigilant in ensuring that evaluation results are disseminated promptly.

Conclusion

The evidence presented in this book makes it clear that federal social programs are ineffective. Can we, as taxpayers, live without these federal social programs? The answer is certainly yes. It cannot be just a coincidence that the many multisite evaluations published since 1990 and reviewed in this book overwhelmingly find federal social programs are ineffective. Yet many Americans, including politicians and policy experts, believe that federal social programs can make people better. Given the tremendous financial burden and the scientific evidence of failure, why would anyone still want the federal government to attempt to make people better? While

I do not deny that some small-scale social programs are effective, promoters of implementing these programs on a national scale need some humility. The record does not justify their exuberance.

With the federal debt reaching staggering heights, Congress needs to ensure that it is spending taxpayer dollars wisely. Multisite experimental evaluations are the best method for assessing the effectiveness of federal social programs. Yet to date, this method has been used on only a handful of federal social programs. Congress needs to reverse this trend.

Appendix

Model Legislation for Multisite Experimental Evaluations

SEC. *<Insert number>*. EVALUATIONS.
  (a) PROGRAMS AND ACTIVITIES CARRIED OUT UNDER THIS TITLE.—For the purpose of improving the management and effectiveness of programs and activities carried out under this title, the Secretary shall provide for the continuing impact evaluation of the programs and activities, including those programs and activities carried out under section *<Insert number>*. Such impact evaluations shall address—
    (1) Outcomes measures of the effectiveness of such programs and activities in relation to their cost, including the extent to which the programs and activities—
      (A) Improve the *<Insert outcome measures>* of participants in comparison to comparably situated individuals who did not participate in such programs and activities;
      (B) Increase the *<Insert outcome measures>* over the level that would have existed in the absence of such programs and activities; and
      (C) Increase the *<Insert outcome measures>* of participants in comparison to comparably situated individuals who did not participate in such programs and activities;
    (2) The effectiveness of the performance measures relating to such programs and activities;
    (3) The effectiveness of the structure and mechanisms for delivery of services through such programs and activities;
    (4) The impact of such programs and activities on the community and participants involved;
    (5) The impact of such programs and activities on related programs and activities;

(6) The extent to which such programs and activities meet the needs of various demographic groups; and

(7) Such other factors as may be appropriate.

(b) OTHER PROGRAMS AND ACTIVITIES.—The Secretary may conduct impact evaluations of other federally funded programs related to *<Insert policy area (e.g., employment, early childhood education)>* and activities under other provisions of law.

(c) TECHNIQUES.—Impact evaluations conducted under this section shall use appropriate methodology and research designs, including the use of intervention and control groups chosen by scientific random assignment methodologies. In addition, scientific random assignment methodologies shall be used to select the program sites that will undergo the evaluation. For each impact evaluation, the Secretary shall fulfill all the notification and reporting requirements under subsections (e), (f), and (g). The Secretary shall conduct as least 1 multisite control group evaluation under this section by the end of fiscal year *<Insert year>*.

(d) MANDATORY PARTICPATION.—None of the funds authorized or appropriated by Federal law, and none of the funds in any trust fund to which funds are authorized or appropriated by Federal law, shall be allocated to sites that refuse to take part in the multi-site evaluation after chosen by scientific random assignment methodologies for participation in the evaluation.

(e) NOTIFICATION OF IMPACT EVALUATION PROGRESS.—

(1) REPORTS TO CONGRESS.—Not later than 1 year after the date of the enactment of the *<Insert name of Act>*, and annually thereafter, the Secretary shall transmit to the *<Insert two or more House committees>* of the House of Representatives and the *<Insert two or more Senate committees>* of the Senate a report on the progress the Secretary is making in evaluating the programs and activities carried out under this section.

(2) AVAILABILITY TO GENERAL PUBLIC.—Not later than 1 year after the date of the enactment of the *<Insert name of Act>*, and annually thereafter not later than 30 days after the transmission of an annual report under paragraph (1), the Secretary shall make available the reports to the general public on the Internet website of the Department of *<Insert name>*.

(f) REPORTS.—The entity carrying out an impact evaluation described in subsection (a) or (b) shall prepare and submit to the Secretary a draft report and a final report containing the results of the evaluation.

(g) REPORTS TO CONGRESS.—Not later than 30 days after the completion of such a report described in subsection (e), the Secretary shall transmit the draft report to the *<Insert House committees from*

subsection (e)> of the House of Representatives and the *<Insert House committees from subsection (e)>* of the Senate. Not later than 30 days after the completion of such a final report, the Secretary shall transmit the final report to such committees of the Congress. All reports must be made available to the general public on the Department's internet web site within 30 days of being transmitted to such committees of Congress.

(h) DEFINITIONS.—In this section:

(1) IMPACT EVALUATION—The term "impact evaluation" means an evaluative study that evaluates, in accordance with subsection (a), the outcomes of programs and activities carried out under this title, including the impact on social conditions such programs and activities are intended to improve.

(2) SCIENTIFIC RANDOM ASSIGNMENT METHODOLOGIES— The term "scientific random assignment methodologies" means research designs conducted in program settings in which intervention and control groups are—

(A) formed by random assignment; and

(B) compared on the basis of outcome measures for the purpose of determining the impact of programs and activities carried out under this title participants.

(3) CONTROL GROUP.—The term "control group" means a group of individuals—

(A) who did not participate in the programs and activities carried out under this title; and

(B) whose outcome measures are compared to the outcome measures of individuals in an intervention group.

(4) INTERVENTION GROUP—The term "intervention group" means a group of individuals—

(A) who participated in the programs and activities carried out under this title; and

(B) whose outcome measures are compared to the outcome measures of individuals in a control group.

Notes

Chapter 1

1. Patrick McGuinn and Frederick Hess, "The Great Society and the Evolution of the Elementary and Secondary Education Act of 1965," in *The Great Society and the High Tide of Liberalism*, ed. Sidney M. Milkis and Jerome M. Mileur (Boston: University of Massachusetts Press, 2005), 311–312; Jerome M. Mileur, "The Great Society and the Demise of New Deal Liberalism," in *The Great Society and the High Tide of Liberalism*, ed. Sidney M. Milkis and Jerome M. Mileur (Boston: University of Massachusetts Press, 2005), 436.

2. Peter H. Rossi, Mark W. Lipsey, and Howard E. Freeman, *Evaluation: A Systematic Approach*, 7th ed. (Thousand Oaks, CA: SAGE Publications, 2004).

3. Rasmussen Reports, "64% Think Budget Cuts Should Be Considered in Every Government Program," February 28, 2012, http://www.rasmussenreports .com/public_content/business/federal_budget/february_2012/64_think_budget _cuts_should_be_considered_in_every_government_program (December 11, 2012).

4. Rasmussen Reports, "65% Favor Across-the-Board Spending Cuts," November 27, 2012, http://www.rasmussenreports.com/public_content/politics/general _politics/november_2012/65_favor_across_the_board_spending_cuts (December 11, 2012).

5. Dan Balz, "President Tries to Keep Balance as Ground Shifts," *Washington Post*, July 11, 2011, A01.

6. State News Service, "Reid: GOP Leaders Must Decide if They Will Do What Tea Party Wants or What Country Needs," April 4, 2011.

7. Press release, "Release: Sanders on Senate Spending Proposals," Federal Information and News Dispatch, March 9, 2011.

8. eMediaMillWorks Political Transcripts, "The Congressional Hispanic Caucus, The Congressional Black Caucus, and the Congressional Asian Pacific American Caucus Hold a News Conference on the Debt," *Roll Call*, July 20, 2011.

9. Barack Obama, "Remarks by the President at the Associated Press Luncheon," April 3, 2012, http://www.whitehouse.gov/the-press-office/2012/04/03/ remarks-president-associated-press-luncheon (accessed on December 11, 2012).

10. Ibid.

11. Ibid.

12. Tom Harkin, "Statement of Senator Harkin (D-IA) at the Appropriations Labor-HHS-Education Subcommittee Hearing: The Impact of Sequestration on Education," Press release, July 25, 2012, http://www.harkin.senate.gov/press/release.cfm?i=337365 (accessed on December 11, 2012).

13. Joel Klein, "Time to Ax Public Programs That Don't Yield Results," *Time*, July 7, 2011, http://www.time.com/time/nation/article/0,8599,2081778,00.html (accessed on December 11, 2012).

14. Ibid.

15. Isabel V. Sawhill and Jon Baron, "Federal Programs for Youth: More of the Same Won't Work," *Youth Today*, May 1, 2010, http://coalition4evidence.org/wordpress/wp-content/uploads/Viewpoint-Essay-Sawhill-Baron-Youth-Today-May-2010.pdf (accessed on December 11, 2012).

16. Office of Management and Budget, *Historical Tables, Budget of the United States, Fiscal Year 2013* (Washington, DC: U.S. Government Printing Office, 2011), Table 7.1: Federal Debt at the End of Year: 1940–2017, 139–140, http://www.whitehouse.gov/sites/default/files/omb/budget/fy2013/assets/hist.pdf (accessed on December 11, 2012).

17. Congressional Budget Office, *Federal Debt and the Statutory Limit, November 2012*, November 2012, 1, http://www.cbo.gov/sites/default/files/cbofiles/attachments/43736-FederalDebtLimit-11-12-12.pdf (accessed on December 11, 2012).

Chapter 2

1. U.S. Department of the Treasury, Bureau of the Public Debt, "Monthly Statement of the Public Debt of the United States, December 31, 2011," Table 1: Summary of Treasury Securities Outstanding, December 31, 2011, http://www.treasurydirect.gov/govt/reports/pd/mspd/2011/opds122011.pdf (December 11, 2012).

2. David Nakamura, "Obama Asks Congress for Debt Limit Hike," *44* (blog), *Washington Post*, January 12, 2012, http://www.washingtonpost.com/blogs/44/post/after-delay-obama-asks-congress-for-debt-limit-hike/2012/01/12/gIQAA3ADuP_blog.html (December 11, 2012).

3. Congressional Budget Office, *The Budget and Economic Outlook: Fiscal Years 2012 to 2022*, January 2012, x, http://www.cbo.gov/ftpdocs/126xx/doc12699/01-31-2012_Outlook.pdf (December 11, 2012); Congressional Budget Office, *An Update to the Budget and Economic Outlook: Fiscal Years 2012 to 2022*, August 2012, 1, http://www.cbo.gov/sites/default/files/cbofiles/attachments/08-22-2012-Update_to_Outlook.pdf (accessed December 11, 2012).

4. Congressional Budget Office, *The Budget and Economic Outlook: Fiscal Years 2012 to 2022*, January 2012, x.

5. Congressional Budget Office, *An Update to the Budget and Economic Outlook: Fiscal Years 2012 to 2022*, 1.

6. Congressional Budget Office, *The Long-Term Budget Outlook*, June 2009, xii, http://www.cbo.gov/ftpdocs/102xx/doc10297/06-25-LTBO.pdf (December 11, 2012).

7. Office of Management and Budget, *Historical Tables, Budget of the United States, Fiscal Year 2013* (Washington, DC: U.S. Government Printing Office, 2011), Table 7.1: Federal Debt at the End of Year: 1940–2017, 139–140, http://www.whitehouse.gov/sites/default/files/omb/budget/fy2013/assets/hist.pdf (February 13, 2012).

8. Congressional Budget Office, *Federal Debt and the Statutory Limit, November 2012*, November 2012, 1, http://www.cbo.gov/sites/default/files/cbofiles/attachments/43736-FederalDebtLimit-11-12-12.pdf (December 11, 2012).

9. For discussion of the change in the understanding of the U.S. Constitution, see Richard A. Epstein, *How Progressives Rewrote the Constitution.* (Washington, DC: Cato Institute, 2006).

10. Charles R. Kessler, *I Am the Change: Barack Obama and the Crisis of Liberalism* (New York: Broadside Books, 2012).

11. Obama for America, "The Life of Julia," http://www.barackobama.com/life-of-julia (December 11, 2012).

12. For more in-depth exploration of the principles of American Founding and the challenges to it, see James W. Ceaser, "Foundational Concepts in American Political Thought," in *Modern America and the Legacy of the Founding*, eds. Ronald J. Pestritto and Thomas G. West (Lanham, MD: Lexington Books, 2007), 3–31 and Tiffany Jones Miller, "Transforming Formal Freedom into Effective Freedom: Dewey, the New Deal, and the Great Society," in *Modern America and the Legacy of the Founding*, eds. Ronald J. Pestritto and Thomas G. West (Lanham, MD: Lexington Books, 2007), 169–206.

13. Massachusetts Constitution, 1790, Heritage Foundation *First Principles Series*, http://www.heritage.org/initiatives/first-principles/primary-sources/massachusetts-constitution.

14. Declaration of Rights, June 12, 1776, Heritage Foundation *First Principles Series*, http://www.heritage.org/initiatives/first-principles/primary-sources/virginia-declaration-of-rights (December 11, 2012).

15. Thomas G. West, "The Political Theory of the Declaration of Independence," in *The American Founding and the Social Compact*. eds. Ronald J. Pestritto and Thomas G. West (Lanham, MD: Lexington Books, 2003), 108.

16. Ibid., 101.

17. Miller, "Transforming Formal Freedom," 170.

18. Bradley C. S. Watson, *Living Constitution, Dying Faith: Progressivism and the New Science of Jurisprudence* (Wilmington, DE: ISI Books, 2009), 24.

19. Miller, "Transforming Formal Freedom," 171.

20. Ibid.

21. Thomas G. West, "Progressivism and the Transformation of American Government," in *The Progressive Revolution in Politics and Political Science: Transforming the American Regime*, eds. John Marini and Ken Masugi (Lanham, MD: Rowman & Littlefield Publishers, Inc., 2005), 14.

22. Ibid.

23. James W. Ceaser, "Foundational Concepts in American Political Thought," in *Modern America and the Legacy of the Founding*, eds. Ronald J. Pestritto and Thomas G. West (Lanham, MD: Lexington Books, 2007), 19.

24. Frank Johnson Goodnow, "The American Conception of Liberty," in *American Progressivism: A Reader*, eds. Ronald J. Pestritto and William J. Atto (Lanham, MD: Rowan & Littlefield Publishers, Inc., 2008), 62.

25. Ibid., 63.

26. Woodrow Wilson, *Constitutional Government in the United States* (New Brunswick, NJ: Transaction Publishers, 2002), 4.

27. John Dewey, *Liberalism and Social Action* (Amherst, NY: Prometheus Books, 2000); John Dewey, *Individualism Old and New* (Amherst, NY: Prometheus Books, 1999).

28. John Dewey, *Freedom and Culture* (Amherst, NY: Prometheus Books, 1989), 120; John Dewey, *Reconstruction in Philosophy* (Boston: Beacon Press, 1957), 44.

29. Dewey, *Liberalism and Social Action*, 27.

30. Charles E. Merriam, *A History of American Political Theories* (New York: MacMillan Company, 1926), 316.

31. Ibid., 332.

32. John Dewey and James H. Tufts, *Ethics* (New York: Henry Holt and Company, 1910), 438.

33. Dewey, *Liberalism and Social Action*, 34–35; Dewey, *Individualism Old and New*.

34. Dewey and Tufts, *Ethics*, 438.

35. Woodrow Wilson, *The State: Elements of Historical and Practical Politics*. (Boston: D. C. Heath & Co., Publishers, 1910), 633.

36. Dewey and Tufts, *Ethics*, 438.

37. Ibid.

38. Ibid.

39. Dewey, *Liberalism and Social Action*, 35.

40. Ibid., 60.

41. West, "The Political Theory of the Declaration of Independence," 107.

42. Ibid.

43. Katherine Briar-Lawson, Toni Naccarato, and Jeanette Drews, "Child and Family Welfare Policies and Services," in *The Hand Book of Social Policy*, eds. James Midgley and Michelle Livermore (Los Angeles: SAGE Publications, 2009), 315–335; David T. Beito, "This Enormous Army: The Mutual-Aid Tradition of American Fraternal Societies before the Twentieth Century," in *The Voluntary City: Choice, Community, and Civil Society*, eds. David T. Beito, Peter Gordon, and Alexander Tabarrok (Ann Arbor: University of Michigan Press, 2002), 182–203; David T. Beito, "The 'Lodge Practice Evil' Reconsidered: Medical Care through Fraternal Societies, 1900–1930," *Journal of Urban History* 23, no. 5 (1997): 569–600; David T. Beito, *From Mutual Aid to the Welfare State: Fraternal Societies and Social Services, 1890–1967* (Chapel Hill: University of North Carolina Press, 2000).

44. Beito, "This Enormous Army," 182–203; Beito, "The 'Lodge Practice Evil' Reconsidered"; Beito, *From Mutual Aid to the Welfare State*.

45. Beito, *From Mutual Aid to the Welfare State*, 1.

46. Beito, "This Enormous Army."

47. Beito, *From Mutual Aid to the Welfare State*.

48. Ibid., 14.

49. Briar-Lawson, Naccarato, and Drews, "Child and Family Welfare Policies and Services," 328.

50. Beito, *From Mutual Aid to the Welfare State*, 19.

51. Beito, "This Enormous Army."

52. Beito, *From Mutual Aid to the Welfare State*, 228.

53. Jerome M. Mileur, "The Great Society and the Demise of New Deal Liberalism," in *The Great Society and the High Tide of Liberalism*, eds. Sidney M. Milkis and Jerome M. Mileur (Boston: University of Massachusetts Press, 2005), 419.

54. Burton W. Folson, Jr., *New Deal or Raw Deal? How FDR's Economic Legacy Has Damaged America* (New York: Threshold Editions, 2008), 30–33.

55. Ibid.

56. Joan Hoff Wilson, *Herbert Hoover: Forgotten Progressive* (Long Grove, IL: Waveland Press, 1992), 150–151.

57. U.S. Department of Commerce, Bureau of the Census, *Historical Statistics of the United States: Colonial Times to 1970, Part 1* (U.S. Government Printing Office: Washington, DC, 1975), Series D 1-10 Labor Force and Its Components: 1900 to 1947, 126.

58. Ibid.

59. Robert VanGiezen and Albert E. Schwenk, "Compensation from before World War I through the Great Depression," U.S. Department of Labor, Bureau of Labor Statistics, http://www.bls.gov/opub/cwc/cm20030124ar03p1.htm (December 11, 2012).

60. Stanley Lebergott, "Annual Estimates of Unemployment in the United States, 1900–1954," in *The Measurement and Behavior of Unemployment*, ed.

Universities-National Bureau (National Bureau of Economic Research, 1957), 229, http://www.nber.org/chapters/c2644.pdf (December 11, 2012).

61. Ibid, Table 2, 215–216.

62. Ibid.

63. Franklin D. Roosevelt, "Campaign Address on Progressive Government at the Commonwealth Club in San Francisco, California," September 23, 1932, http://www.presidency.ucsb.edu/ws/index.php?pid=88391#axzz1wYMxy6tT (December 11, 2012).

64. Franklin D. Roosevelt, "State of the Union Message to Congress," January 11, 1944, http://www.presidency.ucsb.edu/ws/index.php?pid=16518#axzz1wYMxy6tT (December 11, 2012).

65. Ibid.

66. Ibid.

67. Alan Brinkley, *The End of Reform: New Deal Liberalism in Recession and War* (New York: Vintage Books, 1996), 5.

68. William Voegeli, *Never Enough: America's Limitless Welfare State* (New York: Encounter Books, 2010), 18.

69. Robert Leighninger and Leslie Leighninger, "Social Policy of the New Deal," in *The Hand Book of Social Policy*, eds. James Midgley and Michelle Livermore (Los Angeles: SAGE Publications, 2009), 137.

70. Ibid., 137.

71. Ibid., 138.

72. Ibid.

73. Hugh Helco, "The Political Foundations of Antipoverty Policy," in *Fighting Poverty: What Works and What Doesn't*, eds. Sheldon H. Danziger and Daniel H. Weinberg (Cambridge, MA: Harvard University Press, 1986), 314.

74. Ibid.

75. Ibid., 322.

76. Daniel Friedlander and David H. Greenberg, "Evaluating Government Training Programs for the Economically Disadvantaged," *Journal of Economic Literature* 35 (December 1997): 1812.

77. John A. Andrew, *Lyndon Johnson and the Great Society* (Chicago: Ivan R. Dee, Inc., 1998), 95.

78. Ibid.

79. Eileen Boris, "Contested Rights: The Great Society between Home and Work," in *The Great Society and the High Tide of Liberalism*, eds. Sidney M. Milkis and Jerome M. Mileur (Boston: University of Massachusetts Press, 2005), 116.

80. Patrick McGuinn and Frederick Hess, "The Great Society and the Evolution of the Elementary and Secondary Education Act of 1965," in *The Great Society and the High Tide of Liberalism*, eds. Sidney M. Milkis and Jerome M. Mileur (Boston: University of Massachusetts Press, 2005), 311–312; Jerome M. Mileur, "The Great Society and the Demise of New Deal Liberalism," in *The Great Society and the*

High Tide of Liberalism, eds. Sidney M. Milkis and Jerome M. Mileur (Boston: University of Massachusetts Press, 2005), 436.

81. McGuinn and Hess, "The Great Society and the Evolution of the Elementary and Secondary Education Act of 1965," 311.

82. Michael Reisch, "Social Policy and the Great Society," in *The Hand Book of Social Policy*, eds. James Midgley and Michelle Livermore (Los Angeles: SAGE Publications, 2009), 152.

83. Lyndon B. Johnson, "Remarks at the University of Michigan," May 22, 1964.LBJ Presidential Library. (December 11, 2012).

84. Ibid.

85. Ibid.

86. Lyndon B. Johnson: "Remarks at a Fundraising Dinner in Detroit," June 26, 1964, American Presidency Project, http://www.presidency.ucsb.edu/ws/?pid=26345 (December 11, 2012).

87. Andrew, *Lyndon Johnson and the Great Society*, 13.

88. Ibid., 63.

89. McGuinn and Hess, "The Great Society and the Evolution of the Elementary and Secondary Education Act of 1965," 289.

90. Andrew, *Lyndon Johnson and the Great Society*, 57.

91. Robert H. Haveman, *Poverty Policy and Poverty Research: The Great Society and the Social Sciences* (Madison: University of Wisconsin Press, 1987), 17.

92. Ron Haskins and Isabel Sawhill, *Creating an Opportunity Society* (Washington, DC: Brookings Institution, 2009), Appendix B, 257.

93. Office of Management and Budget, *Historical Tables, Budget of the United States, Fiscal Year 2013* (Washington, DC: U.S. Government Printing Office, 2011).

94. Congressional Budget Office, *Estimated Impact of the American Recovery and Reinvestment Act on Employment and Economic Output from April 2010 through June 2010*, August 24, 2010, http://www.cbo.gov/publication/21671 (December 11, 2012).

95. Office of Management and Budget, *Historical Tables, Budget of the United States, Fiscal Year 2013* (Washington, DC: U.S. Government Printing Office, 2011), Table 1.2, 24–25.

96. Ibid.

97. Ibid.

98. Ibid.

99. Ibid.

100. Ibid.

101. Ibid.

102. Ibid.

103. Congressional Budget Office, *Federal Debt and the Statutory Limit, November 2012*, November 2012, 1, http://www.cbo.gov/sites/default/files/cbofiles/attachments/43736-FederalDebtLimit-11-12-12.pdf (December 11, 2012).

104. Congressional Budget Office, *The 2012 Long-Term Budget Outlook: Federal Debt Held by the Public, 1912 to 2037, June 2012*, 1, http://www.cbo.gov/sites/default/files/cbofiles/attachments/06-05-Long-Term_Budget_Outlook.pdf (accessed December 11, 2012).

105. Ibid., 5.

106. Voegeli, *Never Enough*.

107. Office of Management and Budget, *Historical Tables, Budget of the United States, Fiscal Year 2013*, (Washington, DC: U.S. Government Printing Office, 2011), Table 3.2.

108. U.S. Census Bureau, Population Estimates Program, Population Division, "Historical National Population Estimates: July 1, 1900 to July 1, 1999," June 28, 2000, http://www.census.gov/popest/data/national/totals/pre-1980/tables/popclockest.txt (December 11, 2012).

109. U.S. Census Bureau, Population Division, Table 1: Annual Estimates of the Population for the United States, Regions, States, and Puerto Rico: April 1, 2010 to July 1, 2011 (NST-EST2011-01), release date December 2011, http://www.census.gov/popest/data/national/totals/2011/index.html (December 11, 2012).

110. Carmen M. Reinhart and Kenneth S. Rogoff, *This Time Is Different: Eight Centuries of Financial Folly* (Princeton, NJ: Princeton University Press, 2009), xxxiii.

111. Ibid., 15.

112. Alberto Alesina and Silva Ardagna, "Large Changes in Fiscal Policy: Taxes versus Spending," *Tax Policy and the Economy* 24, no. 1 (2010): 35–68.

113. Ibid., 62.

114. Alberto Alesina, Silva Ardagna, Roberto Peroti, and Fabio Schiantarelli, "Fiscal Policy, Profits, and Investment," *American Economic Review* 92, no. 3 (June 2002): 571–589.

115. Ibid., 572.

116. Ibid.

117. Ibid.

118. Ibid., 584.

119. Silvia Ardagna, "Fiscal Policy Composition, Public Debt, and Economic Activity," *Public Choice* 109 (2001): 301–325.

120. Bertrand Gruss and Jose L. Torres. "Macroeconomic and Welfare Costs of U.S. Fiscal Imbalances," *IMF Working Paper*, January 2012, http://www.imf.org/external/pubs/ft/wp/2012/wp1238.pdf (December 11, 2012).

121. Ibid., 22.

122. Ibid.

Chapter 3

1. U.S. House of Representative, Committee on the Judiciary, Subcommittee on Crime, Terrorism, and Homeland Security, *Reauthorization of the Second Chance Act*, 111th Cong., 2nd Sess., September 29, 2010.

2. Ibid., 70.

3. Ibid.

4. See Karen Bogenschneider and Thomas J. Corbett, *Evidence-Based Policy-making: Insights from Policy-Minded Researchers and Research-Minded Policy-makers* (New York: Routledge, 2010).

5. Ron Haskins, Testimony of Ron Haskins Co-Director of the Center on Children and Families Brookings Institution, and Senior Consultant, Annie E. Casey Foundation before the Committee on the Budget U.S. House of Representatives April 17, 2012, 8, http://budget.house.gov/uploadedfiles/haskinstestimony 4172012.pdf (August 24, 2012).

6. Lawrence Sherman, Denise Gottfredson, Doris Mackenzie, John Eck, Peter Rueter, and Shawn Bushway, University of Maryland Department of Criminology and Criminal Justice, *Preventing Crime: What Works, What Doesn't, What's Promising* (Washington, DC: U.S. Department of Justice, Office of Justice Programs, 1997).

7. Lawrence Sherman, "Conclusion: The Effectiveness of Local Crime Prevention Funding," in Sherman et al., *Preventing Crime*, 1.

8. Lawrence W. Sherman, David Farrington, Brandom C. Welsh, and Doris Layton MacKenzie, *Evidence-Based Crime Prevention* (London: Routledge, 2002).

9. Stewart I. Donaldson, "In Search of the Blueprint for an Evidence-Based Global Society," in *What Counts as Credible Evidence in Applied Research and Evaluation Practice?* eds. Stewart I. Donaldson, Christina A. Christie, and Melvin M. Mark (Thousand Oaks, CA: SAGE Publications, 2009), 2–18.

10. Carol H. Weiss, *Evaluation*, (Upper Saddle River, N.J.: Prentice Hall, 1998), 4.

11. Lawrence B. Mohr, *Impact Analysis for Program Evaluation*, (Thousand Oaks, Cal.: Sage Publications, 2005), 4. Emphasis removed from the original.

12. Peter H. Rossi, Mark W. Lipsey, and Howard E. Freeman. *Evaluation: A Systematic Approach*. (Thousand Oaks, CA: Sage Publications, 2004), 18.

13. William R. Shadish, Thomas D. Cook, and Donald T. Campbell, *Experimental and Quasi-Experimental Designs for Generalized Causal Inference* (Boston: Houghton Mifflin Company, 2002). In addition to experimental and quasi-experimental designs, there are natural experiments and nonexperimental designs. Natural experiments use naturally occurring differences between intervention and comparison groups. Nonexperimental designs, the weakest of the designs, do not use counterfactuals or design elements such as pretests.

14. Rossi, Lipsey, and Freeman, *Evaluation*, 54.

15. Ibid., 54–55.

16. Ibid., 56–57.

17. Ibid., 560–561.

18. Alan Agresti and Barbara Finlay, *Statistical Methods for the Social Sciences* (Upper Saddle River, NJ: Prentice Hall, 1997), 357.

19. Ibid.

20. Ibid.

21. Ibid.

22. Ibid.

23. Mark W. Lipsey, *Design Sensitivity: Statistical Power for Experimental Research* (Newbury Park, CA: Sage Publications, 1990).

24. Donald Campbell and Julian C. Stanley, *Experimental and Quasi-Experimental Designs for Research* (Boston: Houghton Mifflin Company, 1963), 5.

25. Shadish, Cook, and Campbell, *Experimental and Quasi-Experimental Designs for Generalized Causal Inference*, 54.

26. Campbell and Stanley, *Experimental and Quasi-Experimental Designs for Research*, 5.

27. Ibid.

28. Ibid.

29. Ibid.

30. Shadish, Cook, and Campbell, *Experimental and Quasi-Experimental Designs for Generalized Causal Inference*, 60.

31. Campbell and Stanley, *Experimental and Quasi-Experimental Designs for Research*, 5.

32. Shadish, Cook, and Campbell, *Experimental and Quasi-Experimental Designs for Generalized Causal Inference*, 60.

33. Campbell and Stanley, *Experimental and Quasi-Experimental Designs for Research*, 5.

34. Ibid.

35. John S. Goldkamp, Michael D. White, and Jennifer B. Robinson, "Do Drug Courts Work? Getting Inside the Drug Court Black Box," *Journal of Drug Issues* 31, no. 1 (2001): 27–72.

36. Ibid., 32.

37. R. Johnson Byron, *More God, Less Crime: Why Faith Matters and How It Could Matter More* (West Conshohocken, PA: Templeton Press, 2011).

38. Ibid., 110.

39. Campbell and Stanley, *Experimental and Quasi-Experimental Designs for Research*, 5.

40. Shadish, Cook, and Campbell, *Experimental and Quasi-Experimental Designs for Generalized Causal Inference*, 60.

41. Ibid., 83.

42. Ibid.

43. Ibid.

44. Ibid., 84.

45. Rossi, Lipsey, and Freeman, *Evaluation*, 239.

46. Ibid.

47. Gary Burtless, "Randomized Field Trials for Policy Evaluations: Why Not in Education?" in *Evidence Matters: Randomized Trials in Education Research*, eds. Frederick Mosteller and Robert Boruch (Washington, DC: Brookings Institution, 2002), 179–197.

48. Jim Manzi, *Uncontrolled: The Surprising Payoff of Trial-and-Error for Business, Politics, and Society* (New York: Basic Books, 2012), 76.

49. Gary Burtless, "Randomized Field Trials for Policy Evaluations."

50. Ibid., 183.

51. Ibid.

52. David Weisburd, Cynthia M. Lum, and Anthony Petrosino, "Does Research Design Affect Study Outcomes in Criminal Justice?" *Annals of the American Academy of Political and Social Sciences*, no. 578 (November 2001), 50–70.

53. Ibid.

54. David Weisburd, "Ethical Practice and Evaluation of Interventions in Crime and Justice," *Evaluation Review* 27, no. 23 (June 2003): 336–354.

55. Ibid., 350.

56. Shadish, Cook, and Campbell, *Experimental and Quasi-Experimental Designs for Generalized Causal Inference*, 249.

57. Ibid.

58. Ibid., 251.

59. Ibid.

60. U.S. Department of Education, *Federal Pell Grants: Fiscal Year 2011 Budget Request*, undated document, 8–9, http://www2.ed.gov/about/overview/budget/budget11/justifications/p-pell.pdf (July 23, 2012).

61. Office of Management and Budget, *Appendix, Budget of the United States, Fiscal Year 2013* (Washington, DC: U.S. Government Printing Office, 2011), 393, http://www.whitehouse.gov/sites/default/files/omb/budget/fy2013/assets/appendix.pdf (July 23, 2012).

62. Rossi, Lipsey, and Freeman, *Evaluation*, 288.

63. Ibid., 289.

64. Mohr, *Impact Analysis for Program Evaluation*, 135.

65. Ibid, 138.

66. Ibid, 139.

67. Ibid.

68. Beth C. Gamse, Robin Tepper Jacob, Megan Horst, Beth Boulay, Faith Unlu, Laurie Bozzi, Linda Caswell, Chris Rodger, W. Carter Smith, Nancy Brigham, and Shelia Rosenblum, *Reading First Impact Study: Final Report* (Washington, DC: U.S. Department of Education, Institute of Educational Sciences, November 2008).

69. Ibid, 5.

70. Ibid.

71. Ibid., 6.

72. Ibid., 17, 24.

73. Mohr, *Impact Analysis for Program Evaluation*, 135; Rossi, Lipsey, and Freeman, *Evaluation*, 147.

74. Rossi, Lipsey, and Freeman, *Evaluation*, 147.

75. Ibid.

76. Robert J. LaLonde, "Evaluating the Econometric Evaluations of Training Programs with Experimental Data," *American Economic Review* 76, no. 4 (September 1986): 604–620.

77. Ibid., 617.

78. Ibid.

79. Rajeev H. Dehejia and Sadek Wahba, "Causal Effects in Nonexperimental Studies: Reevaluating the Evaluation of Training Programs," *Journal of the American Statistical Association* 94, no. 448 (December 1999): 1053–1062.

80. Ibid., 1053.

81. Jeffrey A. Smith and Petra E. Todd, "Reconciling Conflicting Evidence on the Performance of Propensity-Score Matching Methods," *American Economic Review* 91, no. 2 (May 2001): 112–118.

82. Ibid., 113.

83. Larry L. Orr, Stephen H. Bell, and Jacob A. Klerman, "Designing Reliable Impact Evaluations," in *The Workforce Investment Act: Implementation Experiences and Evaluation Findings*, eds. Douglas J. Besharov and Phoebe H. Cottingham (Kalamazoo, MI: W. E. Upjohn Institute for Employment Research, 2011), 437.

84. Jeffrey A. Smith and Petra E. Todd, "Does Matching Overcome LaLonde's Critique of Nonexperimental Estimators?" *Journal of Econometrics* 125 (2005): 305–353.

85. Ibid.

86. Ibid., 307.

87. Orr, Bell, and Klerman, "Designing Reliable Impact Evaluations," 437.

88. Daniel Friedlander and Philip K. Robins, "Evaluating Program Evaluations: New Evidence on Commonly Used Nonexperimental Methods," *American Economic Review* 85, no. 4 (September 1995): 923–937.

89. Ibid., 935.

90. Wang-Sheng Lee, "Evaluating the Effects of a Mandatory Government Program Using Matched Groups within a Similar Geographic Location," Melbourne Institute of Applied Economic and Social Research, University of Melbourne, November 20, 2006.

91. Roberto Agodini and Mark Dynarski, "Are Experiments the Only Option? A Look at Dropout Prevention Programs," *Review of Economics and Statistics* 86, no. 1 (February 2004): 180–194.

92. Ibid., 192.

93. Elizabeth Ty Wilde and Robinson Hollister, "How Close Is Close Enough? Evaluating Propensity Score Matching Using Data from a Class Size Reduction

Experiment," in *Social Experimentation, Program Evaluation and Public Policy*, ed. Maureen A. Pirog (Association for Public Policy Analysis and Management, 2008), 65–90.

94. Ibid., 86.

95. Ibid.

96. Steven Glazerman, Dan M. Levy, and David Myers, "Nonexperimental versus Experimental Estimates of Earnings Impacts," *Annals of the American Academy of Political and Social Science* 589 (September 2003): 63–93.

97. Ibid.

98. Howard S. Bloom, Charles Michalopoulos, and Carolyn J. Hill, "Using Experiments to Assess Nonexperimental Comparison-Group Methods for Measuring Effects," in *Learning More from Social Experiments: Evolving Analytic Approaches*, ed. Howard S. Bloom (New York: Russell Sage Foundation, 2005), 178.

99. Kevin Arceneaux, Alan S. Gerber, and Donald Green, "Comparing Experimental and Matching Methods Using a Large-Scale Voter Mobilization Experiment," *Political Analysis* 14 (2006): 37–62.

100. Phoebe H. Cottingham and Douglas J. Besharov, "Introduction" in *The Workforce Investment Act: Implementation Experiences and Evaluation Findings*, eds. Douglas J. Besharov and Phoebe H. Cottingham (Kalamazoo, MI: W. E. Upjohn Institute for Employment Research, 2011), 40.

101. Jacub M. Benus, Carolyn J. Heinrich, Peter R. Mueser, and Kenneth R. Troske, *Workforce Investment Act Non-Experimental Net Impact Evaluation*, Columbia, MD: Impaq International, December 2008, http://www.impaqint.com/files/4-Content/1-6-publications/1-6-2-project-reports/Report%20-%204%20-%20Workforce%20Investment%20Act%20Non-Experimental%20Net%20Impact%20Evaluation%20-%20Final%20Report.pdf (December 21, 2012).

102. Steven Schinke, Paul Brounstein, and Stephen E. Gardner, *Science-Based Prevention Programs and Principles, 2002*, U.S. Department of Health and Human Services, Center for Substance Abuse Prevention, Substance Abuse and Mental Health Services Administration, 2002, http://www.eric.ed.gov/ERICWebPortal/contentdelivery/servlet/ERICServlet?accno=ED474651 (June 29, 2011).

103. Elizabeth B. Robertson, Susan L. David, and Suman A. Rao, *Preventing Drug Use among Children and Adolescents: A Research-Based Guide for Parents, Educators, and Community Leaders*, National Institutes of Health, National Institute on Drug Abuse, October 2003, http://drugabuse.gov/pdf/prevention/RedBook.pdf (June 29, 2011).

104. Denise Hallfors, Hyunsan Cho, Victoria Sanchez, Sheren Khatapoush, Hyung Min Kim, and Daniel Bauer, "Efficacy vs. Effectiveness Trial Results of an Indicated 'Model' Substance Abuse Program: Implications for Public Health," *American Journal of Public Health* 96, no. 12 (December 2006): 2254–2259. See also 20 U.S. Code §§ 7112 and 7115.

105. Hallfors et al., "Efficacy vs. Effectiveness Trial Results of an Indicated 'Model' Substance Abuse Program."

106. Ibid., 2257.

107. Ibid., 2258.

108. Ibid.

109. Scott W. Henggeler, Gary B. Melton, and Linda A. Smith, "Family Preservation Using Multisystemic Therapy: An Effective Alternative to Incarcerating Serious Juvenile Offenders," *Journal of Consulting and Clinical Psychology* 60, no. 6 (December 1992): 953–961.

110. Cynthia Cupit Swenson, Scott W. Henggeler, Ida Taylor, and Oliver W. Addison, *Multisystemic Therapy and Neighborhood Partnerships: Reducing Adolescent Violence and Substance Abuse* (New York: Guilford Press, 2005).

111. Charles M. Borduin, Scott W. Henggeler, David M. Blaske, and Risa J. Stein, "Multisystemic Treatment of Adolescent Sexual Offenders," *International Journal of Offender Therapy and Comparative Criminology* 34, no. 2 (September 1990): 105–113; Charles M. Borduin, Barton J. Mann, Lynn T. Cone, Scott W. Henggeler, Bethany R. Fucci, David M. Blaske, and Robert A. Williams, "Multisystemic Treatment of Serious Juvenile Offenders: Long-Term Prevention of Criminality and Violence," *Journal of Consulting and Clinical Psychology* 63, no. 4 (August 1995): 569–578; Scott W. Henggeler, W. Glenn Clingempeel, Michael J. Bronding, and Susan G. Pickrel, "Four-Year Follow-Up of Multisystemic Therapy with Substance-Abusing and Substance Dependent Juvenile Offenders," *Journal of the American Academy of Child and Adolescent Psychiatry* 41, no. 7 (July 2002): 868–874; Henggeler, Melton, and Smith, "Family Preservation Using Multisystemic Therapy."

112. Julia H. Littell, Melanie Popa, and Burnee Forsythe, "Multisystemic Therapy for Social, Emotional, and Behavioral Problems in Youth Aged 10–17," *Campbell Systematic Reviews*, September 21, 2005.

113. Alan Leschied and Alison Cunningham, *Seeking Effective Interventions for Young Offenders: Interim Results of a Four-Year Randomized Study of Multisystemic Therapy in Ontario, Canada* (London, Ontario: Centre for Children and Families in the Justice System, 2002).

114. Terje Ogden and Colleen A. Halliday-Boykins, "Multisystemic Treatment of Antisocial Adolescents in Norway: Replication of Clinical Outcomes Outside of the US," *Journal of Child and Adolescent Mental Health* 9, no. 2 (2004): 77–83.

115. Littell, Popa, and Forsythe, "Multisystemic Therapy for Social, Emotional, and Behavioral Problems in Youth Aged 10–17."

116. Erica B. Baum, "When the Witch Doctors Agree: The Family Support Act and Social Science Research," *Journal of Policy Analysis and Management* 10, no. 4 (Autumn 1991): 603–615; Judith M. Gueron, "The Politics of Random Assignment: Implementing Studies and Affecting Policy," in *Evidence Matters: Randomized Trials*

in Education Research, eds. Frederick Mosteller and Robert Boruch (Washington, DC: Brookings Institution, 2002), 15–49.

117. Lawrence W. Sherman and Richard A. Berk, "The Specific Deterrent Effects of Arrest for Domestic Assault," *American Sociological Review* 49, no. 2 (April 1984): 261–272.

118. Lawrence W. Sherman, *Domestic Violence: Experiments and Dilemmas* (New York: Free Press, 1992); Lawrence W. Sherman, Douglas A. Smith, Janell D. Schmidt, and Dennis Rogan, "Crime, Punishment, and Stake in Conformity: Legal and Informal Control of Domestic Violence," *American Sociological Review* 57 (October 1992): 680–690; Lawrence W. Sherman, Janell D. Schmidt, Dennis Rogan, Douglas A. Smith, Patrick R. Gartin, Ellen G. Cohn, Dean J. Collins, and Anthony R. Bacih, "The Variable Effects of Arrest on Criminal Careers: The Milwaukee Domestic Violence Experiment," *Journal of Criminal Law & Criminology* 83, no. 1 (1992): 137–169.

119. Sherman, *Domestic Violence*.

120. Jim Manzi, "What Social Science Does—and Doesn't—Know," *City Journal* 20, no. 3 (Summer 2010): 14–23, http://www.city-journal.org/2010/20_3_social -science.html (March 14, 2011).

121. Ibid.

Chapter 4

1. Marnie Shaul, "GAO Update on Prekindergarten Care and Education Programs," letter to Senators Michael B. Enzi, Lamar Alexander, and George V. Voinovich, June 2, 2005, http://www.gao.gov/new.items/d05678r.pdf (July 6, 2009).

2. Isabel V. Sawhill and Jon Baron, "Federal Programs for Youth: More of the Same Won't Work," *Youth Today*, May 1, 2010, http://coalition4evidence .org/wordpress/wp–content/uploads/Viewpoint-Essay-Sawhill-Baron-Youth-Today –May–2010.pdf (August 24, 2012).

3. John M. Love, Ellen Eliason Kisker, Christine M. Ross, Peter Z. Schochet, Jeanne Brooks-Gun, Diane Paulsell, Kimberly Boller, Jill Constantine, Cheri Vogel, Allison Sidle Fulingi, and Christi Brady-Smith, *Making a Difference in the Lives of Infants and Toddlers and Their Families: The Impacts of Early Head Start, Volume 1: Final Technical Report*, Princeton, NJ: Mathematica Policy Research, June 2002, 4.

4. Ibid., 192.

5. Ibid., 20.

6. Ibid., 31.

7. Ibid., 39.

8. Ibid., 38.

9. Ibid.

10. Ibid., 55.

11. Ibid.

12. Ibid., Table 1.1, 26.

13. Ibid.

14. Ibid., 145.

15. Ibid., Figure IV.1, 148.

16. Ibid., Figure IV.2, 150.

17. Ibid., Figure IV.3, 152.

18. Ibid., Figure IV.4, 154.

19. Ibid., Figure IV.5, 157.

20. Ibid., Figure IV.7, 169.

21. Ibid., Table V.1, 201.

22. Ibid., Box V.1, 200.

23. Ibid., Table V.1, 201.

24. Ibid., Box V.1, 200.

25. Ibid.

26. Ibid., Box V.1, 200.

27. Ibid., Table V.1, 201.

28. Ibid., Table V.2, 203.

29. Ibid., Table V.3, 207.

30. Ibid., Table V.4, 211.

31. Ibid., Table V.5, 215.

32. Ibid., Box V.5, 214.

33. Ibid., Table V.5, 215.

34. Due to rounding by the authors of the Early Head Start evaluation, the difference between 27.6 and 27.0 is 0.5.

35. Ibid., Table V.5, 215.

36. Ibid., Table V.6, 219.

37. Ibid., Table V.6, 219.

38. Ibid., Table V.7, 221.

39. Ibid., Box V.7, 220.

40. Due to rounding by the evaluation authors, the difference may not entirely add up.

41. Ibid., Table V.8, 227.

42. Ibid., Table V.9, 229.

43. Ibid., Table V.10, 232.

44. Ibid., Table V. 11, 235.

45. Ibid. Table VII.11, 381–385; Table VII.12, 386–388.

46. Ibid., Table VII.11, 381–385.

47. Ibid., Table VII.12, 386–388.

48. Ibid., Table 1.1, 26.

49. Cheri A. Vogel, Yange Xue, Emily M. Moiduddin, Barbara Lepidus Carlson, and Ellen Eliason Kisker, *Early Head Start Children in Grade 5: Long-Term Follow-Up of the Early Head Start Research Evaluation Project Study Sample: Final Report*, OPRE Report # 2011-8 (Washington, DC: Office of Planning, Research, and Evaluation, Administration for Children and Families, U.S. Department of Health and Human Services, December 2010).

50. Ibid., 6.

51. Ibid., Table III.2, 24–25.

52. Ibid., Table II.1, 9–12.

53. Ibid., Table III.3, 26.

54. Ibid., Table III.2, 24–25.

55. Ibid.

56. Ibid.

57. Ibid.

58. Ibid.

59. Ibid., Table III.6, 31–33.

60. Ibid., Table III.7, 34.

61. Ibid., Table III.6, 31–33.

62. Ibid.

63. Ibid.

64. Ibid., Table III.6, 31–33; Table III.7, 34.

65. Ibid., Table III.6, 31–33.

66. Ibid., Table III.6, 31–33; Table III.7, 34.

67. JoAnn Hsueh, Erin Jacobs, and Mary Farrell, *A Two Generational Child-Focused Program Enhanced with Employment Services: Eighteen-Month Impacts from the Kansas and Missouri Sites of the Enhanced Services for the Hard-to-Employ Demonstration and Evaluation Project* (Washington, DC: Office of Planning, Research, and Evaluation, Administration for Children and Families, U.S. Department of Health and Human Services, March 2011), 1.

68. Ibid.

69. JoAnn Hsueh and Mary E. Farrell, *Enhanced Early Head Start with Employment Services: 42-Month Impacts from the Kansas and Missouri Sites of the Enhanced Services for the Hard-to-Employ Demonstration and Evaluation Project*, OPRE Report # 2012-05 (Washington, DC: Office of Planning, Research, and Evaluation, Administration for Children and Families, U.S. Department of Health and Human Services, February 2012), 9.

70. Hsueh et al., *A Two Generational Child-Focused Program Enhanced with Employment Services*, 11.

71. Ibid.

72. Ibid.; Hsueh and Farrell, *Enhanced Early Head Start with Employment Services.*

73. Hsueh and Farrell, *Enhanced Early Head Start with Employment Services*, 17.

74. Hsueh et al., *A Two Generational Child-Focused Program Enhanced with Employment Services*, 1.

75. Ibid., ES–9.

76. Ibid., Table 5.1, 79.

77. Hsueh and Farrell, *Enhanced Early Head Start with Employment Services*, Table 3.1, 34.

78. Hsueh et al., *A Two Generational Child-Focused Program Enhanced with Employment Services*, Table 5.1, 79.

79. Hsueh and Farrell, *Enhanced Early Head Start with Employment Services*, Table 3.1, 34.

80. Hsueh et al., *A Two Generational Child-Focused Program Enhanced with Employment Services*, Table 5.3, 84; Hsueh and Farrell, *Enhanced Early Head Start with Employment Services*, Table 3.3, 39.

81. Hsueh et al., *A Two Generational Child-Focused Program Enhanced with Employment Services*, Table 5.2, 81.

82. Hsueh and Farrell, *Enhanced Early Head Start with Employment Services*, Table 3.2, 36–37.

83. Ibid.

84. Hsueh et al., *A Two Generational Child-Focused Program Enhanced with Employment Services*, Table 5.2, 81–82; Hsueh and Farrell, *Enhanced Early Head Start with Employment Services*, Table 3.2, 36–37.

85. Hsueh et al., *A Two Generational Child-Focused Program Enhanced with Employment Services*, Table 6.1, 98; Hsueh and Farrell, *Enhanced Early Head Start with Employment Services*, Table 4.1, 55.

86. Hsueh et al., *A Two Generational Child-Focused Program Enhanced with Employment Services*, Table 6.3, 107.

87. Hsueh and Farrell, *Enhanced Early Head Start with Employment Services*, Table 4.3, 61.

88. Amy E. Lowenstein, "Early Care and Education as Educational Panacea: What Do We Really Know about Its Effectiveness," *Educational Policy* 25, no. 1 (2011): 92–114.

89. U.S. Department of Health and Human Services, "Head Start Program Fact Sheet," http://www.acf.hhs.gov/programs/ohs/about/fy2008.html (January 14, 2010).

90. U.S. Department of Health and Human Services, Administration for Children and Families, *Head Start Impact Study: Final Report*, xxxviii, http://www.acf.hhs.gov/programs/opre/hs/impact_study/reports/impact_study/hs_impact_study_final.pdf (January 15, 2010).

91. U.S. Department of Health and Human Services, Administration for Children and Families, *Head Start Impact Study: First Year Findings* (Washington, DC, June 2005), 1–5.

92. U.S. Department of Health and Human Services, Administration for Children and Families, *Head Start Impact Study: First Year Findings*, June 2005, http://www.acf.hhs.gov/programs/opre/hs/impact_study/reports/first_yr_finds/first_yr_finds.pdf (January 15, 2010).

93. U.S. Department of Health and Human Services, *Head Start Impact Study: Final Report*, 1–10.

94. U.S. Department of Health and Human Services, Administration for Children and Families, *Head Start Impact Study: First Year Findings*.

95. U.S. Department of Health and Human Services, *Head Start Impact Study: Final Report*.

96. Ibid., xxxviii.

97. Public Law 111–5.

98. U.S. Department of Health and Human Services, *Head Start Impact Study: First Year Findings*, Exhibit 5.1A, 5–14.

99. Ibid., 5–4.

100. Ibid., 5–5.

101. Ibid., 5–6 and Exhibit, 5.1-A, 5–14.

102. Ibid., 5–6.

103. Ibid., Exhibit 5.1A, 5–14.

104. Ibid., 5–7.

105. Ibid., Exhibit, 5.1-A, 5–14.

106. Ibid., 5–8 to 5–9

107. Ibid., Exhibit, 5.1-A, 5–14.

108. Ibid., 5–9.

109. Ibid., 5–9.

110. Ibid., Exhibit, 5.1-A, 5–14.

111. Ibid., Exhibit 6.1-A, 6–6.

112. Ibid., Exhibit 6.2-A, 6–9.

113. Ibid., Exhibit 7.1. 7–6 and Exhibit 7.2, 7–7.

114. Ibid., Exhibit 8.1, 8–9.

115. Ibid., Exhibit 8.2, 8–10.

116. Ibid., Exhibit 8.1, 8–9 and Exhibit 8.2, 8–10.

117. Ibid., Exhibit 8.1, 8–9.

118. Ibid., Exhibit 8.2, 8–10.

119. Ibid., Exhibit 8.1, 8–9.

120. Ibid., Exhibit 8.2, 8–10.

121. U.S. Department of Health and Human Services, *Head Start Impact Study: Final Report.*, 4–21–4–25, Exhibit 4.5.

122. Ibid., 4–26.

123. Ibid., 4–21–4–25, Exhibit 4.5.

124. Ibid.

125. Ibid., 4–10–4–13; Exhibit 4.2.

126. Ibid., 4–10–4–13; Exhibit 4.2.

127. Ibid., 4–9.

128. Ibid., 5–8–5–10; Exhibit 5.2.

129. Ibid.

130. Ibid., 5–4–5–6; Exhibit 5.1.

131. Ibid.

132. Ibid., 5–3.

133. Ibid., 6–6–6–7; Exhibit 6.2.

134. Ibid., 6–3–6–4; Exhibit 6.1.

135. Ibid.

136. Ibid., 7–8–7–10; Exhibit 7.2.

137. Ibid.

138. Ibid., 7–4–7–5; Exhibit 7.1.

139. Michael Puma, Stephen Bell, Ronna Cook, Camilla, Pam Broene, Frank Jenkins, Andrew Mashburn, and Jason Downer, *Third Grade Follow-up to the Head Start Impact Study Final Report* (Washington, DC: Office of Planning, Research and Evaluation, Administration for Children and Families, U.S. Department of Health and Human Services, October 2012), http://www.acf.hhs.gov/sites/default/files/opre/head_start_report.pdf (accessed December 21, 2012).

140. Dan Lips, "Politicizing Preschool," Fox News, December 28, 2009, http://www.foxnews.com/opinion/2009/12/29/dan-lips-heritage-preschool-head-start-politics (January 19, 2010).

141. U.S. Department of Health and Human Services, Administration for Children and Families, "Head Start Impact Study and Follow-Up: Overview," http://www.acf.hhs.gov/programs/opre/hs/impact_study/imptstudy_overview.html (January 14, 2010).

142. Ibid., Exhibit 4.2, 78.

143. Ibid., Exhibit 4.1, 77.

144. Ibid., Exhibit 4.4, 83–84.

145. Ibid., Exhibit 4.3, 81–82.

146. Ibid., Exhibit 4.4, 83–84.

147. Ibid., Exhibit 4.3, 81–82.

148. Ibid., 84.

149. Ibid., Exhibit 4.4, 83–84.

150. Ibid., Exhibit 4.3, 81–82.

151. Ibid., Exhibit 4.5, 85; Exhibit 4.6, 86.

152. Ibid., Exhibit 4.8, 88.

153. Ibid., Exhibit 4.7, 87.

154. Nicholas Zill, Alberto Sorongon, Kwang Kim, Cheryl Clark, and Maria Woolverton, "Children's Outcomes and Program Quality in Head Start," U.S. Department of Health and Human Services, Administration for Children and Families, *Faces 2003 Research Brief*, December 2006, http://www.acf.hhs.gov/

programs/opre/hs/faces/reports/research_2003/research_2003.pdf (January 12, 2010).

155. Donald T. Campbell and Julian C. Stanley, *Experimental and Quasi-Experimental Designs for Research* (Boston: Houghton Mifflin Company, 1963).

156. Valerie E. Lee and Susanna Loeb, "Where Do Head Start Attendees End Up? One Reason Why Preschool Effects Fade Out," *Educational Evaluation and Policy Analysis* 17, no. 1 (Spring 1995): 62–82.

157. Janet Currie and Duncan Thomas, "Does Head Start Make a Difference?" *American Economic Review* 85, no. 3 (1995): 341–364; Eliana Garces, Duncan Thomas, and Janet Currie, "Longer–Term Effects of Head Start," *American Economic Review* 92, no. 4 (September 2002): 999–1012.

158. Currie and Thomas, "Does Head Start Make a Difference?" 341.

159. Robert St. Pierre, Anne Ricciuti, Fumiyo Tao, Cindy Creps, Takeko Kumagawa, and William Ross, *Third National Even Start Evaluation: Description of Projects and Participants* (Abt Associates Inc., 2001), 12.

160. Ibid.

161. Ibid., 13–14.

162. Ibid., 17.

163. Robert St. Pierre, Anne Ricciuti, Fumiyo Tao, Cindy Creps, Janet Swartz, Wang Lee, Amanda Parsad, and Tracy Rimdzius, *Third National Even Start Evaluation: Program Impacts and Implications for Improvement* (Cambridge, MA: Abt Associates Inc., 2003), 153.

164. St. Pierre et al., *Third National Even Start Evaluation: Description of Projects and Participants*, 23.

165. St.Pierre et al., *Third National Even Start Evaluation: Program Impacts and Implications for Improvement*, 75.

166. Ibid., 77–93.

167. Ibid., 76.

168. Ibid., 32.

169. Anna E. Ricciuti, Robert G. St. Pierre, Wang Lee, Amanda Parsad, and Tracy Rimdzius, *Third National Even Start Evaluation: Follow–Up Findings from the Experimental Design Study* (Washington, DC: U.S. Department of Education, Institute of Education Sciences, National Center for Education Evaluation and Regional Assistance 2004).

170. Ibid., 1.

171. St. Pierre et al., *Third National Even Start Evaluation: Program Impacts and Implications for Improvement*, Exhibit 6.13, 179.

172. Ibid.

173. Ibid.

174. Ibid.

175. Ibid.

176. Ibid.

177. Ibid., 165.

178. Ricciuti et al., *Third National Even Start Evaluation: Follow-Up Findings From the Experimental Design Study*, Table 4.2, 38.

179. Ibid.

180. Ibid.

181. Ibid.

182. Ibid.

183. Ibid.

184. Ibid.

185. Susanne James-Burdumy, Mark Dynarski, and John Deke, "When Elementary Schools Stay Open Late: Results from the National Evaluation of the 21st Century Community Learning Centers Program," *Educational Evaluation and Policy Analysis* 29, no. 4 (December 2007): 296–318.

186. U.S. Department of Education, Office of Planning, Evaluation and Policy Development, Policy and Program Studies Service, *21st Century Community Learning Centers Descriptive Study of Program Practices* (Washington, DC, U.S. Department of Education, 2010), ix.

187. James-Burdumy et al., "When Elementary Schools Stay Open Late," 296.

188. U.S. Department of Education, *21st Century Community Learning Centers Descriptive Study of Program Practices*, ix.

189. James-Burdumy et al., "When Elementary Schools Stay Open Late," 299.

190. Ibid.

191. Ibid.

192. Ibid., 297.

193. Ibid., Table 3, 306–307.

194. Ibid., Table 4, 308.

195. Ibid.

196. Ibid.

197. Ibid., Table 5, 309.

198. Ibid.

199. Ibid., Table 6, 310.

200. Ron Haskins and Isabel Sawhill, *Creating an Opportunity Society* (Washington, DC: Brookings Institution, 2009), 213.

201. Barbara Devaney, Amy Johnson, Rebecca Maynard, and Chris Trenholm, *The Evaluation of Abstinence Education Programs Funded under Title V Section 510: Interim Report*, Princeton, NJ: Mathematica Policy Research, April 2002, 3.

202. Haskins and Sawhill, *Creating an Opportunity Society*, 219.

203. Rebecca A. Maynard, Christopher Trenholm, Barbara Devaney, Amy Johnson, Melissa A. Clark, John Homrighausen, and Ece Kalay, *First-Year Impacts of Four Title V, Section 510 Abstinence Education Programs*, Princeton, NJ: Mathematica Policy Research, June 2005, 2.

204. Ibid., Figure II.1, 9.

205. Ibid., Table III.1, 22.

206. Christopher Trenholm, Barbara Devaney, Ken Fortson, Lisa Quay, Justin Wheeler, and Melissa Clark, *Impacts of Four Title V, Section 510 Abstinence Education Programs: Final Report*, Princeton, NJ: Mathematica Policy Research, April 2007, 29.

207. Trenholm et al., *Impacts of Four Title V, Section 510 Abstinence Education Programs*, 13.

208. Maynard et al., *First-Year Impacts of Four Title V, Section 510 Abstinence Education Programs*, Table V.1, 60.

209. Ibid., Table V.2, 61.

210. Ibid., Table V.3, 63.

211. Ibid., Table V.4, 64.

212. Trenholm et al., *Impacts of Four Title V, Section 510 Abstinence Education Programs*, 30.

213. Ibid., Table IV.1, 30.

214. Ibid., Figure IV.1, 31.

215. Ibid., Table IV.2, 32.

216. Ibid., Figure IV.2, 33.

217. Ibid., Figure IV.3, 34.

218. Ibid., Figure IV.4, 35.

219. Ibid., Table IV.3, 36.

220. Ibid., Table IV.4, 37.

221. Douglas Kirby, *Emerging Answers 2007: Research Findings on Programs to Reduce Teen Pregnancy and Sexually Transmitted Diseases* (Washington, DC: National Campaign to Prevent Teen and Unplanned Pregnancy, November 2007).

222. John B. Jemmott, Loretta S. Jemmott, and Gregory T. Fong, "Efficacy of a Theory-Based Abstinence-Only Intervention over 24 Months," *Archives of Pediatrics and Adolescent Medicine* 164, no. 2 (February 2010), 152–159.

223. Ibid., 158.

224. Ibid.

225. David Myers and Allen Schirm, *The Short-Term Impacts of Upward Bound: An Interim Report.* Princeton, NJ: Mathematica Policy Research, May 1997, 1.

226. Ibid., 23.

227. Ibid., 4.

228. Ibid., 7.

229. Ibid.

230. Ibid.

231. U.S. Department of Education, Office of the Under Secretary, Policy and Program Studies Service, *The Impacts of Regular Upward Bound: Results from the Third-Follow-Up Data Collection* (Washington, DC: U.S. Department of Education, April 2004), 11.

232. Ibid., 23.

233. Neil S. Seftor, Arif Mamun, and Allen Schirm, *The Impacts of Regular Upward Bound on Postsecondary Outcomes 7–9 Years after Scheduled High School Graduation: Final Report*, Princeton, NJ: Mathematica Policy Research, January 2009.

234. U.S. Department of Education, *The Impacts of Regular Upward Bound*, Table II.5, 26.

235. Ibid., Table II.6, 27.

236. Ibid., 31.

237. Ibid., 32.

238. Ibid., Table III.2, 37.

239. Ibid., Table III.4, 37.

240. Ibid., Table III.4, 39.

241. Seftor et al., *The Impacts of Regular Upward Bound on Postsecondary Outcomes*, Table III.1, 41.

242. Ibid., Table IV.2, 59.

243. Ibid.

244. Ibid., Table III.1, 41.

245. Ibid., Table IV.2, 59.

246. U.S. Department of Agriculture, Food and Nutrition Service, "SNAP Monthly Data," August 30, 2012, http://www.fns.usda.gov/pd/34SNAPmonthly.htm (September 30, 2012).

247. U.S. Government Accountability Office, *Multiple Employment and Training Programs: Providing Information on Collocating Services and Consolidating Administrative Structures Could Promote Efficiencies* (Washington, DC: U.S. Government Accountability Office, January 2011).

248. U.S. Government Accountability Office, *Multiple Employment and Training Programs*, Appendix II, 47–49; Appendix V, 55–57.

249. Ibid., Appendix II, 47–49; Appendix IV, 53–54.

250. Michael J. Puma and Nancy R. Burstein, "The National Evaluation of the Food Stamp Employment and Training Program," *Journal of Policy Analysis and Management* 13, no. 2 (1994): 311–330.

251. Ibid., 311.

252. Ibid., 314.

253. Ibid., 311.

254. Ibid., Table 2, 322; Table 3, 322; Table 4, 323; Table 5, 323.

255. Ibid., Table 2, 322.

256. Ibid., Table 3, 322; Table 4, 323.

257. Ibid., Table 5, 323.

258. Ibid., Table 6, 324; Table 7, 325.

259. Gayle Hamilton, Stephen Freedman, Lisa Gennetian, Charles Michalopoulos, Johanna Walter, Diana Adams-Ciardullo, Anna Gassman-Pines, Sharon

McGroder, Martha Zaslow, Jennifer Brooks, Surjeet Ahluwalia, Electra Small, and Bryan Ricchetti, *National Evaluation of Welfare-to-Work Strategies: How Effective Are Different Welfare-to-Work Approaches? Five-Year Adult and Child Impacts for Eleven Programs* (Washington, DC: U.S. Department of Health and Human Services, Administration for Children and Families and Office of the Assistant Secretary for Planning and Evaluation; and U.S. Department of Education, 2001), ES–4.

260. Hamilton et al., *National Evaluation of Welfare-to-Work Strategies*, ES–5.

261. Hamilton et al., *National Evaluation of Welfare-to-Work Strategies*, ES–6; Jill Duerr Berrick, "Income Maintenance and Support" in *The Hand Book of Social Policy*, ed. James Midgley and Michelle Livermore (Los Angeles: Sage Publications, 2009), 339–340; Eileen Boris, "Contested Rights: The Great Society between Home and Work" in *The Great Society and the High Tide of Liberalism*, ed. Sidney M. Milkis and Jerome M. Mileur (Boston: University of Massachusetts Press, 2005), 115–144.

262. Hamilton et al., *National Evaluation of Welfare-to-Work Strategies*.

263. Ibid., ES–7.

264. Ibid., ES–1.

265. Ibid.

266. Ibid., 2.

267. Ibid., 1.

268. Ibid., ES–2.

269. Ibid.

270. Ibid.

271. Ibid., ES–3.

272. Ibid., Table 4.1, 86–87.

273. Ibid.

274. Ibid.

275. Ibid., Table 5.1, 111.

276. Ibid.

277. Ibid., Table 5.2, 120.

278. Ibid.

279. Ibid., Table 6.1, 127.

280. Richard Hendra, Keri–Nicole Dillman, Gayle Hamilton, Erik Lundquist, Karin Martinson, Melissa Wavelet, Aaron Hill, and Sonya Williams, *How Effective Are Different Approaches Aiming to Increase Employment Retention and Advancement? Final Impacts for Twelve Models*, MDRC, April 2010.

281. Ibid., 1.

282. Ibid., 2.

283. Ibid., Table 1.1, 3–4.

284. Ibid., 11.

285. Ibid.

286. Ibid., 16–17.

287. Ibid., Table 12, 12.

288. Ibid., 31.

289. Ibid., 2.

290. Ibid., 43.

291. Ibid., 49.

292. Ibid., 80.

293. Ibid., 81.

294. Ibid., 82.

295. Ibid., 91.

296. Ibid., Table 3.3, 56; Table 3.4, 58–59; Table 3.5, 60–61; Table 3.7, 85–86; Table 3.8, 96–97.

297. Ibid.

298. Ibid.

299. Ibid.

300. Ibid., 89.

301. Ibid., 103.

302. Ibid., 105.

303. Ibid., 107.

304. Ibid., 130.

305. Ibid., 142.

306. Ibid., Table 4.3, 115–116; Table 4.5, 134–135; Table 4.7, 147–148.

307. Ibid.

308. Ibid., Table 5.3, 168–169; Table 5.4, 178–179; Table 5.5, 90–191; Table 5.6, 202–203; Table 5.10, 224–225.

309. Ibid.

310. Ibid., 159.

311. Ibid., 162.

312. Ibid., 173.

313. Ibid., 173–174.

314. Ibid., 185.

315. Ibid., 186.

316. Ibid., 197.

317. Ibid., 197–198.

318. Ibid., 219–220.

319. Ibid., Table 5.3, 168–169; Table 5.4, 178–179; Table 5.5, 90–191; Table 5.6, 202–203; and Table 5.10, 224–225.

320. Ibid.

321. Ibid.

322. Paul Amato, "The Impact of Family Formation Change on the Cognitive, Social, and Emotional Well-Being of the Next Generation," *Future of Children* 15, no. 2 (Fall 2005): 75–96; Susan L. Brown, "Family Structure and Child Well-Being:

The Significance of Parental Cohabitation," *Journal of Marriage and Family* 66, no. 2 (May 2004): 351–367; Sarah McLanahan and Gary Sandefur, *Growing up with a Single Parent: What Hurts, What Helps* (Cambridge, MA: Harvard University Press, 1994).

323. Haskins and Sawhill, *Creating an Opportunity Society*, 214.

324. Ibid.

325. Robert G. Wood, Sheena McConnell, Quinn Moore, Andrew Clarkwest, and JoAnn Hsueh, *Strengthening Unmarried Parents' Relationships: The Early Impacts of Building Strong Families*, Princeton, NJ: Mathematica Policy Research, May 2010. A long-term follow-up study will be conducted when the couples' children reach the age of three.

326. JoAnn Hsueh, Desiree Principe Alderson, Erika Lundquist, Charless Michalopoulos, Daniel Gubits, David Fein, and Virginia Knox, *The Supporting Healthy Marriage Evaluation: Early Impacts on Low-Income Families* (Washington, DC: Office of Planning, Research and Evaluation, Administration for Children and Families, U.S. Department of Health and Human Services, 2012).

327. Wood et al., *Strengthening Unmarried Parents' Relationships*, Table 2, 4.

328. Ibid., 3.

329. Ibid., 2.

330. Wood et al., *Strengthening Unmarried Parents' Relationships*.

331. Robert G. Wood, Quinn Moore, Andrew Clarkwest, Alexandra Killewald, and Shannon Monahan, *The Long-Term Effects of Building Strong Families: A Relationship Skills Education Program for Unmarried Parents: Final Report*, (Princeton, NJ: Mathematica Policy Research, November 2012).

332. Wood et al., *Strengthening Unmarried Parents' Relationships*, 7.

333. Ibid., Table 3, 8.

334. Ibid.

335. Ibid.

336. Ibid., xii.

337. Ibid., 12.

338. Wood et al., *The Long-Term Effects of Building Strong Families*, xiii.

339. Ibid., Figure ES.2, vx.

340. Wood et al., *Strengthening Unmarried Parents' Relationships*, Table 7, 16.

341. Ibid., Table A.7, A-10.

342. Wood et al., *Strengthening Unmarried Parents' Relationships*, Table A.3, A-6.

343. Ibid., Table A.8, A-11.

344. Ibid., Table A.8, A-11.

345. Wood et al., *The Long-Term Effects of Building Strong Families*, Table A.3a, A.7; Table A.8a, A.16.

346. Ibid., Table A.7a, A.14.

347. Ibid., Table A.5a, A.11.

348. Ibid., Table A.8, A-11.

349. Ibid., Table A.8, A-11.

350. Wood et al., *The Long-Term Effects of Building Strong Families*, Table A.2a, A-5 and Table A.8a, A-16.

351. Wood et al., *Strengthening Unmarried Parents' Relationships*, Table A.2, A-5; Table A.8, A-11.

352. Wood et al., *The Long-Term Effects of Building Strong Families*, Table A.2a, A-5; Table A.8a, A-16.

353. Wood et al., *Strengthening Unmarried Parents' Relationships*, Table A.8, A-11.

354. Ibid., Table A.8, A-11.

355. Wood et al., *The Long-Term Effects of Building Strong Families*, Table A.2a, A-5.

356. Wood et al., *Strengthening Unmarried Parents' Relationships.*, Table A.3, A-6; Table A.8, A-11.

357. Wood et al., *The Long-Term Effects of Building Strong Families*, Table A3a, A-7; Table A.8a, A-16.

358. Ibid., Table A.5a, A-11.

359. Wood et al., *Strengthening Unmarried Parents' Relationships.*, Table A.3, A.6; Table A.8, A-11.

360. Wood et al., *The Long-Term Effects of Building Strong Families*, Table A3a, A-7; Table A.8a, A-16.

361. Ibid., Table A.5a, A.11.

362. Wood et al., *Strengthening Unmarried Parents' Relationships.*, Table A.3, A-6.

363. Wood et al., *The Long-Term Effects of Building Strong Families*, Table A3a, A-7.

364. Wood et al., *Strengthening Unmarried Parents' Relationships.*, Table A.3, A-6; Table A.8, A-11.

365. Wood et al., *The Long-Term Effects of Building Strong Families*, Table A3a, A-7; Table A8.a, A-16.

366. Wood et al., *Strengthening Unmarried Parents' Relationships.*, Table 10, 21.

367. Ibid., Table A.6, A-9.

368. Ibid., Table 10, 21.

369. Ibid., Table A.6, A-9.

370. Ibid., Table A.3, A-6.

371. Hsueh et al., *The Supporting Healthy Marriage Evaluation*

372. Ibid., 3–7.

373. Ibid., 7.

374. Ibid., Table 2, 14.

375. Ibid., Table 4, 27.

376. Ibid.

377. Ibid., Table 5, 29.

378. Ibid., Table 6, 33.

379. Ibid., Table 5, 29.

380. Ibid., Table 6, 33.

381. Ibid., Table 5, 29.

382. Ibid., Table 7, 34.

383. Ibid.

384. Ibid., Table 6, 33.

385. Ibid., Table 7, 34.

386. Ibid., Table 8, 35.

387. Ibid.

388. William Julius Wilson, *More Than Just Race: Being Black and Poor in the Inner City* (New York: W. W. Norton & Company, 2009), 27.

389. Ibid.

390. Robert J. Sampson and Dawn Jeglum Bartusch, "Legal Cynicism and (Subcultural?) Tolerance of Deviance: The Neighborhood Context of Racial Differences," *Law and Society Review* 32, no. 4 (1998): 777–804.

391. Robert Sampson and Stephen W. Raudenbush, "Systematic Social Observation of Public Spaces: A New Look at Disorder in Urban Neighborhoods," *American Journal of Sociology* 105, no. 3 (November 1999): 603–651.

392. U.S Department of Commerce, U.S. Census Bureau, "Areas with Concentrated Poverty: 2006–2010," *American Community Survey Briefs*, December 2011, Table 1, 2.

393. Ibid., Table 2, 5–6.

394. Larry Orr, Judith D. Feins, Robin Jacob, Erik Beecroft, Lisa Sanbonmatsu, Lawrence F. Katz, Jeffrey B. Liebman, and Jeffrey R. Kling, *Moving to Opportunity Interim Impacts Evaluation: Final Report* (Washington, DC: U.S. Department of Housing and Urban Development, Office of Policy Development and Research, June 2003).

395. Orr et al., *Moving to Opportunity Interim Impacts Evaluation*, 2.

396. Ibid.

397. Lisa Sanbonmatsu, Jens Ludwig, Lawrence F. Katz, Lisa Gennetian, Greg J. Duncan, Ronald C. Kessler, Emma Adam, Thomas W. McDade, Stacy Tessler Lindau, Matthew Sciandra, Fanghua Yang, Ijun Lai, William Congdon, Joe Amick, Ryan Gillette, Michael A. Zabek, Jordon Marvakov, Sabrina Yusuf, and Nicholas A. Potter, *Moving to Opportunity for Fair Housing Demonstration Program: Final Impacts Evaluation* (Washington, DC: U.S. Department of Housing and Urban Development, Office of Policy Development and Research, November 2011).

398. Orr et al., *Moving to Opportunity Interim Impacts Evaluation*, 12.

399. Ibid.

400. Ibid., Exhibit 1.5, 16.

401. Ibid., xiv.

402. Ibid., Exhibit 3.4, 64.

403. Ibid., 49.

404. Ibid., Exhibit 3.3, 61.

405. Ibid., Exhibit 3.5, 66.

406. Ibid., Exhibit 4.2, 77.

407. Ibid., Exhibit 4.3, 61; Exhibit 4.4, 82.

408. Ibid., Exhibit 5.3, 95.

409. Ibid., xv.

410. Ibid., Exhibit 6.3, 110; Exhibit 6.5, 117; Exhibit 6.6, 118; Exhibit 6.7, 119.

411. Ibid., Exhibit 7.3, 129.

412. Ibid., 134.

413. Ibid., Exhibit 8.4, 142.

414. Ibid., Exhibit 8.8, 146.

415. Sanbonmatsu et al., *Moving to Opportunity for Fair Housing Demonstration Program: Final Impacts Evaluation*, Exhibit 2.5, 56.

416. Ibid., Exhibit 2.4, 55–56.

417. Ibid., Exhibit 2.6, 59–61.

418. Ibid., Exhibit 2.10, 63–64.

419. Ibid., Exhibit 2.11, 65.

420. Ibid., Exhibit 3.2, 90–92.

421. Ibid., Exhibit 3.4, 95–97.

422. Ibid., Exhibit 3.2, 90–92; Exhibit 3.4, 95–97.

423. Ibid., Exhibit 3.2, 90–92.

424. Ibid., Exhibit 3.4, 95–97.

425. Ibid., Exhibit 4.2, 115; Exhibit 4.4, 124–125.

426. Ibid., Exhibit 4.3, 121–122.

427. Ibid., Exhibit 4.5, 126–129.

428. Ibid., Exhibit 4.3, 121–122; Exhibit 4.6, 130–132.

429. Ibid., Exhibit 4.2, 115.

430. Ibid., Exhibit 4.4, 124–125.

431. Ibid., 137.

432. Ibid., Exhibit 5.7, 132; Exhibit 5.8, 154; Exhibit 5.9, 155.

433. Ibid., Exhibit 5.7, 152.

434. Ibid., Supplemental Exhibit 5.5, 171.

435. Ibid., Exhibit 5.7, 152.

436. Ibid., Exhibit 5.8, 154–155.

437. Ibid., Exhibit 5.11, 159; Exhibit 5.12, 160; Exhibit 5.13, 161.

438. Ibid., Exhibit 6.5, 196–197.

439. Ibid., Exhibit 6.6, 198.

440. Ibid., Exhibit 6.7, 199–200.

441. Ibid., Exhibit 6.8, 201–202.

442. Ibid., Exhibit 6.9, 203.

443. Ibid., Exhibit 6.10, 204.

444. Ibid., Exhibit 7.3, 225–227.

445. Ibid., Exhibit 7.6, 230.

446. Ibid., Exhibit 7.7, 231–232.

447. Ibid., Exhibit 7.9, 235–237.

448. Ibid., Exhibit 7.8, 233–234; Exhibit 7.9, 235–237.

449. Ibid., 264.

Chapter 5

1. U.S. Government Accountability Office, *Multiple Employment and Training Programs: Providing Information on Collocating Services and Consolidating Administrative Structures Could Promote Efficiencies* (Washington, DC, January 2011), Figure 1, 6.

2. For background on the origins of federal employment programs, see Frank Freidel, *Franklin D. Roosevelt: Launching the New Deal* (Boston: Little, Brown, 1973); William E. Leuchtenburg, *Franklin D. Roosevelt and the New Deal, 1932–1940* (New York: Harper Colophon Books, 1963); Broadus Mitchell, *Depression Decade: From New Era through New Deal., 1929–1941* (New York: Harper Torchbooks, 1969); John Joseph Wallis and Daniel K. Benjamin, "Public Relief and Private Employment in the Great Depression," *Journal of Economic History* 41 (December 1993): 97–102.

3. Leonard P. Adams, *The Public Employment Service in Transition, 1933–1968* (Ithaca: New York State School of Industrial and Labor Relations, Cornell University, 1969); Raymond C. Atkinson, Louise C. Odencrantz, and Ben Deming, *Public Employment Service in the United States* (Chicago: Public Administration Service, 1938).

4. U.S. Department of Commerce, Bureau of the Census, *Historical Statistics of the United States: Colonial Times to 1970*, Part 1 (Washington, DC, 1975), 126.

5. Daniel Friedlander, David H. Greenberg, and Philip K. Robins, "Evaluating Government Training Programs for the Economically Disadvantaged," *Journal of Economic Literature* 35 (December, 1997): 1809–1855.

6. Ibid.

7. Gordon Lafer, *The Job Training Charade* (Ithaca, NY: Cornell University Press, 2002).

8. Ibid., 163; U.S. General Accounting Office, *Moving Participants from Public Service Employment Programs into Unsubsidized Jobs Needs More Attention,* (Washington, DC, October 12, 1979), 1.

9. Lafer, *The Job Training Charade.*

10. U.S. General Accounting Office, *More Benefits to Jobless Can Be Attained in Public Service Employment.*

11. Ibid., i.

12. Ibid., ii.

13. Ibid.

14. Ibid., iii.

15. Friedlander et al., "Evaluating Government Training Programs for the Economically Disadvantaged."

16. Lafer, *The Job Training Charade.*

17. Richard F. Fenno, *The Making of Senator Dan Quayle* (Washington, DC: Congressional Quarterly Press, 1989).

18. Ibid.

19. U.S. House of Representatives. *Report of the Committee on Education and Labor Accompanying H.R. 5320, the Job Training Partnership Act*, House Report 97–537. 97th Congress, 2nd Sess., May 17, 1982.

20. Lafer, *The Job Training Charade.*

21. Ibid.

22. William J. Clinton, "President Clinton Delivers Remarks at Signing Ceremony for the Workforce Investment Act," transcript, Federal Document Clearing House, August 7, 1998.

23. Workforce Investment Act, Public Law 105–220.

24. Dianne Blank, Laura Heald, and Cynthia Fagoni, "An Overview of WIA," in *The Workforce Investment Act: Implementation Experiences and Evaluation Findings*, eds. Douglas J. Besharov and Phoebe H. Cottingham (Kalamazoo, MI: W. E. Upjohn Institute for Employment Research, 2011), 55.

25. Lafer, *The Job Training Charade.*

26. Blank et al., "An Overview of WIA," 49–78.

27. Ibid.

28. Christopher T. King and Burt S. Barnow, "The Use of Market Mechanisms" in *The Workforce Investment Act: Implementation Experiences and Evaluation Findings*, eds. Douglas J. Besharov and Phoebe H. Cottingham (Kalamazoo, MI: W. E. Upjohn Institute for Employment Research, 2011), 81–111.

29. Burt S. Barnow, "Vouchers in U.S. Vocational Training Programs: An Overview of What We Have Learned," *Zeitschrift für ArbeitsmarktForschung* (Journal for Labour Market Research) 42, no.1(2009): 77–78.

30. Burt S. Barnow and Christopher T. King, *The Workforce Investment Act in Eight States*, Nelson A. Rockefeller Institute of Government, 2005, http://www.doleta.gov/reports/searcheta/occ/papers/Rockefeller_Institute_Final_Report2-10-05.pdf; Ronald D'Amico and Jeffrey Salzman, *An Evaluation of the Individual Training Account/Eligible Training Provider Demonstration: Final Report*, Social Policy Research Associates, December 2004, http://wdr.doleta.gov/research/FullText_Documents/2005_02_final_ita_demo.pdf.

31. Barnow and King, *The Workforce Investment Act in Eight States;* Sheena McConnell, Elizabeth Stuart, Kenneth Fortson, Paul Decker, Irma Perez-Johnson, Barbara Harris, and Jeffrey Salzman, *Managing Customers' Training Choices:*

Findings from the Individual Training Account Experiment, Final Report. Mathematica Policy Research, Inc., 2006.

32. Barnow and King, *The Workforce Investment Act in Eight States.*

33. D'Amico and Salzman, *An Evaluation of the Individual Training Account/ Eligible Training Provider Demonstration.*

34. Barnow and King, *The Workforce Investment Act in Eight States.*

35. Ronald D'Amico and Jeffrey Salzman, "Implementation Issues in Delivering Training Services to Adults under WIA," in *Job Training in the United States,* eds. Christopher J. O'Leary, Robert A. Straits, and Stephen A. Wandner (Kalamazoo, MI: W. E. Upjohn Institute for Employment Research, 2004), 101–134.

36. Ibid., 124.

37. Phoebe H. Cottingham and Douglas J. Besharov, "Introduction," in *The Workforce Investment Act: Implementation Experiences and Evaluation Findings,* eds. Douglas J. Besharov and Phoebe H. Cottingham (Kalamazoo, MI: W. E. Upjohn Institute for Employment Research, 2011), 3.

38. Ibid.

39. U.S. General Accounting Office, *Multiple Employment and Training Programs: Funding and Performance Measures for Major Programs* (Washington, DC, April 2003).

40. Ibid.

41. Lafer, *The Job Training Charade.*

42. U.S. General Accounting Office, *Workforce Investment Act: Improvements Needed in Performance Measures to Provide a More Accurate Picture of WIA's Effectiveness* (Washington, DC, February 2002).

43. Ibid.

44. Lafer, *The Job Training Charade,* 113.

45. Blank et al., "An Overview of WIA."

46. U.S. General Accounting Office, *Multiple Employment and Training Programs: Funding and Performance Measures for Major Programs.*

47. David B. Muhlhausen and Paul Kersey, "In the Dark on Job Training: Federal Job–Training Programs Have a Record of Failure," Heritage Foundation *Backgrounder* No. 1774, July 6, 2004, http://www.heritage.org/Research/Reports/ 2004/07/In–the–Dark–on–Job–Training–Federal–Job–Training–Programs –Have–a–Record–of–Failure.

48. U.S. Department of Labor, "Requests for Proposals (RFP) 2007," http://www .doleta.gov/grants/rfp07.cfm (July 18, 2010); U.S. Government Accountability Office, *Employment and Training Administration: More Actions Needed to Improve Transparency and Accountability of Its Research Programs,* GAO–11–285, March 2011, http://www.gao.gov/new.items/d11285.pdf (April 21, 2011).

49. U.S. Government Accountability Office, *Employment and Training Administration: More Actions Needed.*

50. U.S. Government Accountability Office, "Workforce Investment Act: Labor Has Made Progress in Addressing Areas of Concern, but More Focus Needed on Understanding What Works and What Doesn't," Statement of George A. Scott, Director, Education, Workforce, and Income Security, before the Subcommittee on Higher Education, Lifelong Learning, and Competitiveness, Committee on Education and Labor, U.S. House of Representatives, GAO–09–396T, February 26, 2009, http://www.gao.gov/new.items/d09396t.pdf (July 18, 2010); U.S. Government Accountability Office, *Employment and Training Administration: More Actions Needed.*

51. U.S. House of Representatives, Committee on Education and the Workforce, "Committee Approves Vital Job Training Reforms," Press Release, June 7, 2012, http://edworkforce.house.gov/News/DocumentSingle.aspx?DocumentID =298947 (August 3, 2012).

52. U.S. House of Representative, Committee on Education and the Workforce, H.R. 4297, *The Workforce Investment Act of 2012*, 112th Cong., 2nd Sess., April 17, 2012, 1.

53. Ibid., 11.

54. Ibid., 13.

55. U.S. House of Representatives, Committee on Education and the Workforce, "Committee Approves Vital Job Training Reforms," Press Release, June 7, 2012, http://edworkforce.house.gov/News/DocumentSingle.aspx?DocumentID =298947 (August 3, 2012).

56. Burt S. Barnow, "Lessons from the WIA Performance Measures," in *The Workforce Investment Act: Implementation Experiences and Evaluation Findings*, eds. Douglas J. Besharov and Phoebe H. Cottingham (Kalamazoo, MI: W. E. Upjohn Institute for Employment Research, 2011), 209–210.

57. Blank et al., "An Overview of WIA," 64.

58. Ibid.

59. Ibid., 49–78.

60. Ibid.

61. Burt S. Barnow and Jeffrey A. Smith, "Performance Management of U.S. Job Training Programs," in *Job Training in the United States*, eds. Christopher J. O'Leary, Christopher J., Robert A. Straits, and Stephen A. Wandner (Kalamazoo, MI: W. E. Upjohn Institute for Employment Research, 2004), 21–55.

62. Ibid.

63. Ibid.

64. King and Barnow, "The Use of Market Mechanisms."

65. Barnow and Smith, "Performance Management of U.S. Job Training Programs," in *Job Training in the United States*, eds. Christopher J. O'Leary, Christopher J., Robert A. Straits, and Stephen A. Wandner (Kalamazoo, MI: W. E. Upjohn Institute for Employment Research, 2004).

66. Ibid.

67. Blank et al., "An Overview of WIA."

68. Burt S. Barnow, "Exploring the Relationship between Performance Management and Program Impact: A Case Study of the Job Training Partnership Act," *Journal of Policy Analysis and Management* 19, no.1(Winter 2000): 118–141.

69. Blank et al., "An Overview of WIA."

70. Barnow and Smith, "Performance Management of U.S. Job Training Programs."

71. Ibid.

72. Ibid.

73. Ibid.

74. U.S Congress, House of Representatives, Committee on Education and Labor, Subcommittee on Higher Education, Lifelong Learning, and Competitiveness, 2007, Hearing on "Workforce Investment Act: Recommendations to Improve the Effectiveness of Job Training," Hon. Ruben Hinojosa, Chair, Serial No. 110–51, June 28, 2007, 6.

75. Ibid.

76. Kathryn Anderson, Richard Burkhauser, Jennie Raymond, and Clifford Russell, "Mixed Signals in the Job Training Partnership Act," *Growth and Change* 22, no. 3 (1992): 32–48; Kathryn Anderson, Richard Burkhauser, and Jennie Raymond, "The Effect of Creaming on Placement Rates under the Job Training Partnership Act," *Industrial and Labor Relations Review* 46, no. 4 (1993): 613–624.

77. Anderson et al., "The Effect of Creaming on Placement Rates under the Job Training Partnership Act," 620.

78. Barnow and Smith, "Performance Management of U.S. Job Training Programs," 3.

79. King and Barnow, "The Use of Market Mechanisms."

80. Felicity Skidmore, "Overview of the Seattle–Denver Income Maintenance Experiment Final Report," in *Evaluation Studies Review Annual.*, eds. Linda H. Aiken and Barbara H. Kehrer (Beverly Hills, CA: Sage Publications, 1985), 297–326; David Greenberg and Mark Shroder, *The Digest of Social Experiments* (Washington, DC: Urban Institute Press, 2004).

81. Greenberg and Shroder, *The Digest of Social Experiments*, 197–201.

82. Ibid.

83. Robert G. Spiegelman and K. E. Yaeger, "Overview," *Journal of Human Resources* 14, no. 4 (1980): 463–479.

84. Arden R. Hall, "The Counseling and Training Subsidy Treatments," *Journal of Human Resources* 14, no. 4 (1980): 591–610.

85. Ibid.

86. Ibid.

87. Skidmore, "Overview of the Seattle–Denver Income Maintenance Experiment Final Report"; Richard W. West, "Effects on Wage Rates: An Interim Analysis," *Journal of Human Resources*, 14, no. 4 (1980): 641–653.

88. Sheena McConnell, Elizabeth Stuart, Kenneth Fortson, Paul Decker, Irma Perez–Johnson, Barbara Harris, and Jeffrey Salzman, *Managing Customers' Training Choices: Findings from the Individual Training Account Experiment, Final Report*. Mathematica Policy Research, Inc., 2006, xviii.

89. Irma Perez–Johnson, Quinn Moore, and Robert Santillano, *Improving the Effectiveness of Individual Training Accounts: Long–Term Findings from an Experimental Evaluation of Three Service Delivery Models, Final Report*, Mathematica Policy Research, Inc., October 2011.

90. McConnell et al., *Managing Customers' Training Choices: Findings from the Individual Training Account Experiment, Final Report*.

91. Ibid., Table IV.8, 61.

92. Ibid., xviii.

93. Ibid., Table IV.8, 61.

94. Ibid., xviii.

95. Ibid., Table IV.8, 61.

96. Ibid., 85.

97. Ibid., Table VI.1, 87.

98. Ibid., Table VI.2, 91.

99. Ibid., Table VI.1, 87.

100. Ibid., Table VI.1, 87.

101. Ibid., Table VI.2, 91.

102. Ibid., Table VII.3, 104.

103. Ibid., Table VII.2, 104.

104. Ibid., Table IV.6, 56.

105. Ibid., Table IV.6, 56.

106. Ibid., Table IV.6, 56.

107. Ibid., Table IV.6, 56.

108. Irma Perez–Johnson, Quinn Moore, and Robert Santillano, *Improving the Effectiveness of Individual Training Accounts: Long–Term Findings from an Experimental Evaluation of Three Service Delivery Models, Final Report*, Mathematica Policy Research, Inc., October 2011.

109. Ibid., Figures VI.1, VI.2, and VI.3, 82–83.

110. Ibid., Figure VI.5, 85.

111. Ibid., Figure VI.6, 90.

112. Ibid., Figure VI.8, 92.

113. Ibid., Figure VII.1, 97.

114. Ibid., Figure VII.2, 98.

115. Carolyn J. Heinrich, Peter R. Mueser, and Kenneth R. Troske, *Workforce Investment Act Non–Experimental Net Impact Evaluation: Final Report*, Columbia, MD: Impaq International, December 2008, http://wdr.doleta.gov/research/ FullText_Documents/Workforce% 20Investment%20Act%20Non–Experimental %20Net%20Impact%20Evaluation%20–%20Final%20Report.pdf.

116. Ibid.

117. Ibid., Figure V.15, 56.

118. Ibid., 41.

119. Ibid., Figure V.15, 56.

120. Ibid., 41.

121. Ibid.

122. Ibid., Figures VII.13 and VII.14, 70.

123. Perez–Johnson et al., *Improving the Effectiveness of Individual Training Accounts: Long–Term Findings from an Experimental Evaluation of Three Service Delivery Models, Final Report*, 20.

124. Heinrich et al., *Workforce Investment Act Non–Experimental Net Impact Evaluation*, 86.

125. Larry L. Orr, Howard S. Bloom, Stephen H. Bell, Fred Doolittle, Winston Lin, and George Cave, *Does Training for the Disadvantaged Work?* (Washington, DC: Urban Institute Press, 1996).

126. Ibid., 30.

127. Ibid.

128. Ibid.

129. Ibid., 30–31.

130. Ibid., Exhibit 4.8, 111.

131. Ibid., Exhibit 4.8, 111.

132. Ibid., Exhibit 4.18, 127.

133. Ibid., Exhibit 4.9, 112.

134. Ibid.

135. Ibid., Exhibit 4.10, 113.

136. Ibid., Exhibits 4.19 and 4.20, 129 and 130.

137. Ibid., Exhibit 4.4, 103.

138. Ibid.

139. Ibid.

140. Ibid.

141. Ibid.

142. Ibid.

143. Ibid.

144. Ibid., Exhibit 4.15, 121.

145. Ibid.

146. Ibid., Exhibit 5.7, 153.

147. Ibid.

148. Ibid.

149. Ibid.

150. Ibid., Exhibit 5.17, 178.

151. Ibid .

152. Ibid.

153. Ibid., Exhibit 4.7, 109.

154. Ibid., 110.

155. Ibid., 109.

156. Ibid., 131.

157. Ibid., Exhibit 4.22, 132.

158. Ibid.

159. Jacob M. Benus, Terry R. Johnson, Michelle Wood, Neelima Grover, and Theodore Shen, "Self- Employment Programs: A New Reemployment Strategy: Final Impact Analysis of the Washington and Massachusetts Self–Employment Demonstrations," *Unemployment Insurance Occasional Paper No. 95–4*. Washington, DC: U.S. Department of Labor, December 1995.

160. Ibid., ii.

161. Ibid.

162. Ibid., iii.

163. Ibid., iii–iv.

164. Ibid., iv.

165. Ibid., vi.

166. Ibid., 129. According to the authors, "exogenous developments in Massachusetts altered the implementation of the demonstration, especially during the period when cohort three was enrolled. As a result, we concluded that it is not appropriate to combine all three cohorts for the impact analysis."

167. Ibid., Table 7.1, 85.

168. Ibid., Table 7.2, 87.

169. Ibid., Table 7.3, 90.

170. Ibid., Table 7.4, 91.

171. Ibid., Table 7.5, 93.

172. Ibid., Table 7.6, 94.

173. Ibid., Table 7.7, 95.

174. Ibid., Table 7.8, 96.

175. Ibid., Table 7.9, 97.

176. Ibid., Table 7.10, 98.

177. Ibid., Table 7.11, 99.

178. Ibid., Table 7.14, 104.

179. Ibid., Table 7.21, 114.

180. Ibid., Table 7.25, 120.

181. Ibid., Table 7.16, 107.

182. Ibid., 107.

183. Ibid., 108.

184. Ibid.

185. Ibid., Table 7.17, 108.

186. Ibid., Table 7.18, 110.

187. Ibid., Table 8.1, 131.

188. Ibid., Table 8.18, 147.

189. Ibid., Table 8.2, 133.

190. Ibid., Table .16, 147.

191. Ibid., Table 8.3, 134.

192. Ibid., Table 8.16, 147.

193. Ibid., Table 8.4, 135.

194. Ibid., Table 8.16, 147.

195. Ibid., Table 8.5, 136.

196. Ibid., Table 8.17, 149.

197. Ibid., Table 8.6, 137.

198. Ibid., Table 8.17, 149.

199. Ibid., Table 8.7, 138.

200. Ibid., Table 8.17, 149.

201. Ibid., Table 8.8, 139.

202. Ibid., Table 8.17, 149.

203. Ibid., Table 8.9, 140.

204. Ibid., Table 8.18, 150.

205. Ibid., Table 8.10, 141.

206. Ibid., Table 8.18, 150.

207. Ibid., Table 8.11, 142.

208. Ibid., Table 8.18, 150.

209. Ibid., Table 8.12, 143.

210. Ibid., Table 8.18, 150.

211. Ibid., Table 8.14, 145.

212. Ibid., Table 8.19, 151.

213. Ibid., Table 8.15, 146.

214. Ibid., Table 8.19, 151.

215. Jeanne Bellotti, Sheena McConnell, and Jacob Benus, *Growing America through Entrepreneurship: Interim Report*, Impaq International, August 2006, i.

216. Ibid., i.

217. Ibid.

218. Ibid., 12.

219. Ibid., i.

220. Ibid., 20.

221. Ibid., vii.

222. Ibid., viii.

223. Ibid.

224. Ibid., ix.

225. Ibid.

226. Jacob Benus, Theodore Shen, Sisi Zhang, Marc Chan, and Benjamin Hansen, *Growing America through Entrepreneurship: Final Evaluation of Project GATE*, Columbia, MD: Impaq International, December 2009, Figure V.1, 60.

227. Ibid., Figure V.1, 60.

228. Ibid.

229. Ibid.

230. Ibid., Figure V.2, 62.

231. Ibid.

232. Ibid., Figure V.4, 67.

233. Ibid.

234. Ibid.

235. Ibid.

236. Ibid., Figure V.5, 72.

237. Ibid.

238. Ibid.

239. Ibid., Figure V.6, 73.

240. Ibid., Table V.3, 76.

241. Ibid., Table V.4, 78.

242. Ibid., Table V.5, 79.

243. Ibid., Table V.6, 81.

244. Ibid.

245. Ibid., 81.

246. Ibid., Table V.7, 84.

247. Ibid.

248. Ibid., Figure VI.1, 97.

249. Ibid.

250. Ibid., Figure VI.2, 98.

251. Ibid., 99.

252. Ibid., Figure VI.4, 100.

253. Ibid., Figure VI.5, 102.

254. Ibid., Figure VI.6, 103.

255. Ibid., Figure VI.7, 104.

256. Ibid., Figure VI.8, 105.

257. Ibid., Figure VI.9, 106.

258. Ibid., Figure VI.10, 111.

259. Ibid., Figure VI.12, 113.

260. Ibid., Figure VI.11, 112; Figure VI.13, 114.

261. Ibid., Figure VI.14, 115.

262. Ibid., Figure VI.15, 116.

263. Ibid., Table VI.4, 120.

264. Ibid., Table VII.1, 125.

265. Ibid.

266. Ibid.

267. Hilda L. Solis, "Statement of Hilda L. Solis, Secretary of Labor, before the Subcommittee of Labor, Health and Human Services, Education, and Related

Agencies, Committee on Appropriations, United States Senate," May 4, 2011, 3, http://www.appropriations.senate.gov/ht-labor.cfm?method=hearings. view&id=7c49eb6c-2c56-4a15-92da-36f92e1e8ba4 (August, 15, 2012).

268. eMediaMillWorks Political Transcripts, "Rep. Denny Rehberg Holds Hearing on Job Training Programs Budget," *Roll Call*, April 11, 2011.

269. Peter Z. Schochet, John Burghardt, and Steven Glazerman, *National Job Corps Study: The Impacts of Job Corps on Participants' Employment and Related Outcomes* (Princeton, NJ: Mathematica Policy Research, Inc., June 2001), 30.

270. U.S. Department of Labor, Office of the Inspector General, *Job Corps Needs to Improve Reliability of Performance Metrics and Results*, September 30, 2011, 2, http://www.oig.dol.gov/public/reports/oa/2011/26-11-004-03-370.pdf (December 20, 2012).

271. Ibid., 2.

272. Ibid.

273. Ibid.

274. Ibid.

275. Ibid., 3.

276. Ibid.

277. Ibid.

278. Ibid.

279. Ibid.

280. Ibid.

281. Schochet et al., *National Job Corps Study: The Impacts of Job Corps on Participants' Employment and Related Outcomes*.

282. Ibid., Table V.7, 104.

283. Ibid.

284. Ibid.

285. Ibid.

286. Ibid., Table. VI.2, 126.

287. Ibid., Table. VI.3, 127. The numbers reported by the authors are rounded.

288. Ibid.

289. Ibid.

290. Ibid., Table VI.4, 130. The numbers reported by the authors are rounded.

291. Ibid.

292. Ibid., Figure VI.6, 154.

293. Ibid., Figure VI.14, 170.

294. Ibid.

295. Ibid., Table VI.5, 139.

296. Ibid.

297. Ibid., Table VII.6, 207.

298. Ibid., Table VII.8, 212.

299. Ibid., Table VII.9, 215.

300. Ibid., Table VII.10, 218.

301. Ibid., Table VII.1, 184.

302. Ibid.

303. Ibid., Table VII.2, 189.

304. Ibid.

305. Ibid., Table VII.3, 191.

306. Sheena McConnell and Steven Glazerman, *National Job Corps Study: The Benefits and Costs of Job Corps* (Princeton, NJ: Mathematica Policy Research, Inc., June 2001).

307. U.S. Department of Labor, Employment, and Training Administration, "Summary of ETA Fiscal Year 2003 Request," www.doleta.gov/budget/03reqsum .pdf (August 27, 2002).

308. Erik Eckholm, "Job Corps Plans Makeover for a Changed Economy," *New York Times*, February 20, 2007, www.nytimes.com/2007/02/20/washington/ 20jobcorps.html (February 28, 2007); Peter Z. Schochet, Sheena McConnell, and John Burghardt, *National Job Corps Study: Findings Using Administrative Earnings Records Data: Final Report* (Princeton, NJ: Mathematica Policy Research, Inc., October 2003).

309. Schochet et al., *National Job Corps Study: Findings Using Administrative Earnings Records Data: Final Report*, 70.

310. Pedro Carneiro and James Heckman, "Human Capital Policy," NBER *Working Paper* No. 39495, February 2003.

311. Schochet et al., *National Job Corps Study: Findings Using Administrative Earnings Records Data: Final Report*.

312. Office of Management and Budget, *The Appendix, Budget of the United States Government, Fiscal Year 2013* (Washington, DC: U.S. Government Printing Office, 2011), 815.

313. Schochet et al., *National Job Corps Study: Findings Using Administrative Earnings Records Data: Final Report*, 70.

314. Ibid., Table III.5, 66.

315. Ibid., Table III.5, 67.

316. Schochet et al., *National Job Corps Study: The Impacts of Job Corps on Participants' Employment and Related Outcomes*.

317. Ibid., 127.

318. Ibid.

319. Ibid., 139.

320. Ibid.

321. George Cave, Hans Bos, Fred Doolittle, and Cyril Toussaint, *JOBSTART: Final Report on a Program for School Dropouts* (Manpower Demonstration Research Corporation, October 1993), xvii.

322. Ibid.

323. Ibid., 4.

324. Ibid., 32.

325. Ibid., 33.

326. Ibid., Table 4.1, 95.

327. Ibid.

328. Ibid., Table 4.2, 97.

329. Ibid., Table 4.5, 109.

330. Ibid.

331. Ibid.

332. Ibid.

333. Ibid., Table 5.1, 119.

334. Ibid., Table 5.2, 120.

335. Ibid., Table 5.9, 156.

336. Ibid., Table 5.8, 153.

337. Ibid.

338. Ibid., Table 6.1, 180–181.

339. Ibid., Table 6.2, 183–184.

340. Ibid.

341. Ibid.

342. Ibid.

343. Ibid., Table 6.3, 186–187.

344. Ibid., Table 6.4, 188–189.

345. Ibid., Table 6.7, 195–196.

346. Ibid., The numbers reported by the authors are rounded.

347. Ibid.

348. Ibid.

349. Ibid., Table 6.8, 198.

350. Ibid.

351. Ibid., Table 5.13, 176.

352. Ibid.

353. Cynthia Miller, Johannes M. Ros, Kristen E. Porter, Fannie M. Tseng, and Yasuyo Abe, *The Challenge of Replicating Success in a Changing World: Final Report on the Center for Employment Training Replication Cites* (Manpower Demonstration Research Corporation, September 2005), 1 http://www.mdrc.org/publications/453/full.pdf (October, 18, 2011).

354. Ibid., 7–8.

355. Ibid., 9.

356. Ibid., Table 2.3, 32.

357. Ibid.

358. Ibid.

359. Ibid., Table 3.2, 64.

360. Ibid.

361. Ibid.

362. Ibid.

363. Ibid., Table 3.4, 67.

364. Ibid., 33.

365. Ibid., Table 2.5, 37–38.

366. Ibid., Table 3.5, 69.

367. Ibid., Table 3.6, 72.

368. Ibid., Table 2.6, 40–41.

369. Ibid., Table 3.7, 78.

370. Ibid.

371. Ibid.

372. Ibid.

373. Ibid.

374. Ibid., Table 3.8, 81.

375. Ibid., Table 3.7, 78.

376. Ibid.

377. Ibid.

378. Ibid.

379. Ibid.

380. Ibid.

381. Ibid.

382. Ibid., Table 3.8, 81.

383. Ibid., Table 3.7, 78.

384. Ibid.

385. Ibid., Table 2.9, 46–47.

386. Ibid., Table 3.9, 83.

387. Ibid.

388. Ibid.

389. Ibid., Table 3.10, 85.

390. Ibid., Table 3.11, 88.

391. Ibid., Table 3.12, 90.

392. Ibid., Table 3.11, 88.

393. Ibid.

394. Ibid., Table 3.12, 90.

395. Ibid., Table 3.5, 69.

396. Ibid., Table 3.6, 72.

397. Ibid., xi.

398. Allen Schirm and Nuria Rodriguez, *The Quantum Opportunity Program Demonstration: Initial Post Intervention Impacts* (Mathematica Policy Research, June 2004), 1.

399. Ibid., v.

400. Ibid.

401. Ibid.

402. Ibid.

403. Ibid., vii.

404. Ibid., 2.

405. Ibid.

406. Ibid., 4.

407. Ibid., 5.

408. Ibid.

409. Ibid., 6.

410. Ibid., 7.

411. Ibid., 7. Emphasis added.

412. Ibid., Table 2, 22.

413. Ibid., 10.

414. Ibid.

415. Ibid., Table 1, 17.

416. Ibid.

417. Schirm et al., *The Quantum Opportunity Program Demonstration: Final Impacts*, Table 3, 20.

418. Ibid., Table 6, 30.

419. Schirm et al., *The Quantum Opportunity Program Demonstration: Initial Post Intervention Impacts*, Table 2, 22.

420. Ibid.

421. Ibid.

422. Ibid.

423. Ibid.

424. Ibid.

425. Ibid.

426. Ibid.

427. Schirm et al., *The Quantum Opportunity Program Demonstration: Final Impacts* , Table 4, 24.

428. Schirm et al., *The Quantum Opportunity Program Demonstration: Initial Post Intervention Impacts* , Table 3, 23.

429. Ibid.

430. Ibid.

431. Ibid.

432. Ibid.

433. Ibid., Table 4, 26.

434. Ibid.

435. Ibid.

436. Ibid.

437. Schirm et al., *The Quantum Opportunity Program Demonstration: Final Impacts*, Table 8, 32.

438. Ibid.

439. Ibid.
440. Ibid.
441. Ibid.
442. Ibid.
443. Ibid., Table 5, 27.
444. Ibid.
445. Ibid.
446. Ibid.
447. Ibid.
448. Ibid.
449. Ibid.
450. Ibid.
451. Ibid.
452. Ibid., Table 5, 27.
453. Ibid., ix.
454. Ibid., x.

Chapter 6

1. Barack Obama, "President Obama Discusses Efforts to Reform Spending, Government Waste; Names Chief Performance Officer and Chief Technology Officer," White House, April 18, 2009, http://www.whitehouse.gov/the_press _office/Weekly-Address-President-Obama-Discusses-Efforts-to-Reform-Spending (accessed December 20, 2012).

2. Ibid.

3. Peter R. Orszag, "Federal Statistics in the Policy Making Process," *Annals of the American Academy of Political and Social Science* 631 (accessed September 2010): 34–42.

4. Ibid., 34–35.

5. Jeffrey Zients, "Discovering What Works," OMB Blog, August 2, 2010, http:// www.whitehouse.gov/blog/2010/08/02/discovering-what-works (accessed October 2, 2012).

6. Orszag, "Federal Statistics," 35–36.

7. Ibid., 36.

8. Ibid.

9. U.S. Department of Education, "Education Improvement Programs: Fiscal Year 2012 Budget Request," D-34, http://www2.ed.gov/about/overview/budget/ budget12/justifications/d-eipdf (accessed October 2, 2012).

10. Orszag, "Federal Statistics," 41.

11. Ibid., 35.

12. Ibid., 34–35.

13. Gregory D. Kutz, "Head Start: Undercover Testing Finds Fraud and Abuse at Selected Head Start Centers," testimony before the Committee on Education and Labor, U.S. House of Representatives, May 18, 2010, http://www.gao.gov/new.items/d10733t.pdf (accessed October 2, 2012).

14. Zients, "Discovering What Works."

15. National Public Radio *Talk of the Nation*, "Analysis: Explanations and Criticism of President Bush's New Marriage Promotion Plan," transcript, obtained from Westlaw, January 22, 2004.

16. Amy E. Lowenstein, "Early Care and Education as Educational Panacea: What Do We Really Know about Its Effectiveness," *Educational Policy* 25, no. 1 (2011): 92–114.

17. Barack Obama, *The Audacity of Hope: Thoughts on Reclaiming the American Dream* (New York: Crown Publishers, 2006), 257.

18. Lowenstein, "Early Care and Education as Educational Panacea."

19. Ibid., 107.

20. Ibid., 101.

21. Ibid., 102.

22. Ibid.

23. Ibid.

24. Ibid., 107.

25. Robinson G. Hollister, "Opening Statement," in *Social Experimentation, Program Evaluation, and Public Policy*, ed. Maureen A. Pirog (Wiley-Blackwell, 2008), 19–20.

26. Ibid., 20.

27. Ibid.

28. Ibid.

29. Ron Haskins and Isabel Sawhill, *Creating an Opportunity Society* (Washington, DC: Brookings Institution, 2009), 134.

30. Ibid.

31. Lisa Sanbonmatsu, Jens Ludwig, Lawrence F. Katz, Lisa Gennetian, Greg J. Duncan, Ronald C. Kessler, Emma Adam, Thomas W. McDade, Stacy Tessler Lindau, Matthew Sciandra, Fanghua Yang, Ijun Lai, William Congdon, Joe Amick, Ryan Gillette, Michael A. Zabek, Jordon Marvakov, Sabrina Yusuf, and Nicholas A. Potter, *Moving to Opportunity for Fair Housing Demonstration Program: Final Impacts Evaluation* (Washington, DC: U.S. Department of Housing and Urban Development, Office of Policy Development and Research, November 2011), 264.

32. Jim Manzi, *Uncontrolled: The Surprising Payoff of Trial-and-Error for Business, Politics, and Society* (New York: Basic Books, 2012), 202.

33. Office of Management and Budget, *Appendix, Budget of the United States, Fiscal Year 2013* (Washington, DC: U.S. Government Printing Office, 2011), 393.

34. Fred Doolittle and Linda Traeger, *Implementing the National JTPA Study* (New York: Manpower Demonstration Research Corporation, 1990); Judith M.

Gueron, "The Politics of Random Assignment: Implementing Studies and Affecting Policy," 15–49 in *Evidence Matters: Randomized Trials in Education Research*, edited by Frederick Mosteller and Robert Boruch, (Washington, D.C.: Brookings Institution, 2002).

35. Kelly Field, "Senate Votes to Block Upward Bound Evaluation," *Chronicle of Higher Education*, November 2, 2007, http://chronicle.com/article/Senate-Approves-Measure/39801 (accessed December 20, 2012).

36. Kelly Field, "Education Department Agrees to End Controversial Upward Bound Study," *Chronicle of Higher Education*, February 25, 2008, http://chronicle.com/article/Education-Dept-to-End/11688 (accessed December 20, 2012).

37. Ibid.; Consolidated Appropriations Act, 2008, Public Law 110-161, § 519, December 26, 2007.

38. Erica B. Baum, "When the Witch Doctors Agree: The Family Support Act and Social Science Research," *Journal of Policy Analysis and Management* 10, no. 4 (Autumn 1991): 603–615; Gueron, "The Politics of Random Assignment," 15–49.

39. Jim Manzi, "What Social Science Does—and Doesn't—Know," *City Journal* 20, no. 3 (Summer 2010): 14–23, http://www.city-journal.org/2010/20_3_social-science.html (March 14, 2011).

40. Ibid.

41. Christy A. Visher and Jeremy Travis, "Transitions from Prison to Community: Understanding Individual Pathways," *Annual Review of Sociology* 29 (2003): 89–113.

Bibliography

Adams, Leonard P. *The Public Employment Service in Transition, 1933–1968.* Ithaca: New York State School of Industrial and Labor Relations, Cornell University, 1969.

Agodini, Roberto, and Mark Dynarski. "Are Experiments the Only Option? A Look at Dropout Prevention Programs." *Review of Economics and Statistics* 86, 1 (February 2004): 180–194.

Agresti, Alan, and Barbara Finlay. *Statistical Methods for the Social Sciences.* Upper Saddle River, NJ: Prentice Hall, 1997.

Alesina, Alberto, Silva Ardagna, Roberto Peroti, and Fabio Schiantarelli. "Fiscal Policy, Profits, and Investment." *American Economic Review* 92, 3 (June 2002): 571–589.

Alesina, Alberto, and Silvia Ardagna. "Large Changes in Fiscal Policy: Taxes versus Spending." *Tax Policy and the Economy* 24, 1 (2010): 35–68.

Amato, Paul. "The Impact of Family Formation Change on the Cognitive, Social, and Emotional Well-Being of the Next Generation." *Future of Children* 15, 2 (Fall 2005): 75–96.

Anderson, Kathryn, Richard Burkhauser, Jennie Raymond, and Clifford Russell. "Mixed Signals in the Job Training Partnership Act." *Growth and Change* 22, 3 (1992): 32–48.

Anderson, Kathryn, Richard Burkhauser, and Jennie Raymond. "The Effect of Creaming on Placement Rates under the Job Training Partnership Act." *Industrial and Labor Relations Review* 46, 4 (1993): 613–624.

Andrew, John A. *Lyndon Johnson and the Great Society.* Chicago: Ivan R. Dee, Inc., 1998.

Arceneaux, Kevin, Alan S. Gerber, and Donald P. Green. "Comparing Experimental and Matching Methods Using a Large-Scale Voter Mobilization Experiment." *Political Analysis* 14 (2006): 37–62.

Ardagna, Silvia. "Fiscal Policy Composition, Public Debt, and Economic Activity." *Public Choice* 109 (2001): 301–325.

Atkinson, Raymond C., Louise C. Odencrantz, and Ben Deming. *Public Employment Service in the United States.* Chicago: Public Administration Service, 1938.

Balz, Dan. "President Tries to Keep Balance as Ground Shifts." *Washington Post,* July 11, 2011. A01.

Barnow, Burt S. "Vouchers in U.S. Vocational Training Programs: An Overview of What We Have Learned." *Zeitschrift für Arbeitsmarkt Forschung* (Journal for Labor Market Research) 42, 1 (2009): 71–84.

Barnow, Burt S. "Exploring the Relationship between Performance Management and Program Impact: A Case Study of the Job Training Partnership Act." *Journal of Policy Analysis and Management* 19, 1 (Winter 2000): 118–141.

Barnow, Burt S. "Lessons from the WIA Performance Measures." In *The Workforce Investment Act: Implementation Experiences and Evaluation Findings,* edited by Douglas J. Besharov and Phoebe H. Cottingham, 209–231. Kalamazoo, MI: W. E. Upjohn Institute for Employment Research, 2011.

Barnow, Burt S., and Christopher T. King. *The Workforce Investment Act in Eight States, The Nelson A. Rockefeller Institute of Government,* 2005. http://www.utexas.edu/research/cshr/pubs/pdf/Rockefeller_Institute_Final_Report2-10-05.pdf (accessed on December 21, 2012).

Barnow, Burt S., and Jeffrey A. Smith. "Performance Management of U.S. Job Training Programs." In *Job Training in the United States,* edited by Christopher J. O'Leary, Robert A. Straits, and Stephen A. Wandner, 21–55. Kalamazoo, MI: W. E. Upjohn Institute for Employment Research, 2004.

Baum, Erica B. "When the Witch Doctors Agree: The Family Support Act and Social Science Research." *Journal of Policy Analysis and Management* 10, 4 (Autumn 1991): 603–615.

Beito, David T. "The 'Lodge Practice Evil' Reconsidered: Medical Care through Fraternal Societies, 1900–1930." *Journal of Urban History* 23, 5 (1997): 569–600.

Beito, David T. *From Mutual Aid to the Welfare State: Fraternal Societies and Social Services, 1890–1967.* Chapel Hill: University of North Carolina Press, 2000.

Beito, David T. "This Enormous Army: The Mutual-Aid Tradition of American Fraternal Societies before the Twentieth Century." In *The Voluntary City: Choice, Community, and Civil Society,* edited by David T. Beito, Peter Gordon, and Alexander Tabarrok, 182–203. Ann Arbor: University of Michigan Press, 2002.

Bellotti, Jeanne, Sheena McConnell, and Jacob Benus. *Growing America through Entrepreneurship: Interim Report.* Columbia, MD: Impaq International, August 2006.

Benus, Jacob M., Terry R. Johnson, Michelle Wood, Neelima Grover, and Theodore Shen. "Self- Employment Programs: A New Reemployment Strategy: Final Impact Analysis of the Washington and Massachusetts Self-Employment Demonstrations." *Unemployment Insurance Occasional Paper* No. 95-4. Washington, DC: U.S. Department of Labor, December 1995.

Benus, Jacub M., Carolyn J. Heinrich, Peter R. Mueser, and Kenneth R. Troske. *Workforce Investment Act Non-Experimental Net Impact Evaluation.* Columbia, MD: Impaq International, December 2008. http://www.impaqint .com/files/4-Content/1-6-publications/1-6-2-project-reports/Report%20-% 204%20-%20Workforce%20Investment%20Act%20Non-Experimental% 20Net%20Impact%20Evaluation%20-%20Final%20Report.pdf (accessed on December 21, 2012)

Berrick, Jill Duerr. "Income Maintenance and Support." In *The Hand Book of Social Policy,* edited by James Midgley and Michelle Livermore, 336–346. Los Angeles: Sage Publications, 2009.

Blank, Dianne, Laura Heald, and Cynthia Fagoni. "An Overview of WIA." In *The Workforce Investment Act: Implementation Experiences and Evaluation Findings,* edited by Douglas J. Besharov and Phoebe H. Cottingham, 49–78. Kalamazoo, MI: W. E. Upjohn Institute for Employment Research, 2011.

Bloom, Howard S., Charles Michalopoulos, and Carolyn J. Hill. "Using Experiments to Assess Nonexperimental Comparison-Group Methods for Measuring Effects." In *Learning More from Social Experiments: Evolving Analytic Approaches,* edited by Howard S. Bloom, 173–235. New York: Russell Sage Foundation, 2005.

Bogenschneider, Karen, and Thomas J. Corbett. *Evidence-Based Policymaking: Insights from Policy-Minded Researchers and Research-Minded Policymakers.* New York: Routledge, 2010.

Borduin, Charles M., Scott W. Henggeler, David M. Blaske, and Risa J. Stein. "Multisystemic Treatment of Adolescent Sexual Offenders." *International Journal of Offender Therapy and Comparative Criminology* 34, 2 (September 1990): 105–113.

Borduin, Charles M., Barton J. Mann, Lynn T. Cone, Scott W. Henggeler, Bethany R. Fucci, David M. Blaske, and Robert A. Williams. "Multisystemic Treatment of Serious Juvenile Offenders: Long-Term Prevention of Criminality and Violence." *Journal of Consulting and Clinical Psychology* 63, 4 (August 1995): 569–578.

Boris, Eileen. "Contested Rights: The Great Society between Home and Work." In *The Great Society and the High Tide of Liberalism,* edited by Sidney M. Milkis and Jerome M. Mileur, 115–144. Boston: University of Massachusetts Press, 2005.

Briar-Lawson, Katherine, Toni Naccarato, and Jeanette Drews. "Child and Family Welfare Policies and Services." In *The Hand Book of Social Policy,* edited by James Midgley and Michelle Livermore, 315–335. Los Angeles: Sage Publications, 2009.

Brinkley, Alan. *The End of Reform: New Deal Liberalism in Recession and War.* New York: Vintage Books, 1996.

Brown, Susan L. "Family Structure and Child Well-Being: The Significance of Parental Cohabitation." *Journal of Marriage and Family* 66, 2 (May 2004): 351–367.

Burtless, Gary. "Randomized Field Trials for Policy Evaluations: Why Not in Education?" In *Evidence Matters: Randomized Trials in Education Research*, edited by Frederick Mosteller and Robert Boruch, 179–197. Washington, DC: Brookings Institution, 2002.

Campbell, Donald, and Julian C. Stanley. *Experimental and Quasi-Experimental Designs for Research*. Boston: Houghton Mifflin Company, 1963.

Carneiro, Pedro, and James Heckman. "Human Capital Policy." *NBER Working Paper* No. 39495, February 2003.

Cave, George, Hans Bos, Fred Doolittle, and Cyril Toussaint. *JOBSTART: Final Report on a Program for School Dropouts*. New York, NY: Manpower Demonstration Research Corporation, October 1993.

Ceaser, James W. "Foundational Concepts in American Political Thought." In *Modern America and the Legacy of the Founding*, edited by Ronald J. Pestritto and Thomas G. West, 3–31. Lanham, MD: Lexington Books, 2007.

Clinton, William J. "President Clinton Delivers Remarks at Signing Ceremony for the Workforce investment Act." Transcript. Federal Document Clearing House. August 7, 1998.

Congressional Budget Office, *The Long-Term Budget Outlook*, June 2009. http://www.cbo.gov/ftpdocs/102xx/doc10297/06-25-LTBO.pdf (accessed on December 21, 2012).

Congressional Budget Office. *Estimated Impact of the American Recovery and Reinvestment Act on Employment and Economic Output from April 2010 through June 2010*. August 24, 2010. http://www.cbo.gov/publication/21671 (accessed on December 21, 2012).

Congressional Budget Office. *CBO's 2011 Long-Term Budget Outlook*. Washington, DC. June 2011. http://www.cbo.gov/ftpdocs/122xx/doc12212/06-21-Long-Term_Budget_Outlook.pdf (accessed on December 21, 2012).

Congressional Budget Office. *The Long-Term Budget Outlook*. Washington, DC. June 2009. http://www.cbo.gov/ftpdocs/102xx/doc10297/06-25-LTBO.pdf (accessed on December 21, 2012).

Congressional Budget Office. *The 2012 Long-Term Budget Outlook: Federal Debt Held by the Public, 1912 to 2037*. June 2012. http://www.cbo.gov/sites/default/files/cbofiles/attachments/06-05-Long-Term_Budget_Outlook.pdf (accessed on December 21, 2012).

Congressional Budget Office. *An Update to the Budget and Economic Outlook: Fiscal Years 2012 to 2022*. August 2012. http://www.cbo.gov/sites/default/files/cbofiles/attachments/08-22-2012-Update_to_Outlook.pdf (accessed on December 21, 2012).

Congressional Budget Office. *Federal Debt and the Statutory Limit, November 2012.* November 2012. http://www.cbo.gov/sites/default/files/cbofiles/attachments/43736-FederalDebtLimit-11-12-12.pdf (accessed on December 11, 2012).

Cottingham, Phoebe H., and Douglas J. Besharov. "Introduction." In *The Workforce Investment Act: Implementation Experiences and Evaluation Findings*, edited by Douglas J. Besharov and Phoebe H. Cottingham, 1–46. Kalamazoo, MI: W. E. Upjohn Institute for Employment Research, 2011.

Currie, Janet, and Duncan Thomas. "Does Head Start Make a Difference?" *American Economic Review* 85, 3 (1995); 341–364.

D'Amico, Ronald, and Jeffrey Salzman. "Implementation Issues in Delivering Training Services to Adults under WIA." In *Job Training in the United States*, edited by Christopher J. O'Leary, Robert A. Straits, and Stephen A. Wandner, 101–134. Kalamazoo, MI: W. E. Upjohn Institute for Employment Research, 2004.

D'Amico, Ronald, and Jeffrey Salzman. *An Evaluation of the Individual Training Account/Eligible Training Provider Demonstration: Final Report.* Oakland, CA: Social Policy Research Associates, December 2004. http://wdr.doleta.gov/research/FullText_Documents/2005_02_final_ita_demo.pdf (accessed on December 21, 2012).

Dehejia, Rajeev H., and Sadek Wahba. "Causal Effects in Nonexperimental Studies: Reevaluating the Evaluation of Training Programs." *Journal of the American Statistical Association* 94, 448 (December 1999): 1053–1062.

Devaney, Barbara, Amy Johnson, Rebecca Maynard, and Chris Trenholm. *The Evaluation of Abstinence Education Programs Funded Under Title V Section 510: Interim Report.* Princeton, NJ: Mathematica Policy Research, Princeton, NJ, April 2002.

Dewey, John. *Reconstruction in Philosophy.* Boston: Beacon Press, 1957.

Dewey, John. *Freedom and Culture.* Amherst, NY: Prometheus Books, 1989.

Dewey, John. *Individualism Old and New.* Amherst, NY: Prometheus Books, 1999.

Dewey, John. *Liberalism and Social Action.* Amherst, NY: Prometheus Books, 2000.

Dewey, John, and James H. Tufts. *Ethics.* New York: Henry Holt and Company, 1910.

Donaldson, Stewart I. "In Search of the Blueprint for an Evidence-Based Global Society." In *What Counts as Credible Evidence in Applied Research and Evaluation Practice?* edited by Stewart I. Donaldson, Christina A. Christie, and Melvin M. Mark, 2–18. Thousand Oaks, CA: Sage Publications, 2009.

Doolittle, Fred, and Linda Traeger. *Implementing the National JTPA Study.* New York: Manpower Demonstration Research Corporation, 1990.

Eckholm, Erik. "Job Corps Plans Makeover for a Changed Economy." *New York Times*, February 20, 2007. www.nytimes.com/2007/02/20/washington/20jobcorps.html (accessed on December 21, 2012).

eMediaMillWorks Political Transcripts. "Rep. Denny Rehberg Holds Hearing on Job Training Programs Budget." *Roll Call*, April 11, 2011.

eMediaMillWorks Political Transcripts. "The Congressional Hispanic Caucus, The Congressional Black Caucus, and the Congressional Asian Pacific American Caucus Hold a News Conference on the Debt." *Roll Call*, July 20, 2011.

Epstein, Richard A. *How Progressives Rewrote the Constitution*. Washington, DC: Cato Institute, 2006.

Federal Information and News Dispatch. "Release: Sanders on Senate Spending Proposals." Press release, March 9, 2011.

Fenno, Richard F. *The Making of Senator Dan Quayle*. Washington, DC: Congressional Quarterly Press, 1989.

Field, Kelly. "Senate Votes to Block Upward Bound Evaluation." *Chronicle of Higher Education*, November 2, 2007.

Field, Kelly. "Education Department Agrees to End Controversial Upward Bound Study." *Chronicle of Higher Education*, February 25, 2008. http://chronicle.com/article/Education-Dept-to-End/11688 (accessed on December 21, 2012).

Freidel, Frank. *Franklin D. Roosevelt: Launching the New Deal*. Boston: Little, Brown, 1973.

Friedlander, Daniel, and David H. Greenberg. "Evaluating Government Training Programs for the Economically Disadvantaged." *Journal of Economic Literature* 35 (December 1997): 1809–1855.

Friedlander, Daniel, and Philip K. Robins. "Evaluating Program Evaluations: New Evidence on Commonly Used Nonexperimental Methods." *American Economic Review* 85, 4 (September 1995): 923–937.

Folson, Burton W. *New Deal or Raw Deal? How FDR's Economic Legacy Has Damaged America*. New York: Threshold Editions, 2008.

Gamse, Beth C., Robin Tepper Jacob, Megan Horst, Beth Boulay, Faith Unlu, Laurie Bozzi, Linda Caswell, Chris Rodger, W. Carter Smith, Nancy Brigham, and Shelia Rosenblum. *Reading First Impact Study: Final Report*. Washington, DC: U.S. Department of Education, Institute of Educational Sciences, November 2008.

Garces, Eliana, Duncan Thomas, and Janet Currie. "Longer-Term Effects of Head Start." *American Economic Review* 92, 4 (September 2002): 999–1012.

Glazerman, Steven, Dan M. Levy, and David Myers. "Nonexperimental versus Experimental Estimates of Earnings Impacts." *Annals of the American Academy of Political and Social Science* 589 (September 2003): 63–93.

Goldkamp, John S., Michael D. White, and Jennifer B. Robinson. "Do Drug Courts Work? Getting Inside the Drug Court Black Box." *Journal of Drug Issues* 31, 1 (2001): 27–72.

Goodnow, Frank Johnson. "The American Conception of Liberty." In *American Progressivism: A Reader*, edited by Ronald J. Pestritto and William J. Atto, 55–64. Lanham, MD: Rowan & Littlefield Publishers, Inc., 2008.

Greenberg, David, Donna Linksz, and Marvin Mandell. *Social Experimentation and Public Policymaking*. Washington, DC: Urban Institute Press, 2003.

Greenberg, David, and Mark Shroder, *The Digest of Social Experiments*. Washington, DC: The Urban Institute Press, 2004.

Gruss, Bertrand, and Jose L. Torres. "Macroeconomic and Welfare Costs of U.S. Fiscal Imbalances." *IMF Working Paper*, January 2012. http://www.imf.org/external/pubs/ft/wp/2012/wp1238.pdf.

Gueron, Judith M., and Edward Pauly. *From Welfare to Work*. New York: Russell Sage Foundation, 1991.

Gueron, Judith M. "The Politics of Random Assignment: Implementing Studies and Affecting Policy." In *Evidence Matters: Randomized Trials in Education Research*, edited by Frederick Mosteller and Robert Boruch, 15–49. Washington, DC: Brookings Institution, 2002.

Hall, Arden R. "The Counseling and Training Subsidy Treatments." *Journal of Human Resources* 14, 4 (1980): 591–610.

Hallfors, Denise, Hyunsan Cho, Victoria Sanchez, Sheren Khatapoush, Hyung Min Kim, and Daniel Bauer. "Efficacy vs. Effectiveness Trial Results of an Indicated 'Model' Substance Abuse Program: Implications for Public Health." *American Journal of Public Health* 96, 12 (December 2006): 2254–2259.

Hamilton, Gayle, Stephen Freedman, Lisa Gennetian, Charles Michalopoulos, Johanna Walter, Diana Adams-Ciardullo, Anna Gassman-Pines, Sharon McGroder, Martha Zaslow, Jennifer Brooks, Surjeet Ahluwalia, Electra Small, and Bryan Ricchetti. *National Evaluation of Welfare-to-Work Strategies: How Effective Are Different Welfare-to-Work Approaches? Five-Year Adult and Child Impacts for Eleven Programs*. Washington, DC: U.S. Department of Health and Human Services, Administration for Children and Families and Office of the Assistant Secretary for Planning and Evaluation; and U.S. Department of Education, 2001.

Harkin, Tom. "Statement of Senator Harkin (D-IA) at the Appropriations Labor-HHS-Education Subcommittee Hearing: The Impact of Sequestration on Education." Press release, July 25, 2012. http://www.harkin.senate.gov/press/release.cfm?i=337365 (accessed on August 7, 2012).

Haskins, Ron. "Congress Writes a Law: Research and Welfare Reform." *Journal of Policy Analysis and Management* 10, 4 (1991): 616–632.

Haskins, Ron. "Testimony of Ron Haskins Co-Director of the Center on Children and Families Brookings Institution, and Senior Consultant, Annie E. Casey Foundation before the Committee on the Budget U.S. House of Representatives," April 17, 2012. http://budget.house.gov/uploadedfiles/haskinstestimony4172012.pdf (accessed on August 24, 2012).

Haskins, Ron, and Isabel Sawhill. *Creating an Opportunity Society*. Washington, DC: Brookings Institution, 2009.

Haveman, Robert H. *Poverty Policy and Poverty Research: The Great Society and the Social Sciences.* Madison: University of Wisconsin Press, 1987.

Heinrich, Carolyn J., Peter R. Mueser, and Kenneth R. Troske. *Workforce Investment Act Non-Experimental Net Impact Evaluation: Final Report.* Columbia, MD: Impaq International, December 2008.

Helco, Hugh. "The Political Foundations of Antipoverty Policy." In *Fighting Poverty: What Works and What Doesn't,* edited by Sheldon H. Danziger and Daniel H. Weinberg, 312–340. Cambridge, MA; Harvard University Press, 1986.

Hendra, Richard, Keri-Nicole Dillman, Gayle Hamilton, Erik Lundquist, Karin Martinson, Melissa Wavelet, Aaron Hill, and Sonya Williams. *How Effective Are Different Approaches Aiming to Increase Employment Retention and Advancement? Final Impacts for Twelve Models.* New York, NY: MDRC. April 2010.

Henggeler, Scott W., W. Glenn Clingempeel, Michael J. Bronding, and Susan G. Pickrel. "Four-Year Follow-Up of Multisystemic Therapy with Substance-Abusing and Substance Dependent Juvenile Offenders." *Journal of the American Academy of Child and Adolescent Psychiatry* 41, 7 (July 2002): 868–874.

Henggeler, Scott W., Gary B. Melton, and Linda A. Smith. "Family Preservation Using Multisystemic Therapy: An Effective Alternative to Incarcerating Serious Juvenile Offenders." *Journal of Consulting and Clinical Psychology* 60, 6 (December 1992): 953–961.

Henggeler, Scott W., Gary B. Melton, and Linda A. Smith. "Family Preservation Using Multisystemic Therapy: An Effective Alternative to Incarcerating Serious Juvenile Offenders." *Journal of Consulting and Clinical Psychology* 60, 6 (December 1992): 953–961.

Hollister, Robinson G. "Opening Statement." In *Social Experimentation, Program Evaluation, and Public Policy,* edited by Maureen A. Pirog, 19–20. Wiley-Blackwell, 2008.

Hsueh, JoAnn, Erin Jacobs, and Mary Farrell. *A Two Generational Child-Focused Program Enhanced with Employment Services: Eighteen-Month Impacts from the Kansas and Missouri Sites of the Enhanced Services for the Hard-to-Employ Demonstration and Evaluation Project.* MDRC. March 2011.

Hsueh, JoAnn, and Mary E. Farrell. *Enhanced Early Head Start with Employment Services: 42-Month Impacts from the Kansas and Missouri Sites of the Enhanced Services for the Hard-to-Employ Demonstration and Evaluation Project.* OPRE Report # 2012-05. Washington, DC: Office of Planning, Research, and Evaluation, Administration for Children and Families, U.S. Department of Health and Human Services, February 2012.

Hsueh, JoAnn, Desiree Principe Alderson, Erika Lundquist, Charless Michalopoulos, Daniel Gubits, David Fein, and Virginia Knox. *The Supporting Healthy Marriage Evaluation: Early Impacts on Low-Income Families.* Washington, DC: Office of Planning, Research and Evaluation, Administration for Children and Families, U.S. Department of Health and Human Services, 2012.

James-Burdumy, Susanne, Mark Dynarski, and John Deke. "When Elementary Schools Stay Open Late: Results from the National Evaluation of the 21st Century Community Learning Centers Program." *Educational Evaluation and Policy Analysis* 29, 4 (December 2007): 296–318.

Jemmott, John B., Loretta S. Jemmott, and Gregory T. Fong. "Efficacy of a Theory-Based Abstinence-Only Intervention over 24 Months." *Archives of Pediatrics and Adolescent Medicine* 164, 2 (February 2010): 152–159.

Johnson, Byron, R. *More God, Less Crime: Why Faith Matters and How It Could Matter More.* West Conshohocken, PA: Templeton Press, 2011.

Johnson, Lyndon B. "Remarks at the University of Michigan," May 22, 1964. http://www.lbjlib.utexas.edu/johnson/archives.hom/speeches.hom/640522.asp (accessed on December 21, 2012).

Kessler, Charles R. *I Am the Change: Barack Obama and the Crisis of Liberalism.* New York: Broadside Books, 2012.

King, Christopher T., and Burt S. Barnow. "The Use of Market Mechanisms." In *The Workforce Investment Act: Implementation Experiences and Evaluation Findings,* edited by Douglas J. Besharov and Phoebe H. Cottingham, 81–111. Kalamazoo, MI: W. E. Upjohn Institute for Employment Research, 2011.

Kirby, Douglas. *Emerging Answers 2007: Research Findings on Programs to Reduce Teen Pregnancy and Sexually Transmitted Diseases.* Washington, DC: National Campaign to Prevent Teen and Unplanned Pregnancy, November 2007.

Klein, Joel. "Time to Ax Public Programs That Don't Yield Results." *Time,* July 7, 2011. http://www.time.com/time/nation/article/0,8599,2081778,00.html (accessed on September 30, 2012).

Lafer, Gordon. *The Job Training Charade.* Ithaca, NY: Cornell University Press, 2002.

LaLonde, Robert J. "Evaluating the Econometric Evaluations of Training Programs with Experimental Data." *American Economic Review* 76, 4 (September 1986): 604–620.

Lebergott, Stanley. "Annual Estimates of Unemployment in the United States, 1900–1954." In *The Measurement and Behavior of Unemployment,* edited by Universities-National Bureau (National Bureau of Economic Research) 211–242. http://www.nber.org/chapters/c2644.pdf (accessed on July 3, 2012).

Lee, Wang-Sheng. *Evaluating the Effects of a Mandatory Government Program Using Matched Groups within a Similar Geographic Location.* Melbourne Institute of Applied Economic and Social Research, University of Melbourne, November 20, 2006.

Leighninger, Robert, and Leslie Leighninger. "Social Policy of the New Deal." In *The Hand Book of Social Policy,* edited by James Midgley and Michelle Livermore, 133–150. Los Angeles: Sage Publications, 2009.

Leschied, Alan, and Alison Cunningham. *Seeking Effective Interventions for Young Offenders: Interim Results of a Four-Year Randomized Study of Multisystemic Therapy in Ontario, Canada.* London, Ontario: Centre for Children and Families in the Justice System, 2002.

Leuchtenburg, William E. *Franklin D. Roosevelt and the New Deal, 1932–1940.* New York: Harper Colophon Books, 1963.

Lipsey, Mark W. *Design Sensitivity: Statistical Power for Experimental Research.* Newbury Park, CA: Sage Publications, 1990.

Littell, Julia H., Melanie Popa, and Burnee Forsythe. "Multisystemic Therapy for Social, Emotional, and Behavioral Problems in Youth Aged 10–17." *Campbell Systematic Reviews*, September 21, 2005.

Lowenstein, Amy E. "Early Care and Education as Educational Panacea: What Do We Really Know about Its Effectiveness?" *Educational Policy* 25, 1 (2011): 92–114.

Love, John M., Ellen Eliason Kisker, Christine M. Ross, Peter Z. Schochet, Jeanne Brooks-Gun, Diane Paulsell, Kimberly Boller, Jill Constantine, Cheri Vogel, Allison Sidle Fulingi, and Christi Brady-Smith. *Making a Difference in the Lives of Infants and Toddlers and Their Families: The Impacts of Early Head Start, Volume 1: Final Technical Report.* Mathematica Policy Research, Princeton, NJ, June 2002.

Manzi, Jim. "What Social Science Does—and Doesn't—Know." *City Journal* 20, 3 (Summer 2010): 14–23. http://www.city-journal.org/2010/20_3_social-science.html (March 14, 2011).

Manzi, Jim. *Uncontrolled: The Surprising Payoff of Trial-and-Error for Business, Politics, and Society.* New York: Basic Books, 2012.

Marshall, Jennifer, David B. Muhlhausen, Russ Whitehurst, Nicholas Zill, and Debra Viadero. "Is Head Start Helping Children Succeed and Does Anyone Care?" Video feed, The Heritage Foundation, March 22, 2010. http://www.heritage.org/Events/2010/03/Head-Start (July 19, 2010).

Massachusetts Constitution, 1780. Heritage Foundation First Principles Series. http://www.heritage.org/initiatives/first-principles/primary-sources/massachusetts-constitution.

Maynard, Rebecca A., Christopher Trenholm, Barbara Devaney, Amy Johnson, Melissa A. Clark, John Homrighausen, and Ece Kalay. *First-Year Impacts of Four Title V, Section 510 Abstinence Education Programs.* Mathematica Policy Research, Princeton, NJ, June 2005.

McConnell, Sheena, and Steven Glazerman. *National Job Corps Study: The Benefits and Costs of Job Corps.* Princeton, NJ: Mathematica Policy Research, Princeton, NJ, June 2001.

McConnell, Sheena, Elizabeth Stuart, Kenneth Fortson, Paul Decker, Irma Perez-Johnson, Barbara Harris, and Jeffrey Salzman. *Managing Customers' Training Choices: Findings from the Individual Training Account Experiment, Final Report.* Mathematica Policy Research, Princeton, NJ, 2006.

McGuinn, Patrick, and Frederick Hess. "The Great Society and the Evolution of the Elementary and Secondary Education Act of 1965." In *The Great Society and the High Tide of Liberalism*, edited by Sidney M. Milkis and Jerome M. Mileur, 289–319. Boston: University of Massachusetts Press, 2005.

McLanahan, Sarah, and Gary Sandefur. *Growing up with a Single Parent: What Hurts, What Helps.* Cambridge, MA: Harvard University Press, 1994.

Merriam, Charles E. *A History of American Political Theories.* New York, MacMillan Company, 1926.

Michalopoulos, Charles. "Precedents and Prospects for Randomized Experiments." In *Learning More from Social Experiments: Evolving Analytic Approaches*, edited by Howard S. Bloom, 1–36. New York: Russell Sage Foundation, 2005.

Mileur, Jerome M. "The Great Society and the Demise of New Deal Liberalism." In *The Great Society and the High Tide of Liberalism*, edited by Sidney M. Milkis and Jerome M. Mileur, 411–455. Boston: University of Massachusetts Press, 2005.

Miller, Cynthia, Johannes M. Ros, Kristen E. Porter, Fannie M. Tseng, and Yasuyo Abe. *The Challenge of Replicating Success in a Changing World: Final Report on the Center for Employment Training Replication Cites.* Manpower Demonstration Research Corporation, September 2005, 1. http://www.mdrc.org/publications/453/full.pdf (October, 18, 2011).

Miller, Tiffany Jones. "Transforming Formal Freedom into Effective Freedom: Dewey, the New Deal, and the Great Society." In *Modern America and the Legacy of the Founding*, edited by Ronald J. Pestritto and Thomas G. West, 169–206. Lanham, MD: Lexington Books, 2007.

Mitchell, Broadus. *Depression Decade: From New Era through New Deal, 1929–1941.* New York: Harper Torchbooks, 1969.

Mohr, Lawrence B. *Impact Analysis for Program Evaluation.* Thousand Oaks, CA: Sage Publications, 2005.

Muhlhausen, David B. "Job Corps: A Consistent Record of Failure." Heritage Foundation *WebMemo* No. 1374. February 28, 2007. http://www.heritage.org/Research/Reports/2007/02/Job-Corps-A-Consistent-Record-of-Failure (accessed on December 21, 2012).

Muhlhausen, David B., and Paul Kersey. "In the Dark on Job Training: Federal Job-Training Programs Have a Record of Failure." Heritage Foundation *Backgrounder* No. 1774. July 6, 2004. http://www.heritage.org/Research/Reports/2004/07/In-the-Dark-on-Job-Training-Federal-Job-Training-Programs-Have-a-Record-of-Failure (accessed on December 21, 2012).

Myers, David, Robert Olsen, Neil Seftor, Julie Young, and Christina Tuttle. *The Impacts of Upward Bound: Results from the Third Follow-Up Data Collection.* Mathematica Policy Research, Princeton, NJ, 2004. http://www.eric.ed.gov/PDFS/ED483155.pdf (April 29, 2011).

Myers, David, and Allen Schirm. *The Short-Term Impacts of Upward Bound: An Interim Report.* Mathematica Policy Research, Princeton, NJ, May 1997.

Nakamura, David. "Obama Asks Congress for Debt Limit Hike." *44* (blog), *Washington Post*, January 12, 2012. http://www.washingtonpost.com/blogs/44/post/after-delay-obama-asks-congress-for-debt-limit-hike/2012/01/12/gIQAA3ADuP_blog.html (accessed on December 21, 2012).

National Public Radio *Talk of the Nation.* "Analysis: Explanations and Criticism of President Bush's New Marriage Promotion Plan." Transcript from Westlaw. January 22, 2004.

Obama for America. "The Life of Julia." http://www.barackobama.com/life-of-julia (accessed on December 21, 2012).

Obama, Barack. *The Audacity of Hope: Thoughts on Reclaiming the American Dream.* New York: Crown Publishers, 2006.

Obama, Barack. "Remarks by the President at the Associated Press Luncheon," April 3, 2012. http://www.whitehouse.gov/the-press-office/2012/04/03/remarks-president-associated-press-luncheon. (accessed December 21, 2012).

Office of Management and Budget. *Appendix, Budget of the United States, Fiscal Year 2013.* Washington, DC: U.S. Government Printing Office, 2011. http://www.whitehouse.gov/sites/default/files/omb/budget/fy2013/assets/appendix.pdf (accessed on December 21, 2012).

Office of Management and Budget. *Historical Tables, Budget of the United States, Fiscal Year 2012.* Washington, DC: U.S. Government Printing Office, 2011. http://www.whitehouse.gov/sites/default/files/omb/budget/fy2012/assets/hist.pdf (accessed on December 21, 2012).

Ogden, Terje, and Colleen A. Halliday-Boykins. "Multisystemic Treatment of Antisocial Adolescents in Norway: Replication of Clinical Outcomes Outside of the US." *Journal of Child and Adolescent Mental Health* 9, 2 (2004): 77–83.

Orr, Larry L., Howard S. Bloom, Stephen H. Bell, Fred Doolittle, Winston Lin, and George Cave. *Does Training for the Disadvantaged Work?* Washington, DC: Urban Institute Press, 1996.

Orr, Larry L., Stephen H. Bell, and Jacob A. Klerman. "Designing Reliable Impact Evaluations." In *The Workforce Investment Act: Implementation Experiences and Evaluation Findings*, edited by Douglas J. Besharov and Phoebe H. Cottingham, 431–446. Kalamazoo, MI: W. E. Upjohn Institute for Employment Research, 2011.

Orr, Larry, Judith D. Feins, Robin Jacob, Erik Beecroft, Lisa Sanbonmatsu, Lawrence F. Katz, Jeffrey B. Liebman, and Jeffrey R. Kling. *Moving to Opportunity Interim Impacts Evaluation: Final Report.* Washington, DC: U.S. Department of Housing and Urban Development, Office of Policy Development and Research, June 2003.

Perez-Johnson, Irma, Quinn Moore, and Robert Santillano. *Improving the Effectiveness of Individual Training Accounts: Long-Term Findings from an*

Experimental Evaluation of Three Service Delivery Models, Final Report. Mathematica Policy Research, Princeton, NJ, October 2011.

Puma, Michael J., and Nancy R. Burstein. "The National Evaluation of the Food Stamp Employment and Training Program." *Journal of Policy Analysis and Management* 13, 2 (1994): 311–330.

Puma, Michael, Stephen Bell, Ronna Cook, Camilla, Pam Broene, Frank Jenkins, Andrew Mashburn, and Jason Downer. *Third Grade Follow-up to the Head Start Impact Study: Final Report.* Washington, DC: Office of Planning, Research and Evaluation, Administration for Children and Families, U.S. Department of Health and Human Services, October 2012. http://www.acf.hhs.gov/sites/default/files/opre/head_start_report.pdf (accessed on December 21, 2012).

Rasmussen Reports. "64% Think Budget Cuts Should Be Considered in Every Government Program," February 28, 2012. http://www.rasmussenreports.com/public_content/business/federal_budget/february_2012/64_think_budget_cuts_should_be_considered_in_every_government_program (accessed on March 1, 2012).

Rasmussen Reports. "65% Favor Across-the-Board Spending Cuts," November 27, 2012. http://www.rasmussenreports.com/public_content/politics/general_politics/november_2012/65_favor_across_the_board_spending_cuts. (accessed on December 11, 2012).

Reinhart, Carmen M., and Kenneth S. Rogoff. *This Time Is Different: Eight Centuries of Financial Folly.* Princeton, NJ: Princeton University Press, 2009.

Reisch, Michael. "Social Policy and the Great Society." In *The Hand Book of Social Policy*, edited by James Midgley and Michelle Livermore, 151–168. Los Angeles: Sage Publications, 2009.

Ricciuti, Anna E., Robert G. St.Pierre, Wang Lee, Amanda Parsad, and Tracy Rimdzius. *Third National Even Start Evaluation: Follow-Up Findings from the Experimental Design Study.* Washington, DC: U.S. Department of Education, Institute of Education Sciences, National Center for Education Evaluation and Regional Assistance, 2004.

Robertson, Elizabeth B., Susan L. David, and Suman A. Rao. *Preventing Drug Use Among Children and Adolescents: A Research-Based Guide for Parents, Educators, and Community Leaders.* Washington, DC: National Institutes of Health, National Institute on Drug Abuse, October 2003. http://drugabuse.gov/pdf/prevention/RedBook.pdf (accessed on December 21, 2012).

Roosevelt, Franklin D. "Campaign Address on Progressive Government at the Commonwealth Club in San Francisco, California," September 23, 1932. http://www.presidency.ucsb.edu/ws/index.php?pid=88391#axzz1wYMxy6tT (accessed on June 1, 2012).

Roosevelt, Franklin D. "State of the Union Message to Congress," January 11, 1944. http://www.presidency.ucsb.edu/ws/index.php?pid=16518#axzz1wYMxy6tT (accessed on December 21, 2012).

Rossi, Peter H., Mark W. Lipsey, and Howard E. Freeman. *Evaluation: A Systematic Approach.* Thousand Oaks, CA: Sage Publications, 2004.

Rossi, Peter H., Mark W. Lipsey, and Howard E. Freeman. *Evaluation: A Systematic Approach.* Thousand Oaks, CA: Sage Publications, 2004.

Sampson, Robert J., and Dawn Jeglum Bartusch. "Legal Cynicism and (Subcultural?) Tolerance of Deviance: The Neighborhood Context of Racial Differences." *Law and Society Review* 32, 4 (1998): 777–804.

Sampson, Robert, and Stephen W. Raudenbush. "Systematic Social Observation of Public Spaces: A New Look at Disorder in Urban Neighborhoods." *American Journal of Sociology* 105, 3 (November 1999): 603–651.

Sanbonmatsu, Lisa, Jens Ludwig, Lawrence F. Katz, Lisa Gennetian, Greg J. Duncan, Ronald C. Kessler, Emma Adam, Thomas W. McDade, Stacy Tessler Lindau, Matthew Sciandra, Fanghua Yang, Ijun Lai, William Congdon, Joe Amick, Ryan Gillette, Michael A. Zabek, Jordon Marvakov, Sabrina Yusuf, and Nicholas A. Potter. *Moving to Opportunity for Fair Housing Demonstration Program: Final Impacts Evaluation.* Washington, DC: U.S. Department of Housing and Urban Development, Office of Policy Development and Research, November 2011.

Sawhill, Isabel V., and Jon Baron. "Federal Programs for Youth: More of the Same Won't Work." *Youth Today*, May 1, 2010. http://coalition4evidence.org/wordpress/wp-content/uploads/Viewpoint-Essay-Sawhill-Baron-Youth-Today-May-2010.pdf (accessed on August 24, 2012).

Schinke, Steven, Paul Brounstein, and Stephen E. Gardner. *Science-Based Prevention Programs and Principles.* Washington, DC: U.S. Department of Health and Human Services, Center for Substance Abuse Prevention, Substance Abuse and Mental Health Services Administration, 2002. http://www.eric.ed.gov/ERICWebPortal/contentdelivery/servlet/ERICServlet?accno=ED474651 (June 29, 2011).

Schirm, Allen, and Nuria Rodriguez. *The Quantum Opportunity Program Demonstration: Initial Post Intervention Impacts.* Mathematica Policy Research, Princeton, NJ, June 2004.

Schirm, Allen, Elizabeth Stuart, and Allison McKie. *The Quantum Opportunity Program Demonstration: Final Impacts.* Mathematica Policy Research, Princeton, NJ, July 2006.

Schochet, Peter Z., Sheena McConnell, and John Burghardt. *National Job Corps Study: Findings Using Administrative Earnings Records Data: Final Report.* Princeton, NJ: Mathematica Policy Research, Princeton, NJ, October 2003.

Schochet, Peter Z., John Burghardt, and Steven Glazerman, *National Job Corps Study: The Impacts of Job Corps on Participants' Employment and Related Outcomes.* Princeton, NJ: Mathematica Policy Research, Princeton, NJ, June 2001.

Schochet, Peter Z., Sheena McConnell, and John Burghardt. *National Job Corps Study: Findings Using Administrative Earnings Records Data: Final Report.* Princeton, NJ: Mathematica Policy Research, Princeton, NJ, October 2003.

Seftor, Neil, Arif Mamun, and Allen Schirm. *The Impacts of Regular Upward Bound on Postsecondary Outcomes 7–9 Years after Scheduled High School Graduation: Final Report.* Mathematica Policy Research, Princeton, NJ, January 2009.

Shadish, William R., Thomas D. Cook, and Donald T. Campbell. *Experimental and Quasi-Experimental Designs for Generalized Causal Inference.* Boston: Houghton Mifflin Company, 2002.

Sherman, Lawrence W. *Domestic Violence: Experiments and Dilemmas.* New York: Free Press, 1992.

Sherman, Lawrence. "Conclusion: The Effectiveness of Local Crime Prevention Funding." In *Preventing Crime: What Works, What Doesn't, What's Promising*, edited by Sherman, Lawrence, Denise Gottfredson, Doris Mackenzie, John Eck, Peter Rueter, and Shawn Bushway, 1–20. Washington, DC: U.S. Department of Justice, Office of Justice Programs, 1997.

Sherman, Lawrence W., David P. Farrington, Brandom C. Welsh, and Doris Layton MacKenzie. *Evidence-Based Crime Prevention.* London: Routledge, 2002.

Sherman, Lawrence, Denise Gottfredson, Doris Mackenzie, John Eck, Peter Rueter, and Shawn Bushway. *Preventing Crime: What Works, What Doesn't, What's Promising.* Washington, DC: U.S. Department of Justice, Office of Justice Programs, 1997.

Sherman, Lawrence W. and Richard A. Berk. "The Specific Deterrent Effects of Arrest for Domestic Assault." *American Sociological Review* 49, 2 (April 1984): 261–272.

Sherman, Lawrence W., Douglas A. Smith, Janell D. Schmidt, and Dennis P. Rogan. "Crime, Punishment, and Stake in Conformity: Legal and Informal Control of Domestic Violence." *American Sociological Review* 57 (October 1992): 680–690.

Sherman, Lawrence W., Janell D. Schmidt, Dennis P. Rogan, Douglas A. Smith, Patrick R. Gartin, Ellen G. Cohn, Dean J. Collins, and Anthony R. Bacih. "The Variable Effects of Arrest on Criminal Careers: The Milwaukee Domestic Violence Experiment." *Journal of Criminal Law & Criminology* 83, 1 (1992): 137–169.

Skidmore, Felicity. "Overview of the Seattle-Denver Income Maintenance Experiment Final Report." In *Evaluation Studies Review Annual*, edited by Linda H. Aiken and Barbara H. Kehrer, 297–326. Beverly Hills, CA: Sage Publications, 1985.

Smith, Jeffrey A., and Petra E. Todd. "Reconciling Conflicting Evidence on the Performance of Propensity-Score Matching Methods." *American Economic Review* 91, 2 (May 2001): 112–118.

Smith, Jeffrey A., and Petra E. Todd. "Does Matching Overcome LaLonde's Critique of Nonexperimental Estimators?" *Journal of Econometrics* 125 (2005): 305–353.

Solis, Hilda L. "Statement of Hilda L. Solis, Secretary of Labor, before the Subcommittee of Labor, Health and Human Services, Education, and Related Agencies, Committee on Appropriations, United States Senate." May 4, 2011, 3. http://www.appropriations.senate.gov/ht-labor.cfm?method=hearings.view&id=7c49eb6c-2c56-4a15-92da-36f92e1e8ba4 (accessed on December 21, 2012).

Spiegelman, Robert G., and K. E. Yaeger. "Overview." *Journal of Human Resources* 14, 4 (1980): 463–479.

St. Pierre, Robert, Anne Ricciuti, Fumiyo Tao, Cindy Creps, Takeko Kumagawa, and William Ross. *Third National Even Start Evaluation: Description of Projects and Participants.* Abt Associates Inc., 2001.

St. Pierre, Robert, Anne Ricciuti, Fumiyo Tao, Cindy Creps, Janet Swartz, Wang Lee, Amanda Parsad, and Tracy Rimdzius. *Third National Even Start Evaluation: Program Impacts and Implications for Improvement.* Cambridge, MA: Abt Associates Inc., 2003.

State News Service. "Reid: GOP Leaders Must Decide if They Will Do What Tea Party Wants or What Country Needs." April 4, 2011.

Swenson, Cynthia, Cupit, Scott W. Henggeler, Ida Taylor, and Oliver W. Addison. *Multisystemic Therapy and Neighborhood Partnerships: Reducing Adolescent Violence and Substance Abuse.* New York: Guilford Press, 2005.

Trenholm, Christopher, Barbara Devaney, Ken Fortson, Lisa Quay, Justin Wheeler, and Melissa Clark. *Impacts of Four Title V, Section 510 Abstinence Education Programs: Final Report.* Mathematica Policy Research, Princeton, NJ, April 2007.

U.S. Census Bureau, Population Estimates Program, Population Division, "Historical National Population Estimates: July 1, 1900 to July 1, 1999," June 28, 2000." http://www.census.gov/popest/data/national/totals/pre-1980/tables/popclockest.txt (accessed on December 21, 2012).

U.S. Census Bureau, Population Division. "Table 1. Annual Estimates of the Population for the United States, Regions, States, and Puerto Rico: April 1, 2010 to July 1, 2011" (NST-EST2011-01), December 2011. http://www.census.gov/popest/data/national/totals/2011/index.html (accessed on June 20, 2012).

U.S. Department of Agriculture, Food and Nutrition Service. "SNAP Monthly Data," August 30, 2012. http://www.fns.usda.gov/pd/34SNAPmonthly.htm (accessed on September 30, 2012).

U.S. Department of Commerce, Bureau of the Census. *Historical Statistics of the United States: Colonial Times to 1970, Part 1.* U.S. Government Printing Office: Washington, DC, 1975.

U.S Department of Commerce, U.S. Census Bureau. "Areas with Concentrated Poverty: 2006–2010." *American Community Survey Briefs*, December 2011. http://www.census.gov/prod/2011pubs/acsbr10-17.pdf (accessed on December 21, 2012)

U.S. Department of Education, *Federal Pell Grants: Fiscal Year 2011 Budget Request*, undated document, 8–9. http://www2.ed.gov/about/overview/budget/budget11/justifications/p-pell.pdf (accessed on July 23, 2012).

U.S. Department of Education, Institute of Education Sciences, National center for Education and regional Assistance. *Third National Even Start Evaluation: Follow-Up Findings from the Experimental Study Design.* Washington, DC, December 2004.

U.S. Department of Education, Office of the Under Secretary, Policy and Program Studies Service. *The Impacts of Regular Upward Bound: Results from the Third-Follow-Up Data Collection.* Washington, DC, April 2004.

U.S. Department of Education, Office of Planning, Evaluation and Policy Development, Policy and Program Studies Service. *21st Century Community Learning Centers Descriptive Study of Program Practices.* Washington, DC, 2010.

U.S. Department of Health and Human Services, Administration for Children and Families. *Head Start Impact Study: First Year Findings.* Washington, DC, May 2005.

U.S. Department of Health and Human Services, Administration for Children and Families. *Head Start Impact Study: Final Report.* Washington, DC, January 2010.

U.S. Department of Labor. "Requests for Proposals (RFP) 2007." http://www.doleta.gov/grants/rfp07.cfm (July 18, 2010).

U.S. Department of Labor, Office of the Inspector General. *Job Corps Needs to Improve Reliability of Performance Metrics and Results,* September 30, 2011. http://www.oig.dol.gov/public/reports/oa/2011/26-11-004-03-370.pdf (accessed on August 7, 2012).

U.S. Department of Labor, Employment, and Training Administration. "Summary of ETA Fiscal Year 2003 Request." www.doleta.gov/budget/03reqsum.pdf (accessed on December 21, 2012).

U.S. Department of the Treasury, Bureau of the Public Debt. "Monthly Statement of the Public Debt of the United States, December 31, 2011, Table 1: Summary of Treasury Securities Outstanding," December 31, 2011. http://www.treasurydirect.gov/govt/reports/pd/mspd/2011/opds122011.pdf (accessed on June 20, 2012).

U.S. Government Accountability Office, Employment and Training Administration. "More Actions Needed to Improve Transparency and Accountability of Its Research Programs." GAO-11-285, March 2011. http://www.gao.gov/new.items/d11285.pdf (accessed on December 21, 2012).

U.S. Government Accountability Office. *Multiple Employment and Training Programs: Providing Information on Collocating Services and Consolidating Administrative Structures Could Promote Efficiencies.* Washington, DC, January 2011.

U.S. Government Accountability Office. *Employment and Training Administration: More Actions Needed to Improve Transparency and Accountability of Its Research Programs.* Washington, DC, March 2011.

U.S. Government Accountability Office. "Workforce Investment Act: Labor Has Made Progress in Addressing Areas of Concern, but More Focus Needed on Understanding What Works and What Doesn't." Statement of George A. Scott, Director, Education, Workforce, and Income Security, before the Subcommittee on Higher Education, Lifelong Learning, and Competitiveness, Committee on Education and Labor, U.S. House of Representatives, GAO-09-396T. February 26, 2009.

U.S. General Accounting Office. *More Benefits to Jobless Can Be Attained in Public Service Employment.* Washington, DC, April 7, 1977.

U.S. General Accounting Office. *Moving Participants from Public Service Employment Programs into Unsubsidized Jobs Needs More Attention.* Washington, DC, October 12, 1979.

U.S. General Accounting Office. *Workforce Investment Act: Improvements Needed in Performance Measures to Provide a More Accurate Picture of WIA's Effectiveness.* Washington, DC, February 2002.

U.S. General Accounting Office. *Multiple Employment and Training Programs: Funding and Performance Measures for Major Programs.* Washington, DC: April 2003.

U.S. House of Representatives. *Report of the Committee on Education and Labor Accompanying H.R. 5320, the Job Training Partnership Act, House Report 97-537.* 97th Cong., 2nd Sess., May 17, 1982.

U.S. House of Representative, Committee on the Judiciary, Subcommittee on Crime, Terrorism, and Homeland Security. *Reauthorization of the Second Chance Act.* 111th Cong., 2nd Sess., September 29, 2010.

U.S. House of Representatives, Committee on Education and the Workforce. "Committee Approves Vital Job Training Reforms." Press release, June 7, 2012. http://edworkforce.house.gov/News/DocumentSingle.aspx?DocumentID=298947 (accessed on August 3, 2012).

U.S. House of Representative, Committee on Education and the Workforce. *H.R. 4297. The Workforce Investment Act of 2012.* 112th Cong., 2nd Sess., April 17, 2012.

U.S Congress, House of Representatives, Committee on Education and Labor, Subcommittee on Higher Education, Lifelong Learning, and Competitiveness, 2007, Hearing on "Workforce Investment Act: Recommendations to Improve the Effectiveness of Job Training," Hon. Ruben Hinojosa, Chair, Serial No. 110-51, June 28, 2007, 6.

VanGiezen, Robert, and Albert E. Schwenk. "Compensation from before World War I through the Great Depression." U.S. Department of Labor, Bureau of Labor Statistics. http://www.bls.gov/opub/cwc/cm20030124ar03p1.htm (accessed on July 3, 2012).

Virginia Declaration of Rights, June 12, 1776. Heritage Foundation *First Principles Series*. http://www.heritage.org/initiatives/first-principles/primary-sources/virginia-declaration-of-rights.

Visher, Christy A., and Jeremy Travis. "Transitions from Prison to Community: Understanding Individual Pathways." *Annual Review of Sociology* 29 (2003): 89–113.

Voegeli, William. *Never Enough: America's Limitless Welfare State*. New York: Encounter Books, 2010.

Vogel, Cheri A., Yange Xue, Emily M. Moiduddin, Barbara Lepidus Carlson, and Ellen Eliason Kisker. *Early Head Start Children in Grade 5: Long-Term Follow-Up of the Early Head Start Research Evaluation Project Study Sample: Final Report*. OPRE Report # 2011-8. Washington, DC: Office of Planning, Research, and Evaluation, Administration for Children and Families, U.S. Department of Health and Human Services, December 2010.

Wallis, John Joseph, and Daniel K. Benjamin. "Public Relief and Private Employment in the Great Depression." *Journal of Economic History* 41 (December 1993): 97–102.

Watson, Bradley C. S. *Living Constitution, Dying Faith: Progressivism and the New Science of Jurisprudence*. Wilmington, DE: ISI Books, 2009.

Weisburd, David. "Ethical Practice and Evaluation of Interventions in Crime and Justice." *Evaluation Review* 27, 23 (June 2003): 336–354.

Weisburd, David, Cynthia M. Lum, and Anthony Petrosino. "Does Research Design Affect Study Outcomes in Criminal Justice?" *Annals of the American Academy of Political and Social Sciences* 578 (November 2001): 50–70.

Weiss, Carol H. *Evaluation*. Upper Saddle River, N.J.: Prentice Hall, 1998.

West, Richard W. "Effects on Wage Rates: An Interim Analysis." *The Journal of Human Resources* 14, 4 (1980): 641–653.

West, Thomas, G. "The Political Theory of the Declaration of Independence." In *The American Founding and the Social Compact*, edited by Ronald J. Pestritto and Thomas G. West, 95–145. Lanham, Md.: Lexington Books, 2003).

West, Thomas G. "Progressivism and the Transformation of American Government." In *The Progressive Revolution in Politics and Political Science: Transforming the American Regime*, edited by John Marini and Ken Masugi, 13–33. Lanham: Rowman & Littlefield Publishers, Inc., 2005.

Wilde, Elizabeth Ty and Robinson Hollister. "How Close is Close Enough? Evaluating Propensity Score Matching Using Data from a Class Size Reduction Experiment." In *Social Experimentation, Program Evaluation and Public Policy*, edited by Maureen A. Pirog. 65–90. Association for Public Policy Analysis and Management, 2008.

Wilson, Joan Hoff. *Herbert Hoover: Forgotten Progressive*. Long Grove, Ill.: Waveland Press, Inc., 1992.

Wilson, William Julius. *More than Just Race: Being Black and Poor in the Inner City*. New York: W.W. Norton & Company, 2009.

Wilson, Woodrow. *The State: Elements of Historical and Practical Politics*. Boston: DC Heath & Co., Publishers, 1910.

Wilson, Woodrow. *Constitutional Government in the United States*. New Brunswick, N.J: Transaction Publishers, 2002.

Wood, Robert G., Sheena McConnell, Quinn Moore, Andrew Clarkwest, and JoAnn Hsueh. *Strengthening Unmarried Parents' Relationships: The Early Impacts of Building Strong Families*. Mathematica Policy Research, Princeton, NJ, May 2010. http://www.mathematica-mpr.com/publications/pdfs/family_support/BSF_impact_finalrpt.pdf (March 14, 2011).

Wood, Robert G., Quinn Moore, Andrew Clarkwest, Alexandra Killewald, and Shannon Monahan, *The Long-Term Effects of Building Strong Families: A Relationship Skills Education Program for Unmarried Parents: Final Report*. Princeton, NJ: Mathematica Policy Research, November 2012. http://www.acf.hhs.gov/programs/opre/resource/the-building-strong-families-project-the-long-term-effects-of-building (accessed on December 14, 2012).

Index

Page numbers followed by "c" indicate charts.
Page numbers followed by "t" indicate tables.

About the Author

David B. Muhlhausen is a leading expert on the need for evaluating the effectiveness of federal programs, including criminal justice programs, at the Heritage Foundation's Center for Data Analysis. A Research Fellow in Empirical Policy Analysis at the think tank, Muhlhausen has testified frequently before Congress on the efficiency and effectiveness of law enforcement grants administered by the U.S. Department of Justice.

Muhlhausen rose to national prominence in 2001 with the publication of his analysis showing the highly touted Community Oriented Policing Services (COPS) program to be a waste of taxpayer dollars. His research illustrated that COPS had neither put 100,000 new police officers on the street nor reduced violent crime. His work prompted Vice President Joseph Biden, at the time a U.S. senator from Delaware and chairman of the Senate Subcommittee on Crime and Drugs, to call a hearing specifically to investigate Muhlhausen's findings. "I want to have a hearing on what has been, from The Heritage Foundation and other places, criticism that the COPS program does not work," Biden said in opening the hearing.

In addition to testifying on issues such as policing, parole, prisoner re-entry and the death penalty, Muhlhausen in recent years delved into election reform issues. He has produced research on the impact of voter ID laws on voter turnout. His research strongly indicates that voter ID laws have little to no effect on voter turnout. Legislative committees from Kansas and Texas have sought Muhlhausen's expert testimony on voter ID laws.

Muhlhausen joined Heritage in 1999 after serving on the staff for the Senate Judiciary Committee, where he specialized in crime and juvenile justice policies. Prior to that, he was a manager at a juvenile correctional facility in Baltimore. He holds a doctorate in public policy from the University of Maryland–Baltimore County and a bachelor's degree in political science and justice studies from Frostburg State University. In addition to his work at Heritage, Muhlhausen is an adjunct professor at George Mason University, teaching program evaluation and statistical methods to graduate students.

A native of Colorado, Muhlhausen grew up in Maryland. He currently resides in Falls Church, Virginia.